THE
MAGIC CATALOGUE

THE
MAGIC CATALOGUE

A GUIDE TO
THE WONDERFUL
WORLD OF MAGIC

Written and Compiled by

WILLIAM DOERFLINGER

A Sunrise Book
E. P. DUTTON
New York

DESIGNED BY BETTY BINNS

Copyright © 1977 by WILLIAM DOERFLINGER

All rights reserved. Printed in the U.S.A.

Library of Congress Cataloging in Publication Data
Doerflinger, William.
     The magic catalogue.

     1. Conjuring.   I. Title.
GV1547.D56   1977   793.8   77-8355

ISBN: 0-87690-272-7 (cloth)
        0-87690-273-5 (paper)

Published simultaneously in Canada by Clarke, Irwin & Company
Limited, Toronto and Vancouver

10 9 8 7 6 5 4 3 2 1
FIRST EDITION

*To my wife, Anne,
who has played the role
of "spectator" on many
happy occasions*

CONTENTS

Color plates will be found between pages 20 and 21

PREFACE

Magic has been a popular form of entertainment since the days of the Pharaohs. Not even in the golden era of the full evening magic show, however, has the art of mystification been more popular than it is today. Dyed-in-the-wool devotees, to be sure, have always remained faithful to magic as hobby or profession. In recent years, however, the art has been the subject of a new surge of interest and popularity that is attracting to the fraternity of conjurers many new enthusiasts with a serious interest in magic.

The more proficient in the art of magic one becomes, and the more widely one reads in magical literature both new and old, the more fully aware does one become of the extent and variety of the world of magic. It takes time and investigation to discover the many resources which, though often overlooked, are available to the magician who knows where to find them. These resources include the services of magic dealers in all parts of the country and the world, of mail-order suppliers, manufacturers and builders of tricks and illusions, all of whom have increased in numbers in recent years. They further include fine books of magical instruction, magicians' magazines filled with directions for tricks and learned information for collectors, news of other magicians and informative advertisements; societies, clubs and conventions through which one may enjoy the friendship and advice of other magicians.

The Magic Catalogue is intended to fill the need for an over-all guide to the labyrinthian world of magic. As a source book of both historical and current information, it is hoped that it will be helpful to both the newer devotee of the art of magic and the more advanced magician and magic collector. It tells where to turn for the equipment, help, training and information you need to understand the qualities that make for good magic, and to advance more rapidly in the endlessly fascinating world of Houdini and Thurston, Blackstone and Dunninger, Doug Henning and Mark Wilson.

Besides bringing together a variety of factual information about the many-sided world of magic, its tricks and its performers, I have attempted to capture something of the mood and mystique, the color and atmosphere, of this graceful and imaginative art. It is hoped that the short survey of the long and fascinating history of magic and magicians, the descriptions and artwork reproduced from dealers' catalogues and the many photographs, engravings, posters and other memorabilia will help the reader to share in the pleasure and cherished friendships I myself have experienced in the decades since my first venturing into this enchanted world.

In selecting tricks and equipment from modern dealers' catalogues for inclusion in the book, I have emphasized wherever possible effects with which I myself am familiar and which I have found to be especially effective in actual performance. This is not to say, however, that among the thousands of tricks in existence, there are not others that are equally effective. And there are others I would have been glad to include if space permitted. Readers are urged, therefore, to write for the full catalogues of the various dealers. The directory of dealers and "catalogue of catalogues" starting on page 231 will make it easy to do this. All decisions regarding inclusion of items have been my own, and no payment has been received for including any item or product.

For fellow magic collectors and all who are interested in magic history, I have also reproduced many items from older magic catalogues dating from the era of generally fine craftsmanship in magical apparatus. The section on "Antique Magic," in particular, is entirely devoted to this field. It is hoped that these reproductions of antique tricks, and of parts of the old catalogues themselves, will interest collectors and acquaint them with special treasures to watch for—treasures such as Hamley Brothers' Fairy Box or Roterberg's Coffee and Milk Trick.

To thank adequately all those generous people who have given their help and cooperation to make this book possible would almost require another book. To the dealers who have graciously permitted the use in the book of material from their catalogues and advertisements, I am particularly grateful. Many of them have taken time from their busy lives to give me interviews and provide other information from their wide knowledge of magic and magicians. They include Recil Bordner, the late Al Flosso, Jack Flosso, Paul Fried, U. F. ("Gen") Grant, Leola LaWain, Bob Little, Jay Marshall, Dr. Harold R. Rice, Irving Tannen and Steve Tigner. It would be impossible to list here all the dealers who have given their cooperation, but their names are in the directory starting on page 231. Without the enthusiasm, creative imagination and hard work of the dealers who devote their lives to the art, the world of magic could hardly exist.

To Mario Carrandi, collector and dealer in old and rare magic, books and memorabilia, go my special thanks for making available posters, photographs and other items from his collection, lending hard-to-find books, and giving other valuable help and advice. I am grateful also to Clayton Albright, Jack Flosso and Robert Schroeter for letting rare items in their collections be photographed. Other photographs have been provided by the Bettman Archive, J. B. Bobo, Lynn Carver, Jose de la Torre, Terry Graczyk, the Harvard Theatre Collection, William W. Larsen, Jr., Leola LaWain, Jack London, Terry McGinniss, H. Muller, Paul Robert-Houdin of the Musée Robert-Houdin, David Price, Anne Resmond, Marilyn Rey, Dr. Harold Rice, Mickey Sharkey, Sotheby's Belgravia, Tony Spina, Irving Tannen and Eve Thumm.

For facts about the history of the International Brotherhood of Magicians, I am obliged to Thomas M. Dowd, International Treasurer, and Irving M. Lewis, International Secretary. Data concerning the Society of American Magicians were sent by Frank Buslovich. Louis A. Rachow, Curator and Librarian of the Walter Hampden Memorial Library at The Players, New York, made the John Mulholland Collection available for consultation. I am grateful to Pace Barnes for help and advice, to Bonnie Stylides for her invaluable editorial assistance, and to all my other friends at E. P. Dutton for their help and support. My thanks to Betty Binns and her associate, Madeleine Caldiero, for their skillful work in designing the book, and to Charles Sopkin for his encouragement. Nancy Thaler and Louise Fisher have typed most of the manuscript and supplied information. Finally, my affectionate thanks to my son, Tom Doerflinger, for his valuable research in connection with the Harvard illustrations, and to my wife, Anne, for her unfailing help and patience during the long months of preparation of the book.

W.D.

Convent, N.J.
May 1977

IMPORTANT DIRECTIONS FOR PRICING AND ORDERING

Send all inquiries and orders for items described in this book DIRECTLY to the dealer or publication concerned, NOT to E. P. Dutton or the author.

The name of the dealer who published each catalogue item or advertisement reproduced in the book is given below or beside the item, together with the latest prices known up to the time of going to press. When two dealers have the same, or closely similar, company names, the city is also given to avoid confusion. For writing to dealers, however, their complete addresses should be used. These addresses will all be found, listed alphabetically, in the "Directory of Dealers and Catalogues" beginning on page 231.

Owing to the frequent price changes to which all products are subject today, all prices given in the book are subject to change without notice. While the prices are as accurate as possible up to the time of going to press, they are given only as general guides to the prices of the items in question and should be regarded only as such.

For this reason, and also to check the continued availability of an item you wish to order, readers are strongly advised to write to the dealer to determine the exact current price and availability status of the item, enclosing a stamped, self-addressed envelope for reply. This should be done before sending your remittance. Inquire also as to the small additional charge that most dealers make to cover the costs of handling, postage and insurance.

Different dealers' prices for the same item may, of course, also vary somewhat.

THE
MAGIC CATALOGUE

MAGIC THROUGH THE CENTURIES

Magic is one of the oldest of the arts. Its practice is reflected in some of the earliest relics of human culture. Among them are the cave paintings limned by prehistoric people on the walls of caverns deep in the earth of southern France and northern Spain. A figure of a dancing man, wearing the horns and skin of an animal, on a wall of the cave of Les Trois Frères in France is believed to be the portrait of a sorcerer of the Old Stone Age. On the desiccated cliffs of the Tassili-n-Ajjer, deep in the Sahara, colored rock paintings many thousands of years old include pictures of men, women and animals believed to be of magical significance.

Among the Indians of North America, the shaman and medicine man held important positions, and magic pictographs survive on the rocks to tell of man's efforts to control the forces of nature. In the ancient books and legends of Arabia, India and Tibet, tales of wonder-working fakirs and lamas have been handed down for centuries to amaze ordinary mortals.

These are examples of magic involving belief in supernatural forces, and should be distinguished from modern magic or conjuring, practiced by entertainers who use deceptive methods to produce marvelous effects. But the borderline between the two, in earlier times, was a narrow one, with considerable overlapping. This appears to have been the case in ancient Egypt, sometimes called "the

Robert Heller, magician and humorist, enjoyed great popularity in the 1860s and 1870s. Here he holds a tiny tobacco pipe for a Harlequin automaton, while the mechanical clown puffs a cigarette, jumps into and out of its box, turns somersaults, whistles and answers questions. (*Harvard Theatre Collection*)

cradle of magic." The Westcar papyrus in the State Museum in East Berlin records a show given before the Pharaoh Cheops about 3000 B.C., by a magician named Dedi. Dedi is probably the earliest professional magician whose name has been recorded. His home was in Ded-Snefru, and his proficiency in the mystic art brought him fame and prosperity. In the court of Cheops Dedi was warmly received and staged a remarkable show. He caused the severed heads of a goose, pelican and ox to rejoin their bodies, and he made a lion follow him around, to the awe of the beholders.

Other Egyptian wizards are described in the Bible. Exodus, Chapter 7, verses 9–12, tells of a contest between Pharaoh's magicians and Moses and Aaron, leaders of the Israelites. According to the Biblical account, Aaron, as directed by the Lord, "cast down his rod before Pharaoh and his servants, and it became a serpent. Then Pharaoh summoned the wise men and the sorcerers, and they also, the magicians of Egypt, did the same by their secret arts. For every man cast down his rod, and they became serpents. But Aaron's rod swallowed up their rods."

It might perhaps be suspected that this account was purely legendary. But the magician Robert Heller actually saw Egyptian magicians in nineteenth-century Cairo perform the trick of turning rods into serpents. The rods, Heller reported, were really snakes that had been hypnotized or drugged in some way to make them rigid. Throwing a snake on the ground and stroking it with mystic passes, the magician would restore its mobility and it would wriggle away. Heller later gave a vivid account of the trick.

The earliest known depiction of an actual magic trick, in the modern sense of the term, is probably a painting found on the wall of a tomb at Beni Hasan, on the Nile. It shows a magician performing the Cups and Balls. The tomb has now unfortunately been flooded by a dam-building project.

The Cups and Balls is a classic trick. It has been popular throughout almost the entire history of conjuring and is still a favorite of close-up magicians. The performer uses three cups, usually unprepared but of special shape, and several small balls, formerly made of cork but now usually crocheted. By his dexterous handling the magician causes the balls to pass mysteriously from cup to cup, to penetrate through the cups, and finally to change to giant balls, fruit or even small birds.

In ancient Greece, wandering entertainers traveled from one town to another giving exhibitions of sleight-of-hand, juggling and puppet plays in the open air. We know that some of these entertainers were widely popular, the Doug Hennings and Mark Wilsons of their day. One of them, Euclides, was honored by having his statue erected in the Temple of Bacchus at Athens, beside that of the great tragedian Aeschylus. The statue of another such entertainer, Theodosius, also stood in Athens, in the Theater of the Istiaians. He was portrayed holding a small ball.

We know about these performers and their statues from the book *Banquet of the Sages,* by the Greek grammarian Athenaeus. Athenaeus also tells of a third performer, Diophites of Locris, who used bladders filled with wine and milk to simulate the effect of ejecting from his mouth either of those liquids desired by the spectators. Probably Diophites exhibited other tricks as well, for he was popular in his time. So much so that Athenaeus cites him as an example of the poor taste of the Athenians in preferring mechanical inventions to the wisdom of the philosophers.

Ingenious inventions, some of them reminiscent of modern illusions and automatons, were also used by the priests of Greece and other Levantine countries to impress the minds of superstitious worshipers. A number of these fascinating devices are described in the writings of the philosopher Hero of Alexandria. Hero's accounts include illustrations that show exactly how the contrivances worked. The accompanying cuts, based on Hero's diagrams, show several of these ancient mechanical wonders. The Shrine of Bacchus, on its handsome pedestal (FIGURE 1), moved to the front of the temple platform under its

FIGURE 1. The Shrine of Bacchus, self-propelled marvel of Greek ingenuity. This and the next four illustrations are from Albert A. Hopkins, *Magic* (New York, 1897).

FIGURE 2. The Shrine of Bacchus: sectional view of interior of pedestal, showing propelling mechanism.

FIGURE 3. The Shrine of Bacchus: mechanisms for delivering wine and milk and for causing the figures to rotate.

FIGURE 4. When a votive fire was lighted on the altar at right, the doors in this Egyptian temple opened msyteriously, untouched by a human hand, to disclose the figure of the god.

own power when its machinery was activated. When it was in position, the ring of dancing figures around the shrine proper began to revolve. The central figure of Bacchus and surmounting statue of Victory spun around to face the spectators. Libations of wine and milk were spontaneously poured onto the altar, and wreaths appeared on the panels at the sides of the pedestal. This early marvel of ingenuity traveled on wheels concealed under its base. The motive power was furnished by falling sand, inside the pedestal. The sinking sand in turn lowered a heavy weight which pulled a cord wound around the axles (FIGURE 2). Other moving parts were activated by smaller weights, while the liquids issued, through valves, from reservoirs under the conical roof of the shrine (FIGURE 3).

Many Greek and Roman temples were equipped with secret chambers which the priests used to cause mysterious voices to issue through speaking tubes. They also concealed devices that simulated other manifestations, ostensibly from the gods. These mysterious effects were well calculated to awe and amaze ordinary mortals in an age when mechanical devices were almost unknown to the multitudes. A worshiper entering the temple shown in FIGURE 4, for example, was expected to kindle a sacrificial fire on the altar at the right. As the fire burned, the doors of the sanctuary slowly and mysteriously opened, without the touch of a human hand, revealing the image of the god to the awed believer.

The mechanism by which this effect was produced is shown in FIGURE 5. When the fire was kindled the air in the hollow base of the altar, E, expanded with the heat and forced liquid from the sphere below it through a curved pipe into a receptacle whose increasing weight pulled a strong cord wound around two rods. To the upper parts of these rods, above the floor, the doors were attached. As the rods revolved in opposite directions, the doors slowly opened. But there was still more to this in-

FIGURE 1

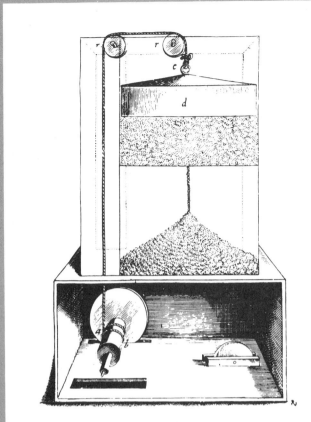

FIGURE 2

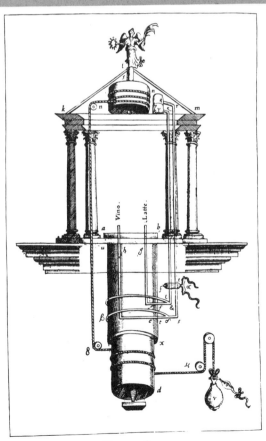

FIGURE 3

FIGURE 4

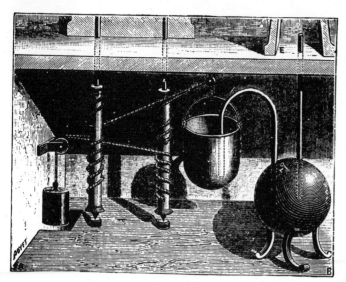

FIGURE 5

FIGURE 5. The cleverly conceived mechanism for opening the sanctuary doors when a fire was kindled on the altar, and closing them when the flames died away.

genious invention. As the fire died down upon the altar, the air inside the altar cooled again and liquid was drawn out of the bucketlike container by the curved pipe, which now acted as a siphon. The rope was pulled in the opposite direction by the counterweight shown in the illustration, and the doors of the sanctuary mysteriously closed.

In pleasure-loving Imperial Rome, wandering sleight-of-hand performers operated much as they did in Greece. They found ready audiences among the throngs of idle citizens enjoying their free bread and circuses, financed by a national treasury filled with revenues from the empire. For the Cups and Balls, Roman conjurers apparently used round pebbles. Their cups were called *acetabulae* (that is, cups for vinegar); hence the performers were known as *acetabularii*.

The Cups and Balls is believed to have come originally from India. It is still a standard effect in the repertories of Hindu street magicians. They use specially shaped, shallow cups with short stems, in place of the deeper cups used by Occidental magicians. The Hindu cups are better shaped for use on the ground, as they can be picked up easily by nipping the stem between two fingers.

Meanwhile, in ancient China, magic was also practiced at temples to awe the simple-hearted worshiper. Joseph Herman Yee has made a study of magic in early

China, on which he reports in *The Chu's Magic*, a beautifully illustrated book/catalogue published by the Chu Magic Studio of Hong Kong. Yee found few references to magic in the more ancient Chinese literature. He attributes this partly to the fact that the Chinese tended in those times to look askance at magic. Magicians, they believed, had sold their souls to devils. Magic was also associated in their minds with chicanery and charlatanism.

Nevertheless, the literature does make it clear that there were itinerant magicians in China some two centuries before Christ, and probably much earlier. Some of these sorcerers, as magicians were called by the Chinese, stationed themselves at the temples. There they used their knowledge of magical principles to hoodwink the superstitious worshipers. Yee writes that they utilized "thermo-dynamic and mechanical" principles, reminding one immediately of Hero's descriptions of temple devices in the Greek world.

"They stationed themselves in temples," Yee writes, "where they concocted stories [that] the gods in their temple could come alive to guide [unsuspecting, superstitious folk] in their problems and/or worries.

"They would ask the folks, who came to the temple seeking an answer to their problems, to pay for temple oil, joss sticks and joss papers, following which the temple gods would either magically move their eyes, raise their hands, nod their heads, or even descend from 'heaven' and answer 'yes' or 'no' to questions asked.

"This was all done by utilizing the power of heat and mechanics."

Yee also discovered an old book entitled *The Chronicle of a Loyang Buddhist Temple (Loyang Chia-Nan Jee)*, written in 523 A.D., which reported on magical illusions performed in and around the city of Loyang. These included various transformations. The skin of a donkey was completely shaved and then restored again. A child was thrown down a well and reappeared mysteriously, uninjured. Seeds were planted and immediately the earth broke open and real dates and melons burst forth.

The Loyang book explained none of these effects. The old-time Chinese magicians guarded their secrets jealously, revealing them only to a single son.

By the seventeenth century magic was popular in China. The author Pu Chu-ling (1640–1715) tells in his *Book of Ghosts* of seeing a magician perform an effect similar to the Indian Rope Trick. The sorcerer threw a rope into the sky and commanded his little son to climb the rope and bring back some peaches from heaven. The boy obeyed and peaches, which were out of season on earth, rained from the skies. They were followed by the boy's severed head, hands, feet, limbs and torso. Sorrowfully, the magician explained that the boy had been caught by heavenly guards and slain for stealing peaches from heaven. The lad, he lamented, was his only son. What was he to do now in his old age? The sympathetic spectators gave generous gifts of money to the poor old man. After carefully putting the money away, the magician collected the boy's remains and placed them in a bamboo case. He mumbled a few magical words and the boy jumped out, as lively as ever.

Such, at least, is the account given by Pu Chu-ling, as cited by Yee. We can hardly be blamed for wondering whether Pu was exaggerating. After all, Indian legends describe the same trick, yet there is no authenticated record of its actually being performed there. If Pu really did see the illusion performed in China, it was probably staged under trees, in whose branches the rope could be held up, at night, or under other special conditions arranged by the magician.

The Middle Ages and Renaissance

With the fall of Rome, Europe entered the long period of cultural decline known as the Middle Ages. Culture was dominated by the Church. Those suspected of witchcraft and trafficking with the devil were mercilessly hunted down, tried, and usually executed. At the same time, magic continued to fascinate the popular mind. Merlin, the great magician, was a central figure in the romances of King Arthur and his Table Round. Merlin was reputed to have transported the great slabs of Stonehenge from far away and erected them in one night. In the old French lays and epics, and in the folktales of Germany and Scandinavia, giants, dwarves, witches and trolls abound. Alchemists like the noted Roger Bacon in thirteenth-century England toiled over smoky braziers and bubbling flasks as they searched for an elusive Philosopher's Stone that would transmute base metals into gold.

Itinerant conjurers continued to show their tricks outdoors in the streets and at fairs, though they were looked upon with disfavor by both the ecclesiastic and civil authorities in England, France and other countries. Even simple sleight-of-hand performers were in danger of being seized by the Inquisition and condemned for practicing witchcraft. Pointing out the harmlessness of these entertainers, Roger Bacon described them and their tricks in language that makes them sound much like the tricks of modern magi and ventriloquists.

The old legends of Charlemagne and his paladins, and travelers' stories brought home from the mysterious East during the Crusades, included tales of sorcery and enchantment. These tales eventually found their way into the Renaissance epics of Ariosto and other poets, and, through them, into the marionette shows of the poor.

It was in the late sixteenth century that the first books in English on conjurers' tricks appeared. The earliest of these was Reginald Scot's *The Discoverie of Witchcraft,* published in 1584. Scot's book contained several chapters explaining the methods used by conjurers and sleight-of-hand artists. It shows that a relatively extensive repertory of effects was known to the magical fraternity of those days. This is also borne out by reports of the spectacular effects performed, as Milbourne Christopher has pointed out, by two noted amateur magicians of the sixteenth century, Boccal, an Italian, and Dalmatius, a Spaniard.

Not all the magicians in those days were poor, wandering street performers. Then, as now, well-to-do men loved magic. Probably the most famous performer of the sixteenth-century wizards was Hieronymus Scotto, an Italian. He received liberal fees for shows which he gave for Queen Elizabeth I of England and others, and was entrusted with important diplomatic missions.

Magic in the Seventeenth and Eighteenth Centuries

From the early books of magic, and from engravings and etchings dating from the seventeenth and eighteenth centuries, we can tell a good deal about the conditions under which ordinary magicians worked.

Usually they exhibited their tricks outdoors, where they would set up folding tables in the street or in a village square. Staples of their performances were the Cups and Balls and card tricks. The insignia of their profession was a loose apron, with a large pocket in the front, called the *gibecière.* The apron was used to carry their balls, cards and other small equipment. The *gibecière* also served as a convenient receptacle into which they could unobtrusively drop palmed balls or other objects. One of these magicians is pictured in the etching, *Il Giocatore di Bussolotti in Roma (The Cups and Balls Player in Rome),* dating from 1821 (page 6).

Some street magicians were also fortune tellers. They could charge a regular fee for this work, whereas at their street shows all that could be done was to pass the hat. Sometimes they would be admitted to homes and palaces to tell fortunes and entertain. Such a scene is shown in the beautiful engraving called *L'Escamoteur (The Conjurer),* believed to be by the French artist Philippe Mercier (1689–1760). The swarthy-faced magician in the picture may be a gypsy, or he may merely have darkened his face to look like one of that mystic race so highly esteemed as fortune tellers. John Mulholland published some years ago in *The Sphinx* the following verses that appeared under an English copy of this engraving:

> With Cups and Balls the juggler plays;
> By turns, this here, that there conveys:
> The Cards, obedient to his words,
> Are by a fillip turned to Birds,

RIGHT TOP: A traveling magician of the early nineteenth century entertains a small audience at a country fair.

RIGHT BOTTOM: The English conjurer and showman Gyngell performed in the early nineteenth century at fairs, in rented rooms in inns, and at London's Vauxhall Gardens.

ABOVE: *The Cups and Balls Player in Rome,* an etching of 1821, shows the magician just reaching the point in the classic trick where the tiny balls change into giant ones. He is wearing the loose apron or *gibecière,* which was the badge of his profession.

RIGHT: *L'Escamateur (The Conjurer),* an engraving attributed to the French artist Philippe Mercier (1689–1760). A conjurer entertains ladies with cups and balls and fortune telling.

His little Boxes change the grain
Trick after trick deludes the train.
He shakes his bag, he shows all fair,
His fingers spread and nothing there,
Then bids it rain with showers of gold,
And now his Iv'ry Eggs are tolde,
But when from thence the Hen he draws
Amaz'd spectators hum applause.

Fair and carnival performers often traveled by wagon. They worked from a stage set up at one end of the wagon, or assembled with trestles, planks and poles on which a canvas background was hung. The early nineteenth-century engraving at the left shows one of those wagon performers. He is wearing a fanciful costume and sporting a diabolical-looking moustache and goatee, as some magicians do today. Many children are among those enjoying the show.

Usually these itinerant magicians made a modest living by passing the hat. But Isaac Fawkes, the leading British fairgrounds performer of his day, had a closed booth and charged an admission fee. Fawkes died in 1731 a rich man, leaving a fortune of £10,000.

Also highly successful was Gyngell, a favorite at fairs in London and the provinces from about 1788 until his death in 1838. The woodcut opposite shows Gyngell in action. Like many magicians of the late eighteenth and early nineteenth centuries he wore an elaborate, plumed cap and suits of colored silk or satin. He was perhaps the greatest of the old-time itinerant conjurers who often depended on the generosity of their audiences rather than charging admission at the door. Sometimes, however, the audience had to pay from 1 to 3 shillings admission to see his show.

During the latter part of the eighteenth century and the earlier years of the nineteenth, magicians tended to use large tables draped to the floor, or almost to the floor. These tables often served to conceal assistants who passed up articles to the performer behind the table or through traps in its top. Many conjurers went in for an array of impressive-looking magical apparatus to heighten the effectiveness of their stage settings. Automatons began to be popular attractions. Some of these were genuine mechanical marvels but others were worked simply by means of cranks turned by hidden assistants.

The most prominent Italian magician in the late eighteenth century was Giuseppe de Willeldal Pinetti (1750–1800). He appeared not only in Italy, but also in France, where he entertained King Louis XVI in 1784. In Paris, interest in magic was high at that time owing to the fame of the charlatan Cagliostro, who claimed that he could actually raise diabolical spirits and perform miracles.

An inventive artist, Pinetti presented a full evening show. He prided himself on the elegance of his suits, which were covered with gold braid and expensive laces.

In the accompanying engraving he is shown performing a trick whose secret seems to have been lost—nailing a chosen card to the wall with a pistol shot. John Mulholland wrote in *The Sphinx* that this effect was performed with a roofing nail which the magician loaded into his pistol. He then tossed the pack of cards into the air and fired through the falling cards. Instantly the chosen card appeared, nailed onto the wall. Mulholland said he did not know how the trick was done.

There are at least two old engravings showing Pinetti performing this feat. Though the composition of the two pictures is different, both show the same stage setting and props: tables with long drapes, candlesticks, a small figure of a man that looks like an automaton, a bottle with a bird on the stopper, chandeliers, rectangular mirrors on the wall at back of the stage. Presumably, therefore, these details are accurate. One of the engravings appears on the next page.

Magic in Europe, 1800–1875

One of the most distinguished magicians during the first half of the nineteenth century was Louis Christian Emmanuel Apollinaire Comte (1788–1859). He was expert with cards and was also noted for his flower tricks. To his talents as a conjurer, Comte added an uncanny ability in ventriloquism. When appearing in a provincial city, he used this talent to play all sorts of practical jokes as he strolled about the streets. After perpetrating some bizarre joke, he would identify himself as Comte, the magician. It was excellent advertising for his show.

Also very popular in Paris was Bartolomeo Bosco, an Italian magician a little younger than Comte. He was born in Turin in 1790 and had led an adventurous life as a soldier in Napoleon's army. Bosco was particularly distinguished for his skill with the Cups and Balls. Bosco's work was described by Jean Eugène Robert-Houdin, the young watchmaker who was destined to become famous as France's leading magician. Robert-Houdin saw Bosco's show in Paris in 1838. After his performance with the Cups and Balls, Bosco announced that he would do the "pigeon trick." He brought forward a black pigeon, and to "punish it for behaving badly," cut off its head on a wooden block. This was done "with or without blood," as the audience preferred. Bosco prevented the flowing of blood by pressing on an artery in the pigeon's neck, or produced bleeding by releasing the pressure. Then a white pigeon was similarly decapitated. Its head was placed in a false-bottomed box with the body of the black pigeon, and vice versa. Bosco then produced from the boxes a live black pigeon with a white head, and a white pigeon with a black head. The audience assumed that the

British conjurers of the late eighteenth or early nineteenth century. They used heavily draped tables and lots of apparatus.

LEFT: The Italian magician Pinetti nails a playing card to the wall with a pistol shot.

ABOVE: Bosco performing with birds in Paris. He clearly used, also, an arsenal of apparatus. (*Bettman Archive*)

two dead pigeons had been restored to life, and they applauded heartily.

Bosco next made a canary bow to the audience by pinching its feet painfully as he held it on his hand. He then offered it to a lady in the audience as a gift, but before reaching her seat, strangled the bird. For a touch of "comedy" he pretended that the lady had killed the bird and that he would be beaten by his wife for coming home without her beloved pet.

Finally, as a climax, Bosco put the dead bird into a box and drew out a live canary. This one he pushed alive into the barrel of a large pistol. The gun was handed to a spectator who was asked to aim and fire. As the shot was fired Bosco lunged with a sword and impaled a duplicate canary on its point, as shown in the accompanying engraving.

Robert-Houdin noted that the spectators were so impressed by Bosco's big reputation as a wonder worker that they simply assumed the various pigeons and canaries had been magically restored to life. They did not realize that he killed bird after bird at every performance. But Robert-Houdin saw the act for what it was. He called Bosco's tricks "bird-murders." (This magician should not be confused with Leon Bosco, the later, comic magician of the Le Roy-Talma-Bosco trio.)

A more elegant French performer was Philippe, whose show Robert-Houdin also attended. Philippe's real name was Jacques André Noé Talon, and he was born in 1802. He began his career as a confectioner. He was working at this trade in Aberdeen, Scotland, when he decided to become a professional magician. Philippe won quick success in the British Isles and his own country. His work was much influenced by a troupe of Chinese conjurers whom he saw in Scotland. He worked in "Chinese" costume, as shown in the engraving on page 10. Philippe is said to have been the first Western magican to perform the Chinese Linking Rings. In this classic feat, eight or more solid steel rings mysteriously link together, unlink, and form a variety of changing combinations and patterns. Another "first" of Philippe's was the production of large bowls of water and goldfish, followed by a quantity of chickens, ducks and other livestock. Philippe's show also featured various automatons. One of these was a harlequin, perhaps somewhat like the one shown in the photograph on page 1.

Another leading magician of the period was Scottish-born John Henry Anderson (1814–1871), who billed himself as "The Wizard of the North." Anderson's work is usually associated with the style of magic typical of the pre-Robert-Houdin period, although both men were ac-

TOP LEFT: Philippe, shown here in one of his Chinese effects, was one of the early French magicians who inspired Robert-Houdin. (*Mario Carrandi Collection*)

TOP RIGHT: The handsome John Henry Anderson, "Wizard of the North," came out of Scotland to delight audiences in England, America and around the world.

LEFT: English translation of the playbill for the premiere of Robert-Houdin's Soirées Fantastiques, from an American edition of the conjurer's *Memoirs* (Philadelphia, Henry T. Coates & Co., 1859), p. 245.

ABOVE: Jean Eugène Robert-Houdin, the "Father of Modern Magic," in 1848. From a lithograph by Léon-Noël in the Musée Robert-Houdin, Blois, France. (*Courtesy of Paul Robert-Houdin*)

tive at much the same time. Anderson is Scotland's most famous magician; and during his career he made and lost fortunes, achieved a fabulous reputation and proved himself one of the most skillful and ambitious publicists in the history of the business. His show was noted for its striking illusions and wealth of costly apparatus.

In 1849 the Wizard of the North gave a command performance for Queen Victoria, Prince Albert and the Prince of Wales at Balmoral Castle. Two years later he crossed the Atlantic for his first visit to America, and enjoyed great success in New York. Later he toured Australia, took his show to Hawaii, and from there traveled to San Francisco and began another tour in the United States and Canada.

Anderson was plagued by fires which destroyed his theaters and equipment on several occasions. He was a master of original advertising techniques and a liberal donor to charities, but he eventually found himself in financial straits which led to bankruptcy and darkened the end of his career. His son, John Henry Anderson, Jr., remained in the United States and enjoyed some popularity here as a magician.

Though all these performers were successful, the most important figure in magic in the mid-nineteenth century was Jean Eugène Robert-Houdin. So original and influential were his contributions to the art that he is known as the "Father of Modern Magic." This marvelous magician was born in the city of Blois, in north central France, December 7, 1805. His name at that time was Jean Eugène Robert, and his father was a watchmaker, whose mechanical ability and skill with tools the boy obviously inherited. "I am inclined to believe," Robert-Houdin later wrote, "that I came into the world with a file or a hammer in my hand, for from my earliest youth, these implements were my toys and delight."

Jean Eugène's father was anxious for his son to be a lawyer, but after a short apprenticeship to a legal firm, the young man's fascination with machinery won out. With his father's consent, he went to live with a cousin in Avaray, and studied watchmaking. One day he entered a bookstore to buy a treatise on clocks and watches. That evening, when he opened the book at home, he found that the proprietor had handed him by mistake a book on conjuring, the *Dictionnaire Encyclopédique des Amusements des Sciences, Mathématiques et Physiques*. Intrigued by what he read in this volume, Jean Eugène took lessons in sleight-of-hand and became an avid amateur magician.

In 1830 young Robert married Josèphe Houdin, the seventeen-year-old daughter of another watchmaker, and added her surname to his own. His bride's father had a watchmaking business in Paris, and Robert-Houdin went to work with him there. As a sideline he sold mechanical toys and magic tricks in a shop connected with his father-in-law's watchmaking establishment.

While working in this way to support his family, Robert-Houdin devoted much time and energy to his great interest, inventing and building intricate mechanical automatons. After many discouragements and privations he succeeded in completing a mechanical man who wrote answers to questions on paper, an artificial singing bird that imitated the song of a nightingale "perfectly," and other ingenious automatons. Two of these he sold at a large profit. He also exhibited a number of his creations at the Exhibition of 1844. King Louis Philippe spent two hours at Robert-Houdin's exhibit and complimented him highly, and he was awarded a silver medal.

His dream, ever since seeing the shows of Comte and Philippe, had been to present a full evening of professional magic entertainment. Now he felt that his automatons were fine enough to grace such a show. Leasing a large room in the Palais Royal, he had it made into a comfortable small theater seating about 200.

There, on July 3, 1845, Robert-Houdin presented the first of his famous Soirées Fantastiques. The program of magic and automatons included a number of his most charming mechanical creations. One of these was the "Orange Tree," which I shall discuss in the section on magic with flowers (page 75). Another was the "Pastrycook of the Palais Royal." From a doorway in a model of the Palais, an automaton appeared carrying on a tray whatever refreshments the spectators requested: brioches, cakes, liqueurs or ices. A woman spectator's own ring mysteriously disappeared from her purse and reappeared in a brioche served by the little pastrycook. The figure would also make the correct change for a gold coin given him in payment for a pastry. This automaton was actually less complicated in its working than most of those invented by Robert-Houdin: his small son was concealed inside the model of the Palais Royal, and placed the items requested on the pastrycook's tray to be carried out through the doorway.

At the first performance of the Soirées Fantastiques, Robert-Houdin was so nervous that he could hardly get through the program. He soon gained confidence, however, and favorable press reviews like the one in *L'Illustration* reproduced on page 76 soon brought such crowds to the little theater that hundreds had to be turned away.

Robert-Houdin's show differed from the conjuring acts of his predecessors not only in the originality of his automatons, but also in a number of reforms he put into effect. These new principles set fresh standards for magicians and helped to establish Robert-Houdin's reputation as father of the modern form of the art. In his *Memoirs* he defines these new principles clearly. First, he insisted on having "an elegant and simple stage, unencumbered by all the paraphernalia of the ordinary conjurer, which looks more like a toyshop than a serious performance." He aimed to abolish "all instruments designed to make up for the performer's want of skill. Real sleight-of-hand must not be the tinman's work but the artist's, and people do not visit the latter to see instruments perform."

Robert-Houdin also dispensed entirely with accomplices in the audience, having "always regarded such trickery as unworthy [of] a real artist." Clear gas jets were used to light the stage, in place of "the thousands of candles whose brilliancy is only intended to dazzle the spectators and thus injure the effect of the experiments." He did away with the long tablecloths reaching down almost to the floor and providing such obvious places of concealment for assistants. Gone from Robert-Houdin's show, too, were the plumed caps and satin or velvet doublets affected by such magicians as Gyngell and Bosco. He determined to abstain "from any eccentric costume" and always appeared, instead, in elegant evening dress. Thus he established a tradition that has been observed by magicians ever since.

"Finally," Robert-Houdin writes, "I wished to offer new experiments divested of all charlatanism, and possessing no other resource than those offered by skillful manipulations, and the influence of illusions."

He concludes: "This was, it will be seen, a complete regeneration in the art of conjuring. . . ."

These new methods that Robert-Houdin believed a performer should follow have since been accepted by nearly all magicians as standard practice.

Two other classic effects that are still popular today originated with Robert-Houdin. He performed both of these with his son Emile. One was the Aerial Suspension, in which the magician's assistant is made to float in the air, supported only by a slender rod, broom or sword under his armpit or shoulders. The other was the Second Sight act, in which Emile, seated on the stage and blindfolded, described in detail personal articles of all kinds handed by members of the audience to his father. (For this effect Robert-Houdin invented an ingenious voice code so natural that it defied detection.)

When the revolution of 1848 forced Robert-Houdin to close his theater in Paris, he went to London, where he was immensely successful. He appeared twice before Queen Victoria and also took his show to Ireland, Scotland, Belgium and Germany.

One of the most dramatic episodes in the great magician's career was still to come. This was his official mission to Algeria in 1856 at the request of the French government. The *marabouts*, a cult of Islamic sorcerers, were stirring up rebellion against French rule in Algeria. To prove to the Arabs that the French brand of magic was more powerful than theirs, a contest between Robert-Houdin and Arab sorcerers was held in a theater in Algiers. The audience of *marabouts* and other Arabs was unfriendly at first but warmed up somewhat when

the French magician caused a basket to fill mysteriously with flowers, produced a shower of gifts from a magic cornucopia, and poured boiling coffee and other drinks from his inexhaustible bottle.

It was now time for Robert-Houdin to impress and even frighten the Arabs by proving to them that he possessed supernatural powers. Therefore he announced that by the strength of his magic he could make even the strongest of them as weak as a child, and invited any man present to come forward for the test.

A powerfully built young *marabout* stepped boldly onto the stage. Robert-Houdin showed him a light but strongly constructed chest, with a handle on top, and asked the man if he could pick it up. The Arab did so effortlessly. Robert-Houdin then announced that he would now make him weaker than a woman, and challenged him to lift the box again. Confidently grasping the handle, the young Arab strained every muscle but could not make the chest budge. He braced his legs for a supreme effort and tugged vainly at the chest. Perspiration broke out on his face and he cursed under his breath. Then his features became contorted, his legs buckled and he began to writhe and twist in agony. Dropping the chest as though it were red hot, he pulled his burnoose over his head and, with a yell, fled from the stage and out of the theater.

Robert-Houdin explains in his recollections that the secret of this illusion, known as the Light and Heavy Chest, was a steel plate concealed in the bottom of the chest, and a powerful electromagnet under the stage. When the current was switched on at a sign from Robert-Houdin, the box was literally held to the stage in a grip of iron. Then, at another signal, an electric current was passed into the handle by means of an induction coil inside the box. The electric shock thus produced was what had sent the Arab screaming toward the exit.

The climax of the exhibition was now to come. Robert-Houdin announced that he possessed a magic talisman that protected him against bullets. He then defied the best marksman in the theater to take a shot at him. A disdainful Arab bounded onto the stage and proudly proclaimed that it would be a pleasure for him to kill the Frenchman. Robert-Houdin handed him a pistol, powder and ball to examine. The Arab agreed that all were in good condition. "I am going to kill you," he announced coldly.

Robert-Houdin had the challenger mark the leaden ball with his knife so that it could be identified, and it was loaded into the pistol with powder and wads. The magician then held up an apple stuck on the point of a knife, and confidently took up his position on the stage, facing the Arab.

"Aim straight for the heart!" he shouted.

The young Arab aimed carefully and fired. Robert-Houdin, untouched, calmly cut open the apple and showed the bullet embedded in it. Then he advanced toward the shocked marksman and had him identify the bullet in the apple as the same one he had marked.

Pandemonium broke out in the hall, and amidst shouts of "Djinn!" and "Satan!" the spectators scrambled out of their seats and speedily emptied the hall. Later the Arab chieftains presented Robert-Houdin with a beautiful inlaid table and a handsome certificate proclaiming the superiority of his magic. The *marabouts* were completely discredited and nothing more was heard about a rebellion against the French government.

This was the effect generally called the Bullet-Catching Trick. Its secret involved substituting by sleight-of-hand a fragile wax bullet, colored to look like lead, for the marked bullet. The real bullet was pressed into a slit in the apple, ready to be produced. When the charge was fired the imitation bullet disintegrated harmlessly.

Robert-Houdin devoted the later years of his life to scientific research. He died at his home near Blois in June of 1871. The Robert-Houdin Museum in Blois contains memorabilia of the great necromancer and some of his automatons and other inventions. His theater in Paris was continued by his son Emile and later passed into the hands of the talented conjurer George Méliès. It was Méliès, an innovative artist, who made some of the earliest motion pictures, including many imaginative short films of fantastic magic effects, and what were perhaps the first movies to tell sustained fictional stories.

One of the few European magicians of the mid-nineteenth century to rival Robert-Houdin in artistry and inventiveness, if not in mechanical ability and showmanship, was an Austrian, Johann N. Hofzinser. He remained primarily an amateur, gave few shows for the general public, and after his death his wife destroyed all of his secrets that she could, in accordance with his instructions. Nevertheless, so charming was Hofzinser's work that records of it had been kept by others, and many of them were rescued from oblivion by a Viennese magic writer, Ottokar Fischer. Hofzinser performed a wide range of different effects in drawing-room magic. He was especially noted, however, for his work with playing cards. His skill in card manipulation was legendary, and luckily Fischer was able to preserve many of the details of these effects in his book entitled *J. N. Hofzinser's Card Conjuring.*

We may now turn temporarily from the magic scene in Europe to see what was happening meanwhile in the New World.

Magic Comes to America: The Earlier Years

During the first half of the eighteenth century, magic crossed the Atlantic and gradually established a beach-head on the puritanical shores of America. In 1734 an advertisement in the New York *Weekly Journal* announced that Joseph Broome, a German conjurer, would show his wonders of sleight-of-hand at a private house in the city. This is the earliest known advertisement for a magician in North America. Many other conjurers came in Broome's wake to try their fortune in the New World. They presented magic, ventriloquism, "educated" or "learned" animals, and mechanical figures. Early in 1798 William Frederick Pinchbeck was exhibiting an educated pig in Boston.

The first well-known magician born in America, however, took his talents back to the Old World and spent his entire professional career in the British Isles and on the continent of Europe. He was Jacob Meyer, who was born in Philadelphia in 1735 to a Jewish family. When he became a convert to Christianity, Meyer adopted the name of his native city. Under the name of Philadelphia he successfully toured the United Kingdom, Germany, Portugal and Spain with his magic act. He appeared in Russia before the Empress Catherine II and in Constantinople before the Sultan Mostapha III. A specialty of Philadelphia's was the production of phantoms, by using a magic lantern to project images on clouds of vapor. Philadelphia's show was typical of its era in its use of a big display of elaborate apparatus.

Advertisements published by showmen in Salem, Massachusetts, newspapers in the autumn of 1804, as shown on page 14, give an indication of the magical and magic-related entertainment of the time. The magician and ventriloquist John Rannie, arriving from Boston where he had enjoyed a run of sixty nights, announced that he would perform a startling watch trick. He would "break with a large hammer ten or twelve gold or silver watches belonging to the company present . . . after which he restores to each lady and gentleman their watches, whole and safe."

Mr. Rannie promised also to exhibit "a philosophical fish" who would "perform many wonderful deceptions, by drawing several cards from the pack, which have been thought of by the company, and also by writing down, with a pen, any words or numbers desired." A cut shows the educated fish patriotically writing the name "Washington" in flowing script.

Mr. Rannie also promised to perform other feats of magic, ventriloquism, balancing and wire dancing.

"Educated" animals were an attraction that had long been popular. At about the same time that Mr. Rannie introduced his fish, a "Learned Goat" was exhibited at the Sign of the Ship Tavern in Salem. The goat combined mathematical with literary accomplishments; it would read, spell, add, subtract, multiply and divide, tell the time and date, distinguish colors and "discover the cards drawn" from a pack by spectators.

Apparently showmen came often to Salem, for only

about six weeks after the Rannie programs, new attractions were being advertised. They included acoustical and optical wonders and several automatons. One of these was a "piece of machinery" representing a small boy, who could "write correctly, dotting and crossing the letters I, and T, with precision and care." There was also an "automaton tumbler" who would perform many antics, turn somersaults and do a hornpipe on a rope or wire. Another mechanical figure, a "Little Magician," was described as characterizing "a foreign Philosopher, holding in one hand a Magic Wand, by the seeming virtue of which he performs many wonders. . . ."

Richard Potter of Massachusetts was appearing in Boston in 1811. He toured the region with a general magic act for twenty years or more. He was one of the best-known magicians then active in the United States.

The attractions most acceptable to American audiences in this period seem to have been those that offered some scientific or cultural significance. "Philosophical experiments" and mechanical automatons intrigued sober Yankees more than mere tricks. Of all the automatons exhibited in America before the Civil War—or indeed after it—none aroused so much interest and speculation as the "Automatic Chess Player." This phenomenon was invented by Baron Wolfgang von Kempelen, exhibited by him in Europe, and brought to America by Johann Maelzel in 1826. This remarkable invention was the almost life-size figure of a turbaned Turk, seated above a chest equipped with sliding doors. When these doors were slid open one after another, the spectators could look inside, where they saw a maze of wheels, gears and other machinery. When the doors were closed again, the Turk would take on any spectator in a game of chess. He would pick up the pieces between his thumb and forefinger and carefully move them to the desired square, or discard them as the case might be. The Chess Player was nearly always victorious in his games. Edgar Allan Poe saw the automaton in Richmond and published a thoughtful essay analyzing the mystery. He divined correctly that the automaton was activated by a human chess player cleverly concealed amid the machinery in the wooden chest. But he failed to explain correctly how the operator was hidden while the machinery was displayed.

Two European magicians were especially popular in America during the 1830s and 1840s. Signor Antonio Blitz, who had previously appeared in many European countries, came here in 1835. So popular was Signor

OPPOSITE: Clippings from Salem, Massachusetts, newspapers describe some of the headliners exhibited in 1804 at the city's Philosophical and Mechanical Museum and in local taverns. (*Author's Collection*)

Blitz that at one time no fewer than thirteen imposters were trading on his name and imitating his repertory.

Another outstanding European artist active in America during this period was Andrew Macallister. Macallister had formerly been an assistant to the French conjurer Philippe, and he brought many of Philippe's finest effects to this country. He presented them and other illusions in a tasteful program divided into two parts which he called the "First Dream" and "Second Dream."

Another performer who first became famous in the Old World but spent much of the later part of his life in America was the gifted and versatile Robert Heller (1826–1878). Heller, whose real name was William Henry Palmer, was born in England, the son of a musician. His magic at first was strongly influenced by that of Robert-Houdin. In 1852 he opened in New York with a program including effects made popular by the French master, such as the "Pastrycook" and "Second Sight." Heller was also a fine pianist and an able composer. For several years, while living in Washington, D.C., he put magic aside to devote himself exclusively to concert work. Later he presented a combined magical and musical program, introducing some illusions into his show. Heller especially endeared himself to his audiences by his dry, humorous style of presenting his magic. He was at the top of his profession in America when he died, suddenly and prematurely, of pneumonia.

One of the chief rivals of Robert-Houdin in England was Carl Herrmann (1816–1887). Born in Germany, Carl was the son of a magician, Emmanuel Herrmann, but he grew up mainly in France. The first member of his family, who formed probably the most famous dynasty of conjurers of all time, to win international acclaim, Carl inaugurated a full evening show in London in 1848. At that time, it must be admitted, his most sensational tricks were "borrowed" from Robert-Houdin. Despite this, his show was received with great enthusiasm. Later he toured Europe and several South American countries, with equal success. In 1861 Herrmann sailed from Cuba to New Orleans. After presenting his show there with great success, he hurried north to New York.

By this time, Herrmann had given up the illusions invented by Robert-Houdin and the other elaborate apparatus he had formerly used. From then on, he depended in his work almost entirely upon manual dexterity. Carl Herrmann entertained Abraham Lincoln and distinguished guests at the White House in 1861. Two years later he returned to England and eventually settled down in Austria to enjoy the fortune he had earned.

The Yankee magician par excellence was Jonathan Harrington (1809–1871). Harrington started performing as a conjurer and ventriloquist when he was only seventeen. For many years he was proprietor of the Old New England Museum in Boston. He toured extensively in New England and was much loved by his audiences, who called him "the funniest man on earth."

Broadway Theatre

MR. E. A. MARSHALL - - - - - - PROPRIETOR
MR. W. R. BLAKE - - - - - - - MANAGER

PRICES OF ADMISSION.

THE GRAND SOIREES
MAGICAL AND PHILOSOPHICAL

Continuing to increase nightly at this Theatre in numbers, Talent & Fashion, each unique and brilliant experiment, being received with the greatest demonstrations of delight and most Rapturous Applause.

MR. MACALLISTER

Will have the honor of giving his Tenth Representation on

Friday Evening, July 6th, 1849

PROGRAMME OF ENTERTAINMENTS.
FIRST DREAM.

1 Dancing Figures, Clown and Harlequin
2 The Travelling Pigeons.
3 The Peacock, a magnificent piece of Mechanism constructed by Mr. McAllister, which at his command will execute every movement as if it was alive; The Peacock will eat, drink, ruffle its feathers spread its wings, fan &c.
4 The CALIFORNIA GOLD BOX, or the secret to fill an empty Money Safe; this experiment will be done in the Parquet.
5 Distribution of Bons Bons from a Handkerchief, for the gratification of the Juvenile Branches.
6 Gloves from a Lady of the audience passed into any of a number of articles placed on a table, and each article so placed afterwards passed indiscriminately from one into the other; This is a Feat of the most extraordinary and pleasing nature.
7 The SPANISH HARLEQUIN, a Mechanism invented by Mr. MacAllister; it will execute different exercises at the word of command, such as Dancing Smoking, Playing, Whistling, &c.
8 GRAND PATRIOTIC FEAT in honor of the day; out of a simple pencil or pencil case Mr. McAllister will produce 500 American Flags, all of which will be presented to the Audience.

Intermission of 20 Minutes between the Parts.
SECOND DREAM.

1 Invisible and visible Plumes.
2 The Marvellous Basket.
3 Spanish Dictionary and Living Exemplifications of the Language.
4 A Present in Expectation.
5 The Aerial Cock, pointing at command of the audience to any hour, and striking the same, composed of a single piece of glass and without works of any kind.
6 To conclude with the unrivalled feat entitled SLEEPING IN THE AIR, a most wonderful Philosophical Experiment—Madame McAllister as the SLEEPING ARAB.

POLYGRAPHIC HALL

ROBERT

HELLER

EVERY EVENING AT EIGHT.

WEDNESDAY AND SATURDAY AFTERNOON at THREE.

THE FAMOUS AMERICAN

CONJUROR!

AND

HUMORIST.

Admission, ONE SHILLING.

John W. Wyman, the magician who specialized in gift shows, performed four times for President Abraham Lincoln. (*Harvard Theatre Collection*)

Another native American magician at the top of his profession was John W. Wyman. Like Robert-Houdin, Wyman was urged by his family to become a lawyer. Instead, he went on the stage in Baltimore and quickly achieved popularity as a magician, ventriloquist, and performer with marionettes. He toured small towns in the eastern states with steady though modest financial success. Wyman specialized in "gift shows" at which prizes of chinaware, furniture, watches and other merchandise and even house lots in New Jersey, were awarded to lucky ticket-holders in a drawing held at the end of the show.

In the latter part of his career, Wyman put more emphasis in his programs on straight magic. He performed for Presidents Martin Van Buren and Millard Fillmore, and entertained Abraham Lincoln four times at the White House.

Wyman was considered an expert on spirit mediums and served on a committee of distinguished citizens who investigated the controversial Fox sisters. In 1848, the two Fox girls reported strange rappings by "spirits" in their home in Hyattsville, New York. Though it was later proven that they had produced the rappings by cracking their toe joints, their claims of producing spirit

manifestations launched the spiritualism movement that created such intense interest in America and Great Britain throughout most of the nineteenth century and on into the twentieth.

Capitalizing on the sensation caused by the Fox sisters, Ira and William Henry Harrison Davenport, brothers from Buffalo, New York, took to the stage with demonstrations of amazing cabinet séances. They allowed themselves to be securely bound by a committee from the audience to benches in a large cabinet. Inside the cabinet were also a variety of musical instruments, slates, bells and other apparatus which the Davenports supposedly could not possibly reach. No sooner were the curtains drawn across the front of the cabinet, however, than the instruments began playing and flying out of the cabinet, writing appeared mysteriously on the slates, and other manifestations ensued.

From America the Davenports took their show to England, where the public became so aroused that riots were started between crowds of believers in spiritualism and skeptics who denounced the Davenports as frauds and charlatans. The British conjurer John Nevil Maskelyne stumbled upon the secret of the Davenports' performances by chance, when he looked into the cabinet and saw one of the brothers, his hand freed, ringing a bell.

Wyman and Maskelyne were among the earliest of the long procession of magicians who campaigned effectively against the deceptions being practiced on a credulous public by fraudulent mediums. Honest performers who made a living by magic resented the charlatans who, by using their methods, claimed supernatural powers. Their exposés of the mediums sometimes took the form of lectures; sometimes séances were staged in magic shows to prove that the conjurer could duplicate the feats of the mediums. So keen was the interest in spiritualism that these exposés were good business for magicians, who could increase their box-office receipts while at the same time satisfying their sense of moral indignation. The campaign of magicians against spiritualists was carried on from the mid-nineteenth century right down to the time of Harry Houdini's intensive activity in that field after World War I.

The Golden Age of the Full Evening Show

The later years of the nineteenth century and the first three decades of the present one saw the culmination of the glamorous full evening magic show. During this period the large stage illusion also reached its fullest development and, in general, was brought to its present high level of impressiveness and sophistication. The major illusions of this era were far more elaborate and

Concealed inside the mysterious Wrestling Cheese of English conjurer P. T. Selbit was a powerful gyroscope that defeated six strong volunteers' efforts to lay the cheese down flat. Selbit featured the trick in vaudeville in 1912. (*Author's Collection*)

COLOR PLATES

1 Harry Kellar walking in the woods, watched by his imps. A poster lithographed by Strobridge.

2 The Great Brindamour toured New England with a show influenced by Alexander Herrmann. Poster lithographed by Strobridge.

3 One of Kellar's most imaginative and animated posters, lithographed by Strobridge.

4 It was in 1894 that Servais Le Roy first performed his Flying Visit illusion, shown in this window card lithographed by Edward Weller of London. In this effect Le Roy mysteriously changed places with his wife in a suspended box, then reappeared from the front of the theater.

5 Aerial warfare between the Le Roy, Talma and Bosco trio, which was organized in 1899, and the Devil. Poster lithographed by Adolph Friedländer of Hamburg.

6 Chung Ling Soo's paper was among the most beautiful of any. Poster lithographed by Horrocks & Co. Ltd. of Ashton-under-Lyme, England.

7 Howard Thurston with a dozen different kinds of animals in a rare poster lithographed by Strobridge for the 1914 season of Thurston's "Wonder Show of the Universe." This poster came in four sections; when joined they made a display about 9 feet high and 7 feet wide.

8 Brochures printed to advertise magicians' lyceum shows were costly and colorful. The Egyptian theme on the cover of this W. W. Durbin brochure recalls his private theater, the American Egyptian Hall, at his home in Ohio.

9 Kar-Mi was the stage name of the American vaudeville performer Joseph B. Hallworth. This poster of 1914, lithographed by National, features an illusion named for Hallworth's wife, Selma, in which a man changed visibly into a woman.

10 An early form of the Passe-Passe Bottle and Glass trick. English, c. 1880–1900.

11 Center: Brass lota, or inexhaustible water vase, decorated with Egyptian motifs. *Right and left:* Chinese Rice Bowls effect; bowls believed to have been imported from China by Martinka & Company.

12 The Cords of Cairo, a rare effect made by the Petrie-Lewis Manufacturing Company and sold by Thayer's, Los Angeles, in the 1920s. It looks somewhat like the Chinese Sticks but works on an entirely different principle.

13 Enameled Baffo box made by Warren Hamilton of Tampa, Florida. A ribbon is stretched through holes in opposite sides of the box. An orange is then placed in the box and the lid closed. A borrowed ring is vanished. When the box is opened both orange and ring are found threaded on the ribbon, the ring in the center of the orange.

2

3

COMEDIANS DE MEPHISTO Co.
LE ROY TALMA BOSCO
THE WORLDS MONARCHS OF MAGIC
THE DEVIL GETS THE WORST OF IT
3229

6

THURSTON
THE GREAT
MAGICIAN
THE WONDER SHOW OF THE UNIVERSE
THURSTON AND HIS PETS

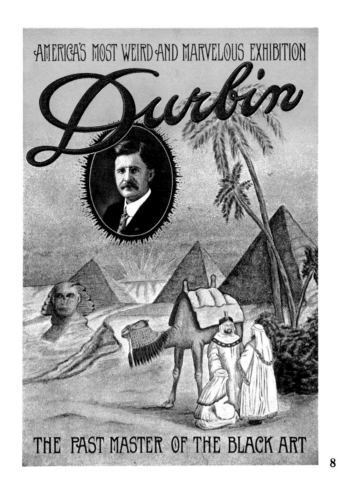

8

9

10

11

12

13

dramatic than the aerial suspensions and productions from cornucopias and portfolios featured by Robert-Houdin and his imitators. Never has the world seen so many magicians of immortal stature as during these golden years of the Herrmanns, Harry Kellar, Maskelyne and Devant, Howard Thurston, Chung Ling Soo, the Great Lafayette, Harry Houdini and their leading contemporaries.

During this era, too, vaudeville was at its height and magic was so popular that often an illusionist and a specialty magician would appear on the same variety bill. Some of the greatest conjurers of the time—men like T. Nelson Downs, the "King of Koins," Horace Goldin and Nate Leipzig—made their reputations in vaudeville.

Alexander Herrmann, known as Herrmann the Great, began his magical career as a youthful assistant to his brother Carl, who was twenty-seven years older. At the age of eight Alexander was appearing in Carl's aerial suspension effect. Later he acted as the medium in his Second Sight act, and with his great natural ability, was trained as Carl's successor in America and the United Kingdom. After a long run of 1000 nights at the Egyptian Hall in London, Alexander Herrmann came to the United States, where he later became a naturalized citizen. A finished performer in every sense, his tall, spare figure, large, dark eyes, and Mephistophelian moustache and goatee made him the very image of the ideal magician. He loved to do magic and would perform amazing impromptu feats of sleight-of-hand on the streets, in restaurants and wherever he went. It was good advertising.

Although Alexander Herrmann was an expert manipulator of cards and coins, many large illusions were featured in his shows. He performed the levitation effect described in the illusion section of this book, with his wife, Adelaide, acting the part of Trilby and himself as the hypnotist Svengali. He also duplicated spirit mediums' feats. Herrmann's version of the Bullet-Catching Trick was even more dramatic than Robert-Houdin's. At the Baldwin Theater in San Francisco, he had five soldiers from a local garrison fire at him simultaneously. He caught their bullets on a china plate. So dangerous was this trick that his wife, Adelaide, begged her husband not to repeat it, but he did perform it again successfully in New York.

In one respect Herrmann departed from the new standards set by Robert-Houdin and regarded as proper by most modern magicians: he often used accomplices in the audience, sometimes as many as five or six in a show. His use of these plants sometimes got him into difficulties. H. J. Burlingame tells in his book *Leaves from Conjurers' Scrap Books* (Chicago, 1891) some amusing anecdotes about Herrmann's stooges. On one occasion, before a show in the South, a rural gentleman was given a marked dollar bill to put in his pocket, together with a ticket for a back row seat. At the proper time in the show, Herrmann borrowed a dollar bill, had it marked, loaded it into a pistol and fired. He then stepped to the footlights and asked if someone in the audience had not felt a strange sensation in his pocket; however, there was no response. Finally seeing his confederate in the back of the theater, Herrmann persuaded him to come up on the stage. He then whispered to him to reveal the dollar note—"Now is the time!" he prompted. Looking confused, the man at last pulled some loose change from his pocket with the words, "Here's all that's left of that dollar note you give me, boss. I done spent part of it for a drink."

Another time, in Chicago, Herrmann's business manager, Frank Curtis, was supposed to arrange for a confederate to occupy a certain aisle seat at each show, wearing a high silk hat of which the magician had an exact duplicate. One night, Burlingame relates, "Herrmann walked down and politely asked the loan of a hat from a man sitting in the usual seat." Not knowing that Frank had neglected to prepare for the hat trick, "the magician took the borrowed hat, kicked it, tore it in pieces, rammed it in a gun and shot it towards the dome. The people looked up and there hung a 'spick and

LEFT TO RIGHT: Carl, Alexander and Leon Herrmann were all handsome men who looked much alike. (*Author's Collection*)

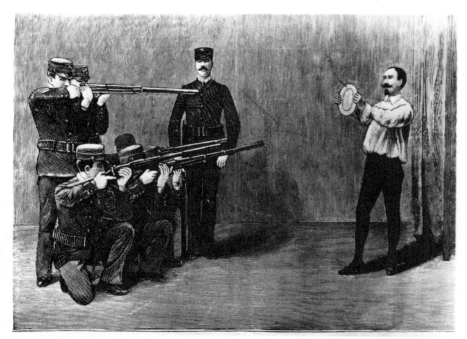

Alexander Herrmann was famous throughout the world as Herrmann the Great. He earned and lost fortunes but always lived in great style. At upper left is a little-known portrait; at upper right he is shown with a birdcage trick; and in the lowest picture, performing the dangerous bullet-catching feat. (*Photos and engraving from Harvard Theatre Collection*)

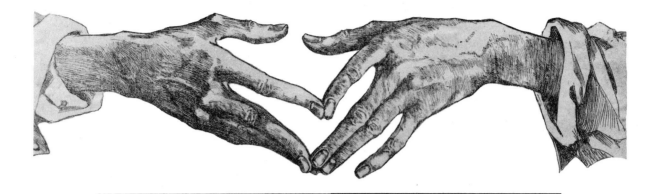

Alexander Herrmann's hands. Drawing by Haydon Jones published in an unidentified newspaper shortly after his death. (*From a scrapbook in the Mario Carrandi Collection*)

span' new hat. It soon fell down, was brushed with a silk handkerchief and handed back to the man from whom it was borrowed. Then only was it discovered that a mistake had been made and the man who had loaned an eight-dollar Dunlap received in return a two-dollar dicer, which just sat on the top of his head. It is unnecessary to state that Frank has never since then neglected his part, as he had to replace the hat which was destroyed."

Despite such occasional contretemps, Herrmann the Great was probably the leading box-office attraction of his time. He earned fortunes and lost them in speculative investments. He shrugged off such financial disappointments and soon recouped his losses. Herrmann traveled in a private car attached to a special train. In another car he carried a team of spirited horses and a beautifully equipped carriage. In each city where he performed, he would drive his fancy rig about the streets as a pleasant form of advertising. At Whitestone Landing, Long Island, he owned an elegant mansion, with his private yacht moored offshore to take him and his guests on summer cruises on the Sound. Whitestone was to become a community of great illusionists, for in later years Howard Thurston, Horace Goldin and Carl Rosini all had homes there.

Heading for a show in Pennsylvania in 1896, Herrmann the Great suffered a fatal heart attack. His last words to his wife were, "I guess I'm not going to get over this. Take the company back to New York." Practically everyone of any importance in the theatrical world attended his funeral.

Immediately after her husband's death, Adelaide Herrmann summoned his nephew, twenty-six-year-old Leon Herrmann, to sail for New York from Paris to work with her in carrying on the show. Leon, who had been performing in Europe, looked much like Alexander, and though he lacked his uncle's inimitable style of presentation, he was welcomed by American audiences. Differ-

ences in temperament prevented Adelaide and Leon from working happily together, however, and after three years they split up their show. Leon, who later aroused his aunt's resentment by billing himself as "Herrmann the Great," died in 1909.

A thorough trouper, Adelaide Herrmann continued to present an elaborate magic act for many years. On one occasion the great illusionist Harry Kellar wrote to her: "Allow me to congratulate you on your grand success. Your very clever work exceeded all that had been told me of your skill. Your manipulation of the Billiard Balls was the finest hand work I ever saw. . . . You certainly are a plucky, hardworking little Woman and the big world must be kind to you."

Adelaide was still active in magic at the age of seventy-five. After finally retiring, she lived in New York until her death in 1932. The three generations of Herrmanns had starred in magic for more than a century.

Meanwhile, in England, another family dynasty had begun to dominate the magic scene. The name Maskelyne, like Herrmann, connoted magic to the British public for nearly a century. The founder and most important member of the dynasty was John Nevil Maskelyne, a descendant of an intellectual family whose ancestors included a former Astronomer Royal. Like Robert-Houdin, young Maskelyne was trained as a clockmaker.

Perhaps it was his scientific and technological turn of mind that led to Maskelyne's becoming involved in the strife between the anti-spiritualists and the spiritualists, and then in professional magic. It was he who managed to look into the mysterious cabinet of the Davenport brothers and discover the secret of their cleverly contrived "spirit" manifestations. It was simple enough, he found: they merely freed their hands from their bonds in the darkened cabinet and then set the high jinks of the spirits in motion.

TOP LEFT: After Herrmann the Great's death his widow, Adelaide, carried on his show.

TOP RIGHT: Leon Herrmann poses for a photo with a poster of his uncle, Herrmann the Great.

LEFT: The gorgeous stage set for Adelaide Herrmann's "Cagliostro" act of 1910 was said to have cost $50,000. (*Photos from Harvard Theatre Collection*)

For some time Maskelyne had been an amateur magician. Now he and a friend, George Alfred Cooke, opened in London a show in which they duplicated the Davenports' "miracles." This launched Maskelyne and Cooke on their popular career. In 1873 Maskelyne leased a theater in Egyptian Hall, the old museum of curiosities in Piccadilly where Alexander Herrmann had played for three years. Maskelyne and Cooke's magic shows at Egyptian Hall soon became a British institution.

Maskelyne was a prolific inventor of illusions. It was he who introduced the first levitation in which a hoop is passed around the body of the lady suspended in midair. In another headline effect he levitated "himself" (actually a dummy that looked exactly like him which was hoisted by black wires) to the dome of the theater. Maskelyne also created a number of automatons which were popular with the public.

In 1902 Maskelyne opened in London a new theater, St. George's Hall, where the tradition of Egyptian Hall was continued for another three decades. Maskelyne's old assistant, Cooke, retired, and his chief collaborator in the later years was David Devant, one of England's greatest conjurers. A captivating performer, clever innovator and shrewd businessman, Devant was co-author with Nevil Maskelyne, J. N. Maskelyne's son, of *Our Magic,* a thoughtful treatise on the principles of effective and artistic presentation of magic as exemplified in the Maskelyne and Devant shows. Devant retired from the stage in 1919. The wand had been broken for John Nevil Maskelyne two years earlier, but magic at St. George's Hall was carried on by his sons, Nevil, Clive, Jasper and Noel until the early 1930s.

However, we are getting ahead of the story. We will have to go back to the 1870s, during the early years of the Maskelyne and Cooke shows in London, to introduce Herrmann the Great's principal rival and one of the most impressive and successful magicians of all time, Harry Kellar. The first of the great international magical celebrities born in America, Kellar led a wonderfully adventurous life. His travels to every continent are unequaled in magical history, and the story of his career reminds one of a novel by Jack London.

His original name was Harry Keller and he was born in Erie, Pennsylvania, in 1849. As a child, after his mother's death, he left home and scrambled for a living as a newsboy on the streets of New York. Taken to upper New York State by a kindly benefactor, he became fascinated with magic and as a teen-ager was employed by a traveling magician, the Fakir of Ava (Isaiah H. Hughes), with whom he worked for six years. From the kindly Fakir, Harry received a good education in magic. He also worked for John Henry Anderson, Jr., and while still quite young he became advance agent and business manager for the Davenport brothers and Fay. The Davenports were so hard to get along with that Kellar

Harry Kellar, the first great American-born illusionist, as he appeared in the earlier part of his career. From a portrait by A. Rimman, reproduced as a theatrical poster by Strobridge. *(Mario Carrandi Collection)*

and William Fay broke with them and struck out on their own. Their act featured a Davenport-type séance and magic performed by Kellar.

When they took this act to Cuba and Mexico, they were astonished and gratified at the enthusiastic response of the Latin audiences to their show. In Mexico, to be sure, they had brushes with bandits and were denounced by an intolerant newspaper as demons, but the big profits they earned made this more than worthwhile.

This success started Kellar on an extensive tour of Central and South America. He learned Spanish and traveled down the west coast, through the Strait of Magellan and up the east coast of the continent to Brazil. En route to England, he was shipwrecked and lost $20,000 in cash and all his apparatus. He managed to get new equipment, including one of the first copies of Buatier de Kolta's Vanishing Birdcage, and sailed for the West Indies and Australia. To avoid the appearance of trading on the name of Robert Heller, he changed the spelling of his last name to Kellar.

During his career Kellar made two complete trips around the world, together with many side excursions to exotic lands. Quick at languages, he learned Dutch, French, and even some Chinese. He took his show to Australia, New Zealand, Indonesia, Hong Kong, Singapore, India, Zanzibar, South Africa. When he appeared in the United States in 1878 business was not good, apparently because people thought of him as an imitator of Heller, who had just died. Another South America tour and his second round-the-world trip, including appearances in Siam, China, Japan and even Siberia, were to intervene before he again returned to America in 1884. This time Kellar's show was an immediate success in New York and after a long run there, he toured the Midwest to packed houses and great acclaim. He continued to be a favorite with the American public for the rest of his career.

The rivalry between Kellar and Herrmann was intense and the two magicians resorted to many stratagems to try to get ahead of one another. As they often appeared in the same cities on much the same dates, their bill posters were kept busy plastering each great magician's paper over that of his rival. Sometimes these layers of posters grew to several thicknesses. Burlingame tells in *Leaves from Conjurers' Scrap Books* how both Kellar and Herrmann would expose each other's tricks, as well as some of their own effects. He also quotes an interview given by Kellar to a reporter describing how he managed to forestall Herrmann while both were playing in Mexico. Herrmann boasted that he had driven Kellar out of Mexico. Kellar, however, managed to rent theaters in Mexico City and the provinces so that he could open in each city a short time before Herrmann.

Kellar did little sleight-of-hand, relying instead upon apparatus tricks and illusions. A perfectionist, he would rehearse every movement of a trick repeatedly, until he had the timing and every minor detail right. Every footstep in his act was planned. One of his greatest illusions was his levitation of a woman, shown in some of his finest posters. It was the levitation invented by Maskelyne, plans of which Kellar apparently obtained from Paul Valadon. That German magician, who had worked for Maskelyne, joined Kellar in 1904. The levitation to the dome of the theater (see page 148) and the Golden Butterfly illusion, a startling vanish of a girl beautifully robed like a butterfly, also originated with Maskelyne. Rivalry in those days was so keen that popular new effects were quickly copied by other magicians. Each performer would present the tricks as "invented by himself." It was part of the game.

Howard Thurston, who had already made a name for himself as a master card manipulator and magical entertainer, arranged to take over Kellar's show as the time for the elder conjurer's retirement approached. In May of 1908, posters appeared on the walls of Baltimore showing Kellar transferring his mantle to the shoulders of Thurston. At a performance in that city on May 16, Kellar formally presented Thurston as his successor.

Kellar had worked hard, as he said, and now he "could afford to take it easy." He lived happily in retirement, appearing on the stage only once more, when Houdini persuaded him to take part in a benefit performance in New York in 1917. Five years later he died, a stalwart and kindly immortal in the annals of magic.

One of the most unusual magicians popular with American audiences at the turn of the century was the Mongolian conjurer Ching Ling Foo. His real name was Chee Ling Qua and he arrived in America in 1898. A magnificent stage and close-up magician, Ching was noted for his production of large bowls of water or small children from an apparently empty cloth. This was an old Chinese trick and Ching Ling Foo was so confident of his Oriental powers that he offered to pay $1000 to any Occidental magician who could duplicate it. Ching's challenge was accepted by William Ellsworth Robinson, an American magician who had assisted Kellar for six years and then spent two years with the companies of Herrmann the Great and after his death, Adelaide and Leon Herrmann. A makeup expert, he often donned a false goatee and moustache and did Herrmann's show for him when the great man wanted to get away to the races. The audience never suspected the substitution. After leaving the Herrmanns, Robinson had operated a bookshop in New York, emphasizing magic books. He had then returned to the stage under the billing of "Robinson, Man of Mystery."

When Robinson offered to do the Oriental trick, Ching Ling Foo hastily withdrew his offer. However, although Robinson had lost his chance of earning $1000, he had come out of the episode with an idea that was to make him famous. He determined to present as fine a Chinese act as Ching's. Under the name of Hop Sing Loo, he performed the new act with the Folies Bergère in Paris in the spring of 1900. A British impresario who was present invited him to bring his act to England, on condition that he use the more euphonious name of Chung Ling Soo. He was billed as "The Marvellous Chinese Conjurer," and his audiences believed that he really was Chinese. His show was a lavish Oriental spectacle, featuring sleight-of-hand, fire-eating and illusions with a Chinese theme. Chung Ling Soo and his old model,

Harry Kellar's most famous illusion was the levitation of a woman invented by John Nevil Maskelyne. (*Poster in the Mario Carrandi Collection*)

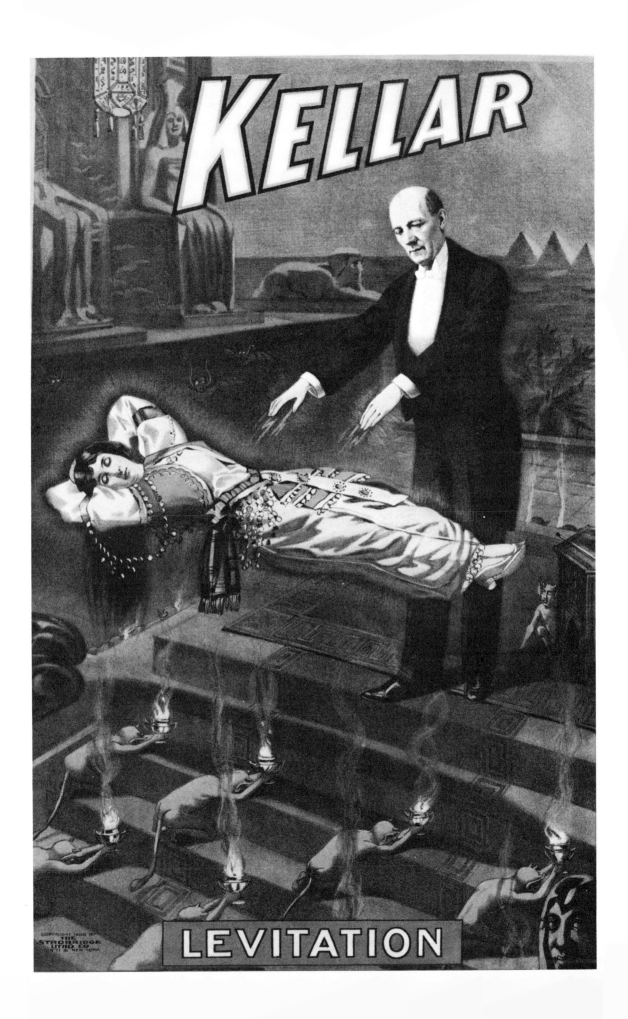

Harry Kellar was the leading American illusionist between Herrmann the Great and Howard Thurston. This rare photograph shows a sensitivity in Kellar's face that few other of his photos captured. (*Harvard Theatre Collection*)

Ching Ling Foo, appeared in London at the same time. Denouncing Chung as an imposter, the real Chinese conjurer once again challenged the stage Chinese to a contest of skill, this time with a purse of £1000.

When Chung Ling Soo and his wife, Dot, who assisted him under the Chinese name of Suee Seen, arrived at the *Weekly Dispatch* office to take up the challenge, Ching Ling Foo failed to show up and again canceled his offer.

This event tended to confirm Chung Ling Soo in the favor of the public. They liked his work and hardly cared whether he was a real Chinese or not. Chung Ling Soo's sumptuously staged and mystifying full evening shows and variety acts were popular attractions on both sides of the Atlantic for years.

One of Chung Ling Soo's feature effects was the Bullet-Catching Trick. Two guns were examined by spectators, who then loaded them with powder and bullets. The magician took up his position at one side of the stage, holding a china plate in his hands. Facing him with the loaded guns were two assistants costumed like Chinese soldiers. At the word of command, they took careful aim and fired at the conjurer. Mysteriously unharmed, the magician caught the bullets on the plate. Chung Ling Soo performed the trick much as Herrmann had done, as shown in the illustration on page 22, except that he used only a two-man firing squad, rather than five.

Like other magicians before him, Chung Ling Soo was tragically betrayed by his own craft. On the evening of March 23, 1918, at the Wood Green Empire Theater in London, he prepared to perform this dangerous trick. Clad in the magnificent robes of a Chinese warlord, he stepped into position and faced the soldiers across the stage. Two British Tommies from the audience carefully inspected and loaded the guns. As the drums rolled, Chung Ling Soo braced himself to catch the bullets on his plate. Two shots rang out and the magician swayed for a moment, then crumpled to the stage. The audience sat stunned; the manager rushed to close the curtains. "I've been shot," Chung Ling Soo gasped as his wife bent over him. "I can't understand it," or "I can't stand it." He was taken to a hospital where he died the following morning.

A Scotland Yard firearms expert examined the two guns. He discovered that each gun actually had two barrels, one of them loaded with a harmless blank charge. Normally, when the trigger was pulled, it was the harmless barrel that fired, and not the one containing the bullet. In one of the guns, however, a screw that plugged a passage between the two barrels had become worn. When the soldier pulled the trigger, both barrels fired and the bullet tore through Chung Ling Soo's body.

Strangely enough, another imitator of Ching Ling Foo also met his death in a theater disaster. He was the Great Lafayette, whose real name was Sigmund Neuberger. Lafayette died in 1911 in a theater fire in Edinburgh from which he was trying to rescue the animals in his act. He was a splendid and highly paid performer, and had he lived he might well have rivaled Howard Thurston in the elaborateness of his illusions and stage settings.

Popular also at the turn of the century was the great Belgian illusionist Servais Le Roy, who came to the United States and performed in America most of his life. Le Roy invented the Asrah illusion, in which a girl is levitated under a cloth and vanishes in the air. He presented a delightful illusion and comedy show with his wife, Talma, and Leon Bosco. He was also noted for his

OPPOSITE: William Ellsworth Robinson (Chung Ling Soo) played the part of a Chinese conjurer so realistically that few people realized that he was actually an American. (*Poster in the Mario Carrandi Collection*)

CHUNG LING SOO
MARVELLOUS CHINESE
CONJURER
JAMES UPTON LTD
ART COLOUR PRINTERS
CAMBRIDGE STREET, BIRMINGHAM

part in the "Triple Alliance" act consisting of himself, Imro Fox and Frederick Eugene Powell.

It was Billy Robinson who, before he became Chung Ling Soo, had been instrumental in arranging a publicity stunt that first made Howard Thurston famous. In 1898, in Denver, Robinson arranged for Thurston to perform his new Rising Cards trick in a private showing for Leon and Adelaide Herrmann and their company. This was an effect in which five chosen cards floated up from the pack to his fingertips. According to news stories, Leon graciously admitted the effect had fooled him. From then on Thurston's publicity called him "The Man Who Mystified Herrmann." It was not mentioned that it was Leon, and not his more famous uncle, Alexander, who had been mystified.

Thurston made his first big hit with his card-manipulation act at Tony Pastor's on 14th Street in New York in 1899. Using the front and back-hand palm and other advanced sleights, he could do incredible things with cards. He could also scale cards to any seat in a theater and would distribute a whole pack that way. He was booked on major American vaudeville circuits, played a triumphant twenty-six-week engagement in London, and performed before royalty on the Continent.

Thurston soon went on from his sleight-of-hand act with cards to the elaborate, full evening illusion shows for which he was chiefly famous throughout the rest of his career. Though he still performed card manipulation, the emphasis in his program was on the newest illusions, presented with a large company and beautiful stage settings.

At times during the 1920s Thurston had four shows playing simultaneously in different parts of the country and in England. He himself headed one company; Harry Jansen (Dante), another; Thurston's brother Harry, a third; and Tampa the Magician, a fourth in the United Kingdom.

Starting with the Leon Herrmann incident, Thurston and his press agents put out many fanciful stories about him, including one to the effect that he had been instructed in magic by holy men in caves high in the Himalayas. Thurston looked on such use of the imagination indulgently, often warning, "Never believe your own publicity."

Even during the Depression, Howard Thurston continued to be a headliner. His last full evening show was in 1931, but the following year he was featured on radio; and in 1934 he staged an elaborate show for President Roosevelt at the White House. That fall he started a farewell tour in vaudeville but suffered a stroke that incapacitated him, and he died in 1936.

Together with Thurston, the outstanding name in magic during the first quarter of this century was that of Harry Houdini. Houdini was not only the greatest

COMEDIANS DE MEPHISTO CO.

LE ROY ★ TALMA ★ BOSCO
WORLDS MONARCHS OF MAGIC.

OPPOSITE TOP: The Great Lafayette, another imitator of the Chinese wizard Ching Ling Foo, died in a theater fire. (*Mario Carrandi Collection*)

OPPOSITE BOTTOM: Great illusionist Servais Le Roy and his wife, Talma, play a trick on their partner, Leon Bosco. (*Poster in the Mario Carrandi Collection*)

RIGHT: Posters appeared in 1908 indicating that the young illusionist Howard Thurston was to succeed the great Kellar. (*Mario Carrandi Collection*)

ABOVE: Illusionist and prestidigitator Howard Thurston (*left*) and master escape artist Harry Houdini. An old composite photograph printed from glass plates. (*Mario Carrandi Collection*)

escape artist of all time, he was also unquestionably one of the greatest showmen. He possessed to an exceptional degree the qualities of dexterity, ingenuity and bravery that are essential for an escape artist. He was responsible for many brilliant innovations in his field of magic. The full evening show he presented in the 1920s combined escapes with general magic and illusions; it was one of the finest ever seen in New York.

Houdini was the son of rabbi, and his real name was Ehrich Weiss. He was born in Hungary in 1874, and brought to America as a small child. He grew up in Appleton, Wisconsin, where his family settled for a time; later he lived in New York.

Houdini became fascinated with magic at an early age, and was working as a magician in Coney Island circuses and museums while still in his teens. It was a hard life. One of young Harry's jobs was to double, between magic turns, as the Wild Man of Borneo. Although Houdini was quite short in stature, he had a powerful physique, and a fierce determination to succeed. He wanted to be able to perform feats that were beyond the reach of the average magician. He took his stage name from the French conjurer, Robert-Houdin, who was then his idol.

While traveling with his young wife Bessie, Houdini found himself stranded in London, with only a few dollars in his pocket. But while there his intense study of handcuffs paid off, for he was able to escape from a pair of the regulation cuffs used by the world-famous Scotland Yard. This feat made Houdini, almost overnight, a headline attraction in England. Later, in Germany, the police were no more successful in thwarting or confining him than their British colleagues had been.

When Houdini returned, eventually, to the United States, his reputation in Europe had preceded him, and he was catapulted quickly into the big time. As an escape artist in vaudeville he commanded top billings and large fees. He also developed a skill in the field of publicity that no other magician has ever equaled. His public exhibitions attracted huge crowds. Again and again he was manacled, shackled, loaded with chains and nailed into packing boxes from which he escaped underwater. He did upside-down escapes from straitjackets while suspended high above crowded streets. His escape from a Chinese torture chest brimming with water, in which he was suspended head down, without room to turn, electrified his audiences. He developed new wonders and spectacular vanishing acts. One of this writer's earliest memories is the magical scene on the stage of the New York Hippodrome when Houdini vanished an elephant.

Harry Houdini was a master at creating an atmosphere of suspense, and making every trick a sensation. I also saw Houdini do the East Indian Needle Trick in his full evening show in New York in 1926, not long before his death. In most magicians' hands this fairly simple trick would be over in a few minutes. The way Houdini did it, inviting a committee of men from the audience to examine his mouth, the needles and thread, and inventing other dramatic business, the trick lasted a good ten minutes and had the audience on the edge of their seats with suspense and apprehension.

During the later years of his life Houdini carried on a tireless campaign against fraudulent mediums. This undertaking, which was filled with sensational revelations and dramatic exposures, made him even more famous. Houdini died prematurely, on October 31, 1926, the victim of an infection caused by an unexpected blow from a college student who was visiting him in his dressing room. Some time earlier the great escape artist had promised his wife and his friends that, if possible, he would send them a signal from the great beyond. Today, each year on Hallowe'en, the anniversary of his death, members of the Society of American Magicians and the International Brotherhood of Magicians in New York make a pilgrimage to Houdini's tomb on Long Island. For many years his widow, Bess Houdini, and many of his friends held hopeful séances on that fateful night. But the signal never came.

Other names, too, stand out as one looks back over the golden years of the full evening show. There was Carter the Great, who began his theatrical career as a talent agent in Chicago, went into magic and took a big show on eight tours around the world. He died in Bombay in 1936. Illusions and memorabilia of Carter's can still be seen at Earthquake McGoon's Saloon in San Francisco (see page 207).

An artistic performer who developed many original effects was Karl Germain (1878–1959) of Cleveland. He gained fame as a lyceum and Chautauqua performer and then moved on to Maskelyne and Devant's St. George's Hall in London to achieve a worldwide reputation. After Germain's retirement from the stage owing to blindness, many of his original effects were presented in the full evening show of his former assistant, Paul Fleming (P. F. Gemill, 1889–1976). Fleming also had a parallel career as professor of economics at the University of Pennsylvania. He presented his charming magic show at colleges and universities throughout the country. He and his brother, Walker Fleming, conducted a magic book business and published the Fleming Classics of Magic, a series of five splendidly edited books by eminent conjurers.

One of the beautfiul posters used by Karl Germain. (*Mario Carrandi Collection*)

Perhaps the longest history of any family dynasty in magic belongs to the distinguished Bambergs of Holland, magicians for six generations. Their prominence in magic goes back to the mid-eighteenth century with Eliaser Bamberg of Leyden, the first in the succession. The next three generations of Bambergs, David Leendert Bamberg; his son, Tobias Bamberg; and *his* son, David Tobias Bamberg, were all highly regarded magicians at the Dutch court.

The next two generations of Bambergs are noted for their work in Chinese costume. Theo Bamberg (1875–1963), who performed under the name of Okito, earned a brilliant reputation as a sleight-of-hand artist, illusionist and creator of tricks and magical apparatus in the Chinese style. He performed throughout Europe and also in the United States, and lived for some time in New York. The beautifully decorated pieces of apparatus built by him and painted with Oriental designs are now valuable collector's items.

Okito's son, David Bamberg, born in 1904, has also had a brilliant career. David grew up in Europe and the United States; he, too, works in Oriental costume, using the stage name Fu Manchu. He has presented elaborate illusion shows with great success throughout Latin America, as well as in the United States and Europe.

Dante, the magician who worked with the Thurston road shows, later became famous independently. He produced *Sim Sala Bim,* a delightful show featuring a wealth of fast-paced illusions. He presented it with great success in the United Kingdom and Europe. When World War II broke out, Dante returned to the United States and in 1940 *Sim Sala Bim* opened in New York. The handsome, genial Dante continued active on the stage and in films for another decade. Eventually he retired to a home in California, where he died in 1955.

Another favorite American magician of the later Golden Age, and probably the leading competitor of Thurston and Dante, was Harry Blackstone. As a young man Blackstone was skillful at woodworking and made trick boxes for August Roterberg, the Chicago magic dealer. His real name was Henri Bouton and he was born in Chicago in 1885. Blackstone began his stage career doing a comedy magic act with his brother, Peter. This grew into a full evening show with Harry as the magician and Peter building the illusions. The show employed a crew of about a dozen people by the 1920s. Blackstone performed in a breezy, informal style, with lots of pretty girls and audience participation in his shows.

In 1926 Blackstone bought a farmhouse on Angel Island in Sturgeon Lake at Colon, Michigan, so that he would have a place to spend his summers and prepare his show for the coming season. His whole company, with all their equipment and livestock, came to the island for the summer. New illusions were rehearsed, scenery painted, and the animals cared for. Blackstone

TOP: Theo Bamberg, famous under the stage name Okito, was the fifth in a family dynasty of noted Dutch conjurers. (*Author's Collection*)

ABOVE: The dashing Dante, whose real name was Harry Jansen, headed one of the Thurston road companies and later scored a great success with *Sim Sala Bim*. (*Mario Carrandi Collection*)

Harry Blackstone. (From *The Sphinx*)

made many friends in Colon, and the village was his home until 1949, when he moved to California. One of the main streets in Colon is now called by his name. Percy Abbott, the magician from Australia who founded Abbott's Magic Manufacturing Company in Colon, first came there as Blackstone's houseguest in the summer of 1927.

The Blackstone show continued to be a leading attraction in American cities for many years. In his later years Blackstone also appeared in films and on radio. His last years were spent in California, where he died in 1965.

Blackstone's art has been carried on by his son, Harry Blackstone, Jr., a dynamic young magician who performs the Vanishing Birdcage and other favorite effects of his father's, as well as new ones, with great spirit and the same ability to involve the audience in his feats. He is a popular figure at the summer Get-Togethers at Abbott's, as well as on the stage, in nightclubs and on television the year round.

Another of the great illusionists is The Great Levante (Leslie George Cole), who now lives in retirement in Sydney, Australia, where he was born in 1892. As a young magician Levante had traveled through Australia and New Zealand. In 1927 he set out on a tour that took him around the world from east to west and ended in England. Levante is a master illusionist and his show featured such tricks as the Human Projectile, in which a large artillery shell containing a girl was apparently fired through a solid metal plate. He is also very skillful at the Substitution Trunk and the Chinese Thumb Tie.

On one memorable occasion in 1939, Levante came to America with a group of British conjurers to attend the convention of the International Brotherhood of Magicians at Kalamazoo, Michigan. Their visit was arranged by Levante's compatriot, Abbott. The British magicians put on a memorable show at the convention and repeated it shortly afterward in New York.

Though many of the noted illusionists have been great travelers, few of them can equal the record of John Calvert. Calvert, a Hoosier born in Indiana in 1911, is as well known in the Levant, the Far East and Europe as he is in the United States. For more than thirty years he has carried on a remarkable career as a magician and movie star on five continents.

Calvert presents a breezy, colorful show with lots of illusions and pretty girls. He has a reputation for finding new and effective ways of presenting effects that might otherwise seem familiar. He is also adept at sleight-of-hand. Calvert probably is unrivaled in the special art of sleeving a coin, and he is said to be able to propel one backward with a snap of his fingers forcefully enough to break a window 6 feet behind him.

In the course of his world travels Calvert has survived many adventures. On one occasion, while flying with his company in his own plane to Nashville, Tennessee, he became confused by ground lights, landed the plane in a field and crashed into a farmhouse. Several of his assistants were injured and he himself suffered a broken leg. Nevertheless he opened next day in Nashville, on crutches. On another trip one of his yachts taking him and his show to Japan barely survived a typhoon in the China Sea. Another of Calvert's yachts was wrecked off the coast of northern Australia when it struck a submerged rock. The true story of the career of John Calvert, with its combination of magic and adventure, is like a tale from the *Arabian Nights*.

The Depression of 1929, the mounting costs of theatrical productions, the growing popularity of the talkies, and the advent of television, all contributed to the decline and, finally, the virtual extinction of the full evening magic show of the Golden Age. For some seventy-five years these beautiful shows, with their exotic costumes and settings, their lovely assistants and handsome performers and their awe-inspiring illusions, opened up for millions a truly magical world of imagination and enchantment. The men and women who created and produced them had to be exceptionally talented, resourceful and dedicated. They deserved the lasting admiration of their audiences, and they received it.

Great Specialists and Club Performers

As new and more difficult sleights were devised and new tricks were invented, the range of magic effects widened and it became impossible for magicians to keep up with all of them. Some of the most distinguished conjurers became specialists in certain fields and are especially remembered for their expertise in a particular branch of magic.

One of the most famous of these specialists was T. Nelson Downs (1867–1938), who became famous at the turn of the century as the "King of Koins." Downs's incredible feats with coins—he claimed that he could easily palm thirty-two half-dollars at a time—made him a vaudeville headliner. Tommy Downs had many friends in the profession with whom he enjoyed exchanging ideas. He was co-author with John Northern Hilliard of *The Art of Magic* (1909), a valuable general treatise, with excellent material on magic with coins and cards and invaluable hints on the principles of showmanship and presentation.

Another master of sleight-of-hand was Nate Leipzig (1873–1939), who was adept with cards, coins and thimbles and in other fields of prestidigitation. Leipzig was especially popular as a vaudeville artist and performer at private functions in the period between the two world wars. He ranks among America's greatest prestidigitators.

An unforgettable personality and one of the greatest of all British and American masters of pure manipulation was Cardini (Richard V. Pitchford, 1899–1973). As a young, aspiring magician fresh from Wales, Pitchford worked as a clerk in Gamage's magic department in London. His first success came in Australia, where he took the stage name Cardini. In the classic form of his act he played the part of an elegant Britisher who has had too many drinks and is confused and irritated by the strange things that keep happening to him: billiard balls appeared unexpectedly between his gloved fingers, clung there, multiplied and changed color; cigarettes appeared from nowhere; his handkerchiefs inexplicably knotted themselves together. Those lucky enough to see Cardini's act never forgot the hilarious spectacle.

In magic with silks, an important specialist and innovator was Ade Duval, whose work is described on page 73.

A very different brand of magic-comedy was performed by another great humorist of the conjuring trade, the crusty, quick-witted and very funny Clarke ("Senator") Crandall of California. For years the Senator held forth at Hollywood's Magic Castle and wrote a popular monthly column for the magic monthly, *The New Tops*. This, and his frequent appearances on the programs of magic conventions, won him a host of friends from coast to coast.

Cardini's skill with billiard balls, coins, thimbles and cigarettes made him one of the greatest prestidigitators of all time. (*Mario Carrandi Collection*)

"Senator" Clarke Crandall of California ranked high among magical humorists. (*Mario Carrandi Collection*)

In the field of mind reading and mentalism, one of the finest performers of the period was Theodore Annemann, who entertained at New York's fabled Waldorf-Astoria. Annemann also edited the influential *Jinx* magazine, in which a great deal of fine magic appeared. The *Jinx* material is still published in book form. Many of Annemann's subtle mental effects are also given in his book, *Practical Mental Effects* (New York, 1944).

An even longer career as a master of mentalism was that of Joseph Dunninger, which spanned the period from the early 1930s to the 1960s. Dunninger started life as a poor boy from the lower East Side of New York. He became interested in magic as a teen-ager and by sheer talent developed a professional act within a few years. At first he appeared in a dime museum and at modest club affairs. By the early 1930s his commanding personality and astounding mental effects made him a much sought-after and highly paid entertainer at exclusive private parties. As a feature of his act, small slips of paper were distributed. On these the audience wrote numbers, words or messages. They then folded the slips and kept them in their own possession. No pads or clipboards, which might register impressions, were used, and nothing was collected. Yet Dunninger, seated before the spectators, could apparently receive impressions of what they had written by second sight. He correctly divined the most complicated messages: personal names and dates, quotations in foreign languages, even algebraic formulas. It was a baffling demonstration.

Later Dunninger extended his operations into the radio and television fields. Here he was enormously successful. Sometimes he would read the minds of people on the other side of the continent. He predicted newspaper headlines, read off the serial numbers on bank notes locked in vaults, and astonished millions of viewers by his uncanny demonstrations of apparent telepathy and precognition.

Off the stage (or out of the TV studio), Dunninger shed the portentous manner of speech he used before the public, and became an informal, pleasant man who enjoyed talking magic with his close friend Al Flosso, the New York coin manipulator and magic dealer, and other magicians. Surely Joseph Dunninger must be ranked as the outstanding mentalist in the history of magic. When he died a few years ago, most of his secrets apparently went with him.

Many magicians of this era appeared most often on the lecture platform or in performances for clubs and societies. Popular at Chatauquas, club entertainments and parties was Al Baker, an all-around magical entertainer who was also a talented ventriloquist and an expert at conjuring for children. Al, who was active well past the age of eighty, has given an amusing sketch of his work, salted with good advice for magicians, in his book, *Magical Ways and Means*.

Well known on the Redpath circuit was another performer highly respected by his fellow magicians, "Silent" Mora. He hailed from Chicago but always worked in Chinese costume. Mora made most of his Chinese-style magical equipment himself, and these ingeniously constructed pieces are still turning up.

Another all-around magician who has left an undying name in the annals of the art was John Mulholland. Originally a teacher, Mulholland entered the magic field by way of the lecture platform, and was a highly effective speaker and magical entertainer for clubs and societies. For many years he edited *The Sphinx*, at that time America's foremost monthly magazine for magicians. John Mulholland was a finished performer, a keen student of the history of magic and a leading collector of magic books, magazines and apparatus. His legacy to his fellow magicians is the magnificent John Mulholland Collection of magic literature and memorabilia housed in the library of his old club, The Players, in New York. A more detailed account of the collection will be found on page 207.

Magic Today

During the decade of the fifties and into the early sixties the art of magic was in at least partial eclipse. The impact of a depression, a world war, and a growing adherence to realism had pushed magic into a corner, where it was left to lie, in dusty abandon, among the playthings of the past. The advent of new forms of entertainment, such as radio and television, had captured the public's interest, and the elegant magician, with his daring and ingenuity, was no longer fashionable. A faithful core of professional and amateur magicians, most of them members of magic societies, upheld the art, but public interest fell off sharply from former years.

However, in recent years there has been a renaissance in the world of magic that may be due, in part, to a growing interest in mysticism, in the occult, in the realm of the unknown. Although the true magician does not usually claim to be a mystic, he appeals to the same instinctive yearnings in human nature—to the love of the mysterious, the fascination with the inexplicable, and the joy of astonishment. The magician's art has also been accorded, in recent years, a brighter ambiance of acceptance and appreciation. The grace, the originality, the drama, the humor, the choreography, the build-up of suspense, the subtle innuendos, the colorful apparatus—all these aspects of the art are once again coming into their own.

One of the brightest stars in the magical firmament today is the magician and actor Doug Henning, who scored such a hit in the musical play, *The Magic Show*, which has enjoyed a long run on Broadway. Its success is a tribute to the lively interest in magic today.

Doug Henning, first star of the smash Broadway hit, *The Magic Show,* sparked a new era in magic with his gasp-provoking talent. (*Wide World Photos*)

Houdini, brought alive again in E. L. Doctorow's novel *Ragtime,* is once again a fascinating figure to the public. Legitimate magic mercifully replaced the baseless witches and Martians in TV serials and commercials. Membership in magic societies and attendance at conventions soared. Magic dealers burgeoned. New magicians stepped into center stage with original styles and illusions. Today the quality of magic performers is as high as it has ever been in the long history of the art, and talented newcomers are everywhere.

Every magician must discover for himself an ambiance, a personality, a unique quality that sets him apart from other performers, and gives him a certain distinction. Doug Henning is the wistful waif. On the stage he has a vulnerable quality that keeps his viewers suspended in a state of hopeful apprehension while he attempts his magical feats. He is then, himself, delighted when, to his great astonishment, the trick happens to succeed. This attitude of childlike wonder and awe is beguiling for the audience, who share in his astonishment and are captivated by his appealing modesty. Here is no slick, assured performer, showing off his prowess, exhibiting his skill. Instead the young magician is right there with them, wondering, attempting, explaining, fascinated, hopeful

and finally, miraculously, triumphant. Doug Henning's modest approach, however, conceals a great wealth of technical prowess. He is one of the most skilled, as well as one of the most colorful performers on the stage today.

A great variety of magic is being presented today, in specialty shows, at benefits, before college audiences, in nightclubs, on television and for organizations and social clubs in small towns and large cities across the country. There is close-up magic and pantomime, comic magic and mentalism, as well as graceful displays, with colored doves and silk scarves, that rely chiefly on the visual. In general the trend today is away from the complex mechanical device, in favor of sleight-of-hand and genuine expertise in the art of deception.

Close-up magic makes use of cards, coins and other small objects. Because it is intimate in nature, without the camouflage of lights and scenery, it requires great dexterity and endless hours of concentration. One of the masters in this field is Albert Goshman. Goshman has performed many times on television, which means that he has two participants from the audience, sitting with him at a small table, and another audience of millions looking over his shoulder. Nevertheless, he relies chiefly on comic and persuasive patter to divert the attention

while his silver coins appear, vanish, reappear, multiply and move about, all seemingly on their own. Goshman has an artful way of involving the participants, even the TV audience, in his act.

One of the most versatile of close-up artists is the greatly gifted Slydini (page 98). One of Slydini's most famous effects is that of the demolished cigarette which he restores instantly, under the intent gaze of the spectator. He also works with paper, silk, balls and coins, and performs many other close-up effects. Slydini is known as the "magician's magician." Although he gives occasional public performances, he devotes much of his time to lecturing and teaching.

An honored figure at the Magic Castle in Hollywood is Dai Vernon, who deserves to be regarded as the dean of American close-up magicians. His skill in every field of prestidigitation is legendary. During his long and distinguished career he has invented many new routines for such classic effects as the Cups and Balls, the Linking Rings, the Coins through the Table, the Chinese Thumb Tie, and others. It takes a high order of imagination to evolve these subtle and often complex routines, in which one move flows into another, one deception lays the foundation for the next, until suddenly a totally surprising climax is reached.

However, there is another important branch of magic in which Dai Vernon is equally adept: card manipulation. He is responsible for many important innovations and original effects in card magic, which have been set forth in several books written for the benefit of other magicians by Vernon's friend Lewis Ganson, British writer and editor.

In 1976 Dai Vernon made a long swing about the United States, lecturing in a number of cities to magicians who paid some $25.00 each for the privilege of hearing "the Professor" explain some of his original secrets. Wherever he went he had reunions with old friends in magic and was received with the honors due to one of the greatest living masters of his art.

Probably no branch of prestidigitation has received more attention from experts today than card manipulation. New sleights and combinations have made card conjuring more complex and difficult. Derek Dingle, an Englishman who now lives in New Jersey, is recognized among America's leading card men. Dingle often lectures at magic clubs, electrifying the members with startling innovations. He frequently entertains at trade shows and large parties, presenting his amazing card deceptions to the accompaniment of a no less original line of humorous patter.

Harry Lorayne, the memory expert, also ranks high among card manipulators. His five books on the subject are filled with enough new sleights and effects to keep a student busy for months. Other noted card experts are Brother John Hamman and Frank Garcia, who is also known for his fantastic effects with sponge balls and dice. Karl Fulves of New Jersey is a fertile source of new card sleights and effects. Many of these he publishes in two magicians' journals under his editorship, *The Pallbearers' Review* and *Epilogue*.

In the coin-manipulation field, Slydini's beautiful work is rivaled by that of Jose de la Torre, of New Jersey (see page 61); Jerry Andrus of Oregon, a highly original performer; and Sam Schwartz and Leonard Greenfader, two prominent amateur magicians of New York.

These are some of the leading practitioners of close-up magic in America today, though there are many others who deserve mention if space permitted. The modern emphasis on sleight-of-hand as distinct from mechanical effects is not confined to close-up work, however, but is also apparent in platform and stage magic.

A fabulous stage act performed entirely by sleight-of-hand is that of Richard Ross of Holland. For sheer artistry and breathtaking surprises Ross's work could hardly be excelled. A handsome young man with curly, blond hair, Ross stands in the front center of the stage beside a small, modern table, and remains in that spot throughout his entire act. His unusual version of the Linking Rings, in which four rings pass through one another and link in mysterious formations, is pure poetry in motion. A gold watch as large as an alarm clock appears mysteriously between his fingers. It multiplies into two, then other watches appear, until finally there are six, almost too many to hold. Original effects with coins

and giant cards make Ross's act still more incredible. He performs with an easy, unhurried grace that enhances the beauty of his prestidigitation. Richard Ross has won many awards in international competition.

Whereas Ross performs the Linking Ring trick with four rings, another leading exponent of this classic effect, Jay Marshall of Chicago, uses traditional sets of eight or more rings. In his hands the gleaming steel rings penetrate each other, linking and unlinking mysteriously to form a rapidly changing series of patterns—a chain, a pyramid, a butterfly with opening and closing wings.

A beautiful phase of modern magic is the common use of graceful, fluttering doves, some pure white, others beautifully colored, which are produced from silks, paper streamers and so on. Some of the new apparatus for the surprise production and mysterious vanishment of doves is also highly ingenious and effective. Leading dove workers at the present time include Bob Downey of Canada (see page 96), the lovely lady magicians Dorothy Dietrich and Celeste Evans, and Bob Dorian (page 90).

One specialty that has undergone many new developments and improvements in recent years is magic with ropes. Not only are cut ropes visibly restored to one piece, but ropes change their length repeatedly and rope circles link together uncannily. Outstanding innovators in rope magic include George Sands of Brooklyn, NY, and Dan Garrett of Georgia, as well as Slydini and Schwartz.

In effects with silks, magic is indebted for many new and charming inventions to Pavel, of Switzerland. More about Pavel's work is told on page 73.

Paper tearing, too, has been developed greatly in late years, notably by Gene Anderson of Texas. More about his innovations will be found in the section on paper tricks.

Another beautiful act with a mystical and poetic quality is presented by Norm Neilson, and consists entirely of magic with musical instruments. A flute disintegrates in his hands into a shower of gleaming particles that shimmer in the spotlight. A white violin balances without apparent support on the edge of a cloth held between Neilson's two hands. When a bow is balanced across the fiddle, it begins to move back and forth and play without human control. Violin and bow sink almost to the stage, rise again to play hide and seek behind the cloth and perch on the magician's shoulder. A large radio set, playing loudly, is carried forward under a shawl and vanishes at the footlights. Finally Neilson produces from the air a trove of silver coins that materialize from nowhere and tinkle melodiously down the steps of a crystal ladder.

Another special branch of magic is entertaining children. Experts in this field who have developed new effects and secrets for children's shows include Frances Ireland Marshall of Chicago, author and editor of many books on the subject, and Bruce Posgate of Toronto, who has lectured on magic for small fry to conjurers' clubs throughout the United States and Canada.

Comedy magic continues to grow increasingly uproarious thanks to the inspired antics of such practitioners of this demanding art as the imaginative Karrell Fox of Michigan; Mike Caldwell, 300-pound master of ceremonies, raconteur and juggler; and Terry Seabrooke of England, who works up a hilarious routine with small boys from the audience who obviously enjoy themselves just as much as Terry does.

Since the death of Dunninger, probably the most popular mental act is the one presented by The Amazing Kreskin. This owlish-looking young man combines ESP effects with an entertaining exhibition of hypnotism in which some thirty people from the audience take part. Kreskin links borrowed finger rings together, reads sealed messages, and while blindfolded, finds the check for his fee for each performance which has been hidden in some unlikely nook or cranny in the auditorium.

An unusual Second Sight demonstration is staged by Jack London of New York and his fourteen-year-old son, Stuart, who, with his back turned, correctly identi-

Mark Wilson, popular West Coast TV magician, receives the Star of Magic Award in New York in October, 1976 from Jack Ferero of Harry Roz-On Ring No. 26 of the International Brotherhood of Magicians. (*Marilyn Rey Photo*)

fies playing cards drawn by people in the audience and personal belongings handed by them to his father. Jack London also presents one of the most effective prediction demonstrations now being performed. A week before his engagement, he gives a locked chest to the chairman of the committee for the event. On the night of the show, the chest is opened on the stage by the committee. Inside it is a cardboard package stapled all around. Attached to this is an affidavit from a notary public attesting that he sealed the package a week earlier. When the package is opened, it is found to contain a prediction by Jack London giving the exact wording of the main headline in the evening newspaper of the show date.

The art of escaping continues to flourish in the hands of The Amazing Randi, who lets himself be hoisted by a giant crane high into the air, and then escapes from a straitjacket. Randi also duplicates Houdini's feat of emerging alive from a milk can filled with water with its lid fastened on with hasps and padlocks.

Norman Bigelow, a younger escape artist, presents an unusually suspenseful act called "The Door of Death." Bigelow lets himself be chained, handcuffed, roped and strapped into a massive cabinet resembling a medieval Iron Maiden, its door studded with fifteen long razor-sharp knives. At the expiration of three minutes on a large, ticking dial that faces the audience, powerful springs automatically bring the lethal door clanging shut. Bigelow's struggle to escape from his bonds in time is a close race against death that leaves the spectators breathless.

The art of the large stage illusion is also alive and well. One indication of this was Doug Henning's work in *The Magic Show*. Also prominent in this glamorous field of magic is Mark Wilson, the West Coast TV illusionist. In Las Vegas, two daring young magicians, Siegfried and Roy, are doing highly original work. Their incredible act features illusions performed with a 10-foot tiger, a huge lion and a sinister-looking black panther. Siegfried and Roy combine the skills of the conjurer with the cool courage of the circus trainer of big cats.

In the field of lavish stage production effects, the leading position is unquestionably held today by the Japanese magician Shimada. He presents an Oriental act full of animation, dance and mystery. For its climax, Shimada has revived an old Chinese tradition of magic with brilliantly colored parasols. He has devised new techniques of producing the vivid, whirling parasols so that they literally seem to materialize from the air in his hands. As one after another spins into sight, Shimada tosses them down until the entire stage is covered with them, creating a magnificent spectacle.

One of the youngest, as well as one of the most gifted and imaginative magicians on the stage today is David Copperfield. He is, himself, an unusually hand-

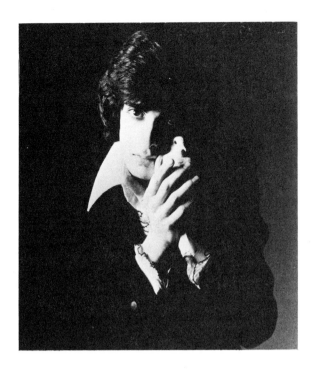

ABOVE: David Copperfield brings together many art forms in a performance that is truly magical. (*Photo courtesy of Tony Spina*)

RIGHT: The symbolic spectre of Death stands close to escape artist Norman Bigelow as he presents "The Door of Death." Chained, handcuffed, roped and strapped into a massive cabinet, Bigelow has exactly three minutes to make his escape before the door, studded with long, razor-sharp knives, automatically clangs shut on him. (*Mickey-"O" Enterprises*)

some young man, tall, slender, with a quicksilver quality, a certain grace and daring that is perfectly adapted to what he has set out to do. Copperfield gives each of his routines a different theatrical tone. One may be choreographed as a dance, with the music, lights and color of a ballet that revolves about an intricate bit of sleight-of-hand. Another may take the form of a drama, with a story line, characters, pantomime and action—a drama that culminates in magic. Still another may have the trappings of broad humor, with himself the buffoon, the butt of the joke, which is, of course, magical. Many of his routines are fantasies, with a dreamlike quality that seems to enfold the magic. Thus young David Copperfield brings together all the art forms in a performance that is, for his audience, magical.

All these men and women, and many more, today demonstrate the time-honored and continuing place of magic in the world of the arts.

MIRACLES IN YOUR POCKET

Impromptu and Close-Up Tricks

Traditionally, most magic catalogues lead off with impromptu and close-up tricks. These are often tricks that can be carried in your pocket. They are ready to use whenever someone who knows you are a magician asks you to "do a trick." As you can never tell when that may occur, to keep your fame as a wizard intact it's sound strategy to carry one or two mind-boggling pocket tricks with you whenever you go out.

There is a wide variety of impromptu tricks available from your magic dealers—tricks with rings, dice, sponge balls, cigarettes, knives, keys and many other familiar objects. Many of these effects are simple and inexpensive, while others, like the Enchanted Ring, shown on page 49, and Ring Flite, on page 50, are precision-made and fairly expensive. An entertaining impromptu exhibition can be given by combining one or two clever pocket tricks with some effects with cards or coins, which you can select from the next two sections of this book.

These intimate effects, done with small objects that could hardly be seen from a distance, are popular not only for informal occasions, but also at magic clubs and conventions, where close-up sessions vie for attention with stage programs. The performer usually sits at a table, with a close-up mat before him, while his audience of ten or twenty people sits around three sides of the table to watch him work. Or, the magician may sit at a smaller

In a close-up session at Tannen's Magic Jubilee, Paul Gertner produces an amazing series of bigger and bigger crystal cubes from a hat. Exhibitions by half a dozen close-up performers are given simultaneously at different locations in the hotel where the convention is held, the magicians rotating to appear in turn before each group of spectators. (*William Doerflinger Photo*)

table while the spectators watch from the usual rows of seats. Some of our finest magicians—men such as Slydini, Dai Vernon and Al Goshman—specialize in close-up magic.

In this section we shall explore some of the best close-up tricks in various categories that can be found today in the magic shops. But first, here is a splendid one you can perform without any special equipment.

The Educated Atoms

This effect is one of the most baffling of close-up tricks. It is especially good as an after-dinner stunt. If, after showing this trick, you politely but steadfastly decline to reveal the secret, your friends will badger you for years to tell them how it is done.

Effect: The magician states that he will attempt an experiment to demonstrate how free atoms can be controlled by the powers of the mind, and taught to spell. Taking an ordinary cube or rectangular lump of sugar from its dish, he hands the sugar cube and a lead pencil to a spectator and asks him to write any two letters or numbers on the sugar cube. He is not to let the magician see what he writes.

When this has been done, the magician takes the sugar cube, written side down, and drops it into a glass of water that has been standing on the table. He then directs the spectator to cover the glass tightly with the palm of his hand and to concentrate upon the initials or numerals he has written on the cube. The wizard explains that as the lump of sugar melts, freeing into the water the atoms of which the sugar and pencil marks are composed, he will attempt to cause the motion of the atoms to be controlled by the force of the spectator's concentration.

In a minute or two the sugar crumbles and dissolves into the water. When it has disintegrated, the magician directs the spectator to remove his hand from the glass, turn it over and look at it. There, in black lead pencil lettering on the palm of his hand, are the same initials or numerals he wrote on the lump of sugar.

Secret: A soft lead pencil (No. 1 or No. 2) should be used. Before beginning, or while the spectator is marking his initials on the cube, unobtrusively moisten the ball of your right thumb with water from some glass or other container that happens to be on the table, or from a wet bit of paper napkin in your pocket. Take the cube from your friend with your right fingers and thumb. As you do so, press your moist thumb against the lettering on the underside of the sugar. This transfers the lettering to your thumb. Transfer the sugar to your left hand and drop it into the glass of water. Then, as if to show the spectator precisely how to place his hand over the glass of water, take his hand in your right hand and while gently moving it toward the glass, press your thumb momentarily against his palm. This should be done fairly firmly but without any sudden pressure, which he would notice. Place his hand over the mouth of the glass and instruct him to hold it there until the sugar dissolves.

The trick is now done, but have him keep his hand in place while you talk impressively about controlling the atoms, as outlined above. To his astonishment, on removing his hand he finds that the atoms from the sugar and graphite have indeed reassembled on his palm just as he marked them on the sugar.

While the sugar is dissolving, you can bring your right hand casually into your lap and wipe any traces of lead off your thumb on a napkin that is already in your lap, or on your clothes. However, the chance of the spectators' noticing your thumb is 1000 to 1. They are so absorbed in the experiment and in your patter about the atoms that they never remember your touching them at all.

"The Parlor Magician" by Charles Dana Gibson.

The uncanniest and most incomprehensible manifestation of the decade! A solid tangible substance with depth and form is created out of NOTHING, yet it is always invisible.

A white handkerchief is shown on both sides and is laid out flat on a table. The four corners are folded toward the center then two more folds are made so that the handkerchief resembles a small but flattened white tent.

Standing away from the table, the magician as well as the spectators watch the handkerchief as something slowly materializes under it. The handkerchief moves as "something" under it takes form. To prove it solid the magician hits it with a spoon. It is audibly solid! Then the magician places his hand on top of the handkerchief and rolls the "nothing" around.

The magician then picks up one corner of the kerchief and whisks it from the table, at the same time shaking it briskly and showing both sides. "Nothing" has returned to nothing! The handkerchief and illustrated instructions. $3.00

THE BONGO BENDER

Now you can bend keys with "animal magnetism" like the famous psychics! At least that is what your audience will believe if you practice a little with Ali Bongo's new, brilliant gimmick. It is hard to be a magician today without being asked to bend keys. The public wants to see it done. Get the Bongo Bender today. $3.50

THE FLOATING-DANCING HANDKERCHIEF

Hanky floats, jumps, dances as tho' alive!!!

A beautiful trick! Easy to do!

Baffling! Mysterious! Astonishing!

Here's a magic effect that's truly a miracle. You hold hankie up by corner, fondle it, talk to it and then command it to dance as you shake it a bit near the floor. Suddenly it floats up, jumps and starts to dance like mad. You can make it waltz, fox trot, rumba and even rock n' roll. Amusing, amazing, unbelievable! But wait! That's not all. While it is dancing you can even walk away from it, even down into audience, and it will continue to dance as if bewitched. Best of all it will dance according to the commands you give it. Especially entertaining when set to music. A big surprise. Very uncanny!

S-80   *Dancing Hanky* **$1.00**

A BIG HIT IN ANY MAGIC SHOW!

Obeys your commands!

HAUNTED MATCH BOXES

Two match boxes are displayed back-to-back. Drawer of one box is open. As the open drawer is closed the other drawer mysteriously opens. A playing card placed between and they still open. Boxes are turned sideways, even separated; and they still open and close. **$4.00**

FLOATING GLASS

Whether you are a professional or amateur magician, you will be thrilled with this fantastic effect. A glass filled with milk, first clings to your finger tips, then actually floats in mid-air. You have full control of the glass at all times, yet no threads or wires are used. Floating Glass complete with several amazing routines ....

(See Directory of Dealers)

Using everyday objects like handkerchiefs, cards and match boxes, the magician can playfully evoke the ghosts of ancient superstition. Would you like to do a "mental" key bending effect similar to the one Uri Geller performs? Then send away for the Bongo Bender, displayed on this page with a selection of other good impromptu and close-up tricks available from magic dealers. These are continued on following pages.

A GREAT POCKET TRICK YOU WILL ALWAYS USE

Jimmy Rogers

I'LL START AGAIN

I'LL START AGAIN: Tricks may come & tricks may go, but the Paddle goes on and on. Why? Because it's one of the best, a standard, and with I'LL START AGAIN, Jimmy Rogers has given us one of the best paddle routines ever, and we know of no better instructions for the paddle move. Three chalk lines are drawn on each side of the paddle and the fun begins. They disappear, jump from top to bottom & back, and reappear every time the performer says, I'LL START AGAIN. Finally, when all lines are erased, a single line running the LENGTH of the paddle suddenly appears! It's fun, it's easy, it's different, and it's a magic classic. You should have it. .... No. 25B ---- $4.00

ABRACADABRA MAGIC SHOP

#255

A paddle as pictured is shown to be empty on both sides. A dime is placed on the paddle. Suddenly, the paddle is given a shake and there is now a dime on both sides! This is repeated with a second and third dime, each time the money doubles until you have six dimes! Six dimes are visibly removed from the paddle, which is again shown empty on both sides. Shake, and a dollar bill appears, which is removed. Shake again, and a $100 dollar bill appears! This is removed and the paddle is once again shown blank. At this point everyone will ask - "How did you do that?" Shake paddle and a mirror appears - "It's all done with mirrors!" EVERYTHING IS COMPLETELY EXAMINABLE! (Money is not included).

THE EMPORIUM OF MAGIC, SOUTHFIELD, MICHIGAN, $4.00

191—COLOR CHANGING KNIFE

A double close-up effect that's tops in impromptu bewilderment!

An attractive white pearl handled pocket knife is shown on both sides. The performer closes his hand over it and it emerges from his fist with a different colored handle, instead of the pearl. Again he shows it on both sides, places it in his fist and it emerges with the pearl handle!

The knife is given for examination and the spectator requested to open the blade. However, he finds it impossible to do so. The performer takes the knife and opens it immediately.

No matter how much the spectator examines the knife, he cannot discover the secrets. Very mystifying and easy to do. $5.00

LOUIS TANNEN, INC.

STOP! DON'T BUY JUNCK IMMITATIONS. THERE HAVE BEEN MANY TRICKS WITH PLASTIC STICKS SET WITH GEMS. WE KNOW BECAUSE WE MADE MOST OF THE BETTER ONES. THIS IS ANOTHER GREAT AND DIFFERENT VERSION. SIX DIFFERENT COLORED GEMS ARE SHOWN ON BOTH SIDES OF A BEAUTIFUL PLEXIGLASS BLACK ROD. SPECTATOR MAKES A SELECTION AND PRESTO CHANGO, ALL THE GEMS CHANGE TO THE SELECTED COLOR. HERE IS A GREAT NEW IDEA THAT IS SURE TO FOOL YOUR FRIENDS.AND CONFUSE YOUR MAGICAL BUDDIES.

MAGIC WORKSHOP, $3.50

TRICKY PADDLES

Consists of two handsome plastic paddles. One of the paddles is seen to have a picture of a magician's hat on BOTH sides. By passing your empty hand over the paddle, a RABBIT magically appears in the hat . . . and the rabbit can be shown on BOTH sides of the paddle. In the same manner, a CIRCLE changes into a SQUARE. Every magician should have a set of TRICKY Paddles. Complete with instructions. . . . .

D. ROBBINS & CO., E-Z MAGIC, $.75.
(See Directory of Dealers)

Few principles in magic have been applied in such myriad different forms as the paddle move. Few are simpler or more deceptive. Older paddle tricks with pictures or "jumping" pegs were forerunners of more elaborate effects. The color-changing knife has inspired many sleight-of-hand routines.

BELOW: Miniature playing cards and the magi's traditional mirrors appear mysteriously on this handsome paddle trick and felt case made by the late John Mulholland, distinguished editor of the now defunct magicians' magazine, *The Sphinx*. (*Author's Collection*)

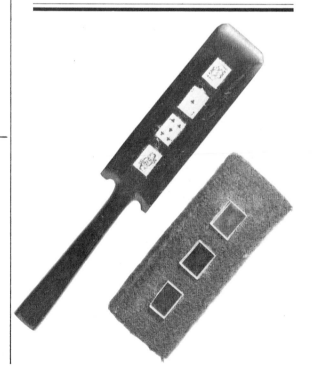

TOPIT!

One second the man has a glass in his hand. The next second, it's GONE!

That's TOPIT! The most amazing vanisher ever conceived. In full view, you can vanish a deck of cards, balls, a glass; any object you can hold in your hand easily, you can vanish.

You can exchange objects, too. There are hundreds of uses for Topit. The foremost exponent of Topit, the late George Davenport, once vanished a live kitten! Our demonstrator, Ross Johnson, was using Topit for every sort of vanish, just a day or two after he first saw it.

This absolutely wonderful gimmick comes with the Topit Handbook, which carefully describes the many uses and tricks possible. Written by Patrick Page, whose work with Topit has to be seen to be believed.

You can use Topit anywhere. Actually, the closer the spectator, the more he is fooled! How about that? Topit and Handbook: **$3.00**

No. 319

TELECOLOR

A genius can not figure this out, yet you can tell ANY selected card even after it is inserted into an envelope and shuffled. This even mystifies experienced magicians. It is unusually clever but easy to perform.
Price only $1.00

200—JUMBO THREE SHELL GAME
VERNET

The ideal close-up trick. Three half walnut shells, and a little ball. The spectators are invited to keep their eye on the shell containing the ball, BUT THEY ARE ALWAYS WRONG. The JUMBO three shell game is so called because the shells used are plastic shells and are a little larger than usual, which makes for EASIER HANDLING, and better visibility from the spectator's viewpoint. Comes complete with illustrated instructions that is easy to understand. Not a difficult trick, but a brilliant one. $4.50

COLOR CHANGING BALLS

This beautiful effect is simple to do but always makes a big hit with every audience! Here is what the audience sees: A red wooden ball is shown, then it is wrapped into a red silk and both are placed into a glass, as seen in the illustration. Performer then shows a green silk, and wraps it around a green ball, which is placed into the second glass. After saying the "magic words" over the glasses, performer removes the red silk and a GREEN BALL is discovered in the glass. When the green silk is removed, a RED BALL is found in the glass. Silks, balls and glasses may all be offered for examination! This is REAL magic! We furnish two 12 inch silks, necessary balls and easy to understand instructions.

Any glasses may be used..............................

LIQUID APPEAR

An absolutely EMPTY glass is shown, then it is placed into the "magic" can. A cover is placed over the can. You say a few "magic words," remove the cover, take out the glass, and IT'S FILLED TO THE TOP with milk (or coca cola, beer, etc.). You can then pour the liquid from the glass. The can may be passed out for examination. No skill required. You will enjoy doing this trick! Everything furnished

---

218—CHINK A CHINK

The apparatus consists of 4 blocks which are placed in a square formation about 10" apart. Performer says Chink a Chink and the 4 blocks magically appear together. Complete with profusely illustrated instructions by Ed Mishell. The perfect pocket trick—get this! ALUMINUM $12.50

157—ENCHANTED RING
Anverdi

ANVERDI—European electronic genius and master plastic manufacturer has given Tannen an exclusive on one of the MOST FANTASTIC CLOSE-UP ITEMS EVER PUT ON THE MAGIC MARKET!!! If there were an award for the best trick of this year—or any year—this effect would walk away with Top Honors!

Working with the simplest of props: a metal ring, a 1" cube of wood with a slot to hold the ring, and a hat pin, you are all set to baffle ANYONE (magicians and laymen alike).

What is written here as to what the spectator sees is EXACTLY what takes place—NOTHING has been added or taken out of this description—

The wooden cube is shown and the metal ring is placed into its slot. The pin is inserted through the hole in the cube to secure the ring into the cube of wood. The spectator SEES the pin holding the ring in place. He can even pull on the ring to see that it is securely held in place. The spectator holds out one finger. The magician places the ring on the spectator's extended finger—the cube is now suspended in midair. The magician now places his palm face up and asks the spectator to touch his palm with the bottom of the cube. The moment the cube touches the magician's palm, IT IS IMMEDIATELY FREE FROM THE RING—which is still held by the spectator!!!!

At this point, all can be handed to the spectator for full and complete examination: the ring, box, and pin!

Remember what we have said at the beginning of this description—NOTHING has been added or taken away from this accurate picture of what the spectator sees. Be the first with one of the most baffling, beautiful penetrations ever devised—truly the "Perfect Penetration"! ANVERDI'S ENCHANTED RING, only $17.50

And worth every penny!

LOUIS TANNEN, INC.

173—THIMBLE JUMBO—Berland

BERLAND'S at it again . . . this time with THIMBLE JUMBO! Imagine this: performer shows hands to be empty . . . SUDDENLY a thimble appears on the first finger of his right hand! He removes the thimble and places it in his pocket. Yet once again from seemingly nowhere a thimble appears on his fingertip! He again removes the thimble and places it in his pocket. But again . . . and again . . . the same effect happens for a total of FOUR thimble productions!!! Yet when the audience thinks the performer is finished suddenly another thimble appears . . . only this thimble is nearly THREE TIMES larger!!! A really JUMBO thimble! A production effect that can be performed with just a little practice! PLUS Berland has included Jumbo Thimble Production Part II with an entirely different routine, complete with gimmicks, an entire act! TWO effects in one!! $5.00

LOUIS TANNEN, INC., AND SAMUEL BERLAND

Sam Berland, Chicago magic dealer, performs his surprising jumbo thimbles effect. (*Terry Graczyk Photo*)

DON ALAN'S BOWL ROUTINE

No. RC7

Don Alan is the "wonder boy" of this decade in magic. You will find many of his tricks and books in our catalogue. He is a very busy professional, with many top TV shows to his credit, plus his own series on TV.

"Don Alan's Bowl Routine" is the trick Don did for the sponsor of his first TV show, and he was hired on the spot. Since then, he considers it his lucky trick and often uses it on TV and in club dates. It's a great trick!

Effect: The beautiful routine uses an engraved brass Indian bowl, sponges, a clear plastic wand and a "bagel" (a hard roll). The sponges appear and multiply and vanish under the bowl and eventually change into the bagel (or any object you desire). How they fool the audience in doing it! What a sensational climax! And how very easy to learn with the good illustrated directions given with it. Very highly recommended. $8.50

MAGIC, INC.

256—RING FLITE

A FEATURE TRICK. Sensational in its IM-PACT on the audience. A ring is borrowed, placed into your palm, which is then closed into a fist. Spectator grasps your wrist. BUT, from the pocket on the other side, you take out a leather KEY CASE. From it drop the keys and hanging among them is the BORROWED RING! Every superlative in the dictionary has been used by delighted owners of this fabulous trick. $20.00

LOUIS TANNEN, INC.

No. 12—Linking Pins

TRULY A CLASSIC IN CLOSE-UP MAGIC— it won the prize as the best trick of 1955. This effect by Jerry Andrus has baffled and entranced everyone who has seen it. JUMBO SIZE SAFETY PINS link and unlink, form chains which seem-ingly melt apart—in fact, they seem to just pene-trate; metal through metal. There are no phony moves in linking the pins. Performer links and unlinks the pins though held in spectator's hands.

We cannot stress too highly the value of this effect to a performer who is interested in better-than-average close-up magic. This is more than just a trick. It is an ENTIRE ROUTINE made possible by a very CLEVER GIMMICK. Complete set of Pins and illus-trated routine **$2.00**

KANTER'S MAGIC SHOP, NOW $4.00

WUNDERBAR

One of the "hit" tricks of the recent IBM convention in Little Rock. A small silver bar is displayed inside a test tube. The bar bobs up and down in the tube and pushes the cork out of the tube. Then the bar jumps from the tube into the performer's hand. The bar then floats in mid air without any apparent support. Many floating moves are possible. Wunderbar can be performed under extreme close up conditions and the spectators will see nothing to reveal how it's done. PRICE--$8.50

MAGIC METHODS

TRI-DIE ✱

A beautiful deception with three dice in a small plastic box. The performer opens the box and displays the dice. One of these is openly removed and the cover placed back on the box. The die is placed in the performer's pocket. When the box cover is removed, the die is back in the box!! It seems imposs-ible for the die to reappear in the box, but it does!! Those performers who are adept at sleight of hand should be able to effectively blend this trick into various sleight of hand tricks they already know which employ dice. Complete with instructions for the basic effect and the nicely made dice box. Price-------------------------------------$8.50

MAGIC METHODS

HOLE-LUCINATION

#566

Here is something very, very different - and that's what you're always looking for, right? You show a large white card (7"x4½") in a frame. It bears a bright red arrow pointing to a hole on the side of the card. The card is withdrawn from its frame and the hole is indicated by putting your finger through it. Then the magic starts. The card is replaced into the frame and, using your finger, you move the hole around the card!--first to the other end of the ar-row, then to the top of the card, and finally to the bottom. As a smash climax, you remove the card from the frame and the hole, now at the bottom of the card, is once again indicated by poking your finger through it!! And the card can be examined. It's new, it's different, it's very clever
Order it today.

THE EMPORIUM OF MAGIC, SOUTHFIELD, MICHIGAN, $12.50

WITH A DECK OF CARDS

"Card tricks enjoy universal popularity with professionals and amateurs alike," a famous New York magic dealer's catalogue pointed out almost a century ago. "Anyone who can amuse and astound a company with simply a pack of cards, is sure to be a most welcome guest at any party."

For proficiency in card magic, apparatus is less important than books and assiduous practice. To mention some of the best books on card work that are currently available, a general, comprehensive work on sleights is *Expert Card Technique*, by Jean Hugard and Frederick Braue. Also recommended are *Close-Up Card Magic* and later card books by Harry Lorayne (see bibliography), Dai Vernon's books on card magic, and Frank Garcia's *Million Dollar Card Secrets* and *Super Subtle Card Miracles*. The *Encyclopedia of Card Tricks*, edited by Jean Hugard, gives hundreds of effects of varying degrees of difficulty. Another basic work on card manipulation, especially gamblers' sleights, is S. W. Erdnase's *The Expert at the Card Table*.

Two of the most valuable works in this field are unfortunately out of print, but used copies are well worth looking out for. They are *Greater Magic* and *The Art of Magic*, both written by John Northern Hilliard, though T. Nelson Downs is the official author of the second.

Most older magicians started out by using the fine, clear descriptions of basic card sleights given by Pro-

Coe Norton performs a classic of magic —the Card Sword effect (*Lynn Carver Photo*)

fessor Hoffmann in his classic work, *Modern Magic*, first published in 1876. Since then, however, many of Hoffmann's sleights have been widely supplanted by later, and sometimes easier, methods of achieving the same effects. Many new methods of palming are described by Hugard and Braue. Advanced card manipulators such as Derek Dingle, Harry Lorayne and Larry West have introduced new and often difficult moves. Also on the advancing frontiers of card magic are Carl Fulves' periodicals mentioned before, *The Pallbearers' Review* and *Epilogue*, both available by subscription or from magic dealers.

Many of the finest and most classic effects in card magic are happy combinations of dexterous handling and ingenious apparatus. Among these are such great tricks as the Rising Cards, for which numerous different methods have been devised, the Card Sword, and the Card Star. It should be added that some of the top card effects listed in dealers' catalogues consist only of the secrets and routines, and do not require any mechanical apparatus. Three outstanding card miracles of this type are Paul Curry's popular trick Out of This World and the effects called Bombay and Premonition, both originated by Eddie Joseph.

On pages that follow are some of the finest card effects from dealers' catalogues. But first some striking tricks in which you apparently teach cards to spell.

One of the most popular and effective groups of card tricks, though old in principle, are those in which a chosen card is revealed by spelling. In this trick a spectator chooses a card and then spells the name of the card, removing one card from the top of the deck for each letter, until, to his astonishment, he discovers the final card is the chosen one.

Various methods have been developed over the years for accomplishing this trick. Some require sleight-of-hand; others do not. The first and most important step is to know what card has been chosen. To do this, after the spectator has chosen his card, hold the deck in your left hand and riffle the cards with your right forefinger. Direct the spectator to replace his card wherever he likes. As he does so, insert your left little finger under the inner end of the chosen card. As your left hand holds the deck out to the spectator to shuffle, open your fingers slightly, thus raising the upper portion of the deck just enough so you can glimpse the chosen card, and let the portions close together again. Even more effective is to *force* the card by any method you know, so that you can let the spectator hold the deck himself as he replaces the chosen card. In either case, he does the shuffling.

Explain that since the trick's effectiveness depends upon a genuine shuffle, you will run through the face-up deck to show that the card is really somewhere in it. Caution the spectator not to tell you which card it is.

When you reach his card, which you know, start silently spelling its name to yourself—for example, "Q-U-E-E-N O-F S-P-A-D-E-S"—one letter for each card that passes from your left fingers to your right. When you reach the card for the last letter, press your left little finger against its lower end and hold a slight break there. After running through the whole deck, turn the cards over. Under cover of this movement casually and unobtrusively cut the cards at the break, and square the deck. (Better still, use the card sleight called "the pass," if you have learned it, to reverse the upper and lower portions of the deck.)

Should the chosen card be so near the top that you run out of cards before completing the spelling, simply go back to the face-up bottom card, as though you are giving the spectator more time, and silently count a few more cards, as needed.

Lay the deck on the table and remark that you are not even going to touch it. Ask the spectator to spell the name of his card aloud, and to remove one card from the top for each letter. When he picks up the card for the last letter, quickly and dramatically ask him to turn it over. His selected card is staring him in the face.

Another snappy variation is to spell two cards. This requires some additional mental counting. First you count the spectator's card. Then note the next card after the spectator's and count its name—for instance, "E-I-G-H-T O-F H-E-A-R-T-S"—to yourself, card by card. After reaching the last letter, cut the deck or make the pass. Tell the spectator he can locate his card by spelling out its name. "Let's suppose," you say, "that you'd chosen the eight of hearts. Just spell its name and lift off one card for each letter." You demonstrate this yourself and, to his surprise, the last card is the eight of hearts.

Then hand him the deck. He continues spelling card by card in the same way. The last card is the one he selected.

Another variation is to let the victim spell his own name rather than that of the card, revealing his chosen card on the last letter as before. First he chooses a card, then inserts it in the pack. After the above procedures, when he spells out his name, he discovers the card he has chosen. It is best to start this trick by telling him to write his name on a large pad. You then explain that writing on the pad will influence the cards.

Another good method, not requiring sleight-of-hand, is to identify the chosen card by means of a key card—the one on the bottom of the pack, which you have noted in advance. Cut the pack from the bottom for the return of the chosen card and drop the key card and its half on the deck on top of the chosen card. As you run through the deck, as above, you can at once identify the chosen card since it is next to the key card. This method, however, doesn't permit shuffling with much safety.

Other variations and different spelling effects may be found in a number of books on card magic.

Abbott's Nu-Power Rising Cards

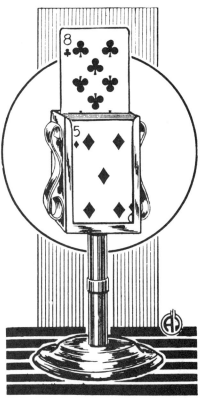

An entirely new concept in Magic's all-time classic — **The Rising Cards.**

NU-POWER is a hidden power that causes card after card to rise out of a deck of cards.

What is it?

So let's check off the methods used in the past — Swiss Motor — Watch Motor — Threads — Wires — Elastics — Catgut — Springs — Weights — Hairs — Moving Rollers — Faked Decks.

NO — It's none of these. It's startlingly **different.**

Created and made at the Abbott plant.

The card holder is as illustrated, made entirely of brass, chrome plated. The holder for cards has no back or front, just a skeleton frame to hold a full deck of cards.

AN ORDINARY DECK IS USED

Here is the effect: Cards are shuffled by a member of the audience. Three or more cards are freely chosen — NO FORCE — and may be initialled — then replaced in the deck, which again is shuffled. Now, without adding or attaching anything or exchanging deck, it is placed in the skeleton frame holder. When YOU are ready, a chosen card rises slowly and gracefully up out of the deck. There's nothing to stop — leave the card in the 'rise' position as long as you like. The card is removed and a second card will rise after a 30-second interval — or a 5-minute interval if you wish.

IT'S UNDER YOUR CONTROL ALL THE TIME

Two, three, and more — 10 cards if you wish — rise in the same way. Definitely this is a self-contained effect.

It can't go wrong on you. It's foolproof. It's so clever, you'll love it.

So the rest is up to you. Send your order today for Abbott's NU-POWER RISING CARDS.

ABBOTT'S MAGIC MFG. CO., $42.00; DELIVERED, $44.50

Deluxe Card Star 1037   US$80

From a pack of shuffled cards, 5 cards are selected by 5 spectators, which are inserted back into the pack and shuffled. Next a 5-pointed chromed brass card star is shown and the pack of cards are thrown against it. Suddenly, the 5 selected cards mysteriously appear on the 5 points of the star. Complete with a Chromed Brass Card Star and a deck of cards.

CHU'S MAGIC STUDIO

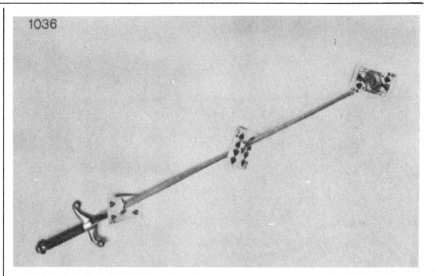

SUPERIOR CARD SWORD   1036   US$40

Magician fans a deck of cards to show them to be all different. Then, three cards are selected by members of the audience and returned to the deck which is thoroughly shuffled. Magician now brings out a sword, and asks a spectator to toss the deck up into the air. Miracle of miracles! The three selected cards are impaled on the sword tip and blade. A beautiful metal sword is supplied.

CHU'S MAGIC STUDIO

Three classic card effects are shown in the advertisements reproduced on this page. Different versions of these effects are available from other dealers.

LEK-TRIK DECK

As used by Dick Oslund, on his hundreds of school shows. This is NOT a sewed together deck.

Especially constructed to enable you to do these card flourishes with the greatest of ease: Cascade or Spring Shuffle, Waterfall Shuffle, Arm Spread and Turnover, Arm Spread with a Toss Up and Catch, Fans.

Can also be used for a comedy finish. Or, you can finish with one of the spectacular flourishes and take your bow. Very versatile deck. No. 507 $ 2.50

MAGIC, INC.

PSYCHEDELIC FANNING DECK

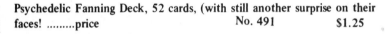

The most magnificent combination of poster colors ever used in a fan deck - brilliant orange, red, pink, blue, yellow, green, white. The most terrific "dance floor" finish ever felt on the surface of cards for fanning. They fan themselves! We think ANYBODY should be an expert with a few minutes with this deck!

Psychedelic Fanning Deck, 52 cards, (with still another surprise on their faces! ....price   No. 491 $1.25

Same deck, especially and expertly cut and round cornered to allow you to show still more color combinations, and finally to create a big double size fan. .....price   No. 492 $2.50

MAGIC, INC.

FANORAMA

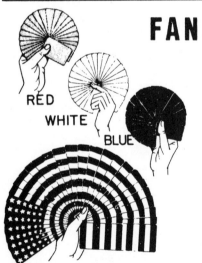

RED
WHITE
BLUE

Colorful
Easy To Do
No Intricate Sleights

FAN ALL RED
FAN ALL WHITE
FAN ALL BLUE

then . . .

FAN IN A **GIANT FAN** — THE STARS AND STRIPES IN a GIANT ROSETTE OF THE **AMERICAN FLAG** IN ALL ITS GLORY

MADE OF DURABLE, GLAZED, CARD STOCK — COMES TO YOU ATTRACTIVELY BOXED AND READY TO PERFORM.

ABBOTT'S MAGIC MFG. CO., $8.50; DELIVERED, $9.00

Brain Wave Deck

This trick created a sensation in **Magical Circles** the instant it appeared on the market. It is, without a doubt, one of the most direct and baffling card tricks of the present day.

A full deck of cards, sealed in their case, is given to a person to hold. Now, that person is told to name ANY CARD. For example, we will say he names five of hearts. Cards are removed from the case and fanned out and to the utter amazement of all onlookers, they find a card reversed in the deck and this card is the FIVE OF HEARTS, or WHATEVER CARD THEY HAPPENED TO NAME, and when they turn this card over they are also surprised to find that the back of the card is of an entirely different color than the rest of the deck.

ABBOTT'S MAGIC MFG. CO., $3.50; DELIVERED, $3.80

The Lek-Trik Deck is an ingenious device for simulating difficult card flourishes. The special decks below it add to the beauty of card fanning. The Sorcerer's Apprentice in Atlanta sells special thin cards for fanning purposes. Most performers find that dusting the cards lightly with fanning powder, sold by dealers, makes fanning easier.

The Brain Wave Deck, described above, is an outstanding mental effect. Joseph Dunninger once called it the greatest card trick ever invented. The Ultra Mental Deck, one of the trick packs listed on the next page, is a similar, though less elaborate, effect.

TRICK DECKS

A "trick deck" is specially prepared in some way to make it very easy to do the trick. Unless otherwise mentioned, the deck can only be used for the trick described. "Trick Decks" are very popular because their effects are so easy to do.

NUDIST DECK.   A deck of blank cards are "printed" into a regular deck by magic. Then the faces disappear, return, backs disappear, return, and deck becomes blank again. Includes presentation. No. 1170 $2.00

ULTRA MENTAL DECK. Another great deck very popular with the men who do it for money. Spectator just thinks of a card and it turns out to be reversed in the deck - and it is the only card reversed. No. 169 $1.50

SIMPLEX RISING CARDS. Three or more cards selected and returned to different parts of the deck rise, one at a time. No. 209 $1.25

BLANKA SVENGALI. Like a Svengali Deck, but the deck can be changed to all blank cards, etc. Ten tricks included. No. 210 $1.25

POP EYED EYE POPPER. The Nu Idea Force Deck. Has no equal, and easy to use. Five great tricks are included with deck. No. 132 $2.00

X RAY CARDS. Tricked in a unique way for various mind reading effects. very easy to use, but baffling to anyone.   No. 211 $1.15

SPLIT DECK. It's two diagonal halves. Cards selected from the two halves by spectators match, for a good climax. No. 175. $2.00

DELAND AUTOMATIC DECK. The classic deck for reading from the back. Also "stripped" for extra effects. Full instructions. No. 176 $1.50

MENE-TEKEL PACK. Cards shown all different. Card selected, replaced in center of pack reappears on top of pack. Number of cards selected can be instantly named by magician. Easy to do. No skill. No. 426. $1.50

DELUXE FOUR ACE TRICK   No. 424

This is the one in which the Aces, placed in different piles, disappear while you are looking at them! Then automatically, they all appear in one pile! Special cards plus matching deck and instructions $1.00

No. 490

Unlimited possibilities with this clever pack of 52 gimmicked cards and the instruction book of 36 tricks. You just add one or more of the gimmicked cards to the regular deck we send, and you are ready for miracles.

Mystifying, entertaining, fascinating, and you will find yourself devising some new ones of your own. Everything in Aviator back cards. The 32 page book compiled by Ronald Haines and John Braun.

No. 490   Everything for only $ 5.00

Zens Fifteen Cards

A masterpiece in card magic. A member of the audience counts fifteen cards from pack, places them into an envelope and into his pocket. Cards are not touched by magician. Another member counts fifteen cards from the pack, and then three more members each select a card which is noted and replaced. These fifteen cards may be shuffled, placed in an envelope and held by the spectator. Magician commands the three selected cards to leave one sealed envelope and appear in the other. Upon opening the envelopes this is found to have been accomplished.

EUREKA DECK (MARKED & STRIPPED)

This deck gives you all the advantages of a marked deck, as well as a stripper for instant location. This doubles the effects possible. Comes bridge size with complete instructions.

$1.50

SVENGALI DECK

Now famous as "TV Magic Cards", these cards will perform over 75 tricks including forces and changes. Turn the entire deck to all same card-the one that the spectator selected! Includes instructions for 10 tricks and the special cards.

$1.50

ZODIACS

PHANTOM CARD BOX

THE PHANTOM CARD BOX IS THE ARISTOCRAT OF LOCK-FLAP CARD BOXES!! MADE FOR PLAYING CARDS . . . This thin model box, in gleaming black with an attractive design on the lid, is a beauty!! Will VANISH AND EXCHANGE playing cards while it is in the hands of the spectator!! Spectator himself may open the box and examine it to his heart's content without finding a thing suspicious!! WITHOUT DOUBT, this is the finest card box for the price that has ever been made'!

- STANDS EXAMINATION!
- NO SKILL REQUIRED!
- CAN BE CARRIED READY TO WORK!
- THIN MODEL, ONLY ONE-HALF INCH THICK!

- THREE CLEVER ROUTINES!
- ATTRACTIVELY PACKAGED!

No. 508
Price $3.00

THE IMPROVED HAUNTED DECK

For those of you who have long loved the Haunted Deck, here is something NEW!! You will love this as does everyone who sees it performed. Instead of the magician holding the deck while the deck mysteriously moves around leaving the three chosen cards protruding from it, the magician in this version places the deck on the FLOOR AND WALKS AWAY FROM IT, leaving it to do its thing! The effect of the deck in the middle of the floor moving around revealing the chosen cards is positively uncanny to behold!! You'll love it and so will your audience. This can be done at extremely close quarters without fear of detection. Complete and ready to work with detailed instructions. $8.00

NEW DELUXE FULL COLOR
INSURANCE POLICY

Here's a fun-filled routine with a special policy which guarantees the successful location of a chosen card. A card is selected, shown to all but the magician, then returned to the deck. The magi then runs through the deck and pulls out what he says is the selected card. He's wrong! So he tries a few more times in vain. Panic sets in so he reaches for his insurance policy and begins to read its purpose and conditions, all of which are comedy lines written on the policy. Finally, he opens the policy to its full size and shows a huge (18" x 22") colorful picture of the chosen card. If it's ready-made laughs you're looking for, your search is over. Get this now! $2.50

324—GWENDOLYN   Senator Crandall

Senator Crandall and his Gwendolyn were a laugh riot at Lou Tannen's Magicians' Jubilee some years back. We are fortunate to be able to put out the apparatus and the Senator's hilarious routine. Gwendolyn, in case you didn't know, is a duck. An educated duck that finds selected cards. She may be made of wood, but her personality is winning. You'll love her and so will your audiences. Gwendolyn comes to you all dressed for action wearing a straw hat, feathers, and is gaily painted. She can pick cards right from your hand or from an easily attached feed box. A beautifully dressed Gwendolyn and Senator Crandall's laugh-filled routine. $26.50
We also have the standard all white Duck with feed box permanently attached for . . . $24.50

The Phantom Card Box is an effective and inexpensixe prop for vanishing or changing cards. You might also be lucky enough to find a used, but still sound, Petrie-Lewis Card Box, which does the same things but can be more freely examined by the spectators. There are less expensive card boxs made of wood, as well as slim, elegant, expensive ones of German silver.

322—SIX CARD REPEAT

This card trick has become a classic. A purely mechanical version that's as easy as it is mystifying. Six cards are counted from hand to hand and then three counted on the table. You should have but three left in your hand. But, no strangely enough, you still have—six! This is repeated five times and each repetition brings mounting amazement! Well made of standard cards and a complete routine is supplied. Absolutely no skill or sleights. We guarantee you'll love it. $2.00

DOUBLE SURPRISE PREDICTION

A spectator looks away as a jumbo prediction card, say the Ace of Spades, is set aside. A deck of ALL Aces is also shown, from which the spectator will have a "free choice". As you go through the deck (Aces), one card is selected. Somehow it's the 10 of Hearts. Audience is surprised! Jumbo card has also changed to the 10 of Hearts.

$4⁵⁰

MYSTERY & ENTERTAINMENT

The card trick you'll be asked to do over and over again.
A spectator selects a card which is then placed on the front of the deck where it can be seen by the audience. The deck is then openly returned to the card case and a rubber band placed around the case. A spectator is told to rub the card case with his finger.
Suddenly, B O O M - a loud explosion is heard coming from the card case.
The case is opened and the cards are removed.

The selected card, still on the front of the deck, has a large hole burned right through its center.

IT EXPLODES RIGHT IN YOUR HANDS, YET IT IS ABSOLUTELY SAFE.
The card case is empty before and after the effect. A really novel way to reveal a selected card. A REAL KNOCK-OUT. Price - $1.50

352—ENGLISH 3-CARD MONTE

We blinked our eyes and didn't believe what we were seeing when Patrick Page of England demonstrated this to us. Be the first to get this English 3 card monte trick. Here is a new slant on the 3 card monte that you will be doing and fooling the boys with, yes! you will be doing it five minutes after reading the instructions. You show 3 cards, two spot cards, the red picture card is in the center. Cards are slowly turned face down and spectator is asked to pick the red picture card, try as he might he always picks the wrong card. Again you show the 3 cards, with the red card in the center. You ask spectator to name the position of the red card. As soon as he says it's in the center he sees it visibly change to a BLACK CARD. You can't help but blink your eyes at the sudden change. You still go further and finish by showing both sides of the cards so they should not get the idea that they are fake cards. Complete with instructions and cards. $2.00

Card In Balloon

A method in which a freely selected marked card appears in the balloon.

Any card is chosen from an unprepared deck. Card is initialed, returned to deck and deck is sealed in the ordinary card case. Balloon is inflated and set in holder. Cards in case are placed on the base of the stand.

BANG! Balloon bursts and the initialed card makes its appearance.

No palming. Apparatus is self-contained. Made entirely in metal and chrome plated.

FAKE GAMBLING ACT

Do you want to apparently expose card sharps? Want to show your apparent skill with a deck of cards? This fake gambling act can do just that for you. You can put on an entertaining demonstration of "How Gamblers Cheat." Give the appearance of being a master of a deck of cards. The methods given require no skill whatsoever. You apparently deal seconds, bottoms, and poker hands—even a blindfold poker deal! Our simple instructions make it so easy! Complete in manuscript form. $2.00

T.V. CARD FRAME

EFFECT: . A card is selected and torn into small pieces. The pieces are placed in an envelope and burned, with the exception of one piece that is given to a spectator to hold. Magician takes ashes and throws them at frame and immediately the selected card appears, restored between the two sheets of plastic, minus the piece that the spectator was holding. The card is now removed from between plastic sheets and the piece of card held by spectator is seen to be the missing corner and fits perfectly.

NBK DISTRIBUTORS, INC., $34.95

No. 306 — THE CARD IN THE CIGARETTE

A card is selected from the pack, and by way of identication it is torn into pieces and a piece handed to party who selected it. The rest of the pieces are now placed into a small envelope for safe keeping. — A cigarette is borrowed and lit, but there is something wrong and inside the cigarette is found the selected card with the one corner missing and that just fits into the card. On examining the envelope for the card, instead is found the tobacco from the cigarette. One of the best effects and now being used by one of our most prominent magicians.

FLOSSO HORNMANN MAGIC CO., $1.00

293—OUT OF THIS WORLD
Paul Curry

A poll of magicians by Fred Braue in "Hugard's Magic Monthly" rates this trick by Paul Curry the best of all card tricks.

Here is the effect. Entirely unaided, a spectator deals a complete deck of cards face down into two piles, placing what he guesses are reds in one pile and blacks in the other—red or black purely a hunch. Several cards may be placed in the same heap one right after the other. Any suspicion of pre-arrangement is killed by the freedom allowed. Believe it or not, when the cards are turned over, one pile is all red, the other is all black.

And so very, very simple, anyone can do it. New improved instructions with various routines and subtleties. $1.00

LOUIS TANNEN, INC.

A CARD TRICK BY PROFESSOR HOFFMAN (FROM *Modern Magic*, LONDON, 1876)

TO MAKE A CARD VANISH FROM THE PACK, AND BE FOUND IN A PERSON'S POCKET.—Slightly moisten the back of your left hand. Offer the pack to be shuffled. Place it face downwards on the table, and request one of the company to look at the top card. Request him to place the back of his left hand upon the cards, and press heavily upon it with his right. In order that he may the better comprehend your meaning, place your own hands as described (*see* Fig. 30), and request him to imitate you. When you remove your left hand, the back being moistened, the card will stick to it. Put your hands carelessly behind you, and with the right hand remove the card. All will crowd round to see the trick. Pretend to be very particular that the person who places his hand on the card shall do so in precisely the right position. This will not only give you time, but draw all eyes to his hands. Meanwhile, watch your opportunity and slip the card into the tail pocket of one or other of the spectators. Now announce that you are about to order the top card, which all have seen, and which Mr. A. is holding down so exceedingly tight, to fly away from the pack and into the pocket of Mr. B., making the choice apparently hap-hazard. On examination

FIG. 30.

your commands will be found to have been fulfilled. It has a good effect, when practicable, to slip the card into the pocket of the same person who is pressing upon the pack.

TOP LEFT: Howard Thurston, the great illusionist, was also a master card manipulator. (*Harvard Theatre Collection*)

TOP RIGHT: Brother John Hammann is one of our finest card manipulators and inventors of magic effects with cards. (*William Doerflinger Photo*)

LEFT: Arthur Emerson, dealer and expert magician, demonstrates a card effect at a magic convention. (*William Doerflinger Photo*)

ABOVE: Mario Carrandi, dealer and collector of rare magic apparatus, displays a fine old Card Star. (*Lynn Carver Photo*)

THERE'S MONEY IN MAGIC

Tricks with Coins and Bills

Since the dawn of history man has dreamed of creating money and riches by magic. The ancient Greek myths of King Midas and Jason's quest for the Golden Fleece appeal to the same fascination with wealth that makes modern audiences love to see a magician plucking gleaming coins from empty air. Coins are both intriguing and convenient objects for sleight-of-hand purposes, and coin magic has ben developed today to a high level of ingenuity and beauty.

Indeed, sleight-of-hand assumes even greater importance with coins than in most branches of the mystic art. Ninety percent of coin effects, including the most baffling and entertaining ones, depend upon skillful manipulation. To become proficient with coins, therefore, you must study the best books on the subject. Chief among these, and the coin man's bible, is J. B. Bobo's superlative, 544-page work, *Modern Coin Magic*, now available in a revised and enlarged edition at $15.00. I also recommend highly the coin sections in Edwin T. Sachs's *Sleight of Hand*, Camille Gaultier's *Magic without Apparatus*, and Henry Hay's *The Amateur Magician's Handbook*. (See the bibliography for publishers and dates of these books.)

Besides studying, you must practice, practice and keep on practicing. But cheer up! Mastery of even the easier coin sleights will enable you to baffle and entertain your lay friends, though probably not yet to fool other

T. Nelson Downs (1867–1938) became one of the world's most popular vaudeville artists through his superlative sleight-of-hand work with coins. He was billed as "The King of Koins."

members of the magical fraternity.

Although sleights are so important in this field, magic dealers offer special equipment that is highly desirable and often essential for performing some of the finest tricks with coins. Magic with money may be divided into the following main categories of tricks:

The Production of Coins: This means plucking coins mysteriously from the air or from spectators' hair, beards, noses and pockets. In the most charming and entertaining of all coin effects, the Miser's Dream or Aerial Treasury, an inexhaustible trove of silver is thus conjured up (see page 62).

Vanishing and Reproduction Effects: In these, a coin, often borrowed and marked, is caused to melt away from the performer's hand or vanish with the aid of a rattle box (page 65), trick paper wrapping, gimmicked coin stand or other apparatus, and reappear in a nest of boxes (page 65), ball of wool, or other impossible locations.

The vanishing and reproducing of bills, a related branch of money magic, can be accomplished by means of such clever devices as the bill vanishing tube (page 65), dummy bill rolled up and sewn in the border of a handkerchief, or the versatile Devil's Handkerchief. The vanished bill, whose serial number has previously been noted, reappears inside a borrowed cigarette, a lemon or a sealed envelope zippered inside the magician's wallet. The handsome Himber-type wallets and other cleverly gaffed wallets for such effects are available from many dealers (see, for example, page 65).

Gimmicked and Special Coins: This field, highly important in modern coin magic, involves the use of special coins which are undetectably gaffed for the performance of amazing effects. Hand-made by skilled jewelers working with exquisite precision, they are expensive but an excellent investment for the wizard who wants to do otherwise impossible feats of coin magic. Johnson Products, P.O. Box 734, Arcadia, CA 91006, are leaders in this field and a number of their beautiful productions, which are carried by most larger magic dealers, are described in detail on pages 63 and 64. Guaranteed Magic, 27 Bright Road, Hatboro, PA 19040, also make similar high-quality coins.

Coin Boxes: These are round brass or nickeled boxes in silver-dollar, half-dollar or quarter size, precision-made by Johnson Products, Guaranteed Magic and others, for sleight-of-hand effects with regular or special coins. Many different boxes and box-and-coin combinations, ranging from simple to complex, can be found at prices varying from a few dollars to $30.00 or more. (See page 63 for examples.)

Other Coin Effects: There are other excellent coin effects that do not fit into any of the above categories. Many of them are performed by pure sleight-of-hand. Available at magic shops are such tricks as Sixth Sense (Abbott's, $6.00), in which the magician can tell whether a coin closed inside a brass box by a spectator is heads or tails; Shattering Coins (Tannen, $5.00), in which ten English pennies vanish from the wizard's hand; the Coin Frame (Magic Emporium, Tarzana, CA, $15.00), in which four vanished coins mysteriously appear behind the glass; and various others.

Examples of coin tricks in all the categories noted above will be found on the following pages. Most of them can be obtained not only from the particular dealer whose description is reproduced, but from other magic depots as well.

TOP RIGHT: Al Flosso (1895–1976), the New York magician and magic dealer, won fame for his hilarious performance of the Miser's Dream. Al was affectionately known as "the Fakir of Coney Island."

RIGHT: Jose de la Torre is believed to be the only magician performing this difficult feat, the Rose of Coins—ten coins appear, one by one, between the fingers. Magician, architect, author and magic dealer, he won three trophies with four minutes of coin manipulation at the combined convention of the Society of American Magicians and the International Brotherhood of Magicians in 1970. The next year he won the Jack Miller Trophy of Ring 26, I.B.M., in New York. (*Olga Maša Photo*)

LATEST COIN PAIL

An extremely smart looking "Champagne Bucket" type pail, chrome plated. with a knob and ring on each side. Made for half-dollar size coins holds twelve in each knob, twenty-four in all. A finger-tip touch releases one coin at a time. Pail is eight inches high and seven inches in diameter.

Performer shows pail to be empty, reaching into the air a coin is seen to appear at his fingertips, it is thrown into the pail with a clang. This is repeated until all twenty-four coins are produced. Performer can walk through the audience producing the coins from various places. No skill required. A precision made quality product.

ABBOTT'S MAGIC MFG. CO., $55.00; DELIVERED, $57.00

NEWEST COIN CATCHER

A simple yet well made device for the endless production of coins from the air. The hand is shown empty and a coin appears at the fingertips. Gimmick is attached to finger and hidden by back of hand. When a coin is produced it is supposedly dropped into a hat or coin pail. An endless number may be produced in this manner. At the finish a shower of coins is poured out of the hat or coin pail.

This gimmick is excellent to use with the "Latest Coin Pail". Holds half-dollar size coin.

VERY EASY-TO-DO

ABBOTT'S MAGIC MFG. CO., $2.00; DELIVERED, $2.50

EXCELLO DROPPER

To be attached to any part of the body just so it is out of sight· A pressure of the palm of the hand releases all coins at one time into the curled fingers.

There is no possibility of any part of this fake "jamming" as a novel principle is used. Neither is there any possibility of coins being released before they are wanted. Holds 20 half-dollar size coins.

ABBOTT'S MAGIC MFG. CO., $7.50; DELIVERED, $8.00

The Miser's Dream, that mystifying and amusing fantasy with coins that has been featured in the programs of many of the greatest magicians, can be performed with different routines, but usually depends upon the employment of certain devices, plus the skill and grace with which the performer handles them. Here, as catalogued by Abbott's Magic Manufacturing Company, are examples of the main types of equipment used in performing this classic effect.

Kellar Dropper

This excellent piece of apparatus is most useful in connection with the popular Aerial Treasury trick, although the resourceful Magician can find various other uses for it.

This Coin Catcher is made to contain about 16 palming coins or U.S. half dollars, and is ·so contrived as to produce them, one at a time, at the tips of the fingers. It is also quite essential to the success of every coin manipulator.

ABBOTT'S MAGIC MFG. CO., $8.00; DELIVERED, $8.50

Palming Coins

These coins are made of the finest metal highly-plated. They have a raised, embossed, special A b b o t t design, milled edges and are regular half-dollar size. The milled edge is an aid for easy palming and as each coin is die made. any quantity of coins are easily stacked without fear of slipping.

ABBOTT'S MAGIC MFG. CO., $3.50 DOZ.; DELIVERED, $4.00 DOZ.

Automatic Coin Wand

The perfect Coin Wand. An invaluable accessory to any Magician.

For producing coins in the air, reaching into spectator's pocket, or into a boy's mouth and producing a full sized coin on the tip of the wand. Coin is removed and can be given for examination.

ABBOTT'S MAGIC MFG. CO., $25.00; DELIVERED, $26.00

CHINATOWN HALF #270

If there is a more beautiful Chinese Coin in the world today, we have yet to see one. This coin is made from solid brass with the Chinese characters engraved into it, after which it is highly polished. The effect is well known. Half dollar is sealed inside envelope and the Chinese Coin is outside. Instantly they change places. Spectator may tear open envelope and remove Chinese Coin. One of the cleanest changes in the entire realm of coin magic. You will receive both coins and our instructions.

CHINATOWN QUARTER #271

Same effect and same beautiful workmanship as in the Chinatown Half with instructions.

THE EMPORIUM OF MAGIC, SOUTHFIELD, MICHIGAN. HALF DOLLAR, $12.50; QUARTER, $10.00

18 THE NEW MAGNETIC SILVER & COPPER

We are constantly striving to improve each item in this catalog. The New Magnetic Silver & Copper was our most recent project. Because of some new machining techniques we are now able to make the shell in this set out of a regular size coin instead of an expanded half. You will perform with more confidence knowing that these coins will defy detection even under the closest scrutiny.

Five different routines are supplied with this trick but the combinations possible with this unique set of coins are limited only by your imagination. Here is just a sample: A drinking glass is held in a horizontal position and two coins are set inside; an English Penny and a Half Dollar. The glass is slowly tipped up causing the coins to slide towards the bottom. When they reach the bottom, the Penny penetrates through the glass and falls on the table leaving just the Half Dollar in the glass.

Effect No. 2   A handkerchief is spread over the mouth of a drinking glass. Two coins are resting on the handkerchief. As they are picked up, one of the coins passes through the handkerchief and drops into the glass. Not one unnatural move from start to finish. It's easy to see why this is one of our most popular items. A four piece set. **$20.00**

JOHNSON PRODUCTS, FROM FLOSSO HORNMANN MAGIC CO.

TWO COPPER & ONE SILVER #924

The standard copper/silver transposition trick given a new face, making any explanation virtually impossible. This is exactly what the spectator sees: Three coins are shown — a Half Dollar, English Penny, and a 20 Centavo piece. Nothing else. The two copper coins are placed in one hand. There can be no suspicion because the spectator can see and hear the copper coins in your hand. Magician closes hand and immediately opens it to reveal the half dollar. Copper coins are tossed onto table, having appeared in the opposite hand. Effect is repeated. Copper coins are picked up and placed in pocket as other hand closes around half dollar. Instantly the hand holding the half dollar is opened revealing the two copper coins. The copper coins are tossed upon the table as the half dollar is removed from the pocket. Everything can be examined with a magnifying glass at the finish. A truly remarkable transposition that will leave your audience utterly spellbound.

JOHNSON PRODUCTS, FROM THE EMPORIUM OF MAGIC, SOUTHFIELD, MICHIGAN

THE NEW HOPPING HALF #570

The five gimmicked coins in the Hopping Half set have always represented one of the biggest values in coin magic. The new improved version now includes two Expanded Coins and a Sun & Moon set. Dozens of tricks can be performed by using the coins separately or you can put them all together and do the mind boggling Hopping Half routine. Briefly: Two coins are shown, a half dollar and an English Penny. One of the coins is dropped into your pocket and it immediately reappears back in your hand. The other coin is placed in your pocket and it too hops back. The effect is repeated again and finally, when the poor spectator is about to give up, you open your hand and to his utter astonishment everything has vanished! With this beautiful set of coins the routine is simple to perform and well worth the $32.50 it would normally cost to purchase the coins separately. At our super low price, it's a steal.

THE EMPORIUM OF MAGIC, SOUTHFIELD, MICHIGAN, $22.50

1 OKITO COIN BOX

This is the classic, the forerunner to all coin boxes. Simple in design and appearance. Highly polished, made from solid brass and perfectly weighted. Coins appear, disappear and penetrate through the box. All of the now famous effects are possible with this gem and no magician should be without an Okito Coin Box. Routine included.

NBK DISTRIBUTORS, INC., $7.50

MAGNA COIN BOX

An Okito Box routine with an endless variety of incredible vanishes, productions, and penetrations plus a knock-out finish. Spectator places coin in box and covers with lid. Box is set on address book and instantly, coin passes through box and address book. Routine is climaxed by spectator seeing five coins in box up until last second when they pass through box and hand. Comes with highly polished, solid brass box, two gimmicked halves, special address book and detailed instructions

THE EMPORIUM OF MAGIC, SOUTHFIELD, MICHIGAN, $26.50

STACK OF QUARTERS

Six quarters are borrowed and placed on back of hand. A dollar bill or piece of paper is formed into a miniature cornucopia and placed over the coins. At the word of command the coins pass through the hand. When cornucopia is removed a stack of dimes is found instead. Here is a trick used by some of our best close up workers. Gimmic coins look natural and are sure to fool. Not too hard and nicely routined. For those looking for good coin tricks we highly recommend the above trick. **Stack of Halfs #972**

THE EMPORIUM OF MAGIC, SOUTHFIELD, MICHIGAN.
QUARTERS, $12.50; HALF DOLLARS, $15.00

Precision-made special coins and coin boxes are one of the few branches of magic in which craftsmanship equal to, or finer than, that of yesteryear is being practiced today. They are made by Johnson Products and others and retailed by various dealers.

TWENTY-ONE CENT TRICK

...Or twenty-cents minus a nickel leaves nothing. Dime, penny, and nickel vanish from your hand without a trace. Easy to do and comes complete. A startling effect at a price that can't be beat.

$6⁰⁰

THE MAGIC SHOP, LOS ALAMITOS, CALIFORNIA

DIME & PENNY

A dime and penny are placed in a spectator's hand. The hand is closed and the dime vanishes.

$2⁵⁰

THE MAGIC SHOP, LOS ALAMITOS, CALIFORNIA

FOLDING HALF

Profile cut half-dollars for coin in the bottle trick and many other fine effects. Finest available.

$5⁰⁰

THE MAGIC SHOP, LOS ALAMITOS, CALIFORNIA

CIGARETTE THRU-QUARTER

Magician borrows a cigarette and a quarter from the audience. Then, slowly pushes the cigarette thru the center of the quarter. Freely displayed with the cigarette in place, the cigarette is removed and with the quarter returned to the audience to be examined.

$7⁵⁰

THE MAGIC SHOP, LOS ALAMITOS, CALIFORNIA

All sorts of seemingly impossible miracles with coins can be performed with these high-quality coin sets offered by many magic dealers.

QUARTER FANTASY

One of the fabulous hits of the Ohio Magi-Fest. This effect flabbergasted all who saw it. Brass box is filled with seven quarters and then covered with lid. Quarters then penetrate through the box and the top of performer's hand. Box is then refilled with quarters and this time placed on top of performer's hand without lid—quarters once again penetrate box and hand. For climax box is again filled with quarters and placed on top of hand; this time box penetrates hand and quarters remain. Magic at its best with complete directions. $15.00

GUARANTEED MAGIC

---

27 SILVER/COPPER/BRASS TRANSPOSITION

A definite break through in psychological subtleties. This takes the basic transposition effect, one step further. A Half Dollar, 20 Centavo, and Chinese Coin are shown. The Half is placed in one hand and instantly it changes places with the Mexican and Chinese coins held in the other hand. The effect is immediately repeated. (The change is extra startling due to the fact that the three coins are so completely different in appearance.) The subtlety we mentioned is the fact that the Chinese Coin has a hole through it. If anyone suspects that the "coins somehow fit together" this feature completely wipes out their theory. This is a trick that can really build you a reputation as an outstanding coin worker.

NBK DISTRIBUTORS, INC., $18.50

---

15 THE LOCKING DOLLAR THIRTY-FIVE TRICK

A dollar and thirty-five cents worth of change vanishes completely leaving only a half dollar. The coins disappear without one false move. The perfect vanish. Machined from solid silver coins and the half that remains can be freely passed for examination.

NBK DISTRIBUTORS, INC., $20.00

---

16 THE LOCKING TWO DOLLAR AND EIGHTY-FIVE CENT TRICK

For the connoisseur of fine magical apparatus. Same effect as above but using two silver dollars, a half dollar, quarter and a dime. All coins are solid silver. Everything vanishes except for one silver dollar and that can be examined with a magnifying glass.

NBK DISTRIBUTORS, INC., $30.00

---

19 VISUAL COIN PENETRATION

We wish you could all see this one "live". It never fails to sell itself on this effect alone. Two clear drinking glasses, a playing card and two Half Dollars are all individually shown. Card is placed on the mouth of one glass and the second glass is set on the card. The two Halves are dropped into upper glass. Yes, the spectators actually see the two coins enter the glass. When they hit the bottom, one coin melts away, penetrating through the bottom of the glass and the card. It is seen and heard as it drops into the lower glass. One coin is dumped from each glass onto the table. You are as clean at the end as you were at the beginning. This is truly the most visual piece of magic we have come across yet. There is just no possible explanation for it. Includes two coins, card and instructions.

NBK DISTRIBUTORS, INC., $16.50

No. 456—Bill Vanishing Tube

This tube operates just the reverse of the Famous Bill Tube, as in this case, the rolled up bill is visibly placed in the tube which is then closed. When anybody opens the tube, it is found to be empty, and the identical bill (may be marked) is produced inside the Famous Bill Tube, or elsewhere, as desired. Also useful to vanish or exchange billets, etc. Precision-made Brass Tube

KANTER'S MAGIC SHOP. COLLECTOR'S ITEM, NOT ALWAYS AVAILABLE

208—THE RATTLE BOX

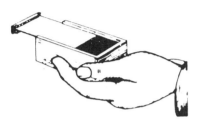

A wonderful vanish for a coin, ring, etc. A handsome box made from solid walnut is shown, the object dropped inside, and the lid closed. When the box is shaken, the object is distinctly heard to rattle around inside, yet at the magician's command the vanish instantly takes place. The object may be reproduced elsewhere immediately. Easy and the finest quality. $5.00

LOUIS TANNEN, INC.

BILL TUBE

This piece of apparatus should be in every magician's gimmick collection because of its many uses. Expertly machined for us, this piece of engineered magic can do great things for you. A lid fits on the tube, a rod goes through holes in the top and tube and this bar is locked in place with a small padlock. People will never figure out how their bill got inside! A great headline prediction can be worked with this! (Mentalists take note!) Like the trusty thumb-tip, a good bill tube is a vital friend to magicians. $12.50

LOUIS TANNEN, INC.

No. 418—Bill in Cigarette

This gives you 12 methods including the latest and original ideas in connection with this ever popular trick of passing a BORROWED DOLLAR BILL INTO A CIGARETTE. Switches, dodges, routines, etc.—a method in which you openly roll a cigarette from tobacco and papers, and cause the bill to be later found inside the very cigarette you have just rolled—and, incidentally, rolled by you with ONE HAND AND WITH EASE! Also tells you what and where to get, a simple little gimmick, that makes it easy to do the preparatory job in fixing up a cigarette for use in any method. Mss.

KANTER'S MAGIC SHOP, $2.00

NESTED BOXES

A new startling pocket trick Consists of four small round plastic boxes, each with a cover A coin is marked for identification You place the coin in your pocket and IMMEDIATELY bring out a Nested Box. When this box is opened, another box appears, then another and another. The MARKED COIN is in the FOURTH and LAST BOX opened! ...

D. ROBBINS & CO., E-Z MAGIC, $1.25.
(See Directory of Dealers)

497—BILL IN LEMON

In this method all difficult moves and sleights are eliminated. A bill is borrowed, numbers on bill copied down. Before this three lemons were shown, one selected, examined and held by anyone. Now the borrowed bill is vanished and found inside the lemon. Performer cuts the lemon open and removes the bill. Very clever gimmick. $10.00

LOUIS TANNEN, INC.

Equipment and a manuscript of instructions for seven classic bill and coin transpositions. These effects rank among the most perplexing mysteries in close-up or platform magic. Unfortunately, the Bill Vanishing Tube is no longer made, but you may be able to find an older one at a magic shop or on a dealer's list of used magic. Another effect no longer manufactured, but highly effective if you can find it, is The Coin in the Silver Boxes. In this trick a borrowed, marked coin vanishes and reappears in a small, locked box inside another box. Both boxes are crisscrossed with rubber bands and enclosed in a leather pouch with a tied drawstring.

47 THE NEW HIMBER WALLET

This is such an incredible utility prop that we wanted to offer the magical profession a top quality wallet and here it is. Hand made from the highest quality black calf leather with an elegant satin lining. It does just about anything such as producing, changing, vanishing, or switching cards, bills, billets, coins etc. Instructions include the famous money printing routine and a very subtle card prediction

NBK DISTRIBUTORS, INC., $25.00

SORCERY WITH SILKS

Mysterious silk effects form one of the most important and captivating branches of contemporary magic. The art of conjuring with silks has made great strides since about 1910. This is due in part to major improvements in the techniques of processing, dyeing and printing silk for magic purposes. The material must be pure silk with all sericin, or weighting, which forms a stiff glaze on the commercial fabric, removed. The silks used in magic are noted for their brilliance of color, beauty of design, and for that most mystifying quality, their remarkable compressibility. There is magic in the very look and feel of these silks.

Sold only by magic dealers, they come in a wide range of sizes, colors, and designs, and in several different weights. Those used for home magic are usually 12 inches square, while silks measuring 18, 24, 27, or 36 inches square show up better in medium-sized halls or large theaters. Mammoth 6-foot squares, 10-foot, 25-foot, and 50-foot rainbow streamers of widths ranging from 6 to 36 inches, and giant flags and banners are available—at a price—for special production effects.

American magicians are indebted for many of the improvements and artistic innovations in this field to a remarkable couple who have devoted themselves to creating magic silks for nearly half a century. Harold and Thelma Rice are owners and operators of the Silk

In the Zombie effect, a gleaming metal ball glides along the edge of a foulard, floats high in the air under the cloth, climbs up the performer's arm, and peeks out from behind the silk or the magician's elbow. Bob Dorian is using a Rice dragon foulard. For a climax, some performers change the Zombie ball suddenly into two bouquets of flowers. (*Lynn Carver Photo*)

King Studios, 640 Evening Star Lane, Cincinnati, OH 45220. Started as a hobby by Harold Rice while majoring in art at college, this enterprise today produces a large part of the silk magic used by the profession. Though their silk effects are used throughout the United States and abroad, the Rices regard quality as more important than quantity and look upon their silks as works of art.

To get started in silk magic and become familiar with the Rices' products, you can save time by sending $1.00 ($1.50 if you wish airmail) to the above address for a copy of the latest Silk King catalogue and price list. I would advise you also to invest, as soon as you can, in one of the most interesting and beautiful of all magic publications, *Rice's Encyclopedia of Silk Magic*, published by the Silk King Studios in three volumes at $20.00 each, with a fourth in preparation. The volumes can be purchased, either singly or as a set, from the Studios or from other dealers. In this work Harold Rice covers both sleight-of-hand with silks and the working and handling of almost all apparatus tricks with silks up to 1962, when the third volume came out. The *Encyclopedia* describes a vast number of effects and secrets of silk magic in its 1542 pages. Its nearly 6000 illustrations were drawn by the magician Francis B. Martineau. It may seem incredible, but Francis Martineau also lettered the entire text of the encyclopedia by hand. It was never set in type but was reproduced in facsimile from his flawless pen-and-ink pages.

Another valuable book published by Silk King is the concise but expert paperback *Thru the Dye Tube* by Harold Rice and W. van Zandt. They detail techniques of changing the colors of silks by pushing them through a paper tube (which is rolled before the audience's eyes and again shown empty at the end of the trick) and other methods. *Walsh Cane Routines,* written as well as illustrated and hand lettered by industrious Mr. Martineau, and published by Silk King Studios, is the last word on cane-to-silk effects and vice versa and other appearing and vanishing cane tricks. In total, Silk King Studios has published eleven paperback books on magic in addition to the three-volume encyclopedia.

Many of the silks and effects in the Rice line are also carried by Mr. Mystic's Magic Corner, Salem, Oregon; and some by Louis Tannen, Inc.; Jeffries Magic Land; Magic, Inc.; Yogi Magic Mart; Abbott's and others. Some are available only from Silk King Studios.

Among individual Rice silks, the Spectrum silks come in many different solid colors; Art Picture silks offer six designs, including a butterfly, clown, devil and beautiful Chinese dragon. Each is produced in various color combinations. Symphony silks feature intricate, colorful geometric patterns. Flash silks display concentric rings dyed in six different color combinations, while Message Silks spell out "Good Night," "Applause Please!" "That's All, Folks," and "Thank You" when produced. There are also card silks for use in card tricks; the American flag and the Jolly Roger; a self-untying serpent silk and others for use with secret miniature spring reels.

Silk King Studios also make up multiple-silk effects, many of which rank among top club and stage feats. I recommend, as especially beautiful and mystifying, the Mismade Flag; the Flag Blendo, in which separate red, white and blue silks change visibly into an American flag; Mr. and Mrs. Green (Meet the Missus), another blendo effect; and the Twentieth Century Silks, in which a flag or silk vanishes and reappears tied between two other silks that were previously knotted together and left in plain view.

Considering the high quality and extensive variety of the Rice silk magic enterprise, one wonders how it has been possible for Dr. Harold Rice to combine his work in silken sorcery with another distinguished career as an educator. He is listed in nearly a dozen *Who's Who* directories, including *Who's Who in America.* He and John Booth are probably the only two magicians listed in *Who's Who in the World.* Previously a president and dean of two colleges, he is now Director of Art Education Graduate Studies at the University of Cincinnati. He must have done it all by magic!

Harold and Thelma Rice, creators of magical silks and proprietors of the Silk King Studios.

RICE'S SYMPHONY PATTERN SILKS

STARLIGHT

MEDALLION

SUNBURST

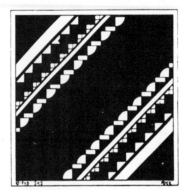

DIAGONAL RAINBOW

SILK KING STUDIOS. 12″ x 12″, $4.00; 18″ x 18″, $10.00; 24″ x 24″, $17.50; 36″ x 36″, $22.50

RICE'S JOLLY ROGER SILK

Our newest creation, this colorful 18″ square was designed for effects requiring a Jolly Roger or Skull and Crossbones silk. Ideal for children's show, safety programs, pirate routines, etc. Perfect for 20th Century effect.

Effectively highlighted with touches of ghastly green, the chalk white skull and crossbones stand out against the dead black background. A blue border frames this deluxe picture silk.

SILK KING STUDIOS, $10.00

RICE'S CARD SILKS

A preference survey disclosed that the King of Spades, Queen of Hearts, and Jack of Diamonds are the court cards most frequently selected by spectators. We now offer these popular cards (and a matching blank card) beautifully printed in four brilliant colors on 18″ silks.

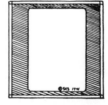

Many novel effects are possible. For example, a selected court card is placed in a card box, and a blank card silk placed in a changing bag. A transposition takes place. The card becomes blank and a court card silk is found in the bag. Can be used in a 20th Century effect, etc. Here is a utility item of 1001 uses!

When ordering, specify cards desired!

SILK KING STUDIOS, COURT CARD SILK AND MATCHING BLANK SILK, $15.00. BLANK SILK ONLY, $7.50

RICE'S ART PICTURE SILKS

FLAME BUTTERFLY

GAY DEVIL

FULL HOUSE CARD SILK

SILK KING STUDIOS,
18″ x 18″, $10.00; 27″ x 27″, $20.00; 36″ x 36″, $30.00

Tannen's Abbott's, the Tricks Company, Ltd. in Japan, The Magic Hands in Germany and others also manufacture excellent silks and silk effects, in somewhat less variety. Some of the German silks are notably beautiful in color. The Magic Hands in Herrenberg stock as many as fifteen different hues. (Color card available.)

Many outstanding silk effects depend entirely on sleight-of-hand and require assiduous practice for smooth performance. One of the most beautiful is the color change through the hand, in which a 12-inch silk is pushed into the top of an apparently empty fist and emerges from the bottom a different color, after which both hands are again shown empty. By using Rice's Palmo ball, a valuable gimmick, this can be done with an 18-inch silk. A classic manipulative effect is the Sympathetic Silks, in which three big silks are tightly knotted together and three others are shown to be separate: the knots pass invisibly from one set to the other. Magic, Inc., sells a simplified, easier version called Knot Control for $6.00. In the spectacular Fountain of Silks, differently colored "hanks" well up one after another from the performer's hand, often climaxed with a bouquet of feather flowers. Also among the finest production effects involving a succession of silks are Rice's Diminishing Silks ($52.50; routine in the Rice booklet, *Capers with Color*, $2.50) and Marconick's Continuous Production of Silks (Magic, Inc., $7.50).

A valuable small book if you don't own the Rice *Encyclopedia*, part of which covers the same ground, is *Reel Magic*, by Albenice. Miniature reels for silk and other effects are expertly manufactured by George Kirkendall and sold by Silk King Studios, Abbott's, Tannen's, and other dealers at about $15.00. Fine reels were formerly made by the late lamented Petrie-Lewis Company (see page 163). A few used ones can still be picked up for around $10.00, but should be tested carefully before buying, as the springs often weaken with age.

P and L reels, unhappily, are but one example of the many pieces of high-quality apparatus for silk effects that are no longer made. Look out for good used examples of the beautiful, red-lacquered P and L Phantom Tube, for the production of silks after the apparently empty tubes have been sealed by spectators with tissue-paper drumheads. Petrie-Lewis made these in 4-inch, 7-inch and 10-inch sizes, with optional double load torpedoes for the larger ones. Watch, too, for P and L's Creative Silks, a small tambourine production; their Utility Tube for producing, vanishing or changing silks; their precision-made Silk Cassette for a seemingly impossible vanish; their Candle Tube, in which a candle changes to a silk; and their Goblin Tube, the only effect in which a *marked* and vanished silk reappears inside a tube sealed with paper drumheads.

In the last few years, unfortunately, prices of silk

Famous school and college magician J. B. Bobo pulls many yards of silk streamer from a small box. His assistant holds a picture silk. The production of seemingly endless streamers from containers too small to hold them is one of the most impressive feats of silk magic. Ade Duval, who specialized in this branch of magic, used to pull hundreds of yards of silk from a tube only 10 inches long by 3 inches in diameter.

Mr. Bobo is the author of *Modern Coin Magic*, one of the great books in magical literature.

have risen so sharply on the world market that some of the finest effects in silk magic, formerly relatively inexpensive, now command high prices while others have been discontinued altogether. It pays, therefore, to watch for silk effects in good condition on the lists of dealers in rare and used magic such as Mario Carrandi, Leola LaWain of the LaWain House of Magic and Robert Nelson (for addresses see pages 231–234). It also pays to watch at magic auctions for treasures of silken sorcery that may soon join Robert-Houdin's automatons and Thayer's Nest of Boxes among the vanished marvels of the past.

The main categories of silk effects are productions, color changes, transpositions, tricks with knots and vanishes. On the next two pages are a variety of effects from dealers' catalogues that are especially recommended.

It is far more magical for a brightly colored silk handkerchief to materialize in your bare hands, or in a box you have just shown empty, than for the hank merely to be picked up off the table for use in a trick.

A bare-hand production of a silk takes a little practice but isn't really difficult. A good method for an opening effect is to attach a 12-inch silk to the buttonhole of your jacket lapel with a fairly weak, black silk thread about 15 inches long. Then accordion-pleat the hank until it forms a little bundle about 1½ inches square, and push it behind your lapel. The loop of thread is left outside; it will not show against a dark coat. After entering, hook your left thumb behind the thread as if reaching to straighten your tie or stroke your lapel. When ready to produce the silk, thrust out both hands, palms forward. The hank appears at your fingertips as if from nowhere, the thread breaking. Try it before a mirror—you'll like it.

A pretty method of producing a 12-inch silk is to roll a bit of newspaper into a cone about 3 inches long and with an opening at the small end just big enough to fit snugly on the tip of your middle finger. Pack the silk into the cone. Keep the middle finger bent toward the palm. Pick up a small rectangle of newspaper measuring about 6 inches by 4 inches, and display it between the thumbs and forefingers of both hands, showing it front and back. Then straighten your middle finger, bringing the loaded cone behind the flat paper. Roll the flat piece into a cone around the loaded one, show that your hands are otherwise empty, tear open the paper and draw forth the silk.

For materializing somewhat larger silks in the hands the best device is probably the Stilwell Hank Ball. This is a thin-walled, hollow ball of metal or plastic, painted flesh color. To the ball is attached a loop of thin catgut about 3 inches long. The ball can thus be either palmed or suspended by the loop from the thumb, so that it hangs down behind the hand. These balls can be loaded with two 15-inch silks. A number of methods for producing silk handkerchiefs with balls and other devices are well described in Professor Hoffman's book, *Later Magic*.

A beautiful old piece of equipment for producing several silks is the Crystal Casket. This is a glass-walled box through which the audience can see clearly, yet several silks visibly materialize inside it, in a flash. These caskets are sold by many dealers. Prices range from about $8.50 to $20.00, depending upon the size, materials and workmanship of the caskets.

In the effect called Swift Silk (Creative Magic, $7.50), colorful silks visibly fill a large, empty, clear goblet.

These silk-producing devices work fast, so the effect ends quickly. A longer routine is offered by a modern miracle marketed at DM 105 (about $45.00) by The Magic Hands studio of Herrenberg, West Germany. This effect is called Champagne Bottle III. In an apparently empty cylinder, a champagne bottle longer than the cylinder suddenly appears. The magician uncorks it with a pop, pours champagne. He then pushes the bottle up into the cylinder, where it instantly turns ino a long, silken streamer that cascades rapidly, yard after yard, to the floor. Finally the cylinder is once again shown empty.

The Magic Hands also offers some of the finest large production banners with telescoping flagstaffs available anywhere.

Vanishing a silk is not difficult. Probably the simplest way is to use the "pull" invented generations ago by the noted French conjurer Buatier de Kolta. This is a pear-shaped cup attached to a length of cord elastic that is fastened to a belt strap at the performer's left side. The elastic passes behind his back and through another strap or safety pin at his right side, where it is held by the pull of the elastic. To vanish a silk the performer gets the cup into his right hand and, holding the silk in both hands in front of his body, works it into the cup. The elastic is hidden by the right sleeve. The cup holding the silk is allowed to fly back invisibly under the coat and after a little further byplay the hands are shown empty.

In place of the pull, a hollow rubber ball with a hole cut in one side can be used. Working the silk into the ball, the performer pretends to place it in his left hand, but really palms it in his right. Reaching for his wand, which is in his pocket or lying on his table, he drops the ball into the pocket or onto a servante (hidden shelf behind a conjurer's table). Touching the left hand with the wand, he shows that the hank is gone. A moment later it is found mysteriously in some other piece of apparatus in which a duplicate silk has been placed.

A comedy effect is Houdini Outstripped. A man volunteer is invited onto the stage, where a rope is tied around his waist and the ends are held by two other volunteers. When they pull on the rope as if to penetrate the victim's waist, his undershorts are apparently

CANE TO DOUBLE SILKS   No. 430

Magician steps forward twirling a black cane taps it on the floor to show it is solid, and then holds it between his hands. It instantly changes to two 24" silks. Do it surrounded. Silks are not included at this low price. $5

COLOR CHANGING CANE TO SILKS

Performer twirls a black cane which suddenly turns bright red. He twirls the red one and it changes into two 24" or four 18" silks! Do it surrounded, any time. Many possibilities of combinations. Everything furnished except the silks. No. 431 $10.00

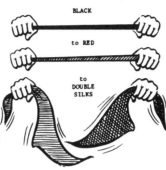

BLACK

to RED

to DOUBLE SILKS

MAGIC, INC.

Silk Wheel
(Tücherrad)

A great visual effect! Two silks are knotted together, and immediately you are able to show seven silks all knotted together to form a large silk wheel.

Without bodyloading!

Colours: Red or Green.

THE MAGIC HANDS, DM 33

CREATION OF MAXIMILIANO LONDONO

Feature   FLAGS

Smashing stage effect in a riot of color which never fails to bring gasps and thunderous applause. A small multi-color strip of paper is passed from hand to hand and torn in half, then in quarters. Paper is crumpled up and immediately changes to a string of beautiful large silk flags of all nations, stretched across magician's body. Doves, silks or other loads can now be produced from string of flags. Particularly good for an opener.

Price $5.00

GUARANTEED MAGIC

Berland's Brilliant
BLITZ!

First performed in Vienna at the F I S M Convention.

Effect: performer enters with a cigarette (unlit) held in one hand, and the other holds a match box. Nothing else is visible. He strikes a match on the box nothing happens . . . once again he tries to light the match, suddenly now the BLITZ. The match changes to a silk . . . the match box changes to three silks now three more silks appear alongside of the single silk reaching among the silks he reaches in and brings out a full size glass of wine!

Complete special silk (you supply 6 of your own silks) necessary gimmicks newly designed. Glass etc. Fully illustrated.

$15.00

Berland's BLITZ production of Silks and Glass of Wine

SAMUEL BERLAND

SUDDEN SILK ON RIBBON

Featured by Tel Smit in his lecture tour, creating an instant demand for this spectacular effect. Equally good for stage, because it looks big, altho it packs small.

A flashy effect. Performer shows length of ribbon, gives it a slight pull between his hands, and suddenly, and to almost certain applause, a silk handkerchief appears tied on the ribbon!

MAGIC, INC., $3.00

RICE'S 50 STAR MIS-MADE FLAG

STANDARD ROUTINE

Performer forms a paper cylinder into which he pushes three silks (red, white, and blue). However, he accidentally (?) drops the blue silk on the floor, and when flag is produced from the cylinder, the blue field is missing as illustrated. The audience enjoys this comedy. Not to be defeated, the performer picks up the blue silk and replaces it and the mis-made flag into the cylinder. Now the flag emerges, perfectly made, with the stars in place.

SILK KING STUDIOS.
JUNIOR SIZE, $25.00. ALSO REQUIRES DYE TUBE, $7.50

SILK KING STUDIOS, INC.

NEW! ✳ STRIPE!

Here is a striking new effect by Warren Stephens. The performer shows a black and red striped tube which is about fifteen inches long and about two inches in diameter. Into the black and red striped tube, the performer pushes a white handkerchief. Suddenly the red stripes on the tube dissapear and the tube is now black and white striped. The handkerchief is blown from the tube and it is now red and white striped. Stripe will be a winner in any program. Very visual and startling. With necessary handkerchiefs and the tube and instructions. PRICE--$22.50
POSTPAID---$24.00

MAGIC METHODS

872—NITE CLUB "BLOW DYE"

Ade Duval

The most beautiful method of dyeing silks ever conceived. An exclusive secret revealed for the first time. Magicians all over the world have seen Duval perform this gorgeous effect and have asked him time and again for his method. Here and now, for the first time anywhere is Ade Duval's own IMPROVED version that can be performed anywhere, under any conditions. This NEW method has never been sold, has never appeared in print. The magician rolls a piece of paper into a tube and thrusts a white silk into the tube. The tube is brought up to the lips, a puff and out comes—A WHITE SILK! (Fooled ya' huh? Thought sumpin' was in the tube.) The white silk is again tucked into the tube, puffed out and Lo and Behold, the silk is RED! Another white silk, puffed out, it's GREEN! Still another white silk, Whoos-s-s, it's YELLOW! The tube is then slit open, and torn up. IT'S EMPTY!! Professional magic, sensational effect, complete with all Ultrasilks necessary, a lucite wand, and Ade Duval's own routine. This effect carries the unqualified endorsement of every magician in the world. $35.00
Same with all gimmicks and routine BUT NO SILKS $18.50

LOUIS TANNEN, INC.

942—SOFT SOAP
Kayton

Here's one of the finest effects in silk magic. It's an Award Winner! A brilliant effect with a perfect sucker finish.

Magician removes three white hankies from his pocket and finds them all spotted with ink. Desiring clean hankies he places them in a soap flake box and closes the top. Then obviously turning the box upside down, he removes three perfectly clean white hankies. The audience screams at this and wants to see the box. Finally, he shows the box and rips it to pieces flinging it into the audience. There are no other hankies in the box. You'll like this. Comes complete with boxes, handkerchiefs, routine, and patter. . . . $13.50
Extra Soft Soap Boxes, $.25 each, per dozen $2.50
NOTE: POSITIVELY NO chemicals or liquids used in the above effect.

LOUIS TANNEN, INC.

pulled off and are seen hanging on the rope. A similar illusion at the expense of a woman spectator is known as the Brassière Trick. Caution: For these little experiments be sure to choose a volunteer with a sense of humor! The tricks are in the $5.00 to $10.00 range.

In many fine effects silks vanish from one place to reappear mysteriously in another. For these tricks duplicates are often used. In Silkola, priced at $10.00, the vanished hank reappears in a capped and previously examined Coke bottle. In Karson's Flash, it is fired from a pistol and visibly materializes knotted around the middle of a long, slender brass rod which the magician's assistant holds above his head with both hands. A silk-vanishing gun will cost about $40.00, but it will enhance your act. It can be effectively used, for example, with a Handkerchief Pedestal, available at some magic shops for about $10.00. On this is set an ordinary-looking tumbler. The glass is covered with a scarf or empty tube. A silk handkerchief is hung over the gun. When the shot is fired, the handkerchief visibly vanishes and is found inside the tumbler.

An old but still favorite effect is the Mutilated Parasol. A colorful parasol is displayed, and a number of silks of various colors are placed into an empty handbag. The parasol is furled and rolled up in a newspaper. When it is drawn out again from the newspaper, hanging from each of its otherwise bare ribs is one of the colored handkerchiefs. They make a pretty display when twirled in the air. The handbag is opened and in it, in place of the silks, is the missing parasol cover. Then, returning the parasol to the paper tube, the transposition is reversed. The Mutilated Parasol is a fairly expensive trick and different models vary considerably in ease of working. Most of them require an assistant.

In one of the newest and most baffling transposition effects, the vanished silk appears inside a transparent, inflated balloon. Truly space-age magic.

The Sympathetic Silks, previously mentioned, is but one example of the many fine handkerchief tricks that involve the magical tying and untying of knots. Tony Slydini's instant dissolving of knots, in his close-up act, is a masterpiece of comedy magic. His studio sells special white silks for this entertaining effect.

Probably no magician has done more to create charming effects of this genre than the original and imaginative Pavel. Czechoslovakian by birth, Pavel now has his studio in Geneva. He has made several tours lecturing before magic groups in the United States. In one Pavel invention, the Blow Tie, three silks are pushed separately into a clear plastic tube. The performer blows into one end of the tube and the hanks sail out into the air—knotted together end to end.

Pavel also drops separate silks into a cone of newspaper formed before the spectators' eyes and pulls them out at the bottom of the cone knotted into a chain. He makes audiences gasp by tying in a 36-inch silk a knot that mysteriously slides down a few inches each time the silk is shaken by one corner. Finally the knot falls bodily off the silk onto the stage, leaving the silk free!

Quadsilk, another Pavel creation (Magic, Inc., $10.00), recalls the Blendo effect, but with a difference. Four differently colored 18-inch silks are shaken together and inexplicably blended into one large silk, checkered in the same four colors. Pavel then picks up a sheet of newspaper, rolls it up, pushes the big silk into it, and out fly the four separate silks again! The newspaper is unrolled and shown empty.

Pavel has written several books explaining the secrets of his effects. In the golden days of vaudeville, the clever American magician Ade Duval draped the entire stage with rainbow-hued silks which he magically produced in his featured act, "Rhapsody with Silks." Today Pavel has inherited his mantle as one of the most innovative masters of the art of sorcery with silks.

Poster used by the great Indian magician P. C. Sorcar, whose fabulous illusion show *Ind-Dra-Jal* (*Magic of India*) made him famous throughout the world. His son, P. C. Sorcar, Jr., has carried on the show since the death of his father in 1971. (*Poster courtesy of Sotheby's Belgravia*)

THE ENCHANTED GARDEN

Magic with Flowers

From ancient times magicians have mystified their audiences by growing real plants and flowers with incredible speed. The mortal who could plant a seed from which a fruit- or flower-bearing shrub grew quickly out of the earth shared in the marvelous mysteries of the natural world.

The possibility of human control over the process of plant growth, by telescoping it in time, lent fascination to one of the most impressive tricks performed by the old-time Hindu fakirs. Thrusting a seed into a little pile of earth as he squatted on the ground in the marketplace, the half-naked fakir would cover the soil with a shawl or basket. After a magical incantation, he lifted the cover to disclose a green shoot pushing up through the soil. Again the cloth or basket was replaced and again it was lifted, this time to reveal a sturdy sapling a foot high. Finally the wonder worker displayed a healthy young mango tree bearing fruit which he distributed to the spectators.

So, at least, ran the reports of travelers returning from the Orient. Seeking an explanation of the mystery, rationalists speculated that the plants must have been hidden in the fakir's loin cloth or robe and cleverly smuggled out under cover of the shawl or basket, but the feat has never been explained with any certainty.

Perhaps it was such travelers' tales that inspired the introduction of illusions with shrubs and flowers into the repertoires of magicians in the West. In any

The Flowering Rose Bush, made by the Petrie-Lewis Manufacturing Company about 1940. On a table stands a plant about 30 inches high, with rich green foliage. At the magician's command, a dozen fresh, real roses grow and flower on the bush in full view of the spectators. The Rose Bush is an extremely rare collector's item. (*Clayton Albright Collection*)

case, magic with flowers has been an important element lending beauty and mystery to the performances of Occidental magicians.

Robert-Houdin, the "Father of Modern Magic," created many marvelous automatons. Describing in his memoirs one of these automatons built about 1845, he writes:

This mechanical piece was preceded by several sleight-of-hand tricks which motivated its appearance on the stage.

I borrowed a lady's handkerchief which I set beside an egg, a lemon and an orange in a row on my table.

I then passed these four objects, one after another, into each other, and when finally they were all united in the orange, I utilized this fruit to compose a mysterious liqueur.

For this, I pressed the orange between my hands, reducing it in size and showing it in different shapes, and finally I made it into a powder which I put into a flagon of spirits of wine.

An orange tree, bare of flowers or fruits, was then brought on. I poured into a small vase a little of the liqueur that I had just prepared, and set it aflame. This I placed beneath the orange bush, and as soon as the vapor reached the foliage it became visibly loaded with blossoms.

Upon a stroke of my wand, these flowers were replaced by fruits which I distributed to the spectators.

One solitary orange remained on the tree. I commanded it to open into four parts, and inside of them one saw the handkerchief that had been entrusted to me. Two butterflies, waving their wings, took it by the corners and, rising into the air, displayed it to the audience.

L'ILLUSTRATION,

Ab. pour Paris. — 3 mois, 8 fr. — 6 mois, 16 fr. — Un an, 30 fr.   N° 125. Vol. V. — SAMEDI 19 JUILLET 1845.   Ab. pour les Dep. — 3 mois, 9 fr. — 6 mois, 17 fr. — Un an, 34 fr.
Prix de chaque N° 75 c. — La collection mensuelle br., 2 fr. 75.   Bureaux, rue Richelieu, 60.   Ab. pour l'Étranger. — 10 — 20 — 40.

M. Robert-Houdin.

La concurrence est partout, mais celle que nous allons signaler n'est pas cette concurrence éhontée qui embouche toutes les trompettes de l'annonce et de la réclame ; elle est au contraire si modeste, que, bien qu'existant déjà depuis quelque temps, l'Illustration sera probablement la première, comme c'est au surplus son rôle et son devoir, à faire connaître à ses lecteurs qu'au n° 164 de la galerie de pierre du Palais-Royal, non loin du théâtre de Séraphin et de l'escalier de cristal, ces deux admirations de l'enfance et de la province, un émule de l'enchanteur Philippe vient d'ouvrir et de consacrer au culte de la magie blanche une charmante petite salle à laquelle M. Martin, jeune architecte de talent, a donné toute la coquetterie et le confortable du plus élégant salon. La fabrication des cuirs repoussés devait déjà à M. Martin ses plus gracieux dessins de meubles.

M. *Robert-Houdin*, le grand prêtre de ce petit temple, marchant sur les traces des Vaucanson et des Maëlzel, est moins un physicien qu'un mécanicien habile, qui, fatigué d'exécuter pour tous les magiciens passés et présents, les ingénieuses combinaisons qui ont fait toute leur réputation, a

pensé qu'il était bien temps pour lui de soumettre directement à la sanction du public une série de récréations d'autant plus perfectionnées qu'il les a préparées pour son propre usage et pour prouver ses talents comme mécanicien.

Cependant, sans avoir la prétention de se poser en prestidigitateur, M. Robert-Houdin démontre que le savoir n'exclut pas le savoir-faire, et après avoir séduit ses spectateurs par les pièces mécaniques les plus compliquées, parmi lesquelles nous devons citer le hibou fascinateur, le valet de trèfle acrobate et surtout l'oranger magique et les papillons escamoteurs qui sont le sujet de notre planche, il parvient, sans autre costume qu'un simple habit noir et **sans** autre appareil qu'un schall et un léger guéridon, à opérer, littéralement sous vos yeux, la fameuse pêche miraculeuse qui, au bazar Bonne-Nouvelle, a fait la vogue et la fortune des soirées mystérieuses du magicien Philippe. Nous lui souhaitons cette vogue et cette fortune ; d'autres la lui prédiront en ajoutant que le temps présent est en général favorable aux escamoteurs : nous dédaignons ce lieu commu**n**.

In another effect Robert-Houdin used a garland of roses suspended horizontally over the stage. Loading into a pistol tube three borrowed pocket watches, two borrowed handkerchiefs and three cards selected by spectators, he fired, and all these objects appeared magically along the garland.

Later in the nineteenth century a trick that did much to establish the reputation of the American magician Harry Kellar (1849–1922) as the leading performer of his day was the illusion known as The Magic Flowers. On an otherwise bare stage were two richly draped circular stands on which sat flower pots. After passing the pots for inspection, Kellar filled them with sand and dropped a few seeds in each pot. He then handed around for thorough inspection a large, thin-walled cone, open at the top and bottom, which was clearly empty. With this cone Kellar covered one of the pots, explaining that darkness helped the seeds to germinate. Sure enough, upon raising the cone a green shoot was seen to have sprouted from the sand. Next covering a pot on the other stand, he lifted the cone to reveal a large

rosebush loaded with real blooms and buds. After again showing the cone empty, Kellar returned to the first stand, where he produced a no less flourishing growth of roses. Assistants clipped the roses from both bushes and distributed them to ladies in the audience.

This beautiful illusion, and the secret behind it, are shown in the accompanying illustrations. On a small shelf behind each of the innocent-looking stands rested a duplicate cone containing a rosebush attached to a lead base, with blooms and buds artfully wired to its branches. When he covered the first pot, Kellar let a small green sprig, weighted so it would stand upright, fall from his hand into the pot. In the act of revealing this sprig, he lowered the cone in a natural manner behind the stand and over the cone concealed there. In a split second he picked up that cone and its hidden bush within the first cone. The rosebush was then released into the pot on the second stand, and another bush was obtained from behind that stand to be revealed on the first table.

To perform this trick smoothly required extreme

LEFT: "Magic Flowers."

BELOW: The mystery explained.

OPPOSITE: In a front-page review in July, 1845, the French magazine *L'Illustration* featured Robert-Houdin's Mysterious Orange Tree and praised his Soirées Fantastiques.

precision of movement and timing. Kellar carefully rehearsed his movements, even outlining on the floor the exact place for every footstep he took throughout the routine. Mainly because of its difficulty, the effect was not often repeated by his successors, but gave way to the use of mechanical cones. In the double walls of these cones, which were now shown "empty" from only the small end, bottomless brass pots holding artificial bushes were released. The bushes swung out on spring arms from the sides of the pots. The effect, while colorful, hardly rivaled Kellar's in mystery. One of these mechanical cones is shown opposite.

Partly under the spell of Kellar's rosebushes, however, magic dealers in the late nineteenth and early twentieth centuries created many other brilliant effects with flowers. It was assumed that flower displays would appeal especially to "the fair sex." Many of these charming and deeply mystifying creations, alas, have vanished permanently, no longer to be found even among collections of magical rarities. On these two pages are shown some of the finest of them, as described and pictured in a catalogue of conjuring apparatus issued by the famous London magical dealers, Hamley Brothers, Ltd. Although this edition of the catalogue came out about 1909, it is probable that many of the illustrations in it date back to the earlier years of the firm, in the era from about 1875 to the 1890s.

The Anatomy of Magic Flowers

Today, as well as in Hamley Brothers' time, two kinds of magic flowers are mainly used, the feather and spring types. Flowers formed from dyed feathers are highly compressible and are generally used for productions from the the sleeve or from a shawl or foulard, as in Hamley's Monster Bouquet. A large bouquet to be produced from a borrowed handkerchief can be arranged on a cloth-covered wire framework which is held flat against the stem by a catch. In this flat form the bouquet can be easily concealed inside the breast of the performer's coat and introduced under the foulard. When the catch is released a spring pulls the bouquet at right angles to its stem. Smaller bouquets are more simply constructed around a wire stem, or formed as a spray.

Flower darts that stick into the floor make showy productions from a borrowed hat or a square circle (page 110). Feather flowers can also be compressed inside canes or candles for transformation effects. Large feather flower pieces such as botania illusions and comic Goofus plants—ugly green stalks that suddenly eject three monster snakes and turn into a handsome bush of flowers —are among the showiest floral display pieces.

No. 5829. **The Mystic Cone and Growth of Flowers.**—The performer first shows the cone, which is made of metal, beautifully japanned, and he puts his arm right through it to prove there is nothing concealed inside—simply a thin metal cone, without any top to it. He now takes a common flower-pot and asks one of the audience to fill it with mould. He then places the cone on the top of the flower-pot, and taking great quantities of various kinds of seeds, he pours them inside the cone until the interior is full; now, making some passes with his wand, he commands the seeds to grow, and removing the cone, reveals a beautiful bouquet of flowers, much higher than the cone, and the seeds have all vanished. The cone stands thirteen inches high and the bouquet of flowers eighteen inches high.

Price **44/-.** *With full directions. Carriage to be paid on receipt.*

No. 5828. **The Fairy Stand of Flowers and Enchanted Cage.**—The performer first shows a beautiful stand full of flowers, some of which he distributes to the ladies to prove they are real; he then borrows a handkerchief and covers over the stand, and immediately produces a large square cage with two live birds in it out of the stand, the flowers remaining undisturbed. The wonderful part of this is that the cage, which is perfectly solid and made of wire, prettily japanned, stands a great deal higher than the stand, whilst the part in which the flowers are arranged is only two inches deep. The cage is the same size square as the stand.

Price **48/-.** *With full directions. Carriage to be paid on receipt.*

No. 5807.   The Inexhaustible Basket of Colour-Changing Flowers.—A SPLENDID STAGE OR DRAWING-ROOM TRICK.—This is one of the most effective tricks ever seen.   You have an ordinary wire *basket*, which you show all round, top and bottom, and then turn it upside down to prove it is quite empty.   It will bear the closest possible inspection, as it is of such beautiful workmanship that the 'cutest conjurer would not discover any deception about it.   The basket looks perfectly natural, and just like any ordinary flower or fancy basket.

To perform this trick you (having shown the basket to be perfectly empty) cover it over, but before you do so, take some *red, white,* and *blue* paper, which you tear up into small pieces and put them into three separate envelopes, which you place on your table in order, thus —*red, white,* and *blue.*   (If the audience like they can themselves place the pieces of paper in the envelopes and seal them down.) You then cover over the basket ; next ask the audience to name the colour they would like to disappear first.   Whichever colour they name (we will say *blue*) you command it to pass, and on opening the envelope the pieces have entirely *vanished*, and on uncovering the basket it is found to be full of *blue flowers.*   These you pour out into any receptacle that will hold them, and show the basket entirely empty as at first.   Again you ask the audience which of the two remaining colours they would like to disappear from the envelopes. This time they say *red.*   Show the pieces in the envelope, let it be stuck down.   Cover over the *basket* once more.   " Presto ! Change ! " Again, when the handkerchief is removed, it is seen that it is full of red flowers and the envelope is quite empty.   Now for the *white ;* but before commanding these to pass into the basket, to prove you do not place anything in it, ask one of the audience to hold it themselves, and not only that, but cover it over.   You then take the *white* pieces of paper out of the envelope, and say that you will vanish them in a different way.   Hold them in your hand, then borrow a match, which you light ; place the paper over the match, and in a flash it has all disappeared, and your hands are entirely empty.   Take the basket from the person who has been holding it, and uncover it, and once more the basket is full of flowers, this time *white* ones.   These can be poured out and the basket once more shown round for inspection. This makes one of the most perfect and effective tricks ever seen, and causes tremendous applause.   It is very easy to perform.

Price **27/6,** *with flowers complete.   With full directions.*
Carriage to be paid on receipt.

No. 5688.   Hamley's Monster Bouquet. —We first show our hands quite empty and arms bare.   Next borrow a lady's shawl, which we show back and front to prove there is no deception about it.   Then simply by shaking it gently, from underneath it we produce a really marvellous bouquet (please notice the size of this), which is 2 ft. 2 ins. in diameter, 5 ft. 6 ins. in circumference, and length 21 ins.   This is made with the very best feathers and flowers.

We make a speciality of feather work of all kinds.

Price **35/-.**   *Post free* **35/5.**

No. 5798.   The Enchanted Candle and Fairy Bouquet.— This is a most novel and elegant illusion, and we can highly recommend it as a pretty and effective addition to a programme.   The performer has on his table two handsome candlesticks, in one of which is a candle burning, the other is empty.   This, he says, is through the carelessness of his assistant ; however, he will perform a little trick with them.   He then shows a small cover, quite empty, and this he stands on the empty candlestick as if it were a candle.   He extinguishes the candle in the other candlestick and covers it with a borrowed handkerchief.   Next he takes a beautiful bouquet, and holding it in the tips of his fingers, he throws it into the air, when, to the astonishment of the audience, it instantly vanishes. He then removes the cover, and behold, there is the candle, where before was only an empty candlestick.   Next he goes to the other, and lifts off the borrowed handkerchief, and the candle has vanished from there, and in place of it is the bouquet fixed upright in the candlestick.   This forms a charming trick, the effect being so pretty and novel.   Highly recommended.

Price **28/6.**   *Pos. free* **29/-.**   *With full directions.*

No. 5797.   The Mysterious Rose Tree and the Three Cards.—Three cards are chosen from the pack by the audience, torn up and placed in a pistol.   The rose tree is brought forward and placed on the table.   One of the company is now asked to fire the pistol at the rose tree, and immediately the three chosen cards appear on the top of the tree, and are taken off and given to the audience.

Price **30/-.**   *Post free* **30/8.**
With full directions.

New and improved principle, very handsome, **36/-.**
Post free **36/9.**

Fancy antique flower effects from Hamley Brothers.

653 –GIANT BOTANIA

An unusual type of Magic. A large tube is shown to be empty and is then placed over a large flower pot. When tube is lifted off the flower pot a large bush of the most beautiful flowers are seen! For sheer, breathtaking beauty, these blossoms are unsurpassable. The Flower Bush produced is larger than the tube. Sorry we cannot show you the beauty.

Small Botania. $125.00
Medium Botania. $195.00
Large Botania. $275.00
Super Jumbo Botania. $325.00

LOUIS TANNEN, INC.

635–GARDEN OF FLOWERS

A self-contained winner for any magician's act. A large silk foulard is shown. Performer thrusts his hand in the folds of the silk and instantly produces a large bouquet! This is followed by another, and still another appears, and finally for good measure, he produces a FOURTH BOUQUET!! FOUR BOUQUETS—NO BODY LOADS! Comes to you complete with foulard and bouquets.

Regular Garden of Flowers $89.50
Garden of Flowers with medium size bouquets. $135.00
Garden of Flowers with GIANT size bouquets. $275.00
New SUPER Garden of Flowers. $365.00

LOUIS TANNEN, INC.

Improved Flower in Buttonhole

Here is a swell opening trick and with this improved method, elastic and body gimmicks are completely done away with. Great for Night Clubs, close-up and intimate shows.

Magician remarks he will show how easy it is to grow a flower by aid of magic. He places the magic seed on his coat lapel, makes a pass with his wand and "like a flash" a beautiful flower appears in the buttonhole. No skill . . . no preparation . . . always ready. It's all in the wand which is chrome-plated and one that can be used throughout the show.

ABBOTT'S MAGIC MFG. CO., $15.00; DELIVERED, $16.00

At the left are two exceptionally colorful flower effects popular with professional magicians. Floral productions along somewhat similar lines can be found in the catalogues of other magic houses also. The surprising trick shown above fits in especially well near the start of a program.

Spring Flowers

Rivaling feather flowers in beauty, if not in durability—although they last quite well if handled gently—are flowers with petals and leaves made of prettily colored tissue paper or silk. Springs cause them to open instantly from a folded condition. When the flowers are folded up and held together a lovely bouquet of two dozen blooms occupies only a very small space.

Some performers prefer spring flowers to the feather variety because of their soft pastel colors. On the other hand, feather flowers are usually larger and more showy.

Spring flowers can be made at home if you are handy at cutting, folding and gluing. To make them properly takes considerable work and skill, however, so the professionally made ones, which are not very expensive, are usually more practical.

Spring flowers are constructed as shown below:

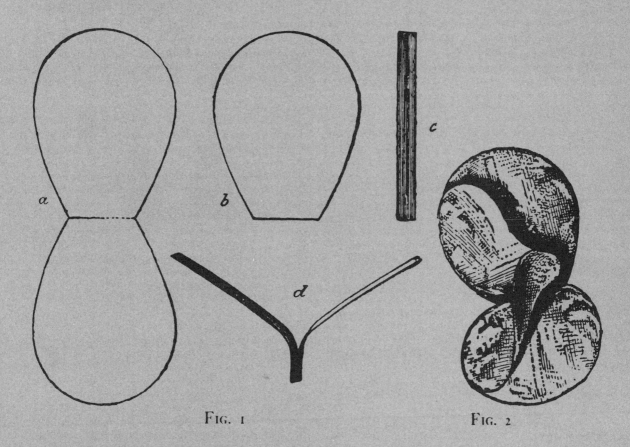

FIG. 1   FIG. 2

Spring flowers can be magically produced in many ways: from a production box, dove pan, square circle or hat; from the fingertips by means of special gimmicks; and in combination with other equipment. Buatier de Kolta, the French magician, introduced the popular trick of forming a plain sheet of paper into a cone, out of which there suddenly wells a profusion of multicolored flowers. On the next page are Messrs. Hamley's announcements of that trick and of the wide variety of spring flowers they sold seventy years ago.

The very useful spring-flower clips (Hamley's No. 5177, following page) are available today from Abbott's, who also stock flowers in several different sizes.

Some of the best spring flowers made in America today are produced by Count Maximiliano Londono, a Brazilian conjurer now living in New York. These are sold by Londono's Magic Novelties Company, 147 West 42nd Street, New York, NY 10036, and also by Tannen's, Guaranteed Magic and others. Cost of twenty-five flowers is about $6.50.

Two fast, colorful effects with spring flowers are The Crystal Flower Tube and The Blockbuster. Sam Berland's Blockbuster is especially designed as an opening trick. This surprising novelty is guaranteed to capture the immediate attention of any audience. Out of an innocent-looking handkerchief you produce, in swift succession, the explosive sound of a shot, a fountain of paper ribbon and lastly, to everyone's amazement, a totally unexpected bouquet of flowers. These effects are shown on page 83.

No. 5177. Flowers of Enchantment.—The performer takes a piece of paper and makes it into a cone before the audience, shows it quite empty, but at once on shaking it over a basket, a shower of beautiful various-coloured flowers proceed from it, filling the basket to overflowing.

Despite unfair competition by small dealers Messrs. HAMLEY BROS. have still the universal reputation for selling the very best goods at the very lowest prices, and their spring flowers are no exception. They are selling their variegated flowers at 2/6 per 100, but the value is the same; in fact, the flowers are absolutely as good in every way as those they sold for 4/6. They do NOT lower the price and give an inferior article. Messrs. HAMLEY simply ask for a trial, and they feel certain of giving satisfaction.

Price **2/6.** *Post free* **2/7** *per* 100.

N.B.—Not less than 100 sold at this marvellously low price.

Large De Kolta flowers, five different colours in each flower, **9d.** *per dozen, or* **5/9** *per hundred.*

Very superior single flowers, elegantly shaded and with silk leaves, **10d.** *per dozen, or* **6/6** *per hundred.*

Superb double flowers, shaded and with silk leaves, **1/-** *per dozen, or* **7/6** *per hundred.*

Rose flowers, various colours, **10d.** *per dozen, or* **6/6** *per hundred.*

Post free **1d.** *extra.*

No. 5177A. Flower Clips.—All magicians who include in their performances the charming and ever popular production of flowers will, we feel sure, recognise the above clever little contrivance as a most welcome boon. Every conjuror who aims at perfection, should progress thereto and keep up-to-date in the magical world by obtaining this. He will find it invaluable for its specified purpose, and it can be put to many other uses by the ingenious conjuror. It is easily fastened and keeps the flowers compact and in perfect condition; it entirely supersedes and does away with all threads, elastic bands, &c., and is easily released by the very slightest pressure, and we can thoroughly recommend it to our customers as invaluable.

Price **6d.** *Post free* **7d.**

Very superior quality, on a different but much better principle.

Price **2/6.** *Post free,* **2/7.**

No. 5178. Primrose Flowers of Enchantment.—Same as the Flowers of Enchantment, but made to represent primroses. A very novel and pretty effect. Suitable for Primrose League Fête Entertainments. Very handsome and large flowers.

Price **2/6** *per dozen. Post free* **2/7.**

No. 5179. The Producing Tulip Flowers.—The performer takes a piece of cartridge paper and makes it into a cone before the audience and shows it perfectly empty (the sleeves of the performer being turned right up and the arms perfectly bare). He then gently shakes it over a basket, umbrella, or table, when a shower of beautiful tulip flowers of various colours proceed from it, making a very big display and filling it to overflowing. The tulips are about 8½ inches long each flower, and most beautifully made, so that a great quantity can be produced at one time. They are made on an entirely different principle than hitherto and will form one of the great effects of the season.

Price **2/6** *per dozen;* **10/3** *per fifty;* **20/-** *per hundred.*

Postage **2d.** *extra.*

No. 5179A. Hamley's New Flower Baskets.—These are the prettiest and most enchanting productions known, and as they take up very little space a dozen or so can easily be produced from a hat, but when set out they make a tremendous and very beautiful show.

Price **5d.** *each. Post free* **6d.** *By the dozen (not less)* **4/-.**

Post free **4/2.**

No. 5180. Hamley's Bouquet Flower Balls.—These splendid garlands are quite new and make a great feature at any entertainment where they are used. There are several ways of introducing them, but perhaps the most effective is from the hat, which has previously been borrowed, it is then shown to the company to prove that there is no deception. On the performer putting his hand in he immediately takes out a most beautiful variegated flower ball about the size of a small melon, and then another and another till he produces at least two dozen, making an enormous show. As the flower balls are produced each can be hung up, having a silk ribbon attached to it. This makes a most pretty effect.

Price **8d.** *Post free* **9d.** *Per dozen (not less)* **5/9.** *Post free* **6/-.**

Strings of 6 Bouquets similar to the above, but brighter and of better quality, **4/-.** *Post free* **4/3.**

No. 5181. Bouquets for the Hat, Plate, &c.—Made up of the above flowers, double, shaded with silk leaves, silk paper flowers, with silk strings attached.

Flowers **1/6** *per dozen, or* **10/6** *per hundred. Postage* **1d.** *extra.*

No. 5182. Bouquet Flowers of Enchantment.—Same as above, but in bunches to represent bouquets. Very effective, with beautifully blended colours, forming a charming variety and great addition to the trick. With silk backs.

Price **7/6** *per dozen. Post free* **7/9.**

Cheaper make, **4/-** *per dozen. Post free* **4/3.**

No. 5183. Bautier de Kolta's New Flowers and Umbrella Illusion.—These flowers are of a new and special make; each one contains five different colours, and can be made to fill an umbrella in one load. Most beautifully finished trick ever performed.

Price **5/9** *per hundred.*

Post free **5/10.**

Complete with skeleton umbrella (fitted round with green or red ribbon), the same as De Kolta's, with brass stand; to take to pieces for travelling.

Price **17/6** *(including the flowers). Post free* **18/-.**

With full directions.

Umbrella and Stand only **12/6.** *Post free* **13/3.**

Antique spring flower effects from Hamley Brothers' *Illustrated Catalogue of Conjuring Tricks,* c. 1909.

Berland's

THE BLOCKBUSTER

#198

Right out of Berland's Lecture, and one of the most surprising and colorful "opening" effects.

A handkerchief is shown empty and draped over the left hand. A lit cigarette is pushed into the handkerchief, a shot is heard and suddenly colored streamers shoot in the air followed by the colorful production of a bouquet of flowers (spring flowers).

In many many public appearances the Blockbuster has proven to be a wonderful opening effect.

Everything to present the effect is supplied: colorful handkerchief, poppers, spring flower bouquet, etc. are furnished.

640—CRYSTAL FLOWER TUBE

One of the prettiest, flashiest, most visual tricks in magic! The production of a large number (up to fifty) colored spring flowers from a crystal-clear Lucite tube! Tube is freely displayed and is unfeked. Then it is capped at each end with pieces of paper held in place by two fancy bands. The capped tube is shown at both ends. It seems impossible for anything to get into the tube, yet SUDDENLY this becomes FILLED WITH FLOWERS. You can break the paper ends and have the flowers shower out into a container. Use your own flowers.

Charles Dickens as Magician

Charles Dickens, the great novelist, loved and performed magic. This has been pointed out by Michael Patrick Hearn in his annotated edition of Dickens' immortal story, *A Christmas Carol*. Mr. Hearn writes:

"Twelfth Night festivities were particularly energetic in the Dickens household because they also celebrated his son Charles Boz Dickens' birthday. For these parties the novelist often invited 'some children of a larger growth' from his wide circle of literary friends. In a letter to a friend, C. C. Felton, December 31, 1842, Dickens announced his plans for one of these entertainments: 'The actuary of the National Debt couldn't calculate the number of children who are coming here on Twelfth Night, in honor of Charley's birthday, for which occasion I have provided a Magic Lantern and divers other tremendous engines of that nature. But best of it is that Forster and I have purchased between us the entire stock in trade of a conjuror. . . . And . . . if you could see me conjuring the company's watches into impossible tea caddies, and causing pieces of money to fly, and burning pocket handkerchiefs without hurting 'em . . . you would never forget it as long as you live.'

"This 'entire stock of a conjuror' was pulled out for several Twelfth Nights to come. 'One of these conjuring tricks,' recalled his daughter Mamie in *My Father As I Recall Him* (1896), 'comprised the disappearance and reappearance of a tiny doll, which would announce most unexpected news and messages to the different children in the audience; this doll was a particular favourite, and its arrival equally awaited and welcomed.' Dickens himself reveled in these demonstrations and he proudly wrote his friend William Macready (then in America) of the marvelous entertainment on Twelfth Night of 1844: 'Forster and I conjured bravely; that a plum-pudding was produced from an empty saucepan, held over a blazing fire in Stanfield's hat without damage to the lining; that a box of bran was changed into a live guinea-pig, which ran between my godchild's feet . . . and you might have heard it (and I daresay did) in America; that three half-crowns being taken . . . and put into a tumbler-glass . . . did then and there give jingling answers to the questions asked of them by me . . . to the unspeakable admiration of the whole assembly.'

"Dickens did not have to exaggerate this response; Mrs. Thomas Carlyle, one of the guests at this particular party, admitted that Dickens was the greatest conjuror she had ever seen."

(*Taken from* The Annotated Christmas Carol, *by Michael Patrick Hearn*, © *1976 by Michael Patrick Hearn. Used by permission of Clarkson N. Potter, Inc.*)

ENTERTAINING CHILDREN

Magic for the Birthday Party Crowd

Children's parties are one of the most active and dependable markets for magic. Birthday parties, parties for the Hallowe'en and Christmas seasons, Sunday schools and school assembly programs all welcome a good magic show. For many of these affairs a part-time or amateur performer is welcome.

The catch is that children are an especially demanding audience. Some performers consider them the toughest of all for a magician. To put on a really entertaining and successful children's magic program takes imagination, careful selection of effects, and a lively and captivating style of presentation, with plenty of fun and humor.

Though children may make a critical audience, their vivid imaginations do enable them to enter easily into the world of make-believe. It's especially important, therefore, for the children's magician to look the part of a magician. A red coat, top hat, showy tie and perhaps a ruffled shirt, worn with dark trousers, will be enough to set the male magician off from the audience's unglamorous fathers and uncles. If you're playing an Oriental role, a jeweled turban or colorful fez goes well with an otherwise Occidental wardrobe. A prettily dressed girl assistant is always an asset with both the boys and the little girls in the audience.

Lady magicians have even more leeway in choosing their costume, be it a simple but romantic-looking dress

William Moreno of New York presents a smooth, well-paced, ten-minute magic act, quite an accomplishment for a lad only four years old. Here he performs at an All-Day Magic Convention in New York. William rehearses his act conscientiously —a good rule for everybody. (*Lynn Carver Photo*)

or a more exotic outfit, perhaps that of a medieval princess, Arabian sorceress, or fairy godmother. A jeweled wand. especially one of those with a lighted electric star at the end (Magic Center, New York, $3.50), underlines her mystical role.

A new sort of attraction more often seen in children's programs in recent years is the magic clown. If you are good at pantomime and don't mind the considerable extra labor of donning a colorful, humorous clown costume and makeup for each performance, you might well consider becoming a magic clown. For a professional or semipro magician to be able to offer this extra attraction in his ads and publicity gives him an extra advantage, especially in appealing to parents or others who are organizing entertainments for small children. There are several fine books on magic clowning that give full details on costumes, props, and clown stunts and humor (see bibliography). Clown makeup and costume props—clown white, red rubber noses, bald heads, giant shoes, and many other items—may be ordered from Magic, Inc.

Attractive-looking magic equipment also helps to establish the proper mood and to attract and hold the children's attention. Display colorful apparatus on nicely decorated tables. Be sure your metal cups, tubes and bowls are brightly polished, your milk pitcher and glassware sparkling, and your silks smoothly pressed. This is important for any type of program.

While glamorous and mysterious costumes and props may help to set the atmosphere for a children's show, always remember that children are alert and intelligent. They appreciate sincerity and being treated as equals, and don't like being played down to. They see a lot of magic, science and sophisticated entertainment on television. Patter stories about giants, dwarves and Peter Rabbit will go over with most modern youngsters only if they're presented with a certain amount of tongue-in-cheek humor.

In playing a children's date, be sure to arrive in time to set up everything you will need, in the correct positions, before the audience is admitted. If the show is in a private home or a small hall without a proper stage and theater seats, ask the hostess beforehand to have the children sit in movable chairs, if possible. Kids sitting on the floor are more apt to start roughhousing or wandering around, and they have an angle of vision that may reveal secrets to them. Seating the children in chairs also helps to keep them from getting uncomfortably close to your table. If they must sit on the floor, lay down a piece of magician's rope 10 feet or so in front of your table and announce that anyone crossing the rope uninvited will automatically turn into a frog.

Take with you one or two large, decorative squares of silk or sateen to throw over your tables and apparatus before you go on. These can also be used to cover your equipment as soon as the show is over, as children are inquisitive and may damage expensive apparatus by handling it.

In a children's entertainment the opening effect is particularly important. It should be fast, fresh and showy, to surprise the spectators, capture their attention and make them realize that you are a real magician.

Plenty of audience participation is also vital in a magic program for children. Care in selecting and handling volunteer assistants will help greatly to insure a smoothly running show. To avoid a mass stampede to the stage, never merely request the assistance of "some" boy or girl from the audience. Instead, point to the particular boy or girl you want and have him or her come up. For comedy tricks at the expense of the volunteer, which will make the audience laugh at him, your best bets are boys who look like hearty extroverts and who won't be too easily embarrassed. Girls enjoy helping with pretty tricks with silks, flowers or flags. Incidentally, what with today's unisex fashions and haircuts, you may not always be successful in identifying the sex of a young volunteer at first glance. To avoid the embarrassment of addressing your new helper as "sir," and then having him bring down the house at your expense by pointing out, "I'm a girl," it's best to establish identity clearly at the outset. When the volunteer joins you ask his or her name, introduce him and have him take a bow and be welcomed with a nice round of applause.

When a wand collapses or a fan breaks apart in his hand, or when water is pumped out of his elbow with the aid of a Magic Funnel, a youthful volunteer assistant has to bear the brunt of the joke. At such times give him moral support and make it clear to the audience that these goings-on are not the child's fault but the result of the magic influences. Never do anything to humiliate a sensitive child who already feels conspicuous on the stage. When the volunteer's part in the show is over thank him politely and have him take another bow. If the assistant is a girl, take her hand gallantly and lead her to the steps going down from the platform, or back into the audience.

A great asset in winning the good will and cooperation of a youthful audience is to give inexpensive rewards to your volunteer assistants. Ideal for this purpose are Magician's Assistant diplomas. When rolled up and secured with small rubber bands these diplomas (Louis Tannen, Inc., $2.50 per package of 50; $4.75 per 100) look like small, white-tipped magic wands. Inside is an arcane-looking certificate admitting the youngster to the Society of Magicians' Assistants, and including your name and telephone number for publicity. These credentials are highly appreciated. Or you can give each child who helps a "free ticket." These printed tickets (Magic, Inc., $1.25 per 100) don't admit one to anything—they're just free. Put your address on the back of each ticket with a sticker or rubber stamp.

If the audience is not too big, announce near the beginning of the show that everyone who helps will get a Magician's Assistant diploma. And be sure to add that *everyone* will get a chance to help before the show is over. This avoids anxiety and scrambling among the audience. See that you keep your word about this by asking, when a new volunteer is needed in the later part of the program, who has not yet helped.

Not all types of magic are appropriate for children's shows. Small children do not understand playing cards and cannot remember the suits and values of selected cards. Nor have they sufficient worldly experience to find it surprising that objects should change places mysteriously. For these very small fry, tricks with animals and special children's effects will probably be most successful.

Mind reading and ESP effects, too, rarely go over with children younger than the teens.

Kids expect a rabbit in a magic show. If you don't produce a real bunny, or at least a guinea pig, use one of the spring rabbits with real fur sold by magic dealers. When properly handled and not displayed too long, they're hard to tell from a real rabbit. The rabbit theme can also be carried out in your picture silks, paper-tearing effects, and apparatus decorated with rabbit pictures.

A very good effect for small children, and one that isn't often seen, is the vanish of a handkerchief over a volunteer's head. This trick, which is easy to do, fools no one in the audience except the lone volunteer, and

EXTRA LARGE MAGIC FUNNEL

No.RC8

One of the most hilarious and scream-provoking kid tricks of all time. Performer shows a large shiny funnel and gets a couple of boys up for helpers. He gives one of the kids a glass of water to drink, then changes his mind and decides he has to get back, quick. The second boy is put to work pumping at the boy's left arm, while performer holds the empty funnel at the boy's right elbow.

The kids start to scream when a big, splashing stream of water begins to run out of the funnel into a glass or pail below. Nice looking aluminum funnel, cannot rust, good capacity, easy handling. Great prop. $10.00

WITCH DOCTOR CAN

WATER IS POURED INTO THE WITCH DOCTOR CAN FROM WHICH THREE COLORED SILKS ARE IMMEDIATELY PRODUCED! WHEN THE WATER IS POURED OUT, IT IS COLORED TO MATCH THE THREE SILKS. (SILKS NOT INCLUDED)

$6.50   26.

BLACK HAND GAG

The kind of stuff that makes kids laugh. A boy is going to help you, and you start to hand him something, then lay it down and look around for a towel. Show it carelessly both sides, then wipe off his hands with it. Shake it out and it is covered with big black dirty hand marks. Sure fire comedy because even the kid involved knows it is a gag.

Special towel to be used over and over. Takes no space to carry. $ 2.50   No. 533

THE GIANT & THE DWARF

A 9" HIGH DWARF, A 17" HIGH GIANT, AND A CASTLE MAKE THIS ILLUSION A DELIGHT FOR CHILDREN ENTERTAINERS! COMES COMPLETE WITH PATTER IN TRUE FAIRY TALE TRADITION!

YOU SEE, IT'S ALL ABOUT THIS DWARF WHO LIVES IN THIS CASTLE, AND ONE DAY THIS GIANT, SEEKING A NEW HOME, COMES UPON THE CASTLE DECLARING THAT HIS HOUSE-HUNTING DAYS ARE OVER, HE TRIES TO TAKE OVER THE CASTLE. BUT THE LITTLE DWARF IS A BIT OF A MAGICIAN HIMSELF...........
$49.95

Watch Your Step

(JACK HUGHES)

Abbott's has Sole American Manufacturing Rights to this Effect

Here is one of the year's most outstanding effects, one that will entertain young and old, and at the same time teach a lesson, a visual lesson in Safety First.

Many Magicians will book shows for schools and children's parties on the strength of this effect alone.

Effect: Two highly decorated stands are shown, and with them some colorful cut-outs of children, boys and girls. The design on one stand is composed of various traffic signals, the other with a huge Red Cross on it to represent a hospital.

Magician patters about the mistakes children make every day, and illustrates the consequences by transferring the cut-outs one by one, to the hospital. At the finish, with a timely word of warning and helpful hints, the performer magically transports the children back to their place of safety. A super kiddies' effect — with a moral — that will be enjoyed by adults as well.

Can be performed quickly or slowly — there's plenty of interest-compelling action throughout, accompanied by a clever patter story in rhyme.

Apparatus is attractively decorated in colors — really good-looking equipment that will add to your setting. Each stand is approximately 14"x12" and ¾" thick.

Can be performed under any conditions — close-up or on the stage.

ABBOTT'S MAGIC MFG. CO., $35.00; DELIVERED, $36.50

always gets a lot of laughs. Facing the victim, you display an unprepared pocket handkerchief. Telling him to keep watching the handkerchief closely, you hold it about 18 inches from his face, almost level with his eyes, and pack it together between your hands. With a sudden forward movement of the hands, throw the handkerchief over his head, to land in back of him on the floor or behind a piece of furniture. The hand movement toward the eyes will cause the victim to blink so that the flight of the handkerchief is invisible to him; it looks as though it simply melted away in your fingers. The onlookers can be counted on to appreciate the effect, especially since it is one they can instantly learn to do themselves. At the end, take the volunteer into the secret and everybody will have learned a trick to take home and work on his friends and relations.

Slydini, the famous close-up magician, has developed this trick into a feature effect which he calls The Flight of the Paper Balls. He uses paper napkins and a seated adult volunteer, tossing the crushed napkins one after another over the head of the bewildered victim until the audience is in hysterics.

For very small children, it's a tremendous help for the magician to be able to vary his straight magic effects with specialities like Punch and Judy or ventriloquism with a cute hand puppet or saucy "vent" dummy. A simpler specialty to learn is balloon magic—twisting balloons to form animals, fruits and other shapes. Older children admire dexterity. They enjoy clever manipulative tricks such as color changes with silks, the Aerial Treasury or Miser's Dream; or, if the spectators are close enough to see clearly, the Cups and Balls with a surprise production of fruits, vegetables, full wine glasses or other unexpected objects for the climax.

For magic programs for school assemblies tricks that not only mystify the children but teach them useful lessons about safety in traffic are popular. One of the best of these effects available is Watch Your Step (page 86), manufactured in the United States by Abbott under a license from the Jack Hughes Magic Company of Norfolk, England.

In almost every show some young spectator can be counted upon to sing out, "I've seen that trick before," even before the effect has gone far enough for anyone to identify it. Also, a child who does know the working of a trick—and it's bound to happen sometimes—won't keep politely quiet as adults usually do, but will try to catch the magician out by announcing that he knows how the trick is done. Bruce Posgate, the Toronto magician who is an expert on conjuring for children, advises the performer in such cases to say calmly, "Well, then, let's keep it a secret between you and me," or "Oh, I didn't know you'd seen it before. In that case, I won't do the trick after all." This brings an outcry of protests from the

majority who *haven't* seen the trick, and want to, which silences the lone carper.

A sure way of turning a children's show into a riot is to attempt to distribute magically produced candy or food of any kind to the audience during your act. However, one closing trick that I have always found to be highly appreciated is baking a cake by magic. For this I use a double-load Dove Pan, also known as a Magic Chafing Dish. This piece of apparatus looks like a plain aluminum baking pan, but is so constructed that its contents can be changed twice without altering the outward appearance of the pan or its cover. For the first substitute load, prepare—or order from the baker—an attractively decorated, single-layer cake just slightly smaller in diameter than the pan. On your table also stands a tin picnic box that contains your "ingredients" for the cake you announce you will bake by magic. Behind this sits your second load, hidden from the audience by the box.

Take a dish towel covered with large, black handprints out of your picnic box and wipe out the empty pan with it "to make sure it's sanitary." Tell the audience you are going to show them how to bake a cake in three minutes. Proceed to drop a series of outlandish ingredients into the pan. For flour, you use a flower from your buttonhole. Instead of baking soda, pour in a little raspberry soda. For "light seasoning," empty a full salt cellar into the mess, then break in an egg and finally add a piece of flash paper to provide heat for the baking. Touch off the flash paper with a match or cigarette and as it flares up clap on the cover to extinguish the fire. This automatically brings the first load into the pan and there is a beautiful cake, decorated to suit the occasion (birthday, Hallowe'en, etc.).

Hastily announcing that the cake will be distributed *after* the show, remove it from the pan by the edges of some silver paper on which it sits. The fact that all eyes are on the unexpected cake gives perfect misdirection to help you bring the second load secretly into the pan by means of the ingenious apparatus. This time you show the pan filled with colored paper plates and napkins and small plastic favors for the party. Unexpectedly a large bunch of spring flowers, for a centerpiece, are released when the weight of the napkins is lifted off them. The gay flowers fill the pan to overflowing. Here is an experiment that offers almost everything a juvenile audience could desire—mystery, comedy, eye appeal, and food.

Double-load Dove Pans are sold by many magic dealers. They are priced in the $18.00 to $25.00 area. Single-load pans are somewhat less expensive and are fine, too, for baking a cake by magic.

A surefire principle upon which practically all children's performers depend for working a youthful audience up into shrieks of excitement is that of the sucker effect. The kids are deliberately led to believe that they

can see through the *modus operandi* of a trick, and keep shouting for the magician to "turn it around" or "open both doors at once," until when he finally does so they are proved wrong. The classic in this genre is the Sliding Die Box. This is a good trick to combine with a hat production. The load is introduced into the hat from a servante (hidden shelf behind the table) after the hat is picked up to roll out onto the table the large die that has mysteriously "returned" to it from the die box.

A newer variation that can be worked on much the same principle as the die box is Run, Rabbit, Run. In this effect the children see the white ears of Peter Rabbit, who has been warned by his mother to stay safe at home, sneaking along behind a brick wall into Mr. MacGregor's tempting but highly dangerous garden. Seeing this, the kids shout to warn the magician, who assures them that Peter is still safe at home. Even as he says this, the kids see the naughty bunny peeking around the corner of Mr. MacGregor's garden wall. Despite these clear evidences of the little rabbit's misdeeds, however, the magician reacts obtusely and persistently feigns innocence until the audience is in an uproar. Finally the performer shows that Peter is in neither the house nor the garden, but has mysteriously vanished to turn up in a previously empty top hat. The outfit for this trick can be purchased from many dealers, in wood or metal, at prices ranging from about $25.00 to $35.00.

Other dependable sucker effects especially suitable for juvenile audiences include Soft Soap (page 72), and The Hippity Hop Rabbits and the Luna Trick (both on page 89).

Many of the effects described in other sections of this book are, of course, excellent for children's shows as well as for adult programs. An extensive class of tricks, however, are those that are devised, decorated and routined almost exclusively for children's shows. Many of them are the inventions of British dealers, who seem to have a peculiar affinity for this sort of effect, usually cut out of fiberboard or plywood and gaily painted in bright colors. Let's look more closely at some of the best effects that dealers on both sides of the Atlantic are offering for the children's entertainer.

Run, Rabbit, Run. The operator holds the board while Peter Rabbit scoots back and forth between his snug home behind the door at left, and Mr. MacGregor's garden at right. His antics bring yells from the juvenile audience. (*Courtesy of Louis Tannen, Inc.*)

HIPPTY HOP RABBITS

THIS OUTFIT CONSISTS OF 2 WOOD CUT-OUT RABBITS, ONE WHITE AND THE OTHER BLACK, AND 2 HEAVY WOODEN COVERS. THE RABBITS CHANGE PLACES BACK AND FORTH SEVERAL TIMES. AUDIENCE <u>THINKS</u> THEY KNOW HOW.. $29.95

JUMBO MILK PITCHER

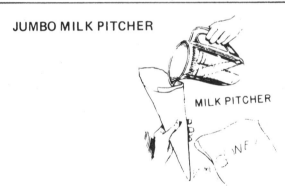

MILK PITCHER

The perfect trick now in PLASTIC, gimmick and all. Use any liquid, nothing to fog the gimmick because it comes out for easy cleaning. A clear colored pitcher is seen full of milk. You tear off a sheet of ordinary newspaper and form it into a cone. With the cone in one hand, and the pitcher of milk in the other, you visibly pour milk from the pitcher into the cone. You step forward with the cone of milk and suddenly swing the open cone right at the spectators. A shower of milk is expected, but nothing comes out of the cone which is perfectly empty. (You may shower your audience with confetti if you wish, as Tony Curtis did in the movie "HOUDINI.") The milk has vanished, leaving no trace. A paper bag can be used instead of a cone. $7.00
Regular smaller milk pitcher $5.00

LUNA TRICK   #677

The "Man in the Moon" (a large wooden disc with a face painted on it), is taken from his home (a prop made up to look like a Cloud) and placed in a second box. (This has two doors, and is finished like a Storm Cloud.) The magician explains that the idea of the trick is to "pass" the Man in the Moon back to his former home, and it is here that the almost endless fun starts!

Tipping the box from side to side, and opening one door at a time, the performer claims that the Moon Man has Vanished! Unfortunately for him, each time the box is tilted a DULL THUD is heard! The kiddies are not slow to tell him that they want to see BOTH doors opened at the same time. After much fun, they are finally opened together, and of course, our little friend has Vanished!

Picking up the original "home cloud," magician boastfully announces that the Moon Man has returned home. BUT . . . Horror of Horrors . . . it is STILL EMPTY. Something has gone wrong, and the performer starts to explain. During the "explanation" . . . the Moon Man PEEPS OVER THE TOP of the Cloud which the performer is holding, and the kiddies shout out. But every time magician turns to have a look at what the kiddies are shouting about the Moon Man drops out of sight! This makes them YELL more than ever. Eventually he is caught, and another HOWLER comes to an end. It is Great Entertainment. . . . Guaranteed 100%.

774—HARVEY AND THE SOLDIER

A SENSATIONAL sucker climax that makes this effect a "must" on your list. A palace guard, resplendent in his RED uniform stands in front of his sentry box. He decides to have a little nap so he sneaks inside the sentry box, but "Harvey" the invisible rabbit is watching so when the soldier comes out his uniform has changed to "BLUE." This will never do, so he begs "Harvey" to change it back to RED. As the story continues the uniform changes from RED to BLUE AND VICE VERSA SEVERAL TIMES! Of course, after two or three times the audience gets wise, (they think!) to the fact that the soldier is RED on one side and BLUE on the other. So they scream and yell for the magician to turn him around. After much misunderstanding, he does; and are they surprised because instead of another soldier, there is "Harvey" finally visible. Soldier and sentry box are beautifully made and decorated. They stand about 12" high. Very showy apparatus. Easy to do. Self-contained. Low, low price for this BIG prop. $12.50

THE FABULOUS FARMYARD

Magic with Animals

People everywhere recognize the rabbit in the hat as the symbol of magic. The creatures of the farmyard—rabbits, ducks, geese, baby chicks and plumed roosters, guinea pigs, dogs—have long been the heart-warming allies of magicians. Children love them especially, and without some trick that includes a four-footed or feathered performer, a children's magic show would hardly be complete.

A striking opening effect for a children's or club show begins with the magician walking on stage with a folded newspaper under his arm. After greeting the audience, he remarks that while waiting in the wings or anteroom he was reading the *Podunk Patriot* (or whatever name the local paper goes by). As often happens, he goes on, there was nothing in the news today. So saying, he unfolds his newspaper—one double-page spread—and shows both sides to the audience. The performer then quickly forms the newspaper into a loose bundle, tears it open and produces a guinea pig.

This effective opening trick is easy to do and requires no special

A dove materializes in the hands of the talented young illusionist Bob Dorian. (*Lynn Carver Photo*)

apparatus. Just before coming on, set your guinea pig on two or three two-page sheets of newspaper. Then form the paper into a bundle around him and tie the bundle securely at the top with strong thread, making a number of turns. Trim off most of the excess paper. Through the turns of thread pass the end of a black thread and with

this make a loop about 15 inches long. Pin this loop to the left shoulder of your vest with a stout safety pin and hang the bundle containing Mr. Guinea Pig under your coat, slightly behind your left arm. Leave your coat unbuttoned. As you show the first side of the newspaper to the spectators, swing your body to the left. Then swing to the right to show the other side, let the bundle swing out from under your coat, catch the thread over your right thumb which holds the paper, and bring the single sheet up around the bundle. Tearing open the paper and unobtrusively breaking the thread, present your pet to the audience.

If this is used as an opener only a few minutes elapse while the animal is in the paper, so he has plenty of air. The newspaper is strong enough to hold a small or medium-sized guinea pig without breaking. A guinea pig is the best pet to use for this trick because it is so docile. A rabbit is not safe to use for this effect because with his strong hind legs, built for hopping, he can kick through the paper. White rats, too, will bite and tear their way out before you can say "Alakazam."

How, then, are rabbits produced? There are many possibilities, depending on the conditions, how you are dressed, the other equipment you are using, and so on. Some methods involve the use of a black cloth bag in which Mr. Bunny remains snugly suspended until he is

Comic magician Leon Bosco has a run-in with a goose in this handsome poster dating from the turn of the century. He was one of the famous trio of Le Roy, Talma and Bosco. Lithograph by Adolph Friedländer, Hamburg. (*Mario Carrandi Collection*)

LEFT: Animal performers of Stan Kramien's touring show "Magic Capades" enjoy the fresh air and sunshine before show time. Two of the troupe's vehicles in the background.

RIGHT: Mars the Magician (Alston Cockrell) and his lovely assistants produce a jumbo rabbit and a trio of exotic birds.

Mars the Magician's bunny is too big to fit into a hat. He had to be materialized from an empty tube.

introduced into the hat under cover of the magician's clothing, a table, or other cover. Floyd G. Thayer's valuable manuscript, "How To Produce a Rabbit from a Borrowed Hat," is sold in mimeographed form by some magic dealers. Other books listed in the bibliography give helpful directions.

Caring for animals properly involves time and expense. Before acquiring them, whether as pets or as co-stars in your magic act, be sure you are prepared to feed them properly, keep their quarters clean and give them the exercise many mammals and birds need. Another question that should be answered in advance is whether there is someone who can care for them while you are away on trips or vacations. Think carefully before taking the plunge, for taking an animal into the household is a long-time commitment that can take much time and energy over the years. If you really enjoy animals, however, or if making your magic act as entertaining as possible is important to you, the investment can be worthwhile.

Guinea pigs and rabbits are among the easiest medium-sized animals to house and use on the platform. Dogs and birds require a greater amount of care. For a serious magical stage show of any size and with many bookings, however, animals are almost essential. In that case, as a rule, a young man or woman in the traveling company is made responsible for the animals, and also acts as assistant on the stage. He or she feeds the livestock, keeps the cages and bedding clean, watches over their health, and makes sure that their coats and plumage are clean and glossy. On the road in pleasant weather, the animals' cages are taken out of the truck or van at each town where the show is booked. The animals are then kept outdoors during the day to get fresh air.

Inventive magicians have devised ingenious pieces of apparatus for the surprise production of animals. Many of these can be purchased at magic dealers' shops. One convenient, multipurpose piece of equipment that can be used for producing a guinea pig or other small animal in a parlor or club show is the drawer box. Another is the bran vase, a beautiful effect which seems to be no longer made and must be obtained, when you can find one, from a dealer in older magic. Such a vase was advertised in Floyd Thayer's *Quality Magic Catalogue No. 7*, of 1928, shown in the Antique Magic section.

No other animal can hope to replace the traditional rabbit as the star attraction in shows for children. Today, however, in magic for general audiences, the rabbit is seen less often than the dove. For sheer beauty as well as surprise, it would be hard to surpass the unexpected, truly magical materialization of a snowy white dove from the folds of a silk handled by a skilled magician. Not only one bird, but a number of them can be made to appear, one after another, to punctuate the performer's program with a series of miraculous materializations, each of

1074—RABBIT WRINGER

A novelty twist to a Rabbit Vanish that is a sure laugh-raiser and still is 100% mystery.

The magician ties a red ribbon around the neck of a live rabbit and places him in a fancy decorated box. Ends of Ribbon are passed through holes in sides of box. Attention is drawn to the roller set in front panel of box. The magician states that to be sure that the rabbit is vanished, he will first flatten him out. As the magician slowly turns the handle, the rabbit (?) is seen to emerge through the rollers, as flat as the proverbial pancake. The box is allowed to fall open and with the exception of the ribbon—IT IS EMPTY!! Now, the flat rabbit is placed in a paper sack, which is crushed—RABBIT HAS VANISHED! and he may be reproduced again from the fancy box—ALIVE AND KICKING!

Nothing better made in the principle used for the vanish, and you have the additional effect of the Flat Rabbit and reappearance of the rabbit back in the fancy box.

Apparatus is finished in black lacquer, trimmed in gold, white rollers, with removable handle. THE OUTFIT IS A BEAUTY! Complete, including Flat Rabbit. $47.50

LOUIS TANNEN, INC.

1134—BOY TO RABBIT

Imagine the publicity that you can get, with this illusion!

MAGICIAN CHANGES A BOY FROM THE AUDIENCE INTO A RABBIT!

The outfit consists of a cabinet on casters. Boy is placed in the cabinet. He can be plainly seen through the open front of same. A cloth is covered over the cabinet and when it is removed, the boy has vanished, and in his place is a live rabbit.

The routine supplied describes the vanishing of the rabbit and the reappearance of the boy back in the audience.

Mr. Smart Magician will realize the full possibilities of the comedy and entertaining features of this original illusion. Cabinet breaks down and is light-weight in construction.

Full workshop plans, plus the routine, and patter. $2.00

LOUIS TANNEN, INC.

RABBIT PRODUCTION . . . . $ 75.00
A small box is shown empty and a rabbit visibly and instantly appears, filling the open front of the box. Will take a good sized rabbit, almost the size of the box itself. Paneled felt finish.

COLOR CHANGING RABBIT . . . . $ 50.00
A fold flat tube is shown on a tray. Produce a white rabbit, (above) and drop him thru the tube. The white rabbit instantly changes into a black rabbit. The tube is folded flat and removed on the tray. Requires two rabbits. Matching paneled felt finish to match set.

GEM PRODUCTION, INC.

mandarin
CABINET

EFFECT: This is a livestock production box which enables the operator to demonstrate it being empty by opening both side doors and holding the open top towards the audience. After the stand is shown thru, the box is placed upon the stand and doors closed. Magician reaches in thru top of box and produces his small rabbit or doves. Doors may again be opened to show inside if desired.

NOTES: The effect can be done surrounded if used per instructions. The box is highly decorated in five colors. Dimensions are: 11¼ X 9" X 9".

Creative Magic Prod. Inc.

BALDWIN, N. Y. 11510

CREATIVE MAGIC PRODUCTS, INC., $48.00

DOVE MAGIC

THIS PAGE IS DEDICATED TO THE DOVE WORKERS AND THE FUTURE DOVE WORKERS OF THE COUNTRY. THIS IS BY NO MEANS OUR COMPLETE LINE OF DOVE ACCESSORIES, SO IF YOU DO NOT SEE AN ITEM THAT YOU ARE LOOKING FOR, PLEASE GIVE US A CALL, OR WRITE US. WE WILL TRY TO BE OF HELP IN ANY WAY POSSIBLE. THANK YOU FOR YOUR CONFIDENCE IN US. LISTED BELOW ARE ITEMS CURRENTLY IN STOCK.

VANISHING DOVE CAROUSEL, Perfect Silent Vanish	$350.00
DOVE CATCHING FROM THE AIR	$139.50
DOVE THROUGH GLASS	$69.50
DOVE TO SILK SENSATION	$12.50
GLOVES TO DOVE, Tray Method	$33.50
RUBBER DOVE, Best Ever Made	$10.00
DOVE FROM RIBBONS	$12.50
DOVAN, Prize Winning Dove Vanish with Dove	$39.50
JOHNNY THOMPSON DOVE HARNESS	$8.50
DOVE-A-MATIC	$24.50
MIRACLE DOVE ACT, Vanish and Reappearance of Two Doves	$69.50
DOVES ON PERCH	$38.50
DOVE BAG	$10.00
DELUXE MODEL DOVE IN BALLOON, Fancy Trim	$59.50
DELUXE DOVE FROM SILK PRODUCTION, No Body Loads	$7.50
TEAR-APART VANISH, Do It Surrounded	$30.00

From Wales, England, comes the fine Dove Magic of THOMAS HYLTON. This young performer is releasing for the first time some of the outstanding secrets of Dove Magic. Each item is made and tested by Mr. Hylton to bring you guaranteed results.

DELUXE DOVE PRODUCTION HARNESS, Great	$10.00
TWIN DOVE PRODUCTION, Best Method Yet	$20.00
DOVE FROM NEWSPAPER, The Perfect Gimmick	$10.00
INSTANT REPEAT DOVE PRODUCTION, Unbelievable	$12.00
COLOR CHANGING DOVE, Beautiful	$15.00
GLOVES TO DOVE, Fantastic	$15.00
BARE-HAND DOVE VANISH TO CANE, Must Wear Tails	$15.00
RABBIT PRODUCTION BAG, Really Made To Hold A Full Grown Rabbit	$15.00
LONDONO'S DOVE HARNESS (each)	$4.50
DELUXE DOVE PRODUCTION	$7.50
HANKY DOVE	$7.50
SUPER DOVE PRODUCTION	$7.50
SIMPLEX DOVE PRODUCTION	$10.00

A page from the catalogue of Louis Tannen, Inc., of New York lists and depicts a number of the best effects in dove magic. This beautiful branch of the magic art has developed greatly in the last twenty-five years.

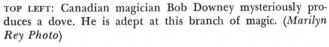

TOP LEFT: Canadian magician Bob Downey mysteriously produces a dove. He is adept at this branch of magic. (*Marilyn Rey Photo*)

TOP RIGHT: He puts the dove, together with several others, into a box resting on a thin table. (*William Doerflinger Photo*)

ABOVE: When all the doves are in the box, Downey fires a harmless, blank pistol at it. (*William Doerflinger Photo*)

RIGHT: Downey then takes the box and table apart piece by piece, showing each piece front and back. The doves have disappeared. (*William Doerflinger Photo*)

Abbott's Super De Luxe DOVE PAN

This Piece of Apparatus Is All That Its Name Implies
STREAMLINED — MODERN

Deceptive to the nth. degree. Each part is spun in one piece, no seams, no joins. A standard effect that is just as popular today as 10 years ago with this beautiful outfit, even more so.

Magi shows pan, breaks two eggs in same, adds a little pepper and salt and flavoring, etc., drops a lighted match into pan and contents flares up. Cover is put on and upon being removed, two live doves, or a small rabbit, makes their appearance . . . Also perfect for making a cake, or candy kisses, etc.

Size of pan is as follows — 10 inches diameter — height of pan 1¼ inches — height of lid 1¼ inches, with a deceptive streamlined raise to knob — in lid. Handle is in black lacquer and is detachable.

ABBOTT'S MAGIC MFG. CO., $43.00; DELIVERED, $45.00

The Dove Pan or Magic Chafing Dish is a versatile piece of apparatus that almost every magician will find useful. An excellent trick can be performed with it by borrowing a lady's ring. This is wrapped in a handkerchief and held by a spectator. The magician's assistant brings on the Dove Pan. Then the handkerchief is opened and the ring is found to have vanished. Eggs and other ingredients for an omelet are dropped into the pan and set ablaze. The lid is clapped on and lifted, and behold! The pan is empty save for a lovely white dove. Tied to a ribbon around the bird's neck is the borrowed ring.

Larger pans are made for producing ducks.

---

which seems more impossible than the one before. The audience has no clue as to how the performer has produced these glamorous birds, or how he has trained them to behave so well.

Dove magic is a special branch of the art which requires expert handling and careful treatment of the birds. Two types of doves are usually used by magicians. The White Java dove is pure white. The Barbary Ring-Necked dove has a gray ring around its neck and a touch of gray or brown in its coloration. Keeping doves healthy and happy is a science in itself. They need plenty of room in which to exercise. Their diet must be carefully watched: they must be fed the proper kinds of seed, diet supplements and grits. They can stand quite low temperatures but are highly vulnerable to heat and draughts. The details of dove husbandry and handling must be learned from special manuals. Those who wish to become dove workers will find an extensive literature at their disposal. Highly recommended books in this field are listed in the bibliography.

Apparatus for dove effects ranges from fairly simple but carefully made harnesses for use in concealing and producing the birds to expensive cabinets for productions and vanishes. An old but ever mystifying effect is Catching Doves with a Net. The performer moves about the stage with an empty fishnet on a long handle, peering into the air until he espies what seems to be an invisible dove. He swings the net and suddenly catches a flapping white dove, which he then taps into a cage held by an assistant. Several doves are caught in this mysterious fashion.

To vanish doves, a different kind of net, known as the Bengal Net, may be used. The apparatus consists of a rectangular banner, with netting in front of it, hanging from a rod about 2 feet long. The bottom edge of the netting is lifted up and hooked to the rod, forming a sort of hammock into which two doves or a large rabbit is placed. At command the netting drops and hangs down as before. The doves or bunny vanish before the spectators' eyes. The magician draws the banner aside so they can see clear through the empty netting.

Perhaps the most elaborate and expensive of all dove effects is the Dove Carousel. Five or six doves are magically produced, and each one is placed on a perch in an ornate metal carousel, about 2 feet high and 2½ feet in diameter, standing on a small table. The merry-go-round is topped with a handsome canopy. When all the perches are occupied by doves the magician sets the carousel slowly rotating. A gay tune from a calliope is heard. Often a bird will spread its wings as if enjoying the ride. Then the performer covers the entire carousel with a colorful foulard and carries it toward the footlights. As he flicks the cloth into the air the music suddenly stops. The carousel and birds have vanished—one of the most beautiful of the myriad effects with doves.

THE ROPE TRICKS

Rope tricks offer a number of advantages. They are mystifying, inexpensive, and adaptable. They can be carried in one's pocket to use as impromptu tricks for a few people, or they can be presented effectively on the stage for a large audience. They show up well even on television. Every magician should have some rope effects in his repertory.

The main classes of rope tricks may be defined as magical tying and untying of knots; penetrations; ropes bewitched to rigidity; stretching and shrinking of rope; and restoring a cut rope into one whole length before the spectators' eyes. Effects in a related branch, escapes from ropes, will be found in the escape section.

Many fine rope tricks depend on pure manipulation. Others require only very simple gimmicks. The principles of rope magic and sleight-of-hand with ropes can best be learned from books on the subject. I particularly recommend the two volumes of Abbott's *Encyclopedia of Rope Tricks;* the chapters on rope magic in Volumes II and V of the *Tarbell Course in Magic;* and Dariel Fitzkee's scholarly booklet, *Rope Eternal.*

To learn to perform rope tricks, first buy a 50-foot hank or two of magician's rope from your friendly neighborhood magic dealer. While ungimmicked, the rope is softer, easier to handle, and shows up better than regular rope.

Slydini does a rope trick. (*Lynn Carver Photo*)

A good way to open the rope part of your program is with the flourish of tying a knot in the end of a rope by merely flicking it in the air. Secretly make a single, loose knot about 5 inches from one end of a 4-foot length of rope. Hold the rope between the second and third fingers of your right hand, with the knot concealed behind the fingers, and the short end showing above your hand. Lift the other end of the rope with the left hand and place it in the right preparatory to flicking it forward. Continuing to patter about knotting a rope the magic way, you flick the unknotted end out and down a couple of times, in what look like vain attempts to perform the feat. Then, the third time, under cover of the hand motion retain the unknotted end in the right fingers, release the knotted one, and take a bow for your uncanny dexterity.

Knotting a rope is beautifully performed in the Czech magician Pavel's trick called The Yellow Knotted Rope (about $12.50; obtainable from many dealers). In another charming Pavel effect, "Fantastic Knot" (Tannen, $4.50), a knot in a red rope is transposed unexplainably into a white rope, where—to prove its genuineness—it is openly untied, leaving a short section of red in the previously completely white rope.

Pavel also invented the clever Rings on Rope.

The rings—three pink ones clipped along one-half of a length of rope, three green clipped along the other half —become intermingled as shown on the next page.

Penetration effects can themselves be divided into several categories. In some of the most entertaining, ropes wound around the neck, waist or leg of the performer or a volunteer assistant are caused to pass through flesh and bone surprisingly and harmlessly. In other penetration tricks, bracelet-sized rings visibly melt onto or off solid ropes, both of whose ends are being securely held. A good kit including two colored plastic rings, rope and directions by Ken de Courcy for a dozen such effects is sold by various magic dealers for about $3.00.

Penetration effects also include those in which knotted circles of rope link and unlink mysteriously in the fashion of Chinese rings. Available from dealers are Peter Warlock's Red and White Ropes, with two linking circles (about $3.00), and the Linking Ropes, with three (about $2.50).

Most famous of all rope effects is the legendary Hindu Rope Trick, said to have been performed by native conjurers in India and China, as described by Pu Chu-ling in the *Book of Ghosts*, previously mentioned. Reports—always secondhand—reached the West of magic *wallahs* who astounded their outdoor audiences by tossing a coil of rope toward the sky, where it remained suspended. Then the conjurer's boy assistant climbed the rope and vanished. When he failed to return, the angry magician, knife in hand, climbed the rope after him. Screams were heard, and presently the boy's severed arms, legs, torso and head thudded to the earth. Descending the rope after them, the wizard collected the scattered parts and placed them in a large basket. As the conjurer chanted incantations the boy, restored to life, arose in one piece from the basket. Then the rigid rope dropped in snaking coils to the earth.

Unfortunately, a fat reward offered to any native magician who could show the trick went unclaimed. We can only regretfully assign the full-blown Hindu Rope Trick to the realm of tall stories. Nevertheless, as a boy I saw Howard Thurston present a replica of it, minus the gory aspects, on a New York City stage in his full evening show. The illusion, while highly dramatic and colorful, was not too mystifying. The young assistant vanished in a cloud of smoke and steam that issued from behind the adjacent theater flies and scenery.

Contemporary attempts to capture at least some of the magic of the fabled Hindu Rope Trick include several other, club-size effects in which pliable ropes grow rigid and stand erect on the floor or on the magician's palm. One of them is shown in this section.

In the field of cut and restored rope tricks, however, you can outdo the finest magicians of the last century with today's improved techniques. Sometimes invisible connecting gimmicks are employed, coupled with ingenious methods of manipulation. Dr. Harlan Tarbell invented several splendid cut and restored rope effects which are described in the fifth volume of his course. Even finer gimmicks than Tarbell possessed for joining severed ropes together are being made today by the Delben Magic Company, P.O. Box 3535, Springfield, MO 65804. These come in two sizes, standard and slim. and are priced at $2.50 a pair. Like all the Delben products I have seen, they are quality items made with old-time precision.

Almost perfect rope restorations, based on entirely different principles, are Bill Neff's Miracle Rope, sold by Abbott's at $5.00, or $5.75 delivered; and Slydini's Own Rope Trick, obtainable from Louis Tannen, Inc., for $12.50. In both of these tricks, the rope is cut before the audience's eyes, restored to one piece, and immediately, without any substitution, tossed out into the audience for examination.

Outstandingly popular among rope tricks at magic clubs in the last several years has been the beautiful effect called The Professor's Nightmare. Using only ungimmicked ropes and sleight-of-hand, the magician causes a short, a medium-length, and a long piece of rope to change in size repeatedly, to equal lengths and quickly back again to their original sizes. Non-elastic ropes are used in this amazing effect. The ropes can be examined by the audience both before and after the trick. Instructions for it are sold by many dealers. It remained, however, for an ingenious Georgia magician, Dan Garrett, to develop the ultimate form of this miracle with rope. In Garrett's version, after the usual Nightmare routine, the short, medium and long ropes are knotted together— yet they still change bizarrely in length, from equal to unequal and back again. Garrett calls the combined routine The Professor's Daydream. He sells it for the modest price of $2.00 without ropes and $3.00 with ropes—one more example of the relative inexpensiveness of most of the mind-boggling magic available to today's performers in the field of rope tricks. A group of them follow.

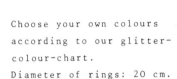

Ring-Miracle   (Ringwunder)

We have produced this trick in a design which will meet
all conditions for stage. Six rings, knotted on a rope,
change their positions. Very effective! Very easy to perform.

Our rings are made of glitter plastic.
Colours for example: red-silver
blue-silver etc.

Choose your own colours
according to our glitter-
colour-chart.
Diameter of rings: 20 cm.

THE MAGIC HANDS, DM 75

622—SUPER-STRETCH ROPE

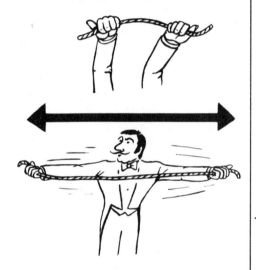

Herpick

Here is the last word in rope effects. It
can be used in any part of a rope routine,
can be examined, and you can do it the
minute you receive this special piece of
rope.

The effect is that you show a small
piece of rope about one foot long—"too
short for the trick"—so you proceed to
stretch the same piece of rope until it is
over FOUR FEET LONG! No sleeve,
pocket, or body work, no switches, you
just stretch it—and it remains the full
length. You may then do your favorite
cut and restored, etc. with it. Remember—it doesn't stretch ONCE, TWICE,
but almost FOUR TIMES its original
length!!! Special rope for 12 performances. $4.50

LOUIS TANNEN, INC.

THE PROFESSOR'S NIGHTMARE   No.396

One of the most popular rope tricks in magic. Used by many
professionals, including ourselves.

The effect is impossible, yet you do it. Show three separate
pieces of rope, each a different length. These are 'stretched'
to equal lengths. But since this is magic, each rope is taken
separately and shown to be a different length. Excellent
magic, enhanced by a very amusing presentation and patter
story about the professor.

Can be done at close range. Tie in with other rope tricks. The rope is furnished, but
when it needs to be replaced, you can use any rope. Highly recommended. $1.50

MAGIC, INC.

CONVINCING ROPE TRICK
AT LAST! Something Really New in Rope Effects

Demonstrated to Walter Harris of
Kalamazoo, said Walter, "I do plenty of
rope tricks but this is the most convincing of them all."
THE REAL CLIMAX TO ALL ROPE ROUTINES
Use Any Rope — Positively Unprepared
No Adhesives — No Rope Gimmicks
Audience see you cut the rope in two
different places and ends of each cut
portion tied. Rope is now in one length
joined at cut sections with knots. Rope
is held at extreme finger tips of right
hand. **Hands are otherwise empty.**
Rope is simply passed through the left
hand,
AND IT IS RESTORED IN ONE PIECE
Again hands are shown empty. Rope may be tossed out to audience.
Only one rope is used — No pulls of any kind

ABBOTT'S MAGIC MFG. CO., $5.00; DELIVERED, $5.50

LINKING ROPES

The performer shows three lengths of rope which are examined. Each in turn is tied into a loop so that he now holds three single separate loops.

Even though the knots are in full view TWO of the loops link together!!

Suddenly all three are linked together!! The knots are ALWAYS in full view.

An easy to do effect. Ropes and routine supplied; you have nothing extra to buy. $2.50
Stage Size $4.00

RAINBOW ROPES

A Londono creation which has become a classic. Red, white, and blue ropes are shown tied together at each end. Ends are untied and retied to show separate ropes. A small flag is waved over ropes; they are drawn through hand and change to a single long rope colored red, white and blue, which is passed out for examination. $3.00

The first trick this clever magician has given to the magical world and like his own performances, it is a gem of perfection. A piece of rope (your own, we don't supply any) is given for examination, then marked and measured. A spectator finds the middle of the rope and gives it back to the performer who immediately cuts the rope in half at that exact spot. Then without making knots or loops the rope is given a flip and, PRESTO! the rope is INSTANTLY restored and tossed out for examination. It is still the same length, same rope! But wait—that isn't all! Again, the spectator finds the center of the rope and the rope is cut. ZIP, faster than lightning the rope is one piece, wholly restored and given to the spectator as a souvenir. Honestly, no amount of description can do this justice. It's terrific. It's perfect. It's real MAGIC! You'll use it in every show. You'll do it just to fool yourself. We have had hundreds of compliments on this miracle but we'll quote just one man: Jean Hugard said, after seeing it twice, "That is the best rope trick I have ever seen in my whole life." This is worth every cent of the price. $12.50

WONDEROPE

THE FABLED RISING ROPE OF INDIA

At last . . . . a practical solution to the Hindu Rising Rope effect.

A rope is uncoiled any time during your show and rises 8 ft. into the air. You may cause it to rise or descend at your will or remain suspended 3 ft. away while you walk around it.

As far as an audience is concerned . . . this is real MAGIC!

These effects and hundreds of others are possible with WONDEROPE, which involves no assistants, no hook-ups to body, table, or stage. At finish you coil rope up and we even give you a version where the same rope is thrown out for inspection!

Remember this self-contained illusion is suitable for club or stage. The illustration on this page gives an accurate idea of how the trick looks to your audience . . . note that top of rope is much higher than hands and that hands are not in contact with rope.

A Miniature Rope Trick—The Straw and String Mystery

Effect: The magician threads a piece of string through a drinking straw, the string hanging out each end of the straw. He then bends the straw double in the middle. Taking a pair of scissors, he cuts through the doubled straw about ¾ inch from the top, obviously severing, at the same time, the string inside it. Yet when the two pieces of straw are fitted together end to end, the whole string is pulled through them freely from one end and emerges uninjured.

Secret: Before presenting the trick, take a razor blade and make a straight cut about 1½ inches long in the middle of one side of the straw. Keep the cut turned away from the audience while threading the string through the straw. A hard, smooth and not too thick cord should be used. Hold the straw between thumb and first finger of the left hand, just below the middle, with cut facing to right. Then bend the straw over toward the right, until its two halves almost come together. The bend should be as close as possible to the middle of the cut, which now faces down.

The right fingers now pull the two hanging ends of the string down slightly, as though to adjust it. This draws the center of the string down through the cut, screened from the spectators by the left forefinger, which holds the straw. Dramatically snip off the empty, top portion of the doubled straw, above the string. Let the audience see the severed ends of the straw for a moment, then place them together, touch them with your wand or say a magic word, and pull out the string magically restored.

Cut and Restored Rope

Take a length of magician's rope about 6 feet long. Magic dealers sell this soft, pliable rope inexpensively, by the hank. Sometimes it's available in bright colors. The Magic Hands offers red, blue and yellow rope as well as white.

To get ready for the cut and restored rope effect, cut from the hank another piece of rope about five inches long. Tie this piece firmly, in a double knot, around the long piece and trim off the ends to make a sliding knot. Arrange the long rope, with the sliding knot about a foot from one of its ends, in such a way that you can readily pick it up with the sliding knot hidden in your left hand. This can be done in either of two ways: (1) coil the rope loosely and place it in your left jacket pocket, with the knot on top, so that you can slip your left fingers under the knot and close them around it as you draw the rope from your pocket to present the trick, or (2) drape the rope over a chair with the knot hidden by the top of the chair back and the main part on the seat.

To perform the effect, face the spectators and pick up the rope with both hands, if using the chair method, left fingers closing around the rope from beneath so as to conceal the fake knot. Jerk the rope hard to show that it is strong. Tie the two ends together in a square knot. Grasping the rope to the left of your left hand, tug it again (as though to show its strength once more), pulling the real knot snugly up against the fake knot that's hidden in your left hand. Hold the two knots together, partly hidden by your left fingers so that they look like a single knot and, with your scissors, trim the ends off the real knot.

Now slide your right hand down to the bottom of the long, looped rope, and tug on it to demonstrate its strength. Reach up with your right hand to your left and, this time, slide the fake knot, hidden now in your right hand, down to the bottom of the loop and tug the loop again. Bring the bottom of the loop, with the hidden fake knot, up to your left hand and lay the two knots together. This leaves a shorter loop hanging down from each side of your left fist. Tug on these loops, both together, at the bottom, again demonstrating solidity. Now let the fake knot, which is around the middle of the rope, fall free from your left hand, keeping the real knot concealed in your hand. You have undetectably switched the fake knot for the real one, and the middle of the rope for what the spectators suppose are the tied-together ends.

Now say you will cut the rope in the middle. With the scissors in your right hand, unmistakably cut through the rope on the right and left sides of your left hand. Holding the rope in your right hand, transfer the scissors to your left hand and deposit them, with the short ends of the rope knotted together, in your left jacket pocket.

Then wind the rope rather tightly around your left hand, sliding the fake knot, as you do so, along and off the rope, keeping it finger-palmed in your right hand. It can either stay there to be disposed of a bit later, or you can leave it in your right jacket pocket as you reach into it for a magic wand or a "pinch of stardust" which you "sprinkle" over the rope before rapidly drawing it off your left hand, completely and mysteriously restored to a single length. Pass the rope out for examination.

PERPLEXITIES WITH PAPER

Conjuring with paper is colorful, entertaining, and lends itself admirably to comedy. It appeals to most people because tissue paper and newspapers are such common, innocent objects and are familiar around the house.

In a simple but effective paper trick with a telling "sucker" twist, the magician holds a strip of red tissue paper about ¾ inch wide and 14 inches long between his left thumb and forefinger. His hands are otherwise quite empty. Tearing the strip to pieces, he squeezes the bits into a small wad, sprinkles them with "magic dust" and suddenly draws out the strip of red tissue paper, fully restored.

The performer now takes the audience into his confidence. He magnanimously demonstrates how he did the trick by having a duplicate strip, folded small, and substituting this for the torn pieces. Thumb-palming the pieces in his right hand, he draws the duplicate strip out from his left.

"There's only one danger," he adds as an afterthought. "If anyone should see the torn pieces you've palmed—well, then you have to use magic." With that he unfolds the "torn pieces" and behold, they too are restored into one long strip.

To do this trick, pleat a strip of red tissue paper to about a 1-inch packet and insert it in a flesh-colored, hollow thumb tip, that indispensable gimmick dispensed by all magic dealers. Lay the thumb tip on your table

Gene Anderson lectures on paper cutting. (*William Doerflinger Photo*)

under the long strip of paper. Get the tip on your right thumb, as you pick up the open strip and display it in your left hand. Tear the strip into pieces, leave the thumb tip cupped in the left fingers, and draw the pleated packet out of the thumb tip with the ball of your right thumb. Substitute the packet for the torn pieces, which you press into the thumb tip and carry away on your right thumb while reaching into your right-hand coat pocket for a pinch of "woofle dust." Ditch the tip in your pocket and palm in the crotch of your thumb a duplicate pleated paper strip from your pocket. Draw out the strip from the left hand, then disclose the "torn pieces" and show them, too, to be inexplicably joined together again.

Closely related to this is the trick of the torn and restored cigarette paper. The British mentalist Al Koran, a master of showmanship, could hold an audience of hundreds spellbound with this trick which employs a tiny cigarette paper.

In Red Ashes (Tannen's, $4.50), a larger strip of red tissue is set afire with a match. As its ashes rise in the heated air and slowly descend, an intact, duplicate strip is plucked from the falling ashes.

Especially easy to work, because entirely self-contained, are what may be called the Chinese Laundry Ticket group of effects. These effects use strips of paper covered with large Chinese or other characters. A good example is Tannen's No Tickee—No Shirtee.

603—NO TICKIE—NO SHIRTEE

The Chinese Laundry Ticket trick up to date with a wonderful comedy climax. Easy to do in the new large size that adds visibility to this clever comedy interlude. The performer tells a story of his trouble with the local laundry, he has his ticket but the laundry doesn't have his shirt. Tearing up the ticket in anger he finds that the laundryman was only kidding, the shirt is ready but now since he has no tickee—no shirtee. Now magic comes to the rescue, the magician fools the laundryman by taking the torn ticket and restoring the pieces so that he has his shirt. Simple, self-contained. 12 tickets. $1.50

LOUIS TANNEN, INC.

668—MULTI-COLOR PAPER PRODUCTION

Another "impossible" surprise effect from the mind of Londono. A strip of pure white tissue paper is torn into pieces. The hands are shown empty except for the torn white paper, which is crushed into a ball and held in one hand. The other hand pulls at the paper and produces a 25 foot, festively-colored streamer. It's an effect by itself, or the multi-color streamer can be used to cover the production of doves, silks, spring flowers, etc. Complete with instructions. (per dozen) $3.50

LOUIS TANNEN, INC.

A sucker twist may be added by dropping a folded paper on the floor. The spectators assume this is the torn-up pieces, but when unfolded it discloses, instead, a picture of a grinning celestial laundryman or a large, printed "STUNG!"

A classic along these lines is the humorous Fresh Fish. The patter, often rhymed, tells the story of a Cockney fishmonger who tears one word after another from the end of his sign reading "Fresh Fish Sold Here Today." Soon he has no sign left—and no trade. Luckily a friendly magician restores the torn-up sign to one piece. Dealers sell packets of a dozen Fresh Fish papers for $1.50 or $2.00.

A curious variation on this trick for gospel magicians is the Scripture Tear (Abbott's, $3.30 delivered). The words "THE BIBLE" are torn to smithereens and amazingly restored, but the performer drops a folded paper to trap the suckers. Unfolded by popular demand, it proclaims "GOD'S POWER." Once again the magician has the last word.

Of all the torn tissue paper tricks, probably the most colorful, most foolproof and most generally effective for either children's or adult audiences are the self-contained tissue-paper-to-hat tricks. Featured by Guaranteed Magic of Hatboro, Pennsylvania, these excellently crafted, charming "hat tears" come in many styles, as shown in this dealer's accompanying ad. Pages 225–226 tell how these paper hats are made by Hatboro women in what almost amounts to a modern cottage industry operated for magicians.

Other tricks in which colored papers are torn up and change to various objects or pictures can be ordered from dealers. There's a wide range of offerings:

	AVAILABLE FROM
Paper panties	Abbott, per dozen $6.00; $6.50 delivered
Double Paper Tear (panties changing to lady's hats)	Abbott, per dozen $6.00; $6.50 delivered
Humpty Dumpty on his wall	Tannen, per dozen $1.50
Skunk	Magic, Inc., per packet $2.00
Santa Claus	Guaranteed Magic, per dozen $5.00
Foxy Paper Tear (top hat with removable rabbit)	Abbott $8.50 doz.; $9.00 delivered
Zebra (from pictures of a black horse and a white horse)	Pavel's Studio

For use with the Milk Pitcher (page 89), Tannen's has Cat Papers: a paper shown blank on both sides is formed into a cone into which milk is poured from the magic pitcher. The milk vanishes from the cone. Where

Gene Anderson displays a giant fir tree torn out of newspaper. (*William Doerflinger Photo*)

has it gone? The paper is flicked open to give the answer: on it now sits a large, well-fed black cat. A supply costs $2.50.

Necromancy with Newspapers

Most talked about trick in the Broadway success, *The Magic Show*, starring Doug Henning, was not the massive Zig-Zag or showy Sawing a Woman in Half illusion, but Henning's effortless, almost casual but mystifying feat of tearing several pages of *The New York Times* to shreds and instantly unfolding them in one piece again.

Many methods for performing the Torn and Restored Newspaper effect are known. The one used by Henning is probably the best. It is called by magicians the Anderson Newspaper Tear and was invented by Gene Anderson, a young chemist and part-time professional magician from Texas who is probably the world's leading expert on tricks and special tears with newspapers. Anderson, who holds a Ph.D. in chemistry and is Manager of Organic Chemicals Development for the Dow Chemical Company, is co-author with Frances Marshall of *Newspaper Magic* (Chicago: Magic, Inc., 1968, $6.50). The reader will find in that book not only detailed directions for the Anderson Newspaper Tear, but also many other good magic effects and feats of tearing and cutting newspapers into surprising and delightful patterns. These include intricate spoked wheels, chains of dolls, 15-foot fir trees, decorated stars, animals, hats and messages. Anderson gives a fast-moving lecture producing amazing things from newspapers and explaining

TROUBLE WIT ROUTINE!

 ① VENETIAN BLIND

 ② FAN
HOLD AT BOTTOM
FAN YOURSELF

 ③ BOW TIE
UNDER CHIN
④ HAIR RIBBON
BEHIND HEAD

 ⑤ DOILY
STRETCH IT TO
MAKE NO SIX

 ⑥ RUG

 ⑦ WINDOW

 ⑧ BIRD BATH

 ⑨ WATER JAR

 ⑩ LOVE SEAT

PARK BENCH STRETCH NO. 10
 ⑪

 ⑫ HASSOCK
TURN UP SIDE
DOWN TO MAKE:
⑬ BOWL

 ⑭ DUST PAN

 ⑮ SCOOP

 ⑯ VASE

 ⑰ SUN BONNET

 ⑱ LAMP SHADE

 ⑲ DE LUXE LOVE SEAT

 ⑳ FIRE PLACE

 ㉑ MORRIS CHAIR
HOLD HAND UNDER
CENTER OF NO. 20

 ㉒ DUMB BELL
REVERSE TO
MAKE NO. 23

PILLOW
 ㉓

 ㉔ SUN HAT
STRETCH TO
MAKE NO. 25

 ㉕ LIFE RAFT

CANDLE STICK & HOLDER
 ㉖ T.W.

㉗ INDIAN HEAD DRESS

his methods. Like his book, his lecture is full of original ideas for magicians.

The Anderson Newspaper Tear is also available separately from magic dealers at about $2.50. Other newspaper tears on the market include Abbott's Torn and Restored Newspaper (half dozen, $5.00; $5.50 delivered); Neil Foster's Center Tear, also sold by Abbott's (supply of papers and instructions, $5.00; $5.50 delivered); Patrick Page's Ten Second Paper Tear (Magic, Inc., $2.00); the Elmsley Newspaper (Magic, Inc., $1.00); and Karrell Fox's Final Edition (Magic, Inc., $2.00).

A flashy feat of paper manipulation is the creation of a tall cornstalk or fir tree (an amusement long antedating the Anderson book). For this take three strips of newspaper—comic papers are more colorful—each made by tearing a double newspaper page horizontally across the middle. Roll the first strip into a tube, and when only about 4 inches of paper are left, insert the end of the next strip between the free end and outside wall of the tube. Keep on rolling this way till all three strips are rolled up.

Then turn the roll upright and tear the upper half of it downward into four strips which are allowed to droop down over the intact lower half of the tube. Insert a finger in the upper hole of the tube, pull the paper gently upward from the center, and you have a beautiful, 4-foot cornstalk with luxuriant foliage.

For variety, after the tube is rolled, hold it horizontally in both hands and with finger and thumb make a tear about halfway through the tube. Turning both hands outward, you get a double tube joined in the middle. Tear the outer sides slightly around to form oval flaps. Then, when the central bridge is pulled gently, the whole thing opens into an ornate Jacob's Ladder.

Strips of newspaper also lend themselves well to the construction of those fascinating one-sided paper rings scientifically known as Möbius bands and long popular with magicians under the name of Afghan Bands. Their construction is detailed in *Newspaper Magic*. A dependable effect for children's shows, the Afghan Bands can also be bought ready-made in paper or cloth. At first inspection they look like simple rings some 6 inches wide and several feet in diameter. When one of them is torn in two around its circumference, two apparently plain rings result. When one of these rings is torn the same way, however, the outcome is a single, and much bigger ring. When the other is torn around, two rings linked together are the result. Paper-tearing races with the Afghan Bands provide good audience-participation stunts for children's entertainments.

Another intriguing old newspaper effect that anyone can construct at home is Clippo. Take a long strip of newspaper about 4 inches wide and coat it with rubber cement which is allowed to dry, then dust it with talcum powder. Shake off the excess powder, then turn the strip over and do the same on the other side. The result will be an innocent-looking strip of paper. If you double the strip and cut a portion of it off with shears, however, the remaining parts can immediately be unfolded and will be found to be perfectly restored to one piece. This effect results from pressure of the scissors pressing the cut edges together so that they adhere.

Clippo strips can be shaped like rabbits with very long necks, or shoes with extremely long toes, to heighten the entertainment.

Troublewit

Not really magic, but a splendid interlude for a magic act, is the device known as Troublewit. Believed to be very old, Troublewit was popularized in Edwardian England by Felicien Trewey and Ellis Stanyon. It is a large sheet of strong paper, measuring about 54 by 36 inches when fully open, but intricately pleated both in wide strips from the long sides toward the center, and then from top to bottom in 1¼-inch pleats. This forms a compact bundle which, when opened out in different ways, and twisted in various directions, can be formed into all sorts of objects: a Venetian blind, church window, table mat, mushroom, candlestick, frying pan, lantern, Welsh hat, water jar, lampshade, lady's bonnet, garden bench, sentry box, and others limited only by the manipulator's imagination. With practice, the various figures can be made to succeed one another with a speed that makes the act look all the funnier and more amazing. Troublewits come already folded out of either white or colored paper. They cost about $7.50. Some of them even glow in brilliant colors in black light—a beautiful effect to heighten this hilarious exhibition of skill and dexterity.

Many other inexpensive and, in the eyes of the layman, completely unexplainable effects with paper will be found in the catalogues of the magic dealers.

MAGIC FOR CLUB AND STAGE

A wide variety of tricks falls into the category traditionally known to magicians as "club and stage" magic. The common denominator here is showmanship. These tricks must be ones that can be projected effectively in a rather large area, such as an auditorium, lodge hall, school assembly room, or regular theater. The size of the apparatus is one criterion. Many club and stage magic tricks have colorful props, which help make them effective. But smaller tricks also fall into this category, especially those with a dramatic quality, such as the "razor-blade" effect, in which the magician puts a packet of imitation razor blades and a long thread in his mouth, and miraculously, brings them all out again, this time strung on the thread.

Many "club and stage" effects can also be presented perfectly well before a small gathering in a private home. Conversely, many of the effects described in other sections of the book—card tricks, coin effects, experiments with silks and paper—are also eminently suited to larger halls. "Club and stage," then, is a catch-all phrase that applies to magic tricks that are colorful, hypnotic or spectacular. We do not include here the "illusions"—tricks involving human beings or large animals or objects. These will be assigned to another category.

Many effects in this category use very finely made and beautiful apparatus. Such effects as the magic guillo-

Gorden and Eve Thumm of Germany are masters at elegant magic for club and stage.

tine (page 121) or alarm clocks (page 111) are strongly made and precisely engineered, and have to be priced accordingly.

Today fewer of these fine medium-sized pieces of magical equipment are made than used to be the case. For this there are two primary reasons. One is the trend away from expert craftsmanship to mass production that has taken place in all industries and has led to the virtual disappearance of the old-time, highly skilled mechanic. The other is the continuing shift in magical fashions from the use of apparatus toward tricks done by prestidigitation.

For the collector at least there will always be a special fascination about the more beautiful "club and stage" effects. Many fine tricks in this category are described in the old-time catalogues of Martinka & Company, August Roterberg, Arthur P. Felsman, Floyd G. Thayer, Conradi, Bartl and others. The Petrie-Lewis Manufacturing Company of New Haven produced such elaborate pieces as The Cords of Cairo, which they made for distribution by Thayer (see Color Plate 12). Warren Hamilton of Tampa, Florida, also made quality effects that were beautifully decorated and painstakingly finished by hand (see Color Plate 13). Another magician who appreciated fine apparatus and carried on the tradition was Richard Himber, the New York inventor and dealer in quality magic.

When we consider the club and stage magic available today, we can hardly do better than to start with production tricks.

We have already touched on hat productions in the section on tricks with animals. However, more should be said on the subject. For hat tricks either a top hat, derby or felt hat with the crown pushed down can be used. For comedy hat productions, the hat should of course be borrowed from an innocent spectator who is discomfited as the magician discovers all sorts of unlikely objects in his hat. In these lean times for the men's hat industry, however, it often happens that no hat is to be found in an audience. It is safer, therefore, to bring a hat of your own and plant it with someone in the audience who will volunteer it when needed. Or else your own top hat, if you wore one on entering, can be used. In either case, since the hat is ungimmicked, the spectators can be allowed to examine it.

The "load" is the term used to refer to the many objects that mysteriously emerge from the hat. There are many ways of getting the load into the hat. It can be secretly introduced into the hat from a special pocket inside the magician's coat, as he bends down to pick up a handkerchief deliberately let fall on the floor; or under cover of some other misdirection. Sometimes the objects to be produced can be lifted into the hat from a servante, usually made of strong felt on a metal frame, at the back of the performer's table. The servante is hidden from the audience by the back drape of the table. Servantes are much less commonly used now than they used to be, but they are convenient and well suited for use in a platform show.

Aside from the servante or special pocket, the secret of the hat production lies largely in the items to be produced. A wide variety of production items is available. There are realistic but highly compressible rubber hot dogs, Coke bottles, ice-cream sundaes and strawberry shortcakes. There are folding satchels, garlands and jumbo dice that lie flat in the hat until lifted out. More expensive, but very effective, is a set of nested alarm clocks, which are extracted from the hat one by one. This looks like an impossible feat, especially if you set each clock ringing shrilly. The clocks' shells contain no mechanism, but the ringing is done with electric bells on the performer's person or table or by using a special ringing clock stand obtainable from magic dealers.

A dozen or two multicolored cloth balls loaded with springs make a dramatic hat production. Not much manufactured today, but often to be found secondhand, are spring vegetables and fruit made of cloth: leafy cabbages, yellow bananas.

A packet of such production goods is made as flat as possible with a good-sized elastic band and lifted into the hat as it rests momentarily at the back edge of the table. A paper coil can be combined with the rest of the load to produce a pinwheel of many yards of colored paper; the performer spins this out of the hat with his wand.

One of the most mystifying hat-production items is the old-fashioned cannonball. It is of hollow zinc, painted dead black, and is so constructed that it can be filled with small candies which the performer produces first.

Two other, newer devices for use in hat productions can be recommended. One is the EZ Hat Loader, described on the next page. Another effective device is the Professional Hat Loader, obtainable from Magic, Inc.

Hat production tricks are strong in both mystery and comedy. Far larger and more colorful productions can be made, however, by using special apparatus. Available from dealers are a variety of cabinets, chests, "square circles," Oriental tubes and other devices for productions. Many of these pieces come beautifully decorated with Oriental or modern motifs to show up spectacularly on the stage. A number of them are shown and described on the pages that follow.

<u>Square Circle Production</u>   (Fantasta)

We have made for you one of the most beautiful small illusions for the stage, a small Fantasta with great production possibilities! The magician shows a cube and a tube completely empty, then he makes appear from it a large quantity of silks, flowers, streamers, umbrellas, bottles and alarmclocks or live animals and many more things.

The Fantasta and tube have glitter finish. The attraction for your show.

Choose your favourite colours from our chart. All colour-combinations are in stock. For example: outside midnight-blue and the tube in gold, green on the outside and the tube in silver. We have two different sizes in stock:

Fantasta A   Size of cube: 6 1/3" x 10 1/2"   Fantasta B   Size of cube: 8" x 15 1/3"

THE MAGIC HANDS. FANTASTA A, DM 115; FANTASTA B, DM 155

One of the most popular devices for producing a large load of silks, animals and other items is the Square Circle, described in a brochure published by The Magic Hands, Herrenberg, Federal Republic of Germany. Gorden and Eve Thumm, owners of The Magic Hands, are shown covering the stage with articles extracted from a large Square Circle. (*William Doerflinger Photo*)

Hat Loader

A magician is not a magician unless he produces something from his hat. With our HAT LOADER, you can produce a large variety of items out of a borrowed hat!! In working the effect, the performer shows a colorful container filled with confetti. Some of the confetti is sprinkled about the hat. A magic pass over the hat, and PRESTO!, the hat is just chock full of stuff!! A realistic egg (wooden), several silk handkerchiefs, a 20 foot garland, and, finally, a glass of milk. Absolutely no body loads! Can be performed away from all tables!

Comes to you with container, wooden egg, milk glass, confetti, and streamer.
EASY TO DO

E-Z MAGIC, FROM HANK LEE'S MAGIC FACTORY, $5.50

980—NEST OF ALARM CLOCKS

A TANNEN EXCLUSIVE

Long unobtainable! A new modern, up-to-date model without those old fashioned bells on the outside. This is a startling production of six alarm clocks. These clocks are spun entirely of light-weight aluminum; six of them weigh just a few ounces and occupy a very small space. Use it for your FINALE. A sensational surprise when produced from a hat, or production box. Here is a magical prop that makes a big DISPLAY.

Nesting Alarm Clocks (each) $5.00
Nest of Alarm Clocks (set of six) $28.50
DeLuxe Nest of Alarm Clocks (complete with display stand and ringing device. . . . . .
. . . . $69.50

Count Artell produces a tower of four alarm clocks! (*Lynn Carver Photo*)

PRODUCTION ITEMS

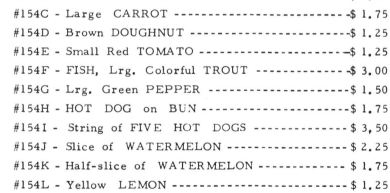

foam

rubber

#154A - Large Red APPLE -----------------------$ 1.50
#154B - Yellow BANANA ------------------------$ 1.25
#154C - Large CARROT -------------------------$ 1.75
#154D - Brown DOUGHNUT -----------------------$ 1.25
#154E - Small Red TOMATO ---------------------$ 1.25
#154F - FISH, Lrg. Colorful TROUT ------------$ 3.00
#154G - Lrg. Green PEPPER --------------------$ 1.50
#154H - HOT DOG on BUN -----------------------$ 1.75
#154I - String of FIVE HOT DOGS --------------$ 3.50
#154J - Slice of WATERMELON ------------------$ 2.25
#154K - Half-slice of WATERMELON -------------$ 1.75
#154L - Yellow LEMON -------------------------$ 1.25
#154M - HAMBURGER ----------------------------$ 1.75

New realistic looking, foam rubber production items in life-like colors. They collapse small and spring instantly to full size and shape when released.

Produced by our own exclusive process.

SMOOTH FINISH * REALISTIC SHAPES * BRILLIANT COLORS

Coe Norton, polished club and stage magician. (*Marilyn Rey Photo*)

CRYSTAL CYLINDER & CHEST

A beautiful Chinese chest is shown empty and a clear plastic cylinder is placed in it so that it sticks up above the top of the box. HI-PRESTO! Open the front door and the cylinder is seen to be full of anything desired, even a live dove. The cylinder is removed and the box is again shown all around. Here is U. F. Grant's routine. The cylinder shown freely and placed in box with front door open. Cylinder visibly filled with ping pong balls. Door closed and silk draped over top of cabinet. Cylinder removed covered with silk. Cabinet shown empty. Silk removed from cylinder and balls are gone! Replace cylinder in cabinet. Open cabinet and it is full of ping pong balls. A great effect and a beautiful outfit.

MAK-MAGIC CO., FROM MIAMI MAGIC, $27.50

1051—CAGE-Y CANISTER

A SUPER SQUARE CIRCLE with an UNUSUAL CLIMAX! A large canister with no top or bottom is shown empty. This is placed in a large square box with no top or bottom, which was also shown empty. A huge production follows—tremendous quantity of silks, flowers, collapsible items, etc. Yet canister may be shown empty at any time. Then for the FINALE, you produce a wire BIRD CAGE large enough to hold 3 live canaries.

Square Box, 11" high, beautifully decorated in 3 colors; Bird Cage, 6½" x 10½". An ingenious feature effect, above par. $38.50

LOUIS TANNEN, INC.

DON ALAN'S COMEDY EGG TRICK

From television's Magic Ranch comes this new trick! An egg is broken into a canister and a card clamped over the top of the can. The can is then inverted and put on top of a boy's head. The performer pretends to forget what comes next and recalls that the instructions for the trick are printed on the card under the can! So he pulls the card out and reads it aloud: "DO NOT REMOVE THIS CARD!"

He then gives the boy an egg beater to beat the egg as it falls down, because he plans to take the can off. When the can is removed, the egg has vanished, much to the boy's relief.

The can is then placed on the performer's hand, lifted off, and standing on his hand is now a tall glass full of candy which may be passed out or given to the boy who has been helping.

Complete with canister, card and glass.

MAK-MAGIC CO., FROM FLOSSO HORNMANN MAGIC CO., $5.50

GRANT'S CONFETTI BOWLS

#328

DO YOU LIKE GOOD CLEAN CUT COLORFUL MAGIC WITH PRETTY APPARATUS? THIS IS IT!

Two beautiful Hi-Lite copper bowls, as illustrated, are used. One is filled with confetti and the two are placed mouth to mouth. When they are separated the confetti has doubled in quantity. This is leveled off, again leaving just one bowl of confetti. Again the two bowls are placed mouth to mouth. HI-PRESTO! The bowls are parted. One bowl is seen to be overflowing with flowers and from the other a dozen or more pretty silks are produced!

Here is a pretty, selfcontained "Oh! So Easy" effect. It can be worked close-up and surrounded. Still, it shows up good at a distance.

Supplied complete with bowls, confetti

THE EMPORIUM OF MAGIC, SOUTHFIELD, MICHIGAN, $8.00

BABY TROUSSEAU PRODUCTION

A guaranteed laugh producer - kids or adults!

Effect: Performer shakes hands with person who helped him, notices a ravel on their collar. When he pulls it, it is really a tape, and as he continues to pull, audience sees that it is a long string of fluttering doll clothes in all colors. This causes a big laugh, which gets bigger when a baby nursing bottle seemingly full of milk, and complete with nipple, shows up on the end of the tape line.

The bottle is light weight white plastic with real big red nipple. Length of clothes and tape fit neatly in the bottle. Instructions explain a good method of loading the bottle right in front of the audience, which is what makes this such a good trick.

Doll clothes are neatly and colorfully made of "silk", ribbon and braid.

Clothes, bottle, nipple and handling instructions for $5.00

MAGIC, INC.

TEMPLE SCREEN $8⁷⁵

An attractive three fold screen, each panel measuring 9 by 12 inches, is shown on the inside, folded flat, then shown on the outside. Audience sees both sides of the panels. The screen is folded into a triangle and a large production follows. Holds a large load, even a rabbit or dove. Folds flat for carrying.

THE MAGIC SHOP, LOS ALAMITOS, CALIFORNIA

IT VANISHES OBJECTS...

IT PRODUCES OBJECTS

MAGIC DRAWER BOX

A wonderful precision made plastic box with a drawer. Vanish cigarettes, pins, matches, coins, silks, etc. A pocket trick that everyone can do to amuse and amaze his friends. Bright Red and Black Size 4"x1½"x3/4".

CREATIVE MAGIC PRODUCTS, INC., $1.50

RISING FLOATING VANISHING GLASS

A glass of liquid is covered with a fancy 18 inch cloth. It clings to the fingers, floats into space, goes way down to the floor, then back to the finger tips.
Then you suddenly grasp a corner of the cloth and toss it high into the air. Glass and contents vanish completely! A most wonderful effect.
If you like VISIBLE, EASY TO DO MAGIC, this is for you. Ready to work.

MAK-MAGIC CO., FROM
JAMES SWOGER HOUSE OF ENCHANTMENT, $8.00

"EVERLASTING" VANISHING WAND

Wrap your wand in a small sheet of paper; twist the ends, and tear it up bit by bit. The missing wand is found in your coat pocket. This 13 inch wand is made of durable plastic and is finely engineered to last. No replacements or shells to buy. Duplicate wand included. **$6⁰⁰**

THE MAGIC SHOP, LOS ALAMITOS, CALIFORNIA

THE VANISHING BIRD CAGE   No.   W2

A breath taking effect with which several performers have gained an international reputation. Used by most leading magicians.

Performer displays an all metal, rigid-appearing bird cage on his outstretched hand. Cage contains a canary. While everyone is watching closely, both the bird and the cage vanish instantly. The cage is not covered in any way. It is there one instant and gone the next.

You can use the famous Harry Blackstone presentation: a group from the audience place their hands on every available bit of cage, so that they cover it entirely with outstretched hands. Suddenly they find their hands empty - THE CAGE IS GONE.

This is the all metal cage with special equipment that makes it vanish like a flash. Comes complete with lifelike rubber canary. Excellent, detailed instructions for easy working. A hit trick! $13.50

MAGIC, INC.

226—DE MUTH SALT SHAKER

We consider this the greatest trick salt shaker ever put out—and best of all it's the simplest salt trick to perform ever devised. Both hands are shown absolutely empty; salt is poured into partly closed left hand. Right hand is kept away from the left. There can be no doubt—the left hand contains the SALT. Without a move of any kind, hand is opened and shown EMPTY. The right hand is shown empty, closed, and a BIG stream of salt pours from the right hand. With the DE MUTH SALT SHAKER you can show hands empty, pour salt into closed left fist and presto you have solid cubes of salt . . . or change salt poured into fist to hand full of NICKELS. The DE MUTH SALT SHAKER has been off the market for 20 years. It sold at that time for $5.00 and it was well worth it. With our more modern and faster machinery we are now able to produce this at a cheaper price. If you want an exciting trick—THIS IS IT! $3.50

LOUIS TANNEN, INC.

#304   COKE GO

COKE-GO "went" because it was so great. Now it's back and as great as ever. A bottle of Coke is placed on your outstretched palm, then partially covered with a white cardboard tube. The top and bottom are still visible. Then a silk is draped over the bottle, whisked away, and Shazam! The coke bottle is still there! So you bring your other hand down on top of the bottle, the bottle vanishes, and the tube is shown empty. If you want, you can even produce a large silk from the tube!

Can be done surrounded, away from all tables, and at any time in the show. This is a precision made super effect for every act.

THE EMPORIUM OF MAGIC, SOUTHFIELD, MICHIGAN, $12.50

THE APPEALING ORANGE BOX

A half dollar is borrowed and marked in any way the spectator desires. Then it is vanished.

A chest about 7 by 12 inches is shown empty. An orange is tied in a bag and placed in the chest, the top of the bag being brought up thru a hole in the cover of the chest, as seen in Fig. 2 of the sketch.

PRESTO! The bag is pulled thru the hole and the orange is gone. The chest is shown empty again. Then from it you produce several oranges which are tossed out. Anyone tosses their orange, and inside is found the borrowed half dollar! A very baffling effect.

Here is a great effect and routine. Comes complete with the chest, bag, etc., together with full instructions.

No. 653

THE LORING CHECKER MYSTERY

A beautiful cabinet decorated in Chinese red and gold, a stack of seven differently colored checkers four inches in diameter, and a handsome cover are seen. The cabinet has back and front doors so one may look right thru it. The doors are opened to show it empty, then three glasses of water and two large silks are produced!

The cover is shown empty and placed in one side of the cabinet. The checkers are placed in the other side, then doors closed. PRESTO! Doors are opened and cover raised. The checkers have changed sides, passing thru the solid partition and the metal cover. The cover is placed over one of the glasses of water on the table. LOOK! The checkers are under the cover and the glass of water is in the cabinet!

The glass now passes back to the cover on the table, while checkers pass into the other side of the cabinet. Finally, the magician nonchalantly produces a fourth glass of water!

A series of miracles, for each side of the cabinet is only a little larger than a single glass. Trick is entirely self contained. Checkers can be shown separate at any time. Highly recommended. Complete except for silks. $ 50.00

RING IN SALT

You show an examined rope. The spectator takes HIS finger-ring and threads it on the rope. You lay your hand around the ring and rope. Ask the spectator to tie the two ropeends together, so there is NO chance for the ring to come off. You give the spectator a saltshaker and ask him to pour little magic salt over your hand. He is asked to hold his hand under yours to catch the ring when you open your hand. Your hand is taken away and there is nothing there but the rope. THE RING IS GONE!!!

The spectator open the saltshaker and pours out the salt, and THERE IN THE SALT IS THE BORROWED RING!!!. Can you think of a stronger CLIMAX?? No subsitution, it's the same ring which the moment before was threaded on the rope. An item of absolutely top quality.

Price incl airmail $15.00
(No personal check)

EL DUCO'S MAGIC
Lergöksgatan 18 S · 214 79 Malmö
Sweden

LEFT TOP: Velma presents one of the most unusual acts offered by any woman magician. She gives the entire program, lasting fifteen or twenty minutes, sitting cross-legged on a high table, in striking Oriental costume. (*Marilyn Rey Photo*)

LEFT: Terry Seabrooke of England, one of the funniest of magi-comedians, with a young volunteer. (*Marilyn Rey Photo*)

ABOVE: Jerry Bergman, comedian and linguist, switches from one language to another as he emcees an I. B. M. show in New York. (*William Doerflinger Photo*)

FAN-TA-SEE

Chinese Fan opened out and an inflated balloon placed on surface of fan. At Performer's Command balloon floats s-l-o-w-l-y up above fan. Back down onto edge of fan and all around it. Then back up above fan ABOVE the performers head. Back down and thru a solid hoop.

SCIENTIFIC - A scientific adaption that does not use a flow-of-air. Fan does not have to be waved to create an air current. This is a very clever adaption.

ONE MAN EFFECT: Pick up fan and put an inflated balloon on it. For home, club or stage shows. Price complete with fan & hoop and balloons, etc.

MIAMI MAGIC, $12.00

FLOATING ELECTRIC LIGHT BULB

No. FP16

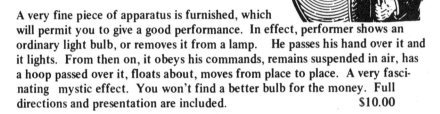

Featured for many years by Blackstone, the famous magician, this trick is one often asked for by committees. A real reputation maker. Not at all difficult to do. Must be done on stage, altho one sequence permits walking in the audience with the floating bulb. Always a thrilling exhibition.

A very fine piece of apparatus is furnished, which will permit you to give a good performance. In effect, performer shows an ordinary light bulb, or removes it from a lamp. He passes his hand over it and it lights. From then on, it obeys his commands, remains suspended in air, has a hoop passed over it, floats about, moves from place to place. A very fascinating mystic effect. You won't find a better bulb for the money. Full directions and presentation are included. $10.00

MAGIC, INC.

THE ZOMBIE BALL

NO ASSISTANTS — NO THREADS
A TRUE CLASSIC OF MAGIC! A
BEAUTIFUL VISUAL EFFECT!

A sparkling, highly polished metal ball rests on a pedestal on the magician's table. Holding a foulard by two corners, magician drapes it over the ball which immediately starts to slowly arise in the air, carrying the foulard with it. Ball is seen to move around under the foulard and eventually floats up into full view. It rests on edge of the material, as illustrated. Again it returns under the foulard and floats back, to come to rest on its pedestal.

Manufactured in highly polished, lightweight aluminum. Supplied complete, with ball, pedestal, gimmick and instructions. (Use your own foulard). $12.50

NEW!! ELECTRIC ZOMBIE! 5" sphere that LIGHTS UP! Complete. $35.00

GUARANTEED MAGIC

ASTRO-SPHERE

Another excellent floating ball effect which is fast becoming a classic is the ASTRO-SPHERE by Tony Spina. In this effect the ball floats in front of and behind the foulard, from one end to the other in a most eerie manner. Finally it floats right up into the performer's hands! The foulard is extremely thin and the ball can be seen at all times. The method is completely different from that of the ZOMBIE. If you want something new in floating ball effects which is totally mystifying, this is for you. Supplied complete with ball, stand, foulard, and routine. $25.00

GUARANTEED MAGIC

Truly magical and deeply impressive are the effects with floating spheres of different varieties shown on this page. Fan-ta-see evokes the fabled mysteries of the Orient. The Floating Electric Light Bulb presents the double mystery of a glowing and floating bulb that drifts far from the magician's hands, returns, hovers, rises high in the air and seems to possess a will all its own. This effect is related to the beautiful floating ball illusion featured in the full evening shows of Howard Thurston and other magicians of an earlier era. The Zombie is one of the most popular effects in modern club magic. It is graceful and mystifying when expertly handled.

1080—RICE BOWLS

A great classic of magic, the Rice Bowls have never failed to charm and bewilder audiences everywhere.

Two metal bowls are shown and both are empty. The Magician pours some rice into one bowl, levelling it off at the top. The second bowl is placed mouth down over the first and when the upper bowl is removed, the rice has increased in a most incredible manner, to double its original quantity.

The excess rice is then pushed aside and the bowl again covered as before. Upon removing the upper bowl once more, a mysterious and startling change is seen to have taken place. The rice has completely vanished and the bowl is now overflowing with water.

One of the truly great standard magical effects of all time, the Rice Bowls is effectively suitable for any type of performance, and is remarkably easy to do. $13.50

1011—FOO CAN

Water or other fluid is poured into a tall metal can. Without covering of any kind, the liquid is caused to vanish from the can which may be turned upside down and twirled upon the wand. Although proved empty, the liquid reappears in the can and may be poured out. Useful in tricks employing liquids such as Hindu Lota, Rice Bowls, Wizard's Funnel, etc. $3.50
DeLuxe Foo Can. $12.50

DELUXE BRILLIANT MAGIC LAMP

A beautiful copper base table lamp that may be used for the "Milk In Lite Bulb" or "Silk In Lite Bulb" effect. Done in a new clean cut manner, close-up or surrounded. Please Note: The large 100 watt bulb gives off a full 100 watt, 110 volt brilliance!
So perfect, it works itself!
In brief: You call attention to the lamp and light it up. Pour milk into a paper bag or cone, using a trick milk pitcher or glass. Crush the paper and the milk is gone. The light goes out. Re move the shade and show it empty. Bulb is seen to be full of milk. The bulb is removed from the socket and the milk poured out. THEN THE BULB IS PLACED BACK IN THE LAMP AND LIT UP AGAIN!
This is a pretty trick when used as the Silk in the Lite Bulb. Or water or colored liquid may be used in the bulb instead of milk. Highly recommended. Work close-up and surrounded.

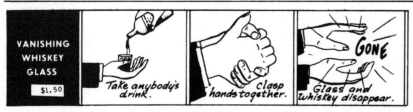

VANISHING WHISKEY GLASS
$1.50
Take anybody's drink. — Clasp hands together. — Glass and whiskey disappear. GONE

Tipsy Turvy Bottles

A Perfect Comedy Trick! Two bottles and two covers shown. Spectator is requested by the magician to "Do as I do." Each places a cover over a bottle. Each bottle and cover are given a half turn. Upon removing covers, the magician's bottle is right side up while spectator's bottle is upside-down. It is repeated with the same results. Becomes screamingly funny.

TRICKY SHAKER

A clear plastic shaker with a chrome cover is shown and placed in a paper bag. Cover is removed and milk poured into the shaker. Suddenly you crush the bag and toss it into the audience! The shaker and milk have vanished! We supply a special collapsible plastic shaker which collapses into the chrome cover when shaker is placed in the bag. Pitcher not supplied since most magi own one. Complete with shaker and special chrome cover.

Double Coke

Two empty cylinders and a can of Coke are shown. From one cylinder, you produce a glass full of UN-COLA (7 UP), from the other a load of silks. Now, the 7 UP is poured into one of the empty cylinders. Lift the cover and it has changed to a glass of Coke. Real liquids in both glasses! Can be done close-up and surrounded. Comes complete with cylinders, glasses, and Coke can.

CHEN LEE WATER SUSPENSION

A metal cylinder is shown to be open at both ends. Water is poured into the top but fails to run out the bottom. Silks may be pushed thru to show there is no obstruction holding the water. Pushing a glass up thru the cylinder, it emerges with the missing water. Cylinder, glass, and gimmick are complete ready to work.

$4.50

Berland's TIPSY BAG!

DRINKS GALORE!
Produce
3 Shot Glasses —
1 or 2 glasses of Wine
followed by a large
Glass of Beer
All out of
one bag!

The trick starts out like an egg bag. Then the drinks start coming, first a cordial for the assistant from the audiance then several shots for you and then for a climax a large glass of beer is also taken out of the bag. Everything complete including illustrated instructions. All best quality.

Price $30.00

Berland's DOUBLE SHOT ROUTINE

#403

PRODUCTION   VANISH

Double shot production and vanish of two shot glasses containing liquid. This really looks like real magic. This has been performed all over the country, including as a close-up trick at the Magic Castle, as well as in the platform room of the Castle. From an unprepared napkin two glasses are produced one at a time. Now they vanish most mysteriously. All this happens away from all chairs tables. Complete with glasses and illustrated instructions.

Abbott's DE-LUXE COFFEE VASE

This outfit consists of a chrome plated vase and chromed metal cover. Vase is shown empty, filled with cotton wool, the metal cover is shown empty and is used to place over vase as a heat control, while the coffee is making — Cover is removed, leaving the cotton wool in view — the shallow lid is put on — removed and magician pours out steaming coffee.

This vase may also be used for the production of silks, etc. Vase is 9 and one-half inches in height, made entirely of metal. DO NOT CONFUSE WITH THE CHEAP FLIMSY IMPORTED TYPE.

No. 5362. **The Passe-passe Trick.**—A wine-glass is shown, and filled with wine. It is then covered over with a handsome brass cover, which has previously been given for examination; when the cover is taken off the glass of wine has disappeared, and in the place of it is a wine bottle, which is lifted up to show there is nothing under it. The bottle is then covered over and changes back to the glass of wine. It is a great improvement to have a pair of these and make the bottle and glass change places from one cover to the other.

Price **2/6** *each, or* **4/3** *per pair. Post free* **2/9** *each, or* **4/7** *per pair.*

Large size, very superior, **3/6** *each, or* **6/6** *per pair. Post free* **3/10** *each, or* **7/-** *per pair.*

No. 1100— Passe Passe Bottles

A splendid trick for either stage or parlor. A bottle of wine, a wine glass and 2 unprepared metal covers are shown. One cover is placed over the bottle, the other cover over the glass. On command, a magical transposition takes place —covers are lifted; bottle and glass HAVE CHANGED PLACES. This can be repeated back and forth, as much as you wish. At finish, covers again shown empty. One of the features is the changing places of the bottle and glass FILLED WITH LIQUID. Large professional size, 11½" inches high. SUPERIOR GRADE. With Enamel Covers

KANTER'S MAGIC SHOP. NO LONGER AVAILABLE.

Comedy Passe Bottles

The same effect as in the regular Passe bottles but with the addition that a stooge steals bottle from the tube without the knowledge (?) of the performer, who is momentarily embarrassed. This by-play is sure-fire laughs. The Passe Passe effect can be repeated even after bottle has been stolen (?)! Bottles are spun brass, natural bottle color, height 10". Covers chrome plated.

ABBOTT'S MAGIC MFG. CO., $55.00; DELIVERED, $57.50

The drawings reproduced on this page, and color illustration 10, show the evolution of a popular club effect, the Passe Passe Bottle and Glass. About 1880 the trick was offered by the London dealer Bland and his successors, Hamley Brothers Ltd., as shown at upper left. It consisted of a bottomless bottle, actually made of thin metal painted black; a glass, over which the bottle shell just fitted to conceal the glass; and a bottle-shaped brass cover. The glass could be picked up inside the bottle, and the bottle inside the cover, by pressing the thin metal walls. Thus, when the cover was lifted, glass and bottle could be made to appear alternately.

By using two such sets, magicians could make bottle and glass apparently change places under the covers. This improved version appears in color illustration 10, though not all the parts are shown. The covers are, of course, both the same size, as are the bottles.

The drawing at center left from the Kanter catalogue shows further improvements that first appeared in the trick about 1910. The suspicious-looking, bottle-shaped covers have been replaced by cylinders open at both ends (or sometimes made with a finger hole in the top). The cylinders can now be shown empty, and a bottle shell inside a cylinder can be picked up with it by pressure of a finger inserted through the top. Since the covers are slightly different in size, they can be nested to prove them empty at the start of the trick. The bottle shells also nest and can be stolen or replaced without visible change. Though the set illustrated is no longer available, quite similar ones are sold by some dealers or can be bought second hand.

In the ultimate form of the trick, called the Comedy version (left, below), the effect proceeds at first as before. Then the conjurer's assistant mischievously steals one of the bottles from inside its cover while the wizard's back is turned. Now the spectators think the performer is sure to be sorely embarrassed—but to everyone's amazement, thanks to a further secret refinement, the trick works anyway!

Fabulous French Arm Chopper!
IT CHOPS-LOPS-&' DROPS!

Any spectator's arm is placed in the chopper. A large solid blade is forced down through the wrist and the spectator's ACTUAL HAND (not a dummy) is seen to drop off into the bag below! One of the most startling effects in the entire realm of magic.

YES - the blade is solid. The ENDS of the same blade extend beyond the sides of the chopper. Any spectator is used. And their actual hand drops. The blade does go clear down, and only one blade is used.

NO - there are no holes in the blade. The blade does not pivot or hinge. The blade is not switched. When the blade comes down, it is not covered. The audience can see the action clearly. The blade apparently slices the hand right off in its downward descent. Oh! It's a scary one alright. Just the kind of trick to make them yell and cover their eyes!

Just to reassure you, the spectator DOES NOT return to his seat with just one hand!

This is a BIG trick. It looks wonderful on the stage, but can be used at a party just as well.

Packs flat, very well made, but light in weight for transporting. Entirely mechanical.

MAK-MAGIC CO., FROM JAMES SWOGER HOUSE OF ENCHANTMENT, $42.50

A surefire laugh-getter for a club program is the magic arm chopper, using a volunteer from the audience. Here is a natural comedy situation that lends itself to entertaining humorous patter. Various models of arm choppers are available; the U. F. Grant model shown above has the advantage that the spectator's hand is actually seen to drop, even though it is unharmed.

A more ambitious form of the chopping trick is the magic guillotine, one example of which appears at right, above. This prop, larger and even more wicked-looking than the arm chopper, makes possible many minutes of byplay, comedy and fun. This realistic-looking, though truly harmless, model is handcrafted by the Delben Company of Springfield, Missouri. It stands more than six feet high.

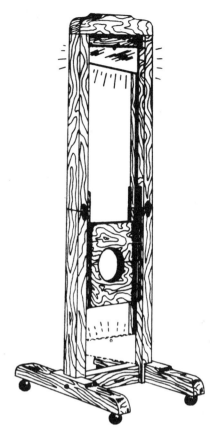

DELBEN CO., $349.00

It's Got
THRILLS
EXCITEMENT
MYSTERY
ACTION
FUN
"A darned good trick."

MAK-MAGIC CO., FROM JAMES SWOGER HOUSE OF ENCHANTMENT

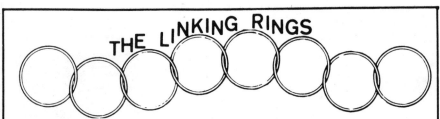

THE LINKING RINGS

A trick almost as old as magic itself. Every magician should own a set of these rings. A trick that has been one of the best loved down the ages it has continued to have a timeless appeal. Steel rings are shown to be solid and are linked and unlinked in a mysterious manner. Various designs may be formed. No matter what linking ring routine you may be doing, this set of 10″ rings will more than fill the bill. Instructions included. Only...................................$28.00

DECEPTIONS UNLIMITED

981—LINKING FINGER RINGS
Richard Himber

Credit to that great man of magic, RICHARD HIMBER, for this wonderful effect of linking borrowed rings together and having them come apart, and immediately hand them out for examination. This effect was featured by AL KORAN at our MIRACLES OF MAGIC SHOW ON BROADWAY and was a tremendous success. The trick is made possible by a secret device and is a beautiful precision-made GOLD RING. Our routines will enable you to do it on the stage or close-up, and completely surrounded. Remember these are the original Himber Linking Finger Rings and they come in two styles.
"STAGGERING" (10 ct. GOLD Signet style ring) $55.00
"TOWERING" (14 ct. GOLD Wedding Band style ring) $65.00

LOUIS TANNEN, INC.

THE PEERLESS BLOCK MYSTERY
GREATEST OF ALL BLOCK TRICKS---FOUR EFFECTS IN ONE

A great, easy to do trick with four effects that can be worked one right after the other!

No.1. Three differently colored blocks are shown separate and solid. Two are stacked on a glass plate, empty cover put over them. (No block is dropped INTO the cover).The third block is wrapped in a handkerchief from which it disappears. Full form of block is seen inside handkerchief up to instant of vanish. Cover is raised and missing block seen between the other two!
No.2. A borrowed hat shown empty. Center block again is vanished from handkerchief and this time found in the hat!
No.3. Three blocks stacked and cover put over them. Immediately it is raised and all the blocks have changed places - to everyone's amazement!
No.4. Cover and borrosed hat are again shown empty. Three blocks are placed in the cover, but when it is raised, the middle block has disappeared! Cover is POSITIVELY empty. Missing block is found in the hat!
Blocks are 3 inch cubes. All good looking props that include cover, special handkerchief, plate glass, blocks, directions,patter, etc. No. 652 $22.50

MAGIC, INC.

Colour-Star-Die
(Colorstarwürfel)

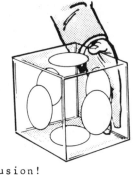

This is a super trick, entirely out of the ordinary! Visible magic! The strongest optical illusion! A three dimensional effect! You show a large crystal die (length of edge: 15 cm) covered with white points. You draw a red, blue or green silk over them and the white points change immediately into the colours of the silks.

A very strong effect! We guarantee that you will be very enthousiastic about this trick!

Three colour-star-dice, three silks 60 x 60 cm red, blue, green.

One single colour-star-die with one silk 60 x 60 cm

THE MAGIC HANDS, DM 50 EACH DIE

> "The ideal conjuring performance is a happy combination of apparatus and sleight of hand."—T. Nelson Downs, *The Art of Magic*, edited by John Northern Hilliard (Chicago, 1909).

VANISHING CANDLE TO SILK

The Magician displays a 15" candle and lights same. He then touches the flame and instantaneously, the candle changes into a silk (use your own silk).

.... $ 8.00

VANISHING LIT CANDLE

The candle is seen in its holder. The Performer covers the candle with a silk. Then he lights the candle and the audience sees it BURNING THROUGH the silk. Removing the candle with the silk from its holder, the LIT CANDLE VANISHES! The Complete Set includes: Candle, Silk, Holder, etc. .... $ 15.00

TWIN VANISHING LIT CANDLES

This is the perfect combination of the two effects above. Also a Complete Set which includes TWO Vanishing Candles, a beautiful silver-looking double holder (packs flat), a gimmicked 18" · 100% pure silk and a wooden stick. .... $ 26.00

LOUIS TANNEN, INC.

HUMAN HEN

The funniest and most baffling trick in magic! Egg after egg (or ping pong balls) are produced from magician's (or friend's) mouth. They are placed into a clear bowl, or tray in plain view of everyone. You can make as many eggs as you wish appear. Mouth is seen empty after each egg is removed. Eggs are real, and can be cracked open to prove so. This trick will keep them laughing, as you act very confused when eggs keep appearing in your mouth. A great routine for kids and adults alike. **Stock No. 1065** **$1.25**

ABRACADABRA MAGIC SHOP

ELLIS WONDER RING

A very popular close up trick with two excellent routines.

Performer can put a solid brass ring on a wand while spectator holds both ends of the wand - and he can take it off under the same conditions! In another routine, the ring is slid on a spectator's thumb. Performer covers thumb with a handkerchief, removes the ring, shows it and puts it away. Spectator sees and feels all this happen, but when handkerchief is pulled off his hand, the ring is back on his thumb! No.532 Standard version, Ellis Ring and inst. $2.50

DeLuxe version, Johnson Products make. Perfectly fitted and machined and balanced. For the pro. No.532A $7.50

MAGIC, INC.

1012—THE ULTRA CANDLE TUBE

The tube that defies detection. The Ultra Candle Tube is not to be compared to the many so-called Candle Tubes which have been placed upon the market. The "Ultra" is beautifully made and can be safely left in the hands of the spectators with the knowledge that it will be impossible for them to discover the secret.

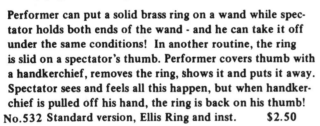

The startling effect that can be performed with this tube is as follows:

The performer passes the tube and cap for minute inspection and upon receiving it again, takes up a lighted candle and inserts it in the tube, into which the candle just fits. Now, before placing the cap on and passing it to a spectator to hold, he shows the candle still inside the tube. A handkerchief is then vanished and the spectator holding the tube is requested to remove the cap. To the astonishment of all they find the candle has mysteriously disappeared and in its place is found the vanished handkerchief. The candle is then produced from the performer's pocket.

The Ultra Tube is finely made and brilliantly nickeled. Get the best when buying a candle tube and see that you get the Ultra. No silk supplied. $24.50

LOUIS TANNEN, INC.

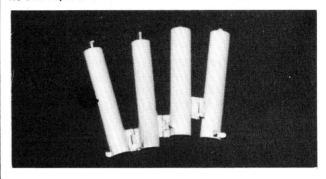

CRYSTAL FIRE BOWL

YES! A CLEAR CRYSTAL BOWL OF FIRE FROM UNDER AN EMPTY FOULARD!

NOW - the magician enters, shows a foulard on both sides, tosses it over his shoulder and from under the foulard he pulls out a clear crystal bowl of fire! A most startling effect.

No batteries, no cigarette lighter units, ALWAYS WORKS! A nice opening effect.

MAK-MAGIC CO., FROM JAMES SWOGER HOUSE OF ENCHANTMENT, $5.00

982–CHINESE STICKS

An old favorite that never fails to prove conclusively the mystic powers of the magician.

Two sticks with cords running through the tops are shown. Attached to the lower ends of the cords are gaily colored tassels, while on the upper ends are small beads. When one cord is pulled down, the other rises synchronously, and vice versa. Pulling the cords back and forth, the magician explains that the cords really run through the sticks and, separating them, this is seen to be true. He then cuts the cord, places the sticks together and has, apparently restored the cord, for when he pulls one cord, the other still rises. At this point, the magician decides to tell the audience how the trick is really done. Holding the sticks apart at the top, but together at the bottom, he explains that the cord passes through one stick, over to the other stick and out the second stick at the top. But imagine the bewilderment of the audience when the magician completely separates the sticks, tucks one under his arm and proceeds to pull the cords back and forth in a most uncanny manner, especially after they were let in on the secret!

Always popular, the Chinese Sticks present an effect that is almost weird in appearance.

Our Chinese Sticks are all top quality, beautifully made, and guaranteed to operate smoothly.

DeLuxe Square, Metal Type	$16.50
Metal 12" set (stage size)	$10.00
Plastic 8" set (parlor size)	$3.00
Large Stage Size, Plastic	$8.50

LOUIS TANNEN, INC.

THE ACROBATIC CANE

No. F-16

You've seen this beautiful effect on TV - it's used by many professionals. Our specially built canes make it easy for you to do, aided by our illustrated, detailed instructions.

A quick, surprising opening, or a short, amusing demonstration of skill during the program. (Only YOU know how easy it is!)

Effect: Performer shows a neat black cane with a white tip and cap. He turns it upside down and holds the ferrule end in his hand. Suddenly the stick leaves his hand of its own accord and turns completely over in the air, the knob end returning to his fingers. Many other exciting and interesting effects are possible, including clinging to the tips of the fingers without visible support. A great trick for pantomime.

Quality made. Breaks in two for packing. Detailed, printed instructions.

Price: $10.00

MAGIC, INC.

Appearing Cane   (Der erscheinende Stock)

Matching our disappearing cane, you can buy our Appearing Cane. You quickly change a silk into a cane or you take the cane from mid-air.

Appearing cane, best quality, steel material, without silk.

THE MAGIC HANDS, DM 28

Berland's Egg BAG WATCH ROUTINE

THE STAND-UP WATCH TRICK

#323

This starts out as an Egg and Bag trick, getting a gentleman from the audience to assist you do the egg and bag trick first, with a new twist — then you suggest that you will do the same trick with the gentleman's watch. The borrowed watch is dropped in the bag and given to the spectator to hold — announce that you will cause the watch to disappear from the bag, take the bag and turn it inside out — watch is gone — after a bit of by-play — performer bares his wrist and on it is the gentleman's watch! Remember, no stooges - the watch that is borrowed is the same one that appears on the performer's wrist.

SAMUEL BERLAND, FROM THE EMPORIUM OF MAGIC, SOUTHFIELD, MICHIGAN, $12.00

1138—VANISHING ALARM CLOCK

A complete mystifying and sensational vanish of an ALARM CLOCK! This is a perfect vanish that is as convincing as it is astounding. Magician exhibits a beautiful gleaming modern alarm clock resting on a thin tray. He throws a foulard over the clock and lifts it off the tray. The alarm is now set RINGING and suddenly the Magician shakes the cloth open, the ringing STOPS, and the clock has COMPLETELY VANISHED leaving no trace. This is real magic, complete with everything you need. $49.50

LOUIS TANNEN, INC.

1034—THE GREAT THUMB TIE

This practical method of Cliff Osman can be performed anywhere and is easy to do. The magician's right thumb is tied with a long piece of thick string, two or more knots being used. The left thumb is then bound tightly to the right thumb and the ends of string tied. The string is drawn SKIN TIGHT around each thumb and all knots are GENUINE. Now, with his thumbs thus tightly bound together, the performer is able to perform a series of amazing tests. Instantly link your arms with those of the spectators, catch solid hoops or rings on your tied arms, pass your hands "through" table legs, etc., and immediate inspection of tied thumbs is possible at any stage. We like this method of Cliff Osman the best. But we also give you additional methods which have been successfully used by various other performers. Comes complete with instructions and three colorful rings and the proper string to perform this classic. $7.50

LOUIS TANNEN, INC.

THAYER's *Catalogue* No. 7

DELUXE MAGIC TEA KETTLE - A Rainbow of Colors

From a beautiful tea kettle, magician pours various colored drinks, 15 to 20 glasses. (Capacity is two quarts). Where do all these pretty colored drinks come from? To show this, magician removes the cover of the kettle and produces a large load of rainbow colored silks. He produces so many they would overflow the kettle if returned to it.

Now the colored drinks are poured back into the kettle and shaken up. Clear water is poured from the kettle (or milk or beer).

Drinks can be handed to audience. "Any Drink Called For" act can be used.

Two excellent routines are included. Kettle is anodized copper, a beauty and durable.
No .   Mailed $10.00

GR9

MAGIC, INC.

THE GREAT HINDU TURBAN MYSTERY   No. 398

Made very popular as a stage trick by leading performers throughout the country. A flashy, showy trick for any kind of performance, but particularly good for club work, schools and acts desiring a touch of the Oriental.

A length of soft white cloth is picked up (or unwound from about the head where it served as a Turban). Two members of the audience stretch it out between them. Performer then takes the turban and cuts it thru the center. The two pieces are then tied together, the ends given to the spectators so as to stretch out the cloth to full length. Performer sets fire to the knot, rubs it between his hands, lets go, and Presto! the turban is fully restored and pulled out at full length for all to see. May be examined. Complete with turban and illustrated directions. $2.00

MAGIC, INC.

SQUARE TO CIRCLE

3.00

Show a metal Square to audience.

IN A FLASH before their Eyes!

It becomes a perfect circle!

FLOSO HORNMANN MAGIC CO.

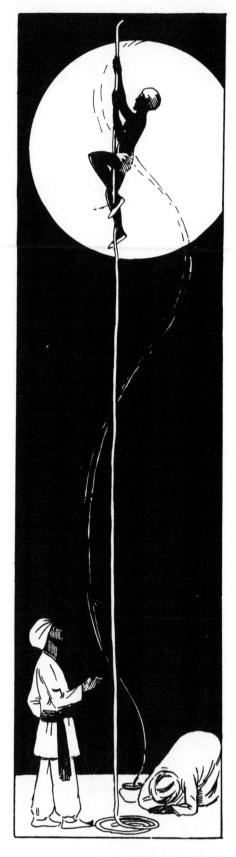

THAYER'S *Catalogue* No. 7

1049—THE FAMOUS EGG BAG

Tricks may come and tricks may go, but the magic of the Egg Bag is eternal. For such is the fate of the truly popular.

The magician shows an attractive bag, inside and out. He places an egg inside the bag, and upon pronouncing the mystic words, causes it to disappear. The bag is turned inside out, banged upon a table, and, in short, everything is done to prove the actual disappearance of the egg. Yet, when the magician places his hand in the bag, he produces the vanished egg.

As a special favor to the audience, the magician fully and carefully explains (?) how the trick is done. Then, following his every move, convinced that they are "in the know," the audience soon discovers the magician has completely fooled them and left them more mystified than before. The bag is again shown empty, and even felt by the spectators, two of whom are then requested to hold the performer's wrists. Where-upon, he reaches into the bag and produces the missing egg, which may again be vanished and changed into a baby chick or any other object.

Of high-quality manufacture and materials, the EGG BAG comes to you complete with an easy-to-do routine that's chock full of comedy situations. No egg supplied. $4.50

Wonderful imitation eggs for above (each). $1.00

LOUIS TANNEN, INC.

RED, WHITE, AND BLUE . . . . $ 150.00
A red box is opened and a white box is removed from within. A blue box is removed from the white box. The white box is shown empty and returned to the red box and a rabbit or dove is placed within the blue box which is held on a tray. The box is covered and placed on top of a little platform on the end of a pole. A toss and the blue box vanishes with its contents. The red box is reopened, the white box removed, and within is found the missing blue box which is opened to find the missing animal.

GEM PRODUCTION, INC.

TOP: "Chinko" Side Stand (*Thayer,* 1928)

ABOVE: "Oriento" Magician's Table (*Thayer,* 1928)

OVERLEAF: Colorful posters or hand-bills for two mid-nineteenth century traveling magic shows—Professor Kerrigan's "Carnival of Novelties" and the spiritualistic show of the Miller Brothers. Bills of this kind are now very rare, for they were printed on cheap paper and have mostly crumbled away with the years. (*Mario Carrandi Collection*)

SAVANNAH THEATRE.

THIS,

Thursday Evening, Jan. 30th.

"This gives me pause."—Shakspeare.
"So wondrous strange the whole might seem the weird fancy of a fairy dream."
"I look upon death to be as necessary to our constitutions as sleep. We shall rise refreshed in the morning."—Dr. Franklin.

SPIRITUALISTS
Pronounce the MILLER BROTHERS mediums of incomparable power.

MATERIALISTS
✳ Admit the evidences of their senses and call them wonderful.

THOSE STRANGE MEN, THE
MILLER BROTHERS

Will Give One More, and Only One More, of their Remarkable Seances

TO-NIGHT

With an Entirely New Series of MANIFESTATIONS.

We copy below a Few Actual Scenes and Endorsements of the Marvelous Manifestations which usually take place at the Seances.

Investigated.

The Investigator

Pre=Vision

...ychometry.

"A gentleman from Shreveport entered the cabinet with the Medium to investigate the phenomena. He went in a respectable young man and came out looking as though he had wrestled unsuccessfully with a Texas cyclone. He declared himself thoroughly satisfied and refused to enter the cabinet again."—New Orleans Picayune.

Prof. KERRIGAN'S
Carnival of Novelties

ILLUSIONS!

MIRACLES!

SCIENCE

WONDERS!

THE GREAT ATTRACTION OF THE AGE!

Under the Management of

MILES BERRY!

THE PUBLIC IS RESPECTFULLY INFORMED

Prof. KERRIGAN

Demonstration of second sight and other feats of mentalism were featured along with illusions in the programs of Charles J. Carter, known as Carter the Great. (*Sotheby's Belgravia*)

MENTAL MARVELS AND SPIRIT MANIFESTATIONS

No branch of magic attracts more respect and popularity today than mentalism. In modern magic programs, mental marvels involving—or seeming to involve—such phenomena as precognition, clairvoyance and telepathy have largely taken the place of the spirit séances featured by many performers of the nineteenth and early twentieth centuries.

For the main cause of this we need look no further than the rise of interest in the study of Extrasensory Perception, a field of investigation which has now won a foothold on the borderline of science. Departments of parapsychology at certain universities, such as Duke and the University of Virginia, may have obtained only limited demonstrable results, but they have at least succeeded in attaining a modicum of scientific respectability.

Professional magicians have also played a considerable part in the rise of interest in ESP. In the 1930s Joseph Dunninger became famous as a society magician in New York and other cities with his impressive demonstrations of what he presented as genuine mind reading. In the 1950s Dunninger's dramatic television programs reached millions of viewers. Dunninger read messages tightly sealed in bank vaults and mysteriously arranged for celebrities in California to reveal the correct totals of numbers suggested by committees in New York. When Dunninger died he took the secrets of his greatest effects with him. Meanwhile, other prominent stage mentalists such as

Poster used by The Great Alexander, mentalist and illusionist from Los Angeles. (*Mario Carrandi Collection*)

The Amazing Kreskin in America and Al Koran in Great Britain were using their own gifts of imagination and showmanship to persuade millions more that there was something to ESP. An audience enjoys seeing a conjurer pull a rabbit out of a hat, but all except the youngest spectators know that rabbits do not really materialize inside hats. An audience seeing a mentalist like Jack London correctly writing on a blackboard the total of three four-digit numbers contributed by three members of the audience and kept in their own possession, is not so sure it isn't done by genuine telepathy.

Modern mentalists perform their tricks by artful methods. Usually they do not claim supernormal powers but make the effect as impressive as skill and showmanship permit, and leave it to the audience to decide whether or not genuine ESP is involved.

It is important in presenting mental effects to avoid using anything that looks like magic apparatus. Equipment usually associated with conjuring would rob a mental effect of its impressiveness. Only simple, everyday, and apparently thoroughly honest and unprepared articles should be employed—such unexciting things as pencils and pens, plain pads, an ordinary-looking clipboard to provide a writing surface for experiments involving written messages. When possible it is better to use, instead of playing cards, which suggest sleight-of-hand, a set of special ESP cards on which the standard symbols used in parapsy-

802—MAGIC CLOCK

Here is something a little different in mental effects. A beautiful hand polished wood box is shown to contain 12 numbers, such as on the face of a clock. The Mentalist instructs a spectator to place dial on any one of the 12 numbers, and close the box. Now taking the box in his hand, and concentrating for several moments, the number is revealed by the Mentalist, who never opens the box. This can be repeated immediately. Close examination of the box will reveal nothing, and is sure to astound your audience. This hand polished box is imported from Germany, and is a delight to own. $20.00

BOB MASON'S "JUST THINK"

This Is A Real Baffler!!! Spectator shuffles a deck and takes a handful of cards, magician never knows how many. Spectator looks over his cards and JUST THINKS OF ONE. He returns the cards to the deck. The magician, during the course of showing the spectator cards one by one, KNOWS INSTANTLY WHEN SPECTATOR IS LOOKING AT HIS MENTALLY SELECTED CARD??? This is a sure fire puzzler. NO SLEIGHTS — NO MATH FORMULAS — NO PREPARATION — USE A BORROWED DECK — YOU NEVER LOOK AT A SINGLE CARD EITHER!!! Mentalists can use a design deck and have a great mental effect. Complete instructions in booklet form. .... **$2 postpaid**

826—TELA-DIE

This is the supreme method for doing some great mind reading. The whole outfit easily fits into your pocket. If you know somebody who's hard to fool, TELA-DIE will fool him. The effect is simple. A die is placed into a box while your back is turned and then returned to performer. Now without your opening the box or getting any sort of a sly peek or using any other devices, you are able to divine and announce the number on top of the die. The secret is very subtle. $10.00

793—CORVELO'S SPECTROMATIC

Here is one of the finest "psychic" effects ever originated, and equally suitable as a trick for pocket or stage. A handsome wood box 4½" x 3" x 1" in size is given to a member of the audience with the request that he remove the cards therein. There are five cards, each bears a different color spot in the center of the card. The spectator mixes the cards, and one is freely selected, noted, and replaced among the others. At one end of the box,  there is a small space between the lid and the body of the box; the spectator is asked to return the cards to the box, one at a time, via the slit. The cards may be put in the box in any order. Magician then names the selected card or causes the card to vanish.

.... $9.50

---

chology experiments—the star, circle, square, plus sign and wavy lines—are printed.

As in any branch of magic, but even more so than in most, mentalism has an extensive literature which the beginner desirous of becoming successful in this work should not fail to study carefully. The *Tarbell Course in Magic* includes much valuable material on mental magic. A basic work in the field is Corinda's *Thirteen Steps to Mentalism*, recently republished by Louis Tannen, Inc., at $15.00. Ted Annemann's book, *Practical Mental Effects*, also contains much fine material. Burling Hull's books on how to answer questions and on the psychology of mental effects and mind-reading acts contain a wealth of valuable inside information. For further information on materials for study, consult the catalogues of magic dealers who handle books.

For many years the leading dealer specializing in mental magic was Robert A. Nelson of Columbus, Ohio. On the death of this dealer a few years ago, many of Mr. Nelson's mental effects and publications were taken over by Micky Hades International of Calgary, Alberta, Canada and Seattle, Washington.

Mental effects may be divided among a number of different categories, depending upon the type of effect and the nature of the equipment used. To begin with, somewhere on the borderline between pocket tricks and mentalism are a group of effects that can best be described as close-up divination tricks. The common denominator here is that the magician uses small items of equipment to demonstrate powers of apparent second sight or divination. He is able to see within closed boxes and sealed envelopes by mysterious methods that baffle the spectator. At the left are several of the best of these effects from dealers' catalogues and advertisements.

Billet Reading

One of the basic feats of the mentalist is the ability to answer questions or to reveal words or phrases written by members of the audience on slips of paper, and ostensibly not seen by the performer. These slips are known to the profession as "billets." They can be used either on the platform or in private séances or "readings" when a client and fortune teller are seated at a table. After being folded or placed in envelopes so that the writing is hidden, the billet or billets are generally collected. The mentalist then contrives to get sight of the concealed message by one of many possible methods, some of which follow:

The One-Ahead System: Holding a folded or sealed billet to his forehead, the performer reads off a fictitious message which is acknowledged by a "plant' 'in the audience. As though to verify the message, the mentalist then unfolds the billet, glances at it, nods, and tosses it aside.

Symbolistic

EFFECT: Magician requests the aid of two volunteers. One is asked to choose a card from a shuffled ESP deck, and hold it against his body. The other is asked to select a number. The freely selected number is counted to on a board and a symbol arrived at. At this point the first spectator turns his card around for all to see and it matches the symbol counted to. Now an envelope which was in view of the audience at all times is opened revealing a prediction that also matches. Effect may be repeated.

NOTES: Comes complete with (9X9') heavy duty plastic laminated board and a deck of official Dr. Rhine ESP cards.

CREATIVE MAGIC PRODUCTS, INC., $10.00

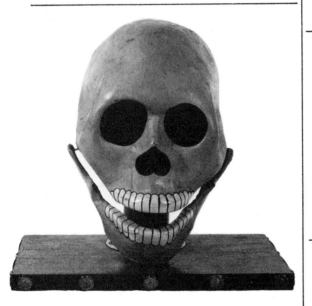

Talking Skull. (*Sotheby's Belgravia*)

837—KEY-R-RECT

From the inventor of
LOCK OF GIBRALTAR
Comes KEY-R-RECT

EFFECT: Performer hands spectators a padlock and five keys that won't open it. Spectator proves this himself. He is then given a sixth key that does open the lock. The keys are now mixed and each one is sealed in an envelope. Performer never touches, or even need see, the lock, keys, or envelopes. Yet, by some strange power, he correctly identifies the envelope containing the key that opens the lock. Terrific on a stage . . . baffling close-up. Uncanny by telephone. Is it ESP? Sixth sense? Witchcraft? No . . . just a mechanical masterpiece that is self-working, foolproof, completely undetectable and made to last a lifetime. Complete with MASTER brand laminated padlock, keys, and four different routines. $13.50

LOUIS TANNEN, INC.

PREDICTA·TOTAL

IS USED ALL OVER THE WORLD

PREDICTA-TOTAL ".5 — One of Bob's greatest effects in the latest, greatest version yet. Mentalist shows and mixes 9 plastic discs (2¾") that bear digits 1 thru 9. These are placed into 9 places on a glare free board (11½" x 11½") with 9 silver pegs. Spectator's direct the placement of the discs and can even bump the other fellows discs into a new position. Finally a spectator turns over the discs and the digits are added as in any addition problem. Their total matches exactly a prediction made before start of trick. This is a very visual effect and has lots of audience participation. KRESKIN featured this on TV. Packs flat in an attache case. Discs are bright yellow with hot stamped numbers. A proven hit all over the world. Now comes with Bob's own personal routine. .... **Complete outfit shipped postpaid $20**

ROBERT MASON PRODUCTIONS

209 Celestial Slate
* FLAP METHOD *

A message mysteriously appears on a previously shown blank slate.

Show the slate blank on both sides, wrap it in a sheet of newspaper and give it to a spectator to hold.

The spectator then unwraps the slate himself and finds the SPIRIT MESSAGE.

Great for 'Ghost', 'Spook', or 'Haunted' effects. Great to reveal the name of a selected card.

SIMPLEX MAGIC, JAMES RAINHO PRODUCTS, $2.50

THREE COLORS

A mind reading trick done with three beads of different colors. Have someone arrange the colors in any order he chooses. He puts them in your hand behind your back. You can bring out any color named. Very easy once you know how to do it. Small enough to carry with you ready to perform any time. D173   75¢

WARNER'S MAGIC FACTORY

ONE OF THE GREATEST BOX OFFICE ATTRACTIONS IN AMERICA

DUNNINGER

HIS AMAZING ABILITY HAS STARTLED THE WORLD

TV — DUNNINGER'S TV RATING 41.9

THE HIGHEST RATED SHOW ON TV

HAZEL BISHOP'S SENSATION — THE DUNNINGER SHOW
2 SEASONS FOR LEVER BROTHERS — RINSO
2 SEASONS FOR THE BIGELOW CARPET CO.
2 SEASONS FOR SHERWIN-WILLIAMS CO. — KEMPTONE

STAGE APPEARANCES

CASINO THEATRE — TORONTO, CANADA

- 20,000 Cheered Him in Buffalo Memorial Auditorium
- 18,000 Were Wildly Enthusiastic in Boston Gardens
- 16,000 Acclaimed Him in St. Louis Arena
- 12,000 Clamored for More in San Francisco Civic Auditorium

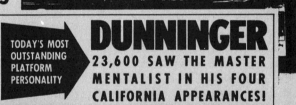

TODAY'S MOST OUTSTANDING PLATFORM PERSONALITY

DUNNINGER 23,600 SAW THE MASTER MENTALIST IN HIS FOUR CALIFORNIA APPEARANCES!

HOTEL AND NIGHT SPOTS

Dunninger Broke Attendance Records for Thirty-One Years in an Eight Weeks' Engagement at New York's Biltmore Hotel.

Played to capacity attendance...

4 weeks at The Versailles — New York
4 weeks at The Cocoanut Grove — Ambassador, Los Angeles, Calif.
6 weeks at The Blackstone Hotel — Chicago, Ill.
2 weeks at The Palmer House — Chicago, Ill.
2 weeks at The Statler — Washington, D. C.
2 weeks at The Chase — St. Louis, Mo.
2 weeks at The Last Frontier — Las Vegas, Nevada

THE AMBASSADOR — LOS ANGELES, CALIF.

THE PRESS...

"Without a doubt Dunninger's act is show business's greatest mystifier since Houdini."
—VARIETY

"Dunninger's act is astounding!" —NEW YORK WORLD TELEGRAM-SUN

"Dunninger is a mighty impressive personality. He's positively uncanny and definitely fascinating."
—MORNING TELEGRAPH

"Dunninger is to telepathy what Alexander Graham Bell was to the telephone."
—CHICAGO SUN

"He had the audience sitting on the edge of their seats."
—LOS ANGELES EXAMINER

"The exhibition is nothing short of marvelous."
—WASHINGTON POST

"Dunninger, the Mentalist, sends patrons from the playhouse wagging their heads and talking to themselves—bringing the first real novelty in Oakland in the last three years."
—POST INQUIRER, OAKLAND

"At the conclusion of Dunninger's performance the applause was deafening for several minutes, forming one of the greatest ovations ever received by an artist in this city."
—VANCOUVER PROVINCE

"As a man of mystery, Dunninger is baffling in the extreme. But he is something more than that. He is preeminently an entertainer."
—INDIANAPOLIS STAR

"His remarkable demonstration in this particular field is deservedly labeled a master achievement."
—BROOKLYN CITIZEN

"You will have the thrill of your life when Dunninger comes on the stage. So far as human intelligence could discover he is the only genuine mind reader on the stage."
—MILWAUKEE SENTINEL

"The weirdest, most uncanny mystery ever presented to the public, is being presented by Dunninger, master of the mind."
—BOSTON AMERICAN

"Dunninger presented feats that were thoroughly mystifying. The audience of skeptics could pick no flaws with his methods of reading their thoughts. Dunninger remains an interesting enigma, if not a minor phenomenon."—NEW YORK TIMES

16,435,310 NEWS STORIES CARRIED ON DUNNINGER BY THE NATIONS PRESS IN ONE YEAR

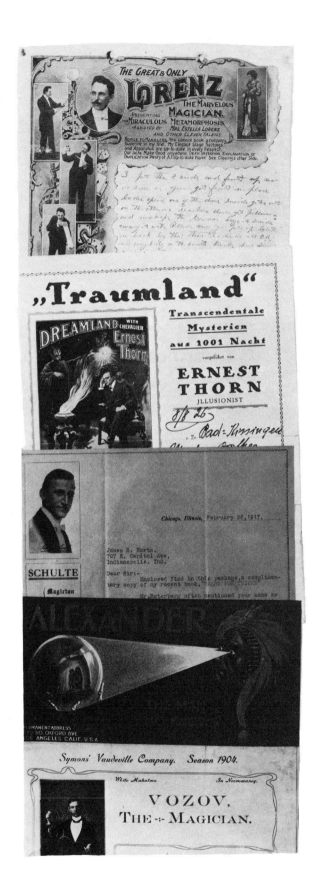

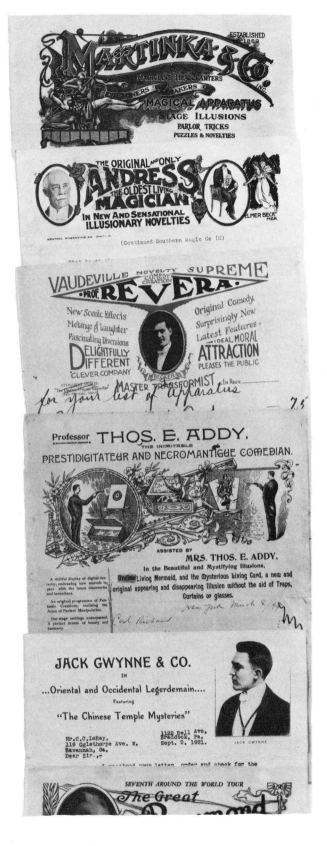

OPPOSITE: Flyer used by Joseph Dunninger, probably the greatest mentalist of all time, at the height of his stage and television career. Dunninger amazed countless millions with his unexplained feats of mind reading and second sight. (*Courtesy of Jack Flosso*)

ABOVE: The colorful and imaginative letterheads used by magicians, mentalists and magic dealers of yesteryear eloquently bespoke the mystery and elegance of their amazing art. (*Mario Carrandi Collection*)

Master mentalist Joseph Dunninger was also a master of showmanship. His magnetic personality deeply impressed his audiences. (*Photo courtesy of Jack Flosso*)

This gives him an opportunity to read the actual question on the billet. He then picks up another billet and proceeds to answer the question he has just read. This time it is an actual message which can be acknowledged by one of the spectators. This is continued as long as desired.

Billet Switching: As he draws the billet toward him across the table to burn it in a small brazier, the fortune teller switches the spectator's billet for a palmed duplicate. He burns the duplicate, meanwhile secretly unfolding the real billet in his lap, reading it quickly, and responding to the message or question.

Real billets may also be switched for duplicates by means of a change bag or similar device. A spectator is then requested to select one of the false slips, all of which bear the same message or number. Or, the magician's assistant can empty the duplicates into a bowl or basket, taking the real ones offstage. There they are opened and their contents signaled to the performer by a small telephonic or wireless device.

The Center Tear: This is used to read the suits and values of cards, initials, numerals, and other very brief messages. The spectator is given a small slip with a printed circle in the middle for him to write in. Taking the billet, the performer folds it in quarters. He then tears it to bits and drops the pieces into a brazier or waste container, but retains in his fingers the corner containing what was the center section. This he reads while shading his eyes with his hand, or in his lap.

The Clipboard: An innocent-looking clipboard is handed to the spectator to write upon. He retains his slip, but the clipboard registers a secret impression of it which can be read after the board is taken back by the performer.

Other subtle methods and devices have been developed. They range from simple and inexpensive ones to costly electronic devices. In expert hands, billet reading is undetectable. Dunninger, as previously mentioned, had his spectators write their messages on slips of paper without any pad, clipboard or other backing, and keep the slips in their own pockets at all times. Yet he was able to read off the most elaborate messages.

Some of the best message-reading devices and other mental effects are shown on the pages that follow.

utissamo

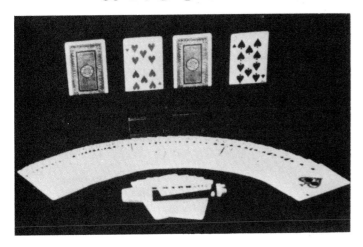

EFFECT: Magician has two spectators each think of a card. He proceeds to write his impression of each on a blank-face card with a marker. The cards are placed in a rack in full view of audience. Magi now produces an ordinary deck of cards and asks spectators to announce their thought of cards. These are removed from deck and placed in rack. When rack is turned, magicians impressions are seen to match the selected cards.

NOTES: Card rack is made of gleaming black and clear lucite and revolves. This is the ultimate in mental card effects. Also available without rack.

CREATIVE MAGIC PRODUCTS, INC., $13.50

NELSON'S MENTAL GIMIC

This fine creation by Nelson-Bergson is an invaluable prop for the magician and mentalist. It is an innocent appearing bulldog type paper clip which is used to hold a prediction. Yet in a flash it will switch the "in view" prediction for another one.

You can have a spectator fold up a $1 and you put it into the clip right in full view. Yet when you wish...that $1 can be switched without any false moves at all.

One fellow hung this from a hook in a plexiglas chest and had a fine Prediction Chest effect.

This is one of the finest utility props ever made for the mentalist. It comes with an 8 PAGE MANUSCRIPT OF EFFECTS AND USES.

Don't confuse this with cheap copies that use rubber bands or elastic. This is top quality and the mechanism is all spring steel and put in place by hand. The extra work involved gives you a piece of magic that will serve you well for many years. Complete outfit................$6.50

ROBERT MASON PRODUCTIONS

Supreme Mind Master

A terrific mental effect that will add strength to any Magic act.

Effect includes a prediction and reading the mind of a member of the audience. No exchanges. Perfect for close-up. Easy to do.

How often have you been asked, "Can you read a person's thoughts?" SUPREME MIND MASTER is the answer.

You first write a prediction on a slate or piece of paper. This is placed in full view of everyone. A deck of cards is shuffled and cut, etc., and then handed to a member of the audience. With the deck in his own hands, he continues with the mixing of the cards. You request the volunteer assistant to remove six cards and to spread these cards. As he thinks of one of the cards, you name it, each card being discarded as named. Five cards are named in this way. One card has been retained by assistant.

You point out that this one card has been left until the last by assistant. He is asked to thing of it. You not only name it, but as he shows it, it proves to be the card that you predicted!

It's a great finish to a most mystifying trick.

ABBOTT'S MAGIC MANUFACTURING CO., $3.00; DELIVERED, $3.50

824—SUPREME
CLIP BOARD

Extra Thin Model

At last, the most perfect clip (impression) board ever offered. Use this board for private readings, theatre work, out of doors, anywhere. Secure all the questions you want, unbeknown to the writers, and without fear of detection. It will withstand the most rigid examination and come through with flying colors. It so naturally resembles a real clip board that it allays suspicion, rather than creates it. Natural wood finish, made by a secret process, that gives perfect appearance. Excellent impressions everytime. Sure fire and easy to load. Holds six to eight questions. This board is unexcelled for private readings.

Finest available method for collecting questions in theatres, lobbies, carnivals, and all places of entertainment. Must be seen to be really appreciated.

The size of the board is approximately 6" x 10", and ¼" or less in thickness. The Supreme Clip Board, complete with extra perforated paper, ready to work $9.50
In lots of six, the usual number for theatres and large clubs $55.00

LOUIS TANNEN, INC.

803—DECEPTIVE TRANSPARENT
CHANGE BAG

AN UNCANNY
TRIPLE FEATURE
MENTAL EFFECT THAT
DEFIES DETECTION!!

Anyone is handed a large sealed envelope to hold. The transparent bag is shown, and in it are placed several different colored silks. Anyone reaches in and pulls out one silk and retains it. The rest of the silks are removed and a handful of coins is tossed into the bag. Three people each reach in and remove a coin, keeping it hidden in their fist. Now several folded slips of paper are placed in the bag, and three people each remove one.

NOW—a spectator opens the large prediction and reads aloud, "I predict the following three things will take place. A person will select a red silk. Two silver and one copper coin will be selected. All names on the slips are different, and the third person will select the name of Dolores. P.S. Al Thatcher took the copper coin!"

This is the impossible come true! The bag is completely transparent. Scores and scores of other effects are possible. The instructions and routine alone are worth the price of the bag. YOU CAN CARRY A COMPLETE ACT IN YOUR POCKET FOR ..
....$3.00

LOUIS TANNEN, INC.

Precognition is knowledge of events before they happen. Some of the finest effects in mental magic simulate this mysterious foreknowledge. A pleasing and easy effect to present is Supersonic Card Prediction, Jr., described below. It was invented by Dr. Stanley Jaks, a well-known mentalist. All the tricks on the opposite page except the New Center Tear Pads also duplicate the uncanny phenomenon of precognition. The book test at lower right is one of a popular and baffling class of tricks in which the performer correctly identifies a single word chosen by apparently fair means from a dictionary or other book. In this case it is presented as a memory test.

The power of precognition is ostensibly at work in what are usually called "prediction" effects. These are among the strongest feats in the repertory of the mentalist. They are often presented as a highlight of the entertainment at large banquets, as well as in magic shows. A month or two weeks before the scheduled event the mentalist hands the head of the sponsoring organization a sealed envelope, stating that it contains a prediction. To make any substitution impossible, the envelope is signed by the official and his associates. They then lock the signed envelope in a safe until the day of the function. The envelope, still sealed, is produced at the climax of the program and opened dramatically. Inside it is found a sheet of paper on which the mentalist, weeks before, has correctly predicted the lead headline in the newspaper published on the day the envelope is opened.

To heighten the drama still further, the signed envelope is often locked inside a strong wooden chest. For advance publicity the chest containing the prediction can be displayed in a local store window or turned over to a bank to be locked in its vault until the day of the demonstration. Two prediction chest effects are described on page 143. They are truly amazing feats.

849—SUPERSONIC CARD PREDICTION JR.

Dr. Jaks

Although the name of this effect suggests something sensational, it hardly conveys the true brain stunning power of this mental marvel. An attractive stand holding five different cards is shown. The cards are each shown to have a different colored spot on the back. You then write a prediction and give it to a spectator to hold. Another spectator is asked to name one of the colors; this colored card is shown to the audience. Spectator now opens prediction which reveals the selected card, as per illustration. Only five cards are used, no switching of cards, no sleight of hand. If you are looking for a good mental trick, this is it. $12.50

LOUIS TANNEN, INC.

by
HEN
FETSCH

MENTAL EPIC

ANY NUMBER . . . WORD . . . CARD

This is undoubtedly one of the finest effects ever to be produced. Our own enthusiasm probably has something to do with the fact that we are selling these faster than the guy can make them. Briefly you show a slate that is marked off into six equal squares. You make three predictions in the top three spaces and cover them with three pieces of cardboard. The spectator's selections are written in the bottom three spaces. On uncovering your predictions they are seen to match the spectator's exactly! Any type of item can be used. Any book, any word, any number, color, design, name, place, date and playing card. In the miracle class, it just doesn't seem possible. Requires absolutely no skill, no effort on your part. Self working, self contained. Unconditionally guaranteed and commended. A super duper knockout.

ABBOTT'S MAGIC MANUFACTURING CO., $25.00; DELIVERED, $26.00

810—ADD-A-NUMBER

Vermyden

Pure, unadulterated mind reading! That's what you'll say when you see this cleverest of all mental effects. Best of all, the entire thing is done for you. AUTOMATICALLY! The Master Mentalist, that's you, declares that he has not only power to read the present, but under certain conditions can predict the future. (The "under certain  conditions" covers you with characters who want you to give them the winner of tomorrow's daily double!) An envelope is introduced and placed in full view of the audience. Three, four, or five members of the audience are asked to give you numbers consisting of as many digits as they wish. These numbers are written on a pad as each spectator gives it to you. Each spectator watches as you write his number on the pad. You now have a column of figures, which when totaled will be in the thousands. The pad is handed to another spectator who totals the column of figures. A total which no one could have possibly foreseen, as not even the numbers had been thought of as yet. The total is announced and anyone is requested to open the envelope which was put on display before ANYTHING was done. Inside is a prediction which matches the spectator's total exactly! An ingenious, self-contained, mechanical marvel that defies detection. Many other applications are possible. A sensational mental effect destined to become an all-time best seller. Complete with pad, pencil, and routine. A mentalist's dream. Large size. A bargain at $12.50

LOUIS TANNEN, INC.

JACK BRIDWELL'S WILL O' THE WITCH

Offbeat mentalism with an occult touch!! Three spectators are invited to help in a strange experiment. As you discuss the famous Salem witch trials, you show a witch doll. Each spectator is given a noose of rope. While you are out of the room, any of the three spectators hangs the witch doll. Upon your return, you take the hanging figure and hold it up in front of each of the three spectators. When the figure is held in front of the guilty party, it begins to swing back & forth...the hanged witch has identified her murderer!! Going one step further, you have a previously written prediction opened - in it is your statement as to which spectator you thought would do the hanging...and needless to say, you are absolutely correct! This is strong stuff, for close-up or on stage. No assistants to code you - it's a one-man effect! The WILL O' THE WITCH will delight both you and your audiences!   Priced at only $5.00

HANK LEE'S MAGIC FACTORY

NEW CENTER TEAR PADS

These are printed especially for us and are nicely made up. You get 100 sheets padded like a salesbook. The astrological design is printed on easy to tear newsprint. Each sheet is 3 3/8" by 5 3/16" making them oblong...which works out fine and does not make center of the sheet obvious at all. You get 100 sheet pad and info on our special tear.
ROBERT MASON PRODUCTIONS,
$1.25 PLUS 25¢ POSTAGE AND HANDLING

MIRACLE BOOK TEST

Performer shows a book of 300 pages and gives it to any spectator for examination. The book contains thousands of different words. Performer states he has memorized all the words. The spectator turns to ANY page and a word is selected. Performer writes a prediction on a piece of paper When the paper is read, It is written on it the EXACT WORD that was selected! A TERRIFIC EFFECT! Complete with 300 page book . . . .

MIRACLE BOOK TEST does not require any memorizing. Can be performed IMMEDIATELY!

D. ROBBINS & CO., E-Z MAGIC, $2.00.
(See Directory of Dealers)

Mind Reading for Two People

By SYDNEY de HEMPSEY

Here is a practical easy-to-learn code that will make the presentation of a Mind Reading act a pleasure.

This code covers the naming of articles, dates on coins, suits and values of cards names, ages, colors, numbers on bills, etc. Best of all, this not a complicated code. It is compiled in easy-to-understand language, and once learned, it is with you for all time.

ABBOTT'S MAGIC MANUFACTURING CO., $2.00; DELIVERED, $2.30

GRANT'S E.S.P.

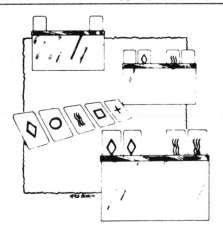

This is the cleanest, most direct mind confounding E.S.P. test of them all! The outfit consists of a clear plastic stand, 6" by 8" in size, with a narrow chrome strip to hold cards upright. Two sets of E.S.P. cards are shown. One set is shuffled face down, the performer picks out two and places them in the stand, backs out. The other set is fanned out face up and two spectators each call out a design. These are placed in the stand alongside the performer's cards. When the performers cards are turned around, they match the spectator's selected cards! A class outfit. No rough and smooth.

MAK-MAGIC CO. FROM JAMES SWOGER HOUSE OF ENCHANTMENT, $3.75

798—CLEARLY MENTAL
Tony Spina

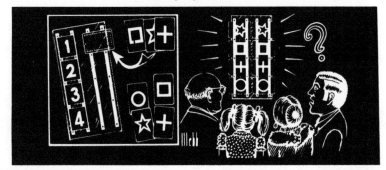

CLEARLY MENTAL by Tony Spina is a sure fire audience tested mental effect that can be a feature item in any act. The premise of the effect is an old one, but updated to 20th century mentalism. The props are simple and innocent looking. A clear sheet of plastic is shown to contain 4 numbers and several strips of elastic to hold cards into place. Four ESP cards with different designs are shown. These are mixed so that the spectator has no idea in which order they are in. The mentalist places these into the Plastic frame, one next to each number. Now taking four duplicate design cards, he mixes these so that once again spectator has no idea in which order they are in. The spectator has an absolutely FREE CHOICE where the remaining four cards should be placed. As each one is placed into position, the suspense keeps building . . . is it possible to predict 4 out of 4? Remember, the spectator tells the Mentalist where to place the cards. No force of any type used. The stunning climax comes when the Plastic frame is turned around. There under the elastic are the 8 ESP cards, each one matching in design. Truly an outstanding effect and a real baffler. $12.50

LOUIS TANNEN, INC.

Second sight is the ability to mentally visualize objects at a distance, unseen by the eyes. Going into the audience, the magician asks people to hand him any personal belongings such as jewels, keys, cards, pens and so on. The medium, sitting on the stage blindfolded and with his or her back turned, describes each object perfectly. *Mind Reading for Two People* is one of the practical books on the subject.

Demonstrations of second sight are often presented by teams composed of a husband, who goes among the audience and has personal belongings handed to him, and his wife, who sits on the stage and acts as the medium. Some of the best second-sight acts have also been presented by father-and-son teams, such as Robert-Houdin and his young son Emile, who scored a success with a demonstration of second sight in the Soirées Fantastiques.

Clairvoyance, related in a sense to second sight, is defined in parapsychology as vision without ocular aid or telepathy, as when, for example, the subject senses the faces of ESP cards that are turned down, or sees events occurring at a distance. Clairvoyance is seemingly combined with precognition in a clever effect called Clearly Mental. It is easy to do and a real puzzler.

811—SIGHTLESS VISION

Revello

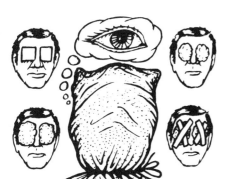

You've read about it. You've heard about it. You've seen it. Now it's yours. The blindfold act that's been baffling television audiences. Just think, the audience places a piece of cardboard over your eyes then plasters it with putty, dough, etc., and covers that with cotton and then adhesive tape. A blindfold is then placed over all this and if that isn't enough a black hood is placed completely over your head and tied around your neck. Yet with this super method, you can drive a car, write and duplicate numbers and names written on a blackboard, play pool, ride a bike, pick out colors named and scores of other impossible feats. Full instructions including hood. $10.00

Another form of second sight is the apparent ability to see through a heavy blindfold, as in the effect at left. The leading exponent of this art is the Oriental magician Kuda Bux. This artist freely reproduces drawings and writings in obscure languages while his eyes are covered with dough, bandaged, taped and blindfolded.

BOB MASON'S ESP CASSETTE MYSTERY
A COMPLETE SELLOUT AT MAGI-FEST

Now . . . THE GREATEST TAPE CASSETTE TRICK YET. TAPE ONLY PLAYS 4 MINUTES AND GIVES YOU A SOCKO FINISH EVERYTIME. This is entirely different than any other tape effect on the market today. Spectator is shown a 4" diagram that contains nine blank squares. Nine ESP symbols are drawn into the nine squares ANYWHERE THAT THE SPECTATOR WANTS THEM DRAWN! Spectator then drops a coin on any square and tape is started immediately. The taped voice then directs the spectator to cross out 3 or 4 squares right off . . . the coin is not on any of these squares. Coin is moved several places . . . voice has spectator cross out designs on various squares . . . coin is not on any of them. Now just one symbol is left . . . the spectator is asked to stare at that symbol AND THE TAPED VOICE ACCURATELY DESCRIBES THE ONLY SYMBOL LEFT! NO GAGS . . . NO JOKES . . . A REAL ESP TYPE EFFECT. CREATED BY A PRO TO GIVE YOU A REAL MENTAL EFFECT WITH A CASSETTE.

A demonstration of precognition on the part of a living performer is impressive. It is doubly so when this uncanny ability is exercised through the once-removed medium of a tape recording made long before the show and played from a cassette, as in Bob Mason's ESP Cassette Mystery.

ANY SYMBOL INTO ANY SQUARE ?

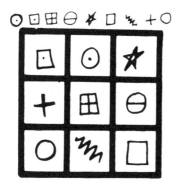

A REAL MENTAL MYSTERY

"I'll take a dozen right now . . . it's great." Betty Nelson, Nelson Enterprises

"Send me an order at once". . . Jim Swoger, Pittsburgh, Pa.

"I rarely endorse anything. This gets my full backing as one of the GREAT TRICKS of 1973." Ed Seguin . . . immediate past president of Magic Dealers Association

"Hey Bob . . . you've got a winner. The ESP Cassette is fast . . . just 4 minutes of real mystery and that finish has got to drive them crazy . . . It is IMPOSSIBLE!!"
Duke Stern

We guarantee you'll be delighted with this ESP Cassette . . . you get it, 2 giant pages of instructions and 150 padded diagrams for only $12 PP.

835—WORD-AMATIC

Sam Schwartz

This is without a doubt, one of the finest mental effects ever put on the market. Mentalist hands 29 index cards to a spectator, each with a different word on it. One of these words is chosen, a completely FREE choice.... Performer now picks up a pad and starts to call off letters and writes these down on the pad. Every letter called by the performer is indeed the same as in the word chosen by the spectator. At no time does the performer ask any questions. The word chosen may contain from 5 to 12 letters, no two words alike. Can you imagine the impact on the audience as you complete the chosen word. This comes to you complete with laminated index cards, grease pencil, 2 special gimmicks, and explicit instructions by Father Brennen. $15.00

822—THE TEST OF THE TIBER

Annemann

You borrow a local telephone directory. A slip of paper and a directory are handed to any spectator who initials the slip of paper. Paper is handed to anyone who writes any number within the limit of the pages in the directory. A second person takes the slip and writes another number, he gives the paper to the one holding the book, who acknowledges his initials, opens the book at the page given and counts to the name at the number given by the second spectator. The performer reveals the correct name from thousands and without an error gives the telephone number and call letters. Nothing to memorize, one person effect. Any book.   . . $1.00

An Abbott Exclusive   # MAIL MENTALISM   (EDDIE JOSEPH)

A Trick That is Terrific is Within Your Grasp!

A card trick — but — Oh! What a card trick!

You don't touch the deck — You don't see the deck — You don't DO the trick — and yet . . . ? If that was all, it would be great. But the presentation is such that your reputation as an outstanding Magician will soar to unknown heights.

And this single trick will increase your engagements — Eddie Joseph, the originator, has used it in this way for years.

You can be thousands of miles away from where the trick is being done. You can have a hundred persons in different parts of the country doing the trick at the same time.

In June, 1948, Eddie Joseph worked this trick on Sid Lorraine — Eddie in Bombay and Sid in Canada. Sid in his TOPS column said that "by air mail letter" he was instructed to freely select a card, then bury it in the deck and deal and lay out — and following the instructions, the card was finally revealed. As Sid put it: "An effective bit of long-distance trickery."

Briefly the effect to the one doing the trick is that he fairly shuffles the deck — at the beginning and during the trick — that he fairly looks at one card. This card is replaced in the deck and is eventually discovered by using the Magic Formula, WHICH IS THE MAGICIAN'S NAME!

Now it sounds unbelievable, but it actually works. So it is tried again — a different card is chosen. It makes no difference — it always works.

IT FOOLS MAGICIANS — and why not, for MAIL MENTALISM is another Eddie Joseph Masterpiece.

PURELY AUTOMATIC IN OPERATION.

Here is how you cash in both in the coin of the realm and in glory. Write a letter to the Chairman of the Club Entertainment Committee, or the Secretary of the Club, Superintendent of Schools, Manager of a Theatre, as follows:

"Dear Mr. ———:

"I dreamed of you last night. I was entertaining your guests at the ———.   They say dreams often come true. I'm writing you to ascertain if this one will. Will you kindly help me to find out?" then the instructions for the card trick. And remember he must use your name for the solution.

Now you must realize that this is not just another card trick.

Again remember that although the one following your instructions has same in writing, try as he will, he cannot find out how the trick is done.

You can telephone the instructions. You do not ask questions. Imagine this on the radio: A name from the phone book and a million persons can do the trick at the same time — and it will fool them.

Jack London's

"PREDICTION CHEST EFFECT"

Gives you the effect of the expensive chests. Use it the day you get it!

EFFECT:
Locked chest is mailed out. At the performance, a committee, opens the chest. Inside is a large envelope containing a dated slip and a package that is thoroughly stapled on all sides. The committeemen check the date the package was sealed. They then open the package. It contains the headlines of the day, written in large letters on an 8½ by 11 sheet of paper. Only one prediction paper is used.
No billet knives or visible gimmicks. Use any chest and lock. PLUS: How to use it at a regular date by bringing the chest to the date! In 8½ by 11 book form, art covers; publicity releases.

Price $35.00

"ALMOST REAL PREDICTION" .... **Price $10.00**

A new mental principle. Still one of my best.

"COMPUTER-MIND" ANY SHUFFLED PACK PEOPLE THINK OF CARDS IN A PACKET AND MIX. LOCATE THEM IN A SURE WAY. . . book form

Price $3.00

Jack London's "SEALED ENVELOPE ACT" (NO ADVANCE INFORMATION USED) Questions on cards sealed in opaque envelopes. Envelopes initialed. Collected in box or basket. Performer mixes envelopes. He then withdraws one envelope at a time — with one hand. He shows both sides of envelope and reads the initials. He answers the question. He is answering the question of the card that is in the envelope in his hand. Card may be immediately removed for verification if desired. No transparency or chemical methods. REMEMBER! One envelope is removed at a time. Only one envelope is in the performer's hand. That is the one he answers. The person's initials are on the envelope; the person's question is in the envelope! In booklet form

Price $5.00

"FANTASTIC MENTAL TEST" Actually three top tests based on a simple move that I developed and used. It leaves you clean. One test for example: People write out tests for performer to do. One is selected and sealed in an envelope yet performer carries out test. In booklet form.

Price $3.50

JACK LONDON

796—CLEAR-VOYANCE

During the past few years we have emphasized the importance of giving an audience something to look at . . . an interesting and colorful piece of apparatus to brighten up the appearance of a mental program. Outstanding in this direction are those great effects of ours: "MENTAL EPIC" AND "DR. JAKS' SUPERSONIC," which are not only fine mysteries, but uniquely VISIBLE. Something which every audience appreciates. Along these lines we offer you . . . CLEAR-VOYANCE!!! A remarkable piece of apparatus that can be used in many ways. To be perfectly frank, it enables you to perform that most important of all principles in mentalism, "ONE AHEAD" BUT, you do it without having to force anything. CLEAR-VOYANCE does the hard work for you. And you don't have to cover it or make any phoney moves! Everything is open and above board, yet, you get hold on their recorded thoughts as easy as pie. The apparatus is easy to handle and requires no sleight of hand whatsoever. Beautifully made in sparkling clear plastic, with gold numbers set on a black frame. Work it completely surrounded. Suitable for close-up, platform, or stage. $32.50

LOUIS TANNEN, INC.

the
World's GREATEST
P R E D I C T I O N
C H E S T

Bob Mason's CHEST is being used all over the world. In a sealed and locked chest, on a folded sheet of paper 8" x 10" is a correct prediction of newspaper headlines, sports result or anything else.

This beautiful walnut chest is a mentalist's dream come true.

Magi does not have to palm anything into the chest. It works almost like a miracle and is a mechanical master-piece.

Ali Bongo, Karrell Fox, Ray Hafler, Anverdi, etc. have all raved about this chest. You will too.

We have sold over three dozen of these. Owners have gotten publicity wherever shown.
The current price is $200.00 plus postage.

If you are seriously interested. Send us one dollar for pictures, complete details and answers to any questions you may wish to ask before buying.

"This is the greatest chest I've seen anywhere in the world"
Art Emerson

ROBERT MASON PRODUCTIONS

Psychic Effects with Cards

Many fine psychic effects are performed with playing cards. Two of the best "mental" decks, the Brainwave and the Ultra-Mental Decks, have already been presented in the card-trick section. Another startling mental mystery can be worked with the special cards known as the Telomatic Deck.

In this experiment, the magician tosses the audience a deck of cards held together by a strong rubber band. He asks the first spectator who catches it to riffle through the deck, note one card, and toss the deck to someone else. Three cards are thus noted. The performer then proceeds, even before the deck is returned to him, to identify the three noted cards. Price about $2.00.

Thought Control, described in the ad on page 147, is a valuable piece of utility equipment that can be used in many different effects with playing cards or ESP cards.

Spirit Effects

Before the days of ESP, it was spiritualism and mediumship that fascinated those interested in psychic phenomena. Modern spiritualism began with the strange manifestations produced in 1848 by the Fox sisters, who claimed to be mediums, at their home in upstate New York. The Davenport brothers produced phenomena in their even more startling stage show. Their box-office success inspired many other teams of stage spiritualists. Among them were the Miller Brothers, whose dramatic playbill is reproduced on pages 128 and 129.

Harry Kellar worked for a time, as we have seen, with the Davenport brothers' show. Later, breaking away from them, Kellar and William Fay toured with a spook show of their own. Other conjurers denounced the spirit mediums as frauds and presented anti-spiritualistic acts exposing their methods.

In the wake of World War I, spiritualism boomed in England and the United States. Shocked by the deceptions being practiced by fraudulent mediums on the bereaved, Harry Houdini embarked on his famous campaign against fake spiritualists. His erstwhile friend, Sir Arthur Conan Doyle, who had lost a son in the war, was equally passionate in his defense of spiritualism. Houdini, Doyle declared, was a medium without realizing it.

In the magic catalogues of the day, paraphernalia for stage and drawing-room séances abounded. Floyd G. Thayer of Los Angeles, for example, offered a spirit hand that tapped out messages from the beyond, a talking skull, luminous ghostly apparitions, and ingenious spirit slates on which messages were mysteriously chalked by the departed. Some of Thayer's ads for these devices, from his *Quality Magic Catalogue, No. 7*, 1928, appear on this page and the two following ones and in the left-hand column on page 147.

No. 1233. Visions of the Dark

This wonderful effect is sure to create a panic wherever shown. In a dark room entirely surrounded by spectators the performer causes a variety of visionary objects to appear and float around the room in the most ghostly manner possible.

We supply the full outfit complete for performing this weird and sensational effect. It can be used by any one without previous practice and will last for years.

Price $5.00

No. 1246.
The Spirit Trumpet Seance

One of the celebrated effects which usually forms a feature at many of the so-called "dark circles" or spiritualistic sittings is the "trumpet seance." This trumpet is usually a metal sectional affair about 30 inches in length, and through which the supposed voices of the departed ones are heard to talk and whisper, while the trumpet seems to float about the room, sometimes high against the ceiling, sometimes tapping the sitters on the heads, and offering uncanny evidence that it is being manipulated by ghostly power.

We supply a fine metal trumpet with special routine for an act of this nature.

Price, complete......................$5.00

No. 1201. The Multo Parvo Dark Seance

In a strange room without any previous knowledge or preparation you can sit in the center with persons all around you. You request anyone to draw their chair up close, to place their feet upon yours, and their hands upon your knees. You then place their hands upon yours so they could tell if you were to make any move whatsoever.

The lights are then turned out. Almost immediately raps are heard. Bells ring, ghostly lights appear and disappear. A trumpet is made to float in the air, spirit voices are heard, writing appears on slates and other manifestations occur.

This is one of the most mysterious and spooky exhibitions of the one man type. No assistant is used, not even the party sitting with you. Supplied complete with apparatus and instructions as used by famous mediums.

Price $10.00

No. 1239. Ghostly Raps

For many years it has been the ambition of many inventors of things mystical to produce a reliable and practical device for producing raps. Numerous indeed have been such inventions, but very few of them could be considered a success from a practical viewpoint.

With what we now offer you can sit at a table, or stand in any part of a strange room with people all around you. Your hands and feet may be secured with ropes or shackles, if desired, and yet you are able to produce the raps at any time and in any number.

Also at any given time you can change the raps to a sound in imitation of writing between slates with a slate pencil which is a feature never before possible with any other apparatus of a similar nature. The success of this remarkable device is due to its utter simplicity and ease of operation, a feature that places this effect within range of any person.

There is nothing to carry in the hand or pocket; there is no deep breathing or muscular exertion. The mysterious raps can be produced with all eyes on the operator without danger of detection.

Price, complete, ready for use..$15.00

No. 1235.
Medium's Reaching Rod

This accessory has been jealously guarded by professional mediums for years. It is for use in dark room seances, when bells, tambourines trumpets, etc., are made to ring and float in space, although the operator may have been securely tied beforehand.

Finely made of brass it can be carried in the vest pocket. Extends from 8 to 36 inches.

Price $5.00

No. 1237.
Marvelous Talking Skull

This weird, uncanny and mystifying experiment consists of a finely modeled papier mache skull which is placed on a piece of glass, resting across the backs of two chairs.

Upon command, the skull answers questions by opening and closing its mouth, according to the usual code of once for "no" and twice for "yes," etc. Best practical method.

Price, with a finely modeled skull.....$5.00

Superior Talking Skull

Here is a fine skull which is an authentic imitation of the real article. This perfect reproduction from a natural life model is made for those who require the best.

Price $10.00

No. 1245.
The Spirit Hand

A finely modeled and finished papier mache hand is examined and then placed on a piece of glass laid across the backs of two chairs. The hand at once answers questions, tells dates, names of cards, etc. by tapping.

A very wonderful effect.

Price, hand with instructions, $4.50

No. 1272. Thayer's Famous "Dr. Q." Spirit Slates

This is positively and without a doubt the most perfect and baffling Spirit Slate Writing Mystery that has ever been produced up to the present time.

A number of well-known and successful performers have even asserted the fact that a large share of their success and reputation has been derived through the use of this great feature effect.

This is only the set of slates that can be taken directly into the audience and submitted to the most critical inspection, yet may be produced full of writing at the will of the operator.

Think of being able to place two examined blank slates into a spectator's hands to hold, and yet to be able to allow that person to unbind and separate those very same slates a moment later, and to find them both filled with written messages, in answer to their own personal questions!

This can actually be done and is the nearest approach to a real supernatural test demonstration that has been ever accomplished by a magician or medium. These slates in this quality are not to be had elsewhere, this being originally our own effect, and which we alone have the proper facilities for producing. Nothing more wonderful can ever be supplied at any price. Complete in every detail.

Price $25.00

No. 1231. Mysterious Dr. "Q." Dark Trumpet Seance

Without question this is one of the most miraculous of all spiritualistic effects. Uncanny beyond belief. The performer seats himself on an ordinary chair in the center of the room. A small table is placed near him on which are a number of blank cards and an ordinary tin trumpet.

The spectators are requested to take the cards and to write on them the name of some departed friend in the spirit world, also a question, sign their own name, and then place the cards back on the table, written side down.

The performer may be tied to the chair if desired. The lights are turned out and soon the trumpet seems to be floating about. Voices from it call different ones by name and answer their questions, sometimes in whispers and sometimes in louder tones.

The lights can be called for at any time, and the performer will be found in the same position, the cards undisturbed and the trumpet on the table. This marvelous act requires no confederates. It can be performed in any strange room, at a moments notice, without a chance of failure.

The principle is so new and novel that other effects of this nature fall far short in comparison in the creative impression of genuine phenomena. Complete in every detail with apparatus, instructions and lecture.

Price $10.00

No. 1247. A Voice From The Great Beyond

This beautiful bronze vase is endowed with the power to talk and answer questions. All a person has to do is to place the spout of the vase to his ear, when a mysterious voice calls them by name, and talks with them on any subject. The vase may be handed from one to another, and to each and every one the voice talks with them in a personal way. Questions may be written and still the voice will answer each and every question with marvelous and unfailing accuracy.

There is nothing attached to the vase in anyway. It is open for free examination at all times. In fact, it need not even be handled by anyone other than the spectators themselves, and the performer can be out of the room under guard if desired.

It is positively one of the most weird and uncanny effects in the entire realm of the mysterious. As a mystery for the home there can never be its equal.

We have installed this outfit in many fine homes in this vicinity and several well-known "movie" folks of Hollywood are among its most satisfied and enthusiastic owners.

Price, outfit complete in every detail..$75.00
Price, vase alone, fully equipped.....$35.00

No. 1218. The Houdini Jumbo Slate

As designed and used by the late Harry Houdini.

It is made like a real slate, but the slate panel is made of ¼ inch 3-ply hardwood in a black slate finish. Size 12x16 inches. It is fitted with an aluminum flap which is light in weight and will not warp.

The flap is covered on the reverse side with newspaper in accord with the usual slate of this character so that the desired effect can be accomplished with ease. This slate is suitable for use with chalk only.

Price $5.00

No. 1217. Great Silent Thought Transference

This act of the mental mystery variety causes a sensation wherever produced. Although not a word is spoken other than remarks of introduction, the desires of the audience are obeyed with quick and telling results.

With definite accuracy the dates of coins are given, the time indicated by a watch, with

detailed particulars as to its kind, style of case, factory number, etc.

While a number of these tests may be similar to others the method of conveying the information is altogether different. This one comprises a number of suitable tests that may be easily learned, due to the simple and easy system by which the proper workings of the act are acquired.

It is something that will not require a large amount of study and constant practice to master, and is suitable for the most refined audiences.

Complete detailed instructions.
Price $1.00

No. 1222. The Mysterious Ink Bottle

With this ordinary ten cent ink bottle some slips of paper and a few pencils, etc., on your table you are ready to deliver a real test of your mediumistic power.

A person is invited to write a question on a slip of paper, which is then folded up, placed in the ink bottle and the stopper put in place.

Hardly has the paper been placed in the bottle than the performer at once answers the questions written on the paper, yet when the bottle is opened the paper is found intact and unmolested.

The bottle never leaves the table nor the spectators sight for a single instant. No wax or carbon impressions, and no confederate.

Useful in many other effects as well.

One of the celebrated "Dr. Q." specialties.
Price $1.50

Here are three more modern mental effects:

818—THOUGHT CONTROL

Richard Himber

Well, here is another one from magic's most prolific magic mind. A wonderful twist on an old idea. Magician has a card selected from a set of symbol cards, these cards are shown to have all different type symbols on them. He then introduces a secretary wallet and opening wallet he takes out an envelope, this envelope is handed to spectator. (Magician does not touch the selected card or the envelope after this.) Selected card is turned over and let's say that the triangle symbol was selected. Now spectator opens up the envelope and finds that the same symbol was also chosen by the magician. If you want to, you can immediately repeat the trick with a regular deck of cards. We highly recommend this Richard Himber miracle. Complete with wallet and cards. $12.50

LOUIS TANNEN, INC.

CRYSTAL VISION

An effect that is novel, and for close-up work cannot be surpassed. A spectator selects a card and notes same. Performer informs the spectator that he is going to give him PSYCHIC POWER. He exhibits a beautiful crystal ball, showing it freely on all sides. The spectator is asked to gaze into the center of the crystal, when a picture of the CHOSEN CARD slowly MATERIALIZES in the crystal. A bewildering experiment.

PRICE $3.00

GUARANTEED MAGIC

807—SPIRIT BELL

A SELF-WORKING MIRACLE WITH NEW EXTRA LOUD BELL

Even if the low price didn't immediately make this a terrific bargain, those who know would tell you to get one quick at any price. This is a classic effect recognized by magicians the world over, as one of the outstanding feats of all time, a collector's item that was bringing $75.00 or more because of its scarcity. It's now available once more, made better than ever. Not $75.00, not $50.00 but a low $42.50.

Magician or mentalist (it's good for either) shows a small bell mounted on a tripod and a large glass. They can actually be passed for a rigid inspection if you desire. The bell is then covered by the inverted glass and placed on a table or held on the hand, it doesn't matter. Magician has cards selected, numbers written, and questions asked by the spectators. The bell now rings (while covered by the glass) and tells the names of the selected cards by ringing the number of times there are spots, indicates the numbers written, and answers the questions by ringing once for yes and twice for no. Included with the apparatus is also a delightful lie detector routine that is a laugh riot. A self-contained trick requiring no threads, wires, assistants, or stooges. Entirely mechanical, and we guarantee that no amount of examination will reveal the secret. The mechanism is 100% indetectible. $42.50
NEW Electronic Spirit Bell (entirely different in principle) $175.00

LOUIS TANNEN, INC.

Harry Kellar's show consisted almost entirely of illusions. Nowhere was Kellar more popular than in South America. This poster in English and Spanish features the levitation of the magician to the dome of the theatre. The illusion was performed by using a dummy and invisible wires. (*Harvard Theatre Collection*)

STAGE ILLUSIONS

Illusions are magical effects involving a human being or a large animal or object such as an automobile or piano. Featuring pretty girls and pleasantly chilling fantasies, they are the *pièces de résistance* of full evening magic shows. They made the fame of such great performers as Buatier de Kolta, the Herrmanns, Kellar, Carter, Thurston, Dante and Blackstone. Today they are featured in elaborate acts by such popular magicians as Doug Henning and Siegfried and Roy. One or two illusions often serve to climax the acts of expert club performers.

The three upper drawings on page 151 show the working of "The Vanishing Lady," an illusion invented by Buatier de Kolta. The lady sits in a plain chair standing on a sheet of newspaper. She is covered with a large cloth, her outline plainly visible beneath it. Suddenly the performer jerks the cloth away and she is gone.

The innocent-looking chair is faked (FIGURE 1) by means of a hinged frame of thin, black wire which the lady pulls over her head and shoulders (FIGURE 2) while the cloth is being adjusted. Other wires simulate the outline of her knees. The chair has no cross rod between its legs and its seat is made to lower down, permitting the lady to slip away through traps in the newspaper and the stage (FIGURE 3). She is already gone minutes before the magician, after appropriate build-up, flicks away the cloth to reveal her startling vanishment.

Harry Rouclere performs the Asra illusion. (*Mario Carrandi Collection*)

The three lower illustrations show the levitation of a woman, as performed by Herrmann the Great. The magician rests a plain board on the backs of two chairs (FIGURE 4). A lady enters and, with the aid of a footstool, mounts and reclines on the board. The performer makes hypnotic passes and the lady appears to slumber. Both chairs are removed, and the board and lady remain suspended in the air without support (FIGURE 5). Slowly she rises higher in the air and floats there. Then her body begins to pivot as her position changes from a horizontal to a slanting one, with her head higher than her feet, and vice versa. She returns to the horizontal, gradually sinks, and the board again comes to rest on the chairs. Awakening from her trance, the lady is helped to the floor. The magician then lifts the board from the chairs, shows it all around and throws it down onto the stage.

The explanation of the illusion is seen in FIGURE 6. On a strong frame behind the backdrop, a movable slide works up and down. Through the slide runs an iron bar with flat jaws at one end. This bar is pushed between the drapes and the performer, standing behind the board, guides the rod so that it grips the board, while he is adjusting the lady's gown and bouquet. The assistant behind the scene raises the slide to levitate the lady, and partly rotates her in midair by means of the double handles. She is then lowered again, the bar is withdrawn, and the performer can walk between the board and the backdrop, remove the board from the chairs and show that everything is plain and unprepared.

A rod with long, horizontal bends in it can be used to permit passing a hoop over the floating lady.

On the following pages will be found many great illusions offered by magic dealers. Most of them are available either as workshop plans for use in home construction, or as completely built and decorated illusions.

Other illusions, including some of the most effective and ingenious ones, appear in the section on antique magic, starting on page 163.

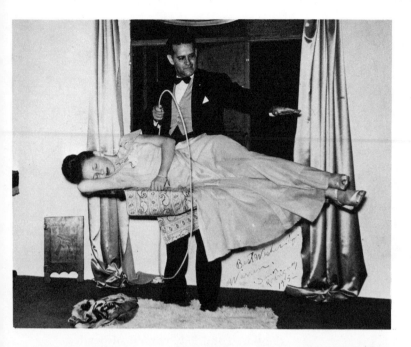

LEFT: The levitation of a lady is performed by Señor Rodriguez.

BELOW LEFT: Sawing a woman in two has been the most popular of all illusions ever since its invention in 1921.

BELOW: The prolific Joseph Buatier de Kolta (1845–1903), invented not only the disappearing lady illusion shown on the opposite page, but also many other classic magical effects, including spring flowers, the handkerchief pull and the vanishing birdcage. (*Photos from Mario Carrandi Collection*)

FIGURE 1

FIGURE 2

FIGURE 3

FIGURE 4

FIGURE 6

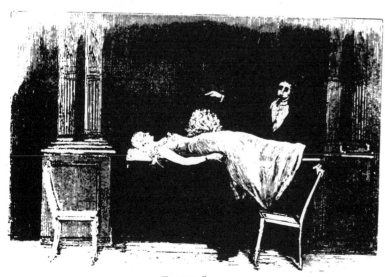

FIGURE 5

These drawings explain two famous illusions, as described at the beginning of this section. (*Illustrations from Albert A. Hopkins,* Magic: Stage Illusions and Scientific Diversions, *New York, 1897*)

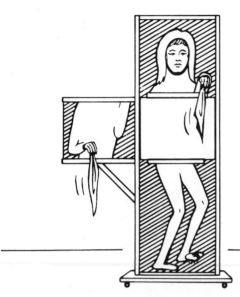

1172—ZIG-ZAG ILLUSION

Here it is! The most talked about illusion of the year . . . ZIG-ZAG—and it is ready for immediate delivery. This brain child of Robert Harbin is just what you need to get your show off the ground. Be the first in your area to "knock them for a loop."

This illusion can be done under any and all conditions . . . IT IS COMPLETELY ANGLE PROOF!! ZIG-ZAG is one of the most baffling illusions ever conceived. Take it from us, if you're looking for the perfect illusion to start you off in the presentation of illusions, THIS IS IT!!!

Superior Professional Model, ready for immediate delivery . . . .
. . . . $1195.00 F.O.B. New York

NOTE: There are no workshop plans available for Zig-Zag.

LOUIS TANNEN, INC.

1191—THE CANNON AND CRYSTAL BOX

Standing on one side of stage is a large cannon, and on the other side is a platform with a number of sheets of plate glass.

Performer builds up a box of glass on the platform (as per Crystal Box). A large hoop covered with paper and having cross feet so that it stands in an upright position, is placed in front of the glass box. Next, he introduces a lady assistant and loads her into the cannon—taking aim at the glass chest, he fires the cannon—a flash, a puff of smoke, a large hole is torn in paper hoop, and the assistant is seen reclining in the Crystal Box.

Workshop Plans $5.00
Superior Professional Model, made to order . . . . Price upon request

LOUIS TANNEN, INC.

1192—PHANTOM WHITE CARGO CAGE

Here is an illusion that has a variety of uses and is limited only by the imagination of the performer.

A long narrow box with bars in front like a cage is seen resting on a thin table that is raised high off the floor on legs. A girl assistant enters the box and can be seen at all times. At the magician's command, while in full view, without a covering of any sort, she vanishes instantly. The box is then broken down flat proving her complete absence.

The process can be reversed by building the box in front of the audience and at a pistol shot the girl appears instantly and visibly and jumps out of the box to the stage. A A wonderful illusion for traveling shows.

Workshop Plans $2.50
Superior Professional Model, made to order . . . . Price upon request

LOUIS TANNEN, INC.

1190—NEW "FLYTO" ILLUSION

Two handsome grill-work cabinets occupy opposite sides of stage.

Assistant enters No. 1, where she remains fully visible through the open grill-work. Front curtain is pulled down, inside of cabinet lights up showing her shadow within. She then walks over to opposite side and enters cabinet No. 2—same business with curtain and lights to show shadow on that side.

PISTOL SHOT—her shadow vanishes and appears back in cabinet No. 1. Then passe-passe—(sucker effect) with shadow, finally opening door of cabinet No. 2 and showing girl still there.

Once more the shadow vanishes in cabinet No. 2 and appears in cabinet No. 1, and when this door is now opened, the same girl steps forth, while cabinet No. 2 is then shown entirely empty.

Borrowed handkerchief can be tied around girl's arm if desired, thus proving no "doubles" are used. One of the greatest illusion cabinets ever invented, and something to baffle magicians.

Workshop Plans $5.00
Superior Professional Model, made to order . . . . Price upon request

LOUIS TANNEN, INC.

THE VANISHING GIRL

A two-fold screen is assembled in the presence of audience. Screen consists of open frames, permitting audience to see right through. Girl stands on the platform and magician covers her with a large sheet. This is quickly pulled away, the girl has vanished. A good finish to any platform or stage act.

Famous Substitution Trunk

For many years a feature act of the late Houdini. A trunk is examined by a committee. Performer steps into a bag which is tied and sealed, and thus secured, performer is locked in the trunk which is roped around all sides. A cabinet is placed around the trunk. Assistant standing outside, suddenly darts inside, draws the curtain and claps her hand, One—Two—Three! The curtain flies open and there stands—not the assistant, but performer himself, minus his coat. The trunk is immediately unroped and unlocked, lid opened, and the bag untied revealing the assistant therein, wearing performer's coat. Quick work, and always a sensation. The use of the bag is optional.

WORKSHOP PLANS $1.00

GIRL IN THE PUMPKIN

A lattice work enclosure is built in full view of the audience on a low platform. A mammoth pumpkin with the front cut out like a Jack-O-Lantern is then placed on a pedestal shaped like a corn stalk that rests in the center of the platform. A girl then steps into the pumpkin through a top opening where her face remains in full view through the Jack-O-Lantern front.

The pumpkin is now lifted by handles on the sides and brought forward to the front of the stage. At a command from the magician the pumpkin is shown empty, the girl having vanished completely. Workshop Plans   **$1.00**

Abbott's Improved
GIRL IN FISH BOWL

This is one of the most intriguing illusions extant — for theatre lobbies, show windows, etc. It holds the crowds and causes endless talk and discussion as to the how and why.

The Effect: A large fish bowl and inside the bowl is a young lady — very much alive although she is only inches tall.

Now in the old method you looked through a reducing lens. This not only required a lot of space but the fish bowl was behind the mirror. In our improved method, no lens is used, very little space is needed, and the fish bowl is in full view so that spectators looking into the bowl see the girl — or you can have a display of live miniature rabbits diminutive in size.

We ship illusion to you complete, including lights to plug in, knock-down cabinet, and special two-gallon capacity fish bowl, all ready to set up and go to work.

SAWING A LADY IN TWO

The performer's lady assistant is placed in the box with her feet and ankles projecting from one end and her head from the other. Her feet and head are then secured with stocks which slide down in metal grooves at each end of the box By means of an ordinary crosscut saw, the box is then cut exactly in half, after which the two sections of the box are separated and moved some distance apart. Only one lady is used.
Master blue print plans

$1.00

The Buddha Chests

A large decorated box on four legs is shown, all four hinged sides of which are opened down to show empty.

Next, a smaller box is shown in the same manner, and then nested within the larger one. Paper top is then placed on and secured with metal hoop band.

Suddenly a girl bursts through the paper top and jumps to the floor.

Sensational, quick, self-contained and works anywhere.

FLOSSO HORNMANN MAGIC CO., WORKSHOP PLANS, $1.00

-The Artist's Model

Performer places a picture frame covered with white paper to represent canvas on a nearby easel such as those used by artists. Donning a smock, a large bow tie and tam, he seizes palette and brushes, and begins a sketch on the paper. Punching holes at various spots, he produces silks, flags, etc. As a climax, a beautiful model bursts through the paper and is assisted to the stage by performer

WORKSHOP PLANS $1.00

FLOSSO-HORNMANN MAGIC CO.

The Sensational MAK-MAGIC

DeVoe
PRINCESS OF AIR!

SENSATIONAL RELEASE **CRASHES** THRU THE MAGICAL **HORIZON!!**

NEVER BEFORE SUCH A CLIMAX ON ANY LEVITATION!

GIRL FROM AUDIENCE ON ALTAR BOARD SUSPENDS IN MID AIR...

MAGI STEPS AWAY AND FIRES SHOT...
BOARD CRASHES TO FLOOR...
GIRL STAYS SUSPENDED IN AIR!!

Solid hoop passed over body... Not a set piece. Can be rolled out to any spot...Audience on 3 sides, not directly in back. Magi free to walk about while girl is suspended. Lightweight Aluminum gimmick all packs down for easy transporting...

only **$265.00**
PLUS SHIPPING

MAK-MAGIC CO.

Dagger Chest

An attractive cabinet, large enough to accommodate a person's head, is shown. The front panel is removed so that spectators have a clear view of the interior. Front panel replaced, back door of cabinet is opened. Cabinet is now placed over victim's head . . . back door closed. TWENTY metal daggers are impaled through cabinet at every conceivable angle. The front panel is removed showing the cabinet filled with daggers . . . the head has vanished. You may even walk the victim down the aisle in this condition.

The front panel is replaced, daggers withdrawn and cabinet removed. The victim's head is intact.

Daggers are lacquered in red and white . . . cabinet in red, black and gold.

ABBOTT'S MAGIC MANUFACTURING CO., $90.00; DELIVERED, $95.00

Headless Woman

This elaborate outfit must not be confused with cheaper-made versions. No mirrors are used. This is a strong feature. Girl is seen, as illustrated, all enclosed in a portable cloth cabinet. The instrument panel is very elaborate and when it is operated, the colored liquid in the clear glass jars bubbles with life and action — making this a most colorful, as well as a completely mystifying illusion.

Girl's hands and feet move, showing that she is very much alive. All metal tubes are chromed. Outfit is complete, including the cabinet.

A FEATURE illusion for a sideshow.

ABBOTT'S MAGIC MANUFACTURING CO., $1,100.00 FOB COLON, MICHIGAN

ABBOTT'S MODERNISTIC AMPUTATION

A modernistic cabinet, as pictured, with open front, with the exception of a small section at the very center. ANYONE from the AUDIENCE steps forward and rolls their sleeves back and place their arm into the cabinet. Next two SOLID blades the width of the cabinet are passed for examination and these same two blades are visibly pushed right down through the center section of the cabinet, completely filling every inch of space of the width of the cabinet. NOW, to the utter amazement of all (magicians included) the small doors at front and rear of center section where the blades have been pushed through are opened and the CENTER PORTION OF THE VICTIM'S ARM HAS COMPLETELY VANISHED. Still you see the arm on side of the blade and the wrist and hand on the other side. Victim is still able to move his fingers and hand. The magician looks right through the cabinet from the rear, through the space where the arm is missing. For those who think there are mirrors used, magician breaks down that theory by pushing his own hand and arm right through the very space where arm is missing.

Magician removes blades and allows person to pull his arm out, none the worse for taking a major part in the strange operation. Audience see him remove his arm visibly, it never leaves their sight for one fraction of a second.

ABBOTT'S MAGIC MANUFACTURING CO., $135.00 FOB COLON, MICHIGAN

Rod Thru' Body

Just the Illusion that you have been waiting for and it all packs into a suitcase.

A member of the audience may be used, or you may use your own assistant. Body stock, replica of the old Chinese Body Stocks, are placed around the victim.

A solid chrome plated metal tube is shown, fitted into a hole in the stocks and slowly forced through the girl's body from the front and coming out at the back so that both ends of tube are in full view. For further proof that the rod goes completely through the body, liquid is introduced into the front of the tube and seen to flow out at the back.

Tube is withdrawn, stocks removed and victim unharmed.

ABBOTT'S MAGIC MANUFACTURING CO.,
$275.00 FOB COLON, MICHIGAN

15 Great Illusions

Such as Girl in Balloon, Headless Man, Rajah's Tent, Dancing Slippers, Buzz Saw Illusion, Light Bulbs Through Girl, Book of Life, etc.

For the Performer who plays carnivals, circuses, clubs or has a large stage show.

Build your own illusion at small cost. Detailed instruction for each illusion.

ABBOTT'S MAGIC MANUFACTURING CO.,
$2.00; $2.30 DELIVERED.

1175—THE DOLL'S HOUSE ILLUSION

The performance of this illusion is always a pleasurable experience. A magical effect that the audience invariably appreciates. A perfect opening for a magician and his assistant.

The magician exhibits a small doll house raised from the floor on four legs, turns it around, showing all sides. He opens the front showing it filled and completely furnished with miniature furniture, otherwise empty. He removes all the furniture and closes the doors, again he spins it around showing all sides. Lo and behold, at his command, the roof bursts open, the front swings aside to reveal a beautifully costumed girl whose size and weight are twice the capacity of the house itself. The house is a joy to behold, a little gem of a doll house. Finely decorated, inside and out. Folds flat for packing. A guaranteed hit for your show. A perfect effect for clubs.

Workshop Plans $2.50

Superior Professional Model, made to order . . . . Price upon request

LOUIS TANNEN, INC.

Tricks and Illusionettes (Ovette)

A 32-page printed book, profusely illustrated. Contains 13 Magical items having variety, dash and color.

Partial Contents: A Novel Opening, The Waterless Tube, Magic Bunny Rings, Oriental Beach Rack, Stack of Fish Bowls, Oriental Tube, Vanishing Lamp, Candle and Fan, and many more.

Includes many worthwhile suggestions on making many of your own effects.

ABBOTT'S MAGIC MANUFACTURING CO.,
$1.50; $1.80 DELIVERED.

1171—MECHANICAL CUT OFF
BUZZ SAW ILLUSION

The modern up-to-date method of sawing a woman in half. Eliminates all thoughts of two girls being used or a trick box. An illusion for superior shows.

The magician's assistant is placed on a flat board and secured by shackles, under a motor driven buzz saw suspended from a trestle. She remains in full view at all times. The motor is turned on, revolving with a wicked whine. Slowly the saw is swung over until it suddenly rips its way through the girl's body severing the upper and lower parts. A weird and spine tingling effect that leaves the audience gasping with horror and finally with relief when the girl is restored to life without bodily harm.

A sensational effect to say the least and an entirely safe and improved method that eliminates all hazard. A feature illusion with many of our leading magicians. Ask anyone who has seen Riciardi!

Workshop Plans $5.00
Superior Professional Model, made to order . . . . Price upon request

LOUIS TANNEN, INC.

1209—THE BIRTH OF CHLORIS

The effect of this illusion is very pleasing to the eye and puzzling to the mind of the audience.

Standing in the center of a brightly lighted stage is a neat four-legged table. Upon this table rests a fancy flower pot containing flowers, in the direct center of which is a beautiful large closed tulip.

A burning candle in a long holder at each corner of the table adds to the illumination of the setting so that a clear and uninterrupted view may be had beneath and all around the table.

At command the tulip slowly opens and as it does so, a beautiful young lady arises from its center until her head and shoulders are in full view. A very charming effect.

Workshop Plans $3.00
Superior Professional Model, made to order . . . . Price upon request

LOUIS TANNEN, INC.

Electric Chair

This outfit consists of a specially-made chair and instrument box. The chair is wired to the instrument box and then plugged into a regular circuit. Spectators are told that the girl is immune to thousands of volts of electricity. Sparks shoot out from her fingers. A light bulb is lighted while held in her hand, also lighted when socket section of light bulb is held in her mouth . . . a torch is lighted at her finger-tips. The effects that you can get with this apparatus are many and varied.

The chair is correctly made, and is absolutely harmless to the individual working it.

ABBOTT'S MAGIC MANUFACTURING CO.,
$1,000.00 FOB COLON, MICHIGAN

Vanishing Dog

An illusion that can be constructed at a minimum expense.

Size is regulated by the size of dog used. Outfit represents a regular-looking dog kennel. Dog is placed in the kennel . . . a shot fired and Presto, the dog has vanished.

Full working secret and drawings.

ABBOTT'S MANUFACTURING CO., $2.00

The Sphinx Illusion, c. 1875.

THE ART OF ESCAPING

Most dramatic of all forms of magic is the escape. In most branches of the art, the only thing at stake is the magician's ability to deceive and entertain. But if he is an escape artist his life may be at stake, while he attempts to free himself from a submerged packing box or a sealed milk can filled with water, or tries valiantly to wriggle out of a straitjacket that is suspended high above the stage.

Because of this potential for disaster, no other form of magic, not even mentalism, lends itself so well to the professional magician's ceaseless quest for the kind of publicity that will bring him highly paid bookings and draw crowds at the box office. The escape artist at times works directly with the public, through outdoor performances and challenge tests that are supervised by public officials, lay committees, or businessmen. He challenges police chiefs to confine him in handcuffs, jailers to lock him in a cell; he defies commercial enterprises to produce a cast-iron boiler, a sealed mailbag, or a massive safe that will hold him. He is a favorite of reporters eager to find a story, and of theater operators anxious to increase business by offering drama and suspense.

Success as an escape artist requires dexterity, physical strength, great stamina, resourcefulness, and ingenuity. It also requires a detailed and comprehensive knowledge of locks, handcuffs and rope ties. The escapologist who claims that he can escape from any kind of manacle

A rare Houdini poster ligothraphed by Strobridge. (*Mario Carrandi Collection*)

must be familiar with scores of different types, both antique and modern, and he must maintain an extensive collection of picks and tools.

These attributes of skill, resourcefulness and courage were possessed in abundance by Harry Houdini, the greatest performer of escapes in the entire history of magic. In the first section of this book (pages 30–33) we outlined Houdini's adventurous career. One can hardly think of another figure in show business whose personality lives on so sharply and clearly, even half a century after his passing.

Among the most baffling feats performed by Houdini were his amazing challenge escapes. Countless experts—professional packers and riggers, policemen, straitjacket manufacturers—challenged him to escape from their heavy wooden boxes, involved rope ties, welded boilers, wet sheets and other forms of confinement. He always escaped.

Edward Ehre of Sarasota, Florida, co-editor of the *Best Sports Stories* anthologies, was about seven years old when he and his brother went to see Houdini's act at the Temple Theater in Rochester, New York. Mr. Ehre recently recalled the experience for the writer. The Ehre boys had tickets for seats in the second balcony which their father, a tailor, had received in return for displaying a Houdini showcard in his shop window. They got to the theater early and joined about ten other people of all ages who

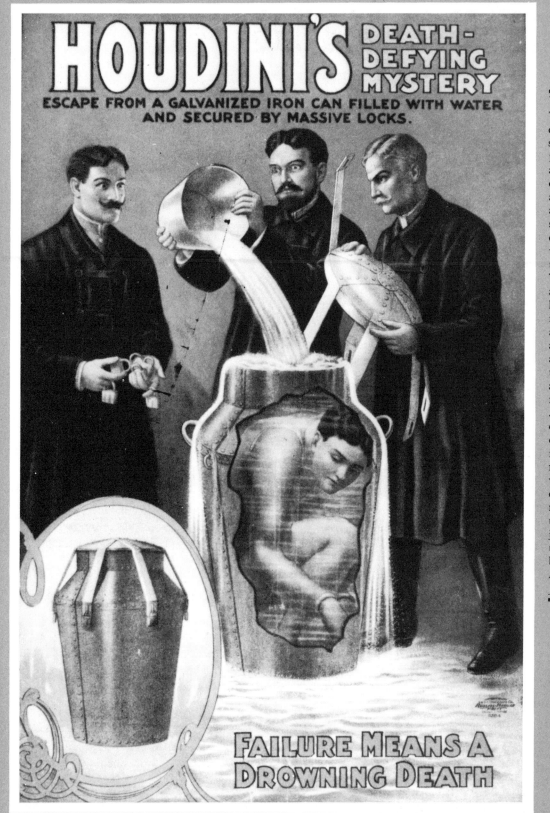

HOUDINI'S DEATH-DEFYING MYSTERY

ESCAPE FROM A GALVANIZED IRON CAN FILLED WITH WATER AND SECURED BY MASSIVE LOCKS.

FAILURE MEANS A DROWNING DEATH

This dramatic poster features Harry Houdini's famous stunt of escaping from a steel milk can overflowing with water poured into it by a committee from the audience. As Houdini performed it, the escape was a masterpiece of endurance and suspense. He would first tell the audience to hold their breaths for sixty seconds while he immersed himself in the can without the top on. After his head went under water the committee filled up the can to compensate for the spillage. The seconds dragged by and, one after another, the spectators gave up trying to hold their breaths any longer. Reappearing, Houdini caught his breath, looked around and finally gave the signal for the actual test. He disappeared into the can and the committee could see his head under the water. The lid was pressed on and clamped down, a curtain drawn. A minute went by . . . a minute and a half . . . two minutes. Remembering their own failure to go even one minute without breathing, the spectators grew panicky. Finally, someone shouted a plea to rescue Houdini immediately, else it would be too late. Others joined in the outcry, pandemonium broke out, the manager and stage hands rushed onto the stage with wrenches and axes . . . just as Houdini staggered from behind the curtain, dripping, panting, exhausted, but alive. *(Poster courtesy of the Houdini Magical Hall of Fame)*

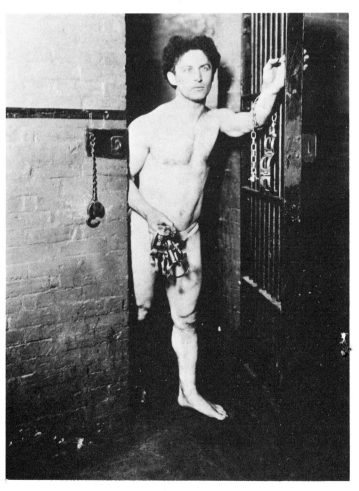

were waiting at the stage door to see Houdini arrive. When the great escape artist appeared he asked all the "stage door Johnnies," in the most friendly way, if they would be interested in earning a couple of dollars. Everyone enthusiastically agreed and Houdini ushered them all inside. They were instructed to wait in the wings until Houdini's act began; then he called them all onto the stage and introduced them to the audience as local people who would see that everything was done fairly.

Several employees of Rochester's biggest department store then came on stage in carpenters' clothes, bringing heavy lumber, tools and plenty of big nails. With these, they constructed a massive box about as long as a coffin, while the other local people watched. Houdini, wearing a business suit, climbed in. The top was solidly nailed on and the box bound with rope or chains. A screen was placed around it and for ten minutes the orchestra played while everyone waited in suspense. Suddenly Houdini emerged from the screen, disheveled and perspiring, but free. The box was intact.

"Remember, the men who built the box were all local fellows," Mr. Ehre marveled. "Houdini shook hands with us all and his business manager gave each of us two dollars, which was a fortune in those days. I've always wondered how he did it. There couldn't have been any false panel in the box because they built it right in front of us. And there wasn't enough room inside the box to give Houdini leverage space enough to work on it."

A number of escape effects which can be used in magic acts are shown in these pages. The secrets of Houdini's great effects, however, mostly died with him, despite various books that have explained some of them. His methods remain cloaked in mystery, but his personality stands out, keen, smiling and friendly, across the years.

TOP LEFT: Harry Houdini (1874–1926), the greatest escape artist of all time. (*Mario Carrandi Collection*)

LEFT: The prison cell that could hold Houdini was never built. Here he emerges from a cell in which he was locked stark naked and loaded with chains and shackles. He is carrying the fetters.

LOCK PICKING SET
Contains 32 Picks, Tension wrenches and Extracters.
Our No. 41 Instructions included - $37.50 ppd.

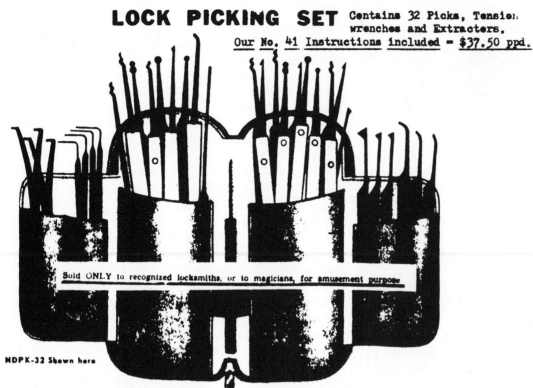

Sold ONLY to recognized locksmiths, or to magicians, for amusement purpose

NDPK-32 Shown here

THESE PICKS are made by the world's largest producer and have been the standard preference for many years.

A UNIQUE COLLECTION, IN THE PICK SET LINE

PRYNCE E. WHEELER

AUSTRALIAN BELT AND MUFF

We are now making up this fine escape item, which has now been off the market for several years. This is as sensational as the Straight Jacket for full view escaping and is ure to create interest and is decidedly different. This outfit consists of a wide leather belt, whichfastens in the back, with large leather loops and heavy chains and rings. The arms and wrists are enclosed in the leather loops and securely fastened with the chains and padlocks.

Escape is made quickly in a matter of seconds and in full view, if desired. Everything is bonifide - no trick chains, locks or buckles - and can be completly examined before and after.

Made of heavy full-grained leather, heavy duty hardware and chrome plated chains.

With complete instructions .... $27.50 ppd.

PRYNCE E. WHEELER

THE MASTER METHOD FOR ESCAPEING FROM HANDCUFFS

The basic method, or secret, of this has been only lightly touched on in the past, and present, publications but never has there been a more completly written explanation than this one...everything most completely explained. This is the Master Method of Escape!

Price $1.00 ppd.

PRYNCE E. WHEELER

X-L SPIRIT SPIRIT TIE

For those who are looking for a practical, and the very best, rope tie. AND, for those that have tried, and fooled around with ties that have been on the market, and have found them so impractical!

This is the best that I have ever see and it has fooled some of the fellows that are well posted in the game!

This is not a complicated, or tricky, appearing tie AND there are no phony moves to secure slack!

The X-L Spirit Spirit Tie is simple and secure looking ...it looks like a secure tie, which would hold anyone!

IN OPERATION: Your wrists are encircled, and bound, with a length of rope TIGHTLY, and securly. They can even try to pull your wrists apart after you are tied; they will not give! It just takes a few seconds under cover and you are out of the rope and tie! Perfect for sack escapes or any demonstration of Escape abilities; and has great Comedy possibilities!

Only a limited number of instructions are printed up ...so, if you are looking for a Pope Tie, that you can and will be able to use ...look no further; THIS IS IT!

X-L SPIRIT SPIRIT ROPE TIE
fully explained and illustrated ....$2.50 P.P.

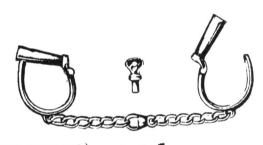

(HIATT-ENGLAND)   Nr. 8-E

DARBY PTN. NON-ADJUSTABLE LEG IRONS.

Famous, no nonsense, English Leg Irons and type much used by Houdini in Escape work.

Companion iron to Handcuffs shown else where.

A heavy Leg Iron with heavy connecting step chain..

Price ....$35.00 ppd..

"ESCAPE KING" MAGIC EQUIPMENT

"THE HANDCUFF KING ACT and SENSATIONAL ESCAPES". $8.00 postpaid. Exclusive limited edition,

The HANDCUFF KING ACT and SENSATIONAL ESCAPES is a greatly expanded and enlarged new edition, with over 100 illustrations showing keys, master keys, lock picks and gimmicks for use in handcuff escapes, including methods of jail escapes and publicity stunts, along with various sensational escape features like the 20 foot chain escape using borrowed locks. How to fix handcuffs for instant release, as required in underwater escapes after jumping from bridge or piers, or enclosed in box tossed into the ocean or river. The new Burling Hull escape from straight jacket WHILE HANGING UPSIDE DOWN ON ROPE FROM UNDERNEATH A HELICOPTER TRAVELING ALL OVER THE CITY TO PROMOTE PUBLICITY FOR SPORT SHOWS AND VARIOUS NATIONAL AND STATE EVENTS. Replaces the old Houdini escape, hanging from the yardarm from only one building. The Helicopter Escape is seen from all over the entire city, exciting curiosity about the man seen hanging from a rope under helicopter making escape from straight jacket.

ORIGINALY INTENDED TO SELL FOR $8.00, BUT NOW ONLY...........$5.50 ppd. Ins'd.

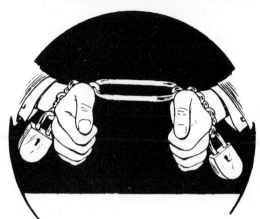

A POSITIVE HIT
With All Magicians!
Abbott's CHAIN HANDCUFFS

An escape feature that is SOCKO ENTERTAINMENT.

Solid steel chains permanently fastened to a welded connecting link and two padlocks are given for examination. A spectator is helpless with them on. Now you have the chain handcuffs locked on your wrists, **behind your back.** In a matter of seconds **you are FREE!** — or — with a committee on the stage, you perform stunts that cause fun and laughter — hands appear on shoulders, spectators' pens and handkerchiefs are taken from their pockets — and no matter how often they inspect the Magician's hands, he is always securely handcuffed. As a finale, Magician gives handcuffs, still securely locked, to spectators for further examination.

A SENSATIONAL FINISH !

One second Magician is securely handcuffed; the next second he calmly walks forward, and — to the amazement of all — it is seen that both volunteer helpers are handcuffed to each other — and they can be freed only by unlocking the CHAIN HANDCUFFS! What a surprise! Audiences will rave about it! A few minutes to master — always ready — **no** assistants — no preparation. All parts plated.

ABBOTT'S MAGIC MANUFACTURING CO., $11.00; DELIVERED, $12.00

The Ghost Walks

A flat board is shown. Board is coffin shaped and fitted with a series of holes, reinforced with metal grommets. It is stained a spooky green with a life-size skeleton in silver. Magician explains that the skeleton represents the "ghost" of a departed Escapologist.

The board, together with a length of chain and a padlock, are carefully examined. Magician now steps up against the board and permits members of the audience to fasten him securely to the board by means of the chains. As the chains are passed through the metal rimmed holes, the sound is very spooky. Suddenly Magician calmly walks free of the chains. This is accomplished IN FULL VIEW.

Board measures approximately 30 x 72" and breaks down for packing. Weight including everything, 25 pounds. Can be set ready to work in two minutes. Workshop Plans available.

ABBOTT'S MAGIC MANUFACTURING CO.,
$100.00 FOB COLON, MICHIGAN. PLANS, $3.00

DID YOU KNOW. . .

The Smith & Wesson Company has placed on the market an allegedly pick-proof handcuff known as Maximum Security.

Each cuff has only ONE KEY, thus making the use of the key system obsolete. The only method of escape is to pick open this allegedly pick-proof cuff.

The method and tools are explained in:

THE BIGELOW COURSE IN ESCAPE ARTISTRY
LESSON TWO
THE STRAIT JACKET & MAXIMUM SECURITY

You will learn:

> How to Escape Jackets
> Applying Ropes
> Rigs & Suspensions
> More On Cuffs
> Maximum Security Cuff

Only $13.00

Don't Forget:
Lesson One . . . How to Pick Police Handcuffs.
EXPERT MANIPULATION OF HANDCUFFS
Only $15.00

Also available: Handcuff Pick Set $12.00; Mini Pick Set $5.00; Pro Shim for Handcuff $1.50; Bridge Jumper Cuff $20.00; Houdini Photos (4) $2.00 each; Siberian Chain Escape $2.00; 33 Rope Ties and Chain Releases $2.00; Houdini On Magic $2.50; Secrets of Houdini $2.50; Regulation Double Locking Handcuffs $12.50; Bigelow Photo $1.00.

MICKEY-"O" ENTERPRISES
606 Fifth Avenue, Dept. LR, Brooklyn, N. Y. 11215
Add $1.00 for postage on all orders. NY residents add sales tax.

MICKEY-"O" ENTERPRISES

ANTIQUE MAGIC AND CATALOGUES

A special group in the magic world are the collectors. They collect old-time magical apparatus, posters, catalogues and memorabilia. They are fascinated by the rare and colorful creations of the master magic craftsmen of the nineteenth and early twentieth centuries. Collectors are also, necessarily, students of magic history. They enjoy researching the lives and careers of magicians and preserving their personal letters, photographs and other memorabilia.

No one who examines fine old pieces of magic can fail to be impressed by the high order of imagination and craftsmanship they represent. Usually these pieces were handmade by skilled machinists, cabinet makers, watchmakers or jewelers. Even less expensive tricks, such as the popular billiard-ball vases, were turned from boxwood and are far more pleasing than the cheap plastic articles so common today.

Among the dealers who manufactured and imported the finest magic certain names stand out. In London, in the second half of the last century and the early years of the present one, there were Bland's; their successors, Hamley Brothers; and the magical department of Gamage's, under the direction of Will Goldston. A country especially noted for intricate mechanisms, finely constructed, was Germany. There Carl Willmann, János Bartl, and Conradi were "names to conjure with." In the United States, the preeminent dealer and headquarters

Magical Antiques. *Left to right:* Bran vase by Donald Holmes; Thayer rice-to-orange vase (wood, hand-turned, originally with natural finish, but later gilded); nineteenth-century burning globe; Davenport cabinet. (*Mario Carrandi Collection*)

for magic in America was Martinka & Company of New York and Ossig, Germany. Headed by brothers Francis and Antonio Martinka, the firm was established in 1873 and continued to operate independently until 1919, when it was bought by Houdini. Pages from its magnificent catalogue of 1898, and views of its showroom and construction shop, appears on pages 168-171. Martinka's was eventually combined with the Hornmann Magic Company, operated by Otto Hornmann at 270 West 39th Street and later at 470 Eighth Avenue, New York. After Hornmann's death the combined Hornmann-Martinka concern was carried on at 304 West 34th Street by Frank Ducrot. He in turn passed it on to Al Flosso, the great coin worker, and it is operated today by Al's son, Jack.

Other outstanding dealers about the turn of the century included Yost of Philadelphia, August Roterberg of Chicago, W. D. Leroy of Boston, and the Mysto Company, the "Magical Mechanicians" of New Haven. Mysto also had a store in New York. A few years later John N. Petrie (1870–1954), who was associated with Mysto, established in New Haven the Petrie-Lewis Manufacturing Company. This firm produced and sold a consistently high-quality line of magical apparatus and supplies for roughly half a century. Petrie-Lewis apparatus is now highly collectible. The Mysto trademark was associated later with

163

a highly successful line of boxed collections of magic tricks for children. The old Mysto catalogue (pages 186–187), however, is full of fine apparatus.

In Chicago, Arthur P. Felsman, who succeeded August Roterberg about 1915, maintained high standards and published beautiful catalogues. In California, one of the great American careers as a magic manufacturer and dealer began in 1902 when a young man named Floyd G. Thayer, an expert in the field of wood turning, began to produce fine hand-turned and hand-finished magical apparatus of wood. From 1907 on, Thayer devoted his full time to manufacturing and selling magic. He started at Pasadena; later he and a young magician and magic writer, Louis F. Christianer, opened the Magic Shop of the West in Los Angeles. Their handsome, photographically illustrated catalogue, *Magical Woodcraft,* is now a rare collector's item.

Floyd Thayer then established the Thayer Magic Manufacturing Company, with headquarters at 334 South San Pedro Street in Los Angeles. He continued to make a number of fine pieces of wooden apparatus and also sold magic from other sources. These included a number of items made by Petrie-Lewis, and many imported ones.

From the 1920s to the 1940s the handsome, thick Thayer catalogues with their wealth of effects in every branch of magic were a mainstay of the art in America. Many of Thayer's fine, hand-turned wooden items were sold with a tasteful natural finish. These were not too practical for the theater, however, as they did not make a "flash" on the stage. In the 1940s the Thayer company was taken over by William W. Larsen, Sr., and his family. They also acquired Thayer's home, a beautiful residence with a splendid magic theater. The Larsens continued the business at this headquarters in the Wilshire district, as the Thayer Studio of Magic. Thayer pieces of this period tend to be more brightly painted.

Two splendid workmen, the Owen brothers, who made some of the finest Thayer pieces, continued to operate independently. This company has now become Owen Magic Supreme. Based in Alhambra, California, it maintains the Owen Brothers tradition of superior craftsmanship and elegantly designed magic, including many illusions.

Donald Holmes of Kansas City also built especially beautiful apparatus, from about 1915 to the early 1920s.

In Philadelphia, a line of magnificent precision apparatus of brass, mainly small but elegant pieces for coin tricks, was produced by Carl Brema. In England, John Martin, a watchmaker, made beautiful, intricate, custom apparatus until his death about 1950. His pieces are now much prized.

In the coin field, the tradition of precise, quality workmanship is still being carried on today by such firms as Johnson Products of Texas and Guaranteed Magic of Pennsylvania. Generally speaking, unfortunately, standards of magical manufacture today have suffered, as in almost every other field, from the trend away from the old-time craftsman, skilled with his hands and proud of his standards, to items of cheaper materials

(*Mario Carrandi Collection*)

"THE WORLD'S ACRAZE FOR SOMETHING NEW"

CHAS. L. BURLINGAME'S

A-LOG

OF

Entirely New and Superior Wonders,

IN THE ART OF

HIGH GRADE PRESTIDIGITATION,

ANTI-SPIRITUALISTIC ILLUSIONS,

CONJURING NOVELTIES,

SENSATIONAL FEATURES.

CHAS. L. BURLINGAME,

5800 LA SALLE ST., Englewood, Cook Co., Ill.

ESTABLISHED IN 1872.

LEFT AND ABOVE: Charles L. Burlingame of Illinois used this whimsical letterhead and catalogue cover in the 1880s.

20   C. L. BURLINGAME'S CATALOGUE OF NOVELTIES.

97.—THE WINGED NUMBERS.

A fine anti-spiritualistic trick, first time offered for sale in America. Any person writes any number he pleases on a slip of paper, seals it in an envelope which performer holds in flame of candle until consumed, then loads the ashes in his pistol and shoots at a white handkerchief held by another person, and the same number appears in centre of the handkerchief. A sensational trick and startling effect.   Price............ 3 00

98.—THE CELEBRATED BANK NOTE TEST.

A splendid sensational trick, and first time offered for sale. To write on a black board the number of a bank note brought by a perfect stranger and sealed in an envelope by him. Performer never sees note from beginning to end. Not to be had elsewhere. Failure impossible. Price........... 3 00

99.—THE SPIRIT PITCHER.

Performer invites a committee of four, five or six persons on stage, hands each one an empty glass, shows an ordinary pitcher of water and pours out for committee, first, one-half of them wine, the other half water, then all wine, then all water, then all wine again, you taking "something with them" each time, but not like theirs, you being "temperate." All from same pitcher. First-class for anti-spiritualists. Full secret.. 3 00

100.—REDMONDI'S SPIRIT CARD TRICK.

For cabinet or canopy only. Medium in canopy at once selects any number of cards drawn by audience. New and fine effect. Price... 3 00

101.—THE READING OF FOLDED PAPERS.

To read folded papers written on by audience. Improved method, with new writing on the arm. A trick that satisfies the audience. For experienced performers. Price.... .... 3 00

Rare Magic. Three small turned wood tricks, including (*upper left*) Morrison's Pill Box, in which a ball is made to vanish and reappear in a small wooden pedestal; (*upper right*) color-changing and vanishing egg; (*below*) improved ball and hammer trick, about 1910. (*Sotheby's Belgravia*)

mass-produced by machinery. Much of the less expensive magic now comes from Japan and Taiwan.

Since the 1960s, however, individual craftsmanship has been carried on by more people everywhere, and this movement has not been without its effect in magic. In Springfield, Missouri, for example, Ben D. Stone's Delben Company makes fine apparatus almost entirely by hand, including a two-hole wrist chopper and handsome die boxes and other pieces in wood with natural finish.

The last quarter of the nineteenth century and the first quarter of the present one, when so much elegant apparatus was made, also saw the production of outstanding magic posters. Some of the beautiful posters used by Kellar, Thurston, Servais Le Roy and others appear in this book. These posters were made by the lithographic process, the artist's original painting being transferred to stone, from which the colored sheets were printed. The colors of these fine lithographs are as bright

today as they were half a century or more ago. Lithography was expensive even in those days, however: the poster cost somewhere in the neighborhood of 10 cents apiece, and since thousands of them were used, only top professional magicians could afford them. The larger ones were printed in sections called "sheets." A really large one may be 9 feet high or more and cover half the side of a barn.

The Tiffany of poster lithographers, Harry Kellar used to say, was the Strobridge company, who made practically all his "paper." The Strobridge headquarters were in New York, with branch offices in Cincinnati and London. The London operation was phased out about 1880, I am informed by Mario Carrandi, dealer in rare magic and authority on magic posters. Early in the second decade of the century the New York operation was moved to Cincinnati. The last Strobridge posters were made for the Barnum and Bailey circus about 1921. After a devastating fire in Cincinnati, the firm closed

Left to right: Botania tube, chrome plated, for the magical growth of flowers: Arabian burning globe; cotton-to-coffee vase; early Passe Passe Bottle and Glass set. (*Sotheby's Belgravia*)

down. Most of the beautiful posters used by Thurston, Kellar's successor, after 1921 were made by Otis Lithographs, in which the magician had an interest.

Almost all the artists of the beautiful magic posters remain anonymous. One exception to this is the early Kellar poster (page 25) based on a painting by A. Rimman. Most magicians' paper was full of colorful detail. Mario Carrandi points out that in those days, when people did more of their moving about on foot and less by auto, they used to enjoy looking at poster details from close to. It was Kellar, Carrandi reports, who introduced the characteristic imps seen in most of his and Thurston's paper. The artists, however, were responsible for the little philosopher goblins who are shown in Thurston's posters, scratching their heads and consulting a weighty tome in a vain search for an answer to the question, "How does he do it?"

Most of the magic manufacturers and dealers mentioned above, as well as many others, published extensive catalogues which were revised at fairly frequent intervals. The most common size of these catalogues was about 9 inches high by 5 or 6 inches wide. Others were pocket-sized and some, especially the Hamley and Gamage catalogues, much larger in trim size. The catalogues of the larger companies ran to around 200 pages or more. They were extensively illustrated with engravings and linecuts and often also with photographs of tricks, the dealer's establishment, and contemporary magicians. These old magic catalogues make fascinating as well as informative reading, and they are prized today by magic collectors. Some of the most interesting of them are shown in the pages that follow.*

* All the catalogues in this section of the book are from the author's collection. The companies that issued them have since ceased operations or, in one or two cases, been absorbed in newer organizations. Needless to say, the tricks advertised in this section are no longer available, except perhaps occasionally from a dealer in rare magic. I have reproduced the original prices to show the bargains once available.

ILLUSTRATED AND DESCRIPTIVE CATALOGUE OF NEW AND SUPERIOR CONJURING WONDERS

MAGICAL APPARATUS. INGENIOUS PUZZLES, SCIENTIFIC AND OTHER NOVELTIES. ETC. OF MARTINKA & CO., The only World Manufacturers and IMPORTERS in this line. 493 Sixth Ave. N.Y. AND OSSIG, Germany.

Established 1873.

LEFT: Cover of the Martinka & Company catalogue of 1898, one of the most beautiful magic catalogues ever published.

RIGHT: At the turn of the century, Martinka & Company, established in 1873, was the magic headquarters of America. *Above:* The main part of the construction room. *Below:* The Martinka showroom. Both drawings from the 1898 catalogue.

289. The Marvelous "Fan," or The Four Seasons.

Performer gives a handsome cedarwood fan to a lady to hold. On opening, it is seen that on one side are painted lovely spring flowers and on the other side summer roses. The lady closes the fan, and upon opening it again it is found, to every one's astonishment, that both of the former pictures have vanished, and in place of the spring flower is now a fall scene, and instead of the roses a winter landscape. The pictures are all artistically hand painted......................Price, **$2.00**

290. Plate, Flour and Dove.

Eggs and flour are mixed on a plate, and same is covered with another plate, and uncovering the plate instantly, live pigeons, with previously borrowed rings attached to their necks, appear, the flour having completely vanished.

Price, **$3.00**

291. The Mysterious Half-Dollar.

A genuine half-dollar is pushed from the outside into a gentleman's hat, and shown to be sticking through it. It is pulled out again in full view of the spectators, and the hat returned uninjured. This is a great improvement on the old style penetrative coin, as the half-dollar can always be shown in full size. A very fine mechanical trick......Price, **$1.50**

ABOVE AND OPPOSITE: Pages from the Martinka catalogue of 1898.

520. The Mystic Pillar and the Flying Cards.

The performer shows a finely chased and nickel plated pillar, which he places upon the table. A card is selected, returned to the pack and placed at the foot of the Mystic Pillar. Now the performer commands the whole of the pack of cards to fly in the air. The command is obeyed, for all the cards fly into the air, and the selected card is seen to leave the others and fly into the hand of the figure on top of the pillar. It is quite impossible to convey the enchanting effect of this beautiful trick. . . . . , Price, **$15**

521. Fairy Vase and Magic Cards.

A handsome vase of flowers is shown to the audience, and some of the flowers are taken from it and presented to the ladies to show that they are real. The audience is now asked to choose three cards from a pack. These are burned, and the ashes sprinkled over the flowers, when instantly the cards reappear perfect, standing on the flowers, and are then taken out and given to the audience to see if they are the same cards. . . Price, **$7 50**

522. Mysterious Chest of Drawers.

A beautiful little chest of drawers is shown, and the drawers taken out and given to the audience for examination. Four cards are now selected by the audience, and one placed in each drawer, which are then replaced in the chest. The cards are now commanded to disappear one a time, each drawer being shown perfectly empty as they disappear. The cabinet can also be used for other transformation tricks. Price, **$25**

No. 5596.—The Unfortunate Sunshade.—The performer borrows a sunshade and a pocket handkerchief. He wraps the sunshade in a piece of newspaper and gives it to a gentleman to hold, and then tears the handkerchief into strips and wraps them in another piece of paper and gives that to another gentleman to hold; a change is now commanded to take place, and, opening the parcel that contained the sunshade, the cover is found to have disappeared, leaving only the bare ribs, from each of which hangs a strip of the handkerchief, and in the other parcel is found the cover. The strips of handkerchief are taken off and placed in another apparatus and restored.

Price **7/6.** *Post free* **8/-.** *With full directions.*
Superior quality **18/6.** *Post free* **19/-.**

No. 5597. The Fairy Flower Stand. — A neat metal stand is freely given for examination, and some mould and seed is placed on it; an empty tin cover, less than one inch high, is placed over it, the performer makes a few passes with his hand, and lifting off the cover there appears a beautiful bouquet of flowers, quite five inches high.

Price **8/6.** *Post free* **9/-.** *With full directions.*
Superior quality, very handsome, **12/-.** *Post free* **12/8.**

No. 5597A. The Fairy Triple Changing Bouquet.—A large bouquet of white flowers is shown. It is then covered with a red handkerchief, and upon removing the handkerchief the flowers are seen to have assumed that colour. A blue handkerchief is now taken and with it the bouquet is again covered, which also is removed, and this time the flowers have changed from red to blue. This makes a good effect, because of its size and pretty colouring.

Price **8/6.** *Post free* **8/10.**

No. 5598. The Charmed Pack of Cards and Handkerchief.—The performer first shows a little case, into which he places his pack of cards, for which it is just the size; he then closes it and asks a lady to hold it. Now he takes a silk handkerchief, and showing his hands empty and having his sleeves turned up, he slowly rubs it in his hands until it disappears, and in its place there is the pack of cards; then asking the lady to open the case, she finds, to her surprise, that the cards have vanished and there is only the silk handkerchief in it, which entirely fills it. Very pretty and effective.

Price **5/6.** *Post free* **5/9.** *With full directions.*

No. 5598A. The Latest Colour Changing Handkerchief.—The performer borrows a silk handkerchief, say red in colour. He then shows both hands perfectly empty. He takes a corner of the handkerchief in his left hand and draws it through his closed fingers two or three times. He then says he will change it into, say, blue. He draws it again through his fingers, and, to their astonishment, the audience see that as it is drawn through the closed hand the part that remains is red, and as fast as it comes through it is changed in colour, being now a beautiful dark blue. The effect of this trick is most pretty, and, owing to the excellence of the apparatus we supply, can be very easily performed, which enables it to be very gracefully done. We can highly recommend this very pretty trick.

Price **8/6.** *Post free* **8/8.**

No. 5599. The Marvellous Appearance of Three Cards on the Back of any Chair.—This trick can be performed with any chair. You bring forward a chair and ask any one to examine it. You then take a pack of cards and ask three people to choose one each, place in the pack and shuffle. Next command them to pass, when instantly they appear on the back of the chair (which has been examined). Take the cards off and ask the audience if they are the ones that they chose, and again give the chair for examination. This trick is worked without a confederate or assistant.

Price **6/3.** *Post free* **6/6.** *With full directions.*

No. 5599A. The Latest Changing Billiard Ball and Handkerchief Trick.—The performer shows an ordinary billiard ball and holds it in his right hand. Next he, with his left, picks up a silk handkerchief. He then commences to wave his arms gently up and down, and suddenly a change is seen to have taken place, the billiard ball in the right hand having changed to a handkerchief and the handkerchief in the left hand having changed to a billiard ball. The hands are then shown empty with the exception of the articles mentioned, which are freely shown to the audience.

Price (in ivorine) **6/6** *complete. Post free* **6/9.**

No. 5600. Producing Eggs from a Borrowed Hat.—The performer in this trick borrows a gentleman's silk hat, turns up his sleeves and shows his arms quite bare and hands empty. He then shows the hat to the audience, and turns it mouth downwards to prove that it is quite empty. He holds the hat at arm's length with the left hand. His right hand again he shows perfectly empty and then places it in the hat and brings out a real egg, which he places on a plate. Then again he puts his hand in and brings out another, and places this also on the plate, till he produces six or seven, all the while holding the hat with the mouth downwards. He then asks the audience to select one and break it to prove that they are real eggs, and they can examine the hat as much as they please. This is a most astonishing trick.

Price **5/6.** *Post free* **5/8.** *With full directions.*

No. 5600A. The Latest Changing Flag Illusion.—A Stars and Stripes Flag is taken and held by the two top corners. It is distinctly shown, quite slowly, back and front. The performer then waves it gently to and fro, when in a flash it is seen to have changed to the Union Jack, which is again shown both sides. This change is remarkable for its quickness and incomprehensibility. There is no false move, yet it is impossible for the audience to solve. We can highly recommend it.

In two sizes :—No. 1. 18 inches square, price **7/6.** *Post free* **7/9.**
No. 2. 32 „ „ „ **24/-.** *„* **24/3.**

5—2

ABOVE AND OPPOSITE: Pages from the *Illustrated Catalogue of Conjuring Tricks* issued by Hamley Brothers, Ltd., London, about 1909.

No. 5782. **The Fairy Box for Florins.**—Four florins are borrowed and placed in the box, which a lady is asked to hold. At the desire of the performer they leave the box one by one (the lady opening it each time) until all have disappeared. They are then produced from elsewhere. This trick works very well in conjunction with the Florin Wand (No. 5095). The mechanism of this beautiful trick will excite great admiration, and being manufactured by our own workmen, we can guarantee each to be of the best finish, and not at all likely to get out of order. Handsomely covered with plush, and with gilt mounts, on an entirely new principle, enabling the performer unseen to gain possession of the marked coins, which may be placed in the box by the audience. It can be used with either florins or half-crowns.

Price **24/6.** *Post free* **24/9.** *With full directions.*
Very Superior Quality, Nickel-Plated, to reproduce the Coins,
Price **52/6.** *Post free,* **52/10.**

No. 5783. **The Horn of Plenty, or Magic Cornucopia.** — A large cornucopia, beautifully ornamented and japanned, is given to the audience for thorough examination. The performer places it down and waves his wand over it three times; then, lifting it up, he proceeds to distribute from it flowers, bonbons, sweets, toys, &c., in seemingly endless profusion, thus proving it really to be a "horn of plenty." When all are distributed, he again shows it empty, as at first. THIS FORMS A VERY BEAUTIFUL AND EFFECTIVE WAY OF DISTRIBUTING GIFTS.

Price **39/6.** *With full directions.*
Very superior, elegantly japanned, **60/-.**
Carriage to be paid on receipt.

No. 5784. **The Red, White and Blue Dyeing Handkerchief and the Union Jack Flag.**—Three white handkerchiefs are shown to the audience. A piece of white paper, which is given for examination, is then rolled into a cylinder, and held in the left hand of the performer, who then takes one of the handkerchiefs and pushes it right through the paper cylinder to show that the latter is quite empty; he takes it again and pushes it through the cylinder, and to the astonishment of the company they see it coming out at the top red, then the other two white handkerchiefs are pushed through and come out respectively blue and white; these three handkerchiefs are then placed over the back of a chair and the paper opened to prove that there is nothing concealed in it; it can also be examined before and afterwards. It is now taken again and rolled into a larger cylinder, which is held in the left hand as before, but this time the performer picks up the three handkerchiefs all at one time, namely, red, white and blue— the national colours—and pushes them through the paper cylinder, when, to the amazement of the company, they are seen appearing at the other end. But no, they are mistaken; certainly the colours are the same, but this time the handkerchiefs have disappeared, and in their place is seen a beautiful Union Jack Flag, which the performer shows to the audience. He remarks that England is larger than that, so takes and pushes the flag through and pulls it out at the top, when to the astonishment of the company it seems to have grown four times the size—in fact, into a large Union Jack Flag, which the performer shakes and holds up before all the company, showing it back and front. The paper cylinder is then opened and shown quite empty.

Price **21/6.** *Post free* **21/9.** *With full instructions.*

No. 5784A. **The Marvellous Dove Tub Illusion.**—The performer takes and shows freely to the audience a handsome enamelled jug which is full of water. Any of the audience that pleases may put his hand into the jug, and thus ascertain that it is quite unprepared. Then an elegant tub, enamelled in the same way as the jug, is also shown, and may be examined as closely as possible. The tub is put down and the jug is placed into it. The performer then draws up his sleeves and shows his hands empty, and arms perfectly bare, and, if desired, also buttons up his coat. He takes the jug and simply pours out some water, when, to the astonishment of the audience, out fly two very pretty doves.

This trick is essentially suitable for either drawing-room or stage; there is no mess and no trouble in connection with it, and it is extremely simple to work. Moreover, it is very useful in connection with any tricks wherein doves are used, as the doves can be produced from the tub with a ring, watch, or any other similar article tied round the neck. We can highly recommend this pretty and fascinating trick. *Price complete,* **24/-.** *Carriage to be paid on receipt.*

No. 5785. **The Magi's Rose Tree.**—Very novel. The performer takes from his Magic Portfolio, which is only 3 inches deep, a large rose tree, in a sexagon-shaped pot, which is handsomely painted. The flower pot and tree stand 2 feet 4 inches high, and the pot is 6½ inches in diameter. THIS HAS A VERY PRETTY EFFECT, AND IS ALSO AN ORNAMENT TO THE STAGE.

Price **34/-.** *Post free* **34/6.**
With full directions.

No. 5786. **The Wonderful Round Flying Cage.**—This cage, which has been hanging up all the evening, is taken down by the performer, who holds it in one hand simply by the ring at the top, when suddenly, without covering it in any way, it vanishes entirely. The cage is beautifully made of metal, silver-plated, and works with the greatest ease, and can be used more gracefully than the square one.

Price **27/6.** *Post free* **27/10.**
With full directions.

No. 5787. **The Fairy Canteen and Bird Cage.**—The performer brings forward a large and beautifully japanned canister, from which he distributes a quantity of bonbons, flowers, toys, &c., until it is empty. He then fills it with cotton wool and places two eggs in it; then closing it, he commands a change to take place, and, removing the cover, he produces from it a large cage with two live birds in it. VERY ASTONISHING EFFECT, AS THE CAGE IS AS LARGE AS THE CANTEEN ITSELF. *Price* **28/-.** *With full directions.*

Extra large, very handsome, with **three** *large cages,* **44/6.**
Carriage to be paid on receipt.

HAT TRICKS

Any Hat Trick not mentioned in this Catalogue can be supplied.

No. 141.
The Finger through the Hat.

You borrow a hat from a gentleman in the audience, when you immediately push your finger through the crown; you appear to be sorry for doing such a silly thing, but the owner feels annoyed, and the audience are highly amused at the joke; yet the conjuror returns the hat in a perfect condition.

Price, complete with full instructions, **6**d.
Postage 1d.

No. 142.
The Wandering Die.

A solid die after being inspected by the company placed on the crown of a borrowed hat, which the conjuror holds by the rim. An examined cover, just large enough to put over the die, is then placed over the latter, which upon command passes through the hat and falls upon the floor.

The cover is shown to be quite empty.

Price, complete with full instructions, **6**d.
Postage 3d.

Large professional size, **2/-**   Postage 3d.

No. 143.   The Hypnotised Hat.

The magician makes a few passes over a gentleman's hat, and by allowing his hands to touch the crown of the hat, "Hi Presto," he raises it off the table and swings it about.

This pretty and novel trick is quite easy to learn.
Price, complete with instructions, **1/6**
Postage 1d.

Coils.

Machine rolled best quality, 5 or 6 in., bright colours, **2/-** per doz.   Post 6d.

3 doz., **5/6**
Post free.

No. 144.

6 doz., **10/6**   Carriage paid.

7 or 8 in., plain, white or blue, **2/6** per doz.
Postage 6d.

Mouth Coils, **5½**d. doz.   Postage 1d.
Special offer.   Throwouts, **9**d. doz.   Post 2d.
Sold elsewhere 3/6 per doz.

No. 145.

To create great laughter you cannot do better.

From a borrowed hat you produce a large cabbage or loaf of bread.

Price, complete with full instructions, **1/3**

Postage 3d.

No. 146.
Bundle of Firewood from Hat.

The conjuror produces from a borrowed hat a quantity of articles, including a bundle of firewood.

Price, firewood, with full instructions, **1/6**
Postage 4d.
Improved method, bundle of wood can be shown both ends.   Price **2/-**   Postage 4d.

No. 147.
The Babies for Producing from a Hat.

From any borrowed hat you instantly produce several of these babies, each higher than the hat itself, and you can stand them on a table.

Price, complete with full instructions, **1/6** each.
Postage 3d.

Professional size, nicely dressed, **10/6** each.
Postage 6d.

No. 148.   The Penetrative Cone.

This wonderful Cone is made to pass through a borrowed hat without injuring same.   Highly recommended by the leading magicians.

Complete, **2/6**   Post 3d.

No. 149.   The Enchanted Boxes.

The performer brings from a borrowed hat 12 fancy boxes.
Price, complete with full instructions, **3/-**
Postage 3d.

No. 150.
The Six Fairy Reticules.

Produced from any borrowed hat.

Price, set of 6, complete with full instructions, **3/6**
Postage 4d.

No. 151.
The Merry Pastry Cook.

This is a very novel and undetectable manner of performing the laughable "Pudding in the Hat" trick.   After the hat is borrowed and placed on a cane-seat chair, the performer mixes up a quantity of flower, water, eggs, &c., in a thin silvered plate, and to the discomfiture of the possessor of the hat, deliberately pours the mixture into the latter.   As a true representative of his art, he repairs the damage, then produces a cake from the hat, returning the latter uninjured to its owner.
The newest and best method for performing this trick.
Price, complete with full instructions and large handsome plate, **4/-**   Postage 3d.

No. 152.
Enchanted Flower Garden from Borrowed Hat.

The performer borrows a hat, and to prove it is empty he turns it upside down. Without his hands touching any part of his body, he produces quite a quantity of beautiful flowers which he drops on a table, where they immediately take root standing upright.

Charming effect and easy to perform.

Complete with full instructions, **4/3** per dozen.
Superior quality, **1/-** each, or **10/6**
Postage 3d.

D

LEFT AND RIGHT: Pages from magic catalogues of A. W. Gamage, Ltd., London, c. 1909–1910. Gamage's magic department was directed by the noted conjurer Will Goldston.

Stage Illusions—*continued.*

No. 618. ☞
The Magic Drummer.

This little figure is completely isolated, and represents a regimental drummer upon a very highly ornamental stand, the finish and workmanship being of the very best. The performer has cards selected and dice thrown, all of which are correctly indicated by the figure tapping upon the drum. Questions are answered and dates given by distinct taps upon the drum.

Price, complete with full instructions, **£10 10 0.** Carriage free.

A Star Attraction!
No. 630. The Great Cannon Trick.

This illusion has caused a great stir in magical circles of late and is guaranteed to cause a fine sensation. The effect is as follows :—

The audience is shewn a large cannon upon a solid carriage, a lady is introduced and a borrowed handkerchief tied to her wrist. The performer places the lady into the cannon and immediately fires it at the gallery, where the lady is seen safe and sound with the borrowed handkerchief tied to her wrist.

This forms a really marvellous illusion, as we guarantee that no double is used and that the lady fired into the air is the same to appear in the gallery.

The cannon is made to wheel about the stage and has a very real appearance.

Price complete. **£25 0 0** Carriage forward.

No. 631. The Goldston "Aga" Illusion.

First introduced by Will Goldston.

Price, complete with full instructions. **£35**

Carriage free.

The superb effect of this, the newest "Aga," is unequalled in the annals of conjuring. Not only is it performed in full daylight, but it is performed in full glare of the limelight if need be, and is far in advance of any other method, for, not only does the usual levitation and "ring passing" occur whilst the performer is moving about and in front of the suspended lady, but whilst the body is suspended the performer actually leaves the stage entirely, or stands at the wings, and by the motions of his hands brings the suspended lady to rest upon the couch as at first.

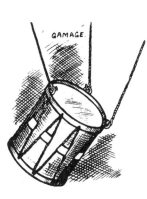

No. 633.
The Enchanted Military Drum.

Nothing different from any ordinary drum is to be observed in this one, which the performer freely shows. It is hung in mid-air, and the "spirits" commanded to beat a military tattoo, which they do in perfect time. The drum now keeps time to music, tells the time, answers questions, etc., in a most astounding fashion; yet it may be handed down for examination at any moment. Automatic and not liable to become disordered.

Price, complete with full instructions—

Small size, **55/-**   Large size, **90/-**

Superior make, **£7 7 0**   Carriage forward.

No. 635. The Second Advent of Rip Van Winkle.

The performer tells the story of Rip Van Winkle—of his sleep for 20 years, etc.—and asserts that he did not die, but made himself invisible, leaving behind him a message informing anyone whom it may concern, that if they will go to the Katskill Mountains, overlooking the Hudson River, they will find a barrel in which he will materialise. The conjuror informs the audience that at great cost he had sent to the Ka skill Mountains and brought the barrel to England. The barrel is then shewn to be absolutely empty, and then the performer proceeds to fasten in each end of the barrel à la tambourine rings. The tub is all the time resting upon trestles in a sort of rack, and beneath this all the audience can see quite clearly, so that no traps can be suspected for an instant. Nevertheless, the performer at once produces from an empty tub a marvellous "load" indeed. for the end of the tub is broken open and out crawls Rip Van Winkle, looking as sleepy as ever—in the shape of a strong man in that character. How Rip Van Winkle gets into the transparently empty tub is a mystery providing a huge ovation for the performer at each performance.

Price, complete with full instructions, **£30**
Carriage free.

No. 632.
Gamage's Black Art Skeletons.

These weird and gruesome objects are beautifully made and fitted to customers' own requirements, to dance, come apart, etc.

They are the finest grade work throughout.

Prices 21/-, 42/- 55/- to **£5 5 0**
Carriage free.

No. 634.
The Headless Countryman.

Price, complete with full instructions, **£25**
Carriage free.

The performer receives a visit from a country farming relative. During conversation, it transpires that "Goiles" has come to town in consequence of his suffering from a terrible toothache. Upon hearing this, the performer volunteers to cure him by a slight operation, which he does by completely severing the countryman's head. Whilst the head which is placed upon a small table rolls its eyes and laments its fate. Eventually the performer corrects his error, and restores the head to its proper resting place. The shock completely cures the toothache, but the countryman makes all speed to get away from such a dangerous relative.

No. 636. The Three Changes.

This marvellous and amazing illusion presents a rapid series of inexplicable changes in which no duplicate people are employed. A Hindoo and a beautiful lady change place from cage to box, from box to platform upon it. From a structure of two tables surmounted by a chair to a cage previously occupied by another person, etc. A large gong is struck, and each time it is done so, some startling and inexplicable change is seen to have taken place. The beating of the gong and its subsequent result is very wierd and sensational.

Price, complete with full instructions, **£100.**

Carriage free.

One of Harry Kellar's most
impressive posters.
(*Mario Carrandi Collection*)

Leroy's Mammoth Pictorial 20th Century Up=to=Date
Illustrated Catalogue

Conjuring
Wonders

Magic
Second Sight

Anti-
Spiritualistic
Illusions

Books, Puzzles, Novelties, Jokes, Etc., Etc.

All that is Latest, Greatest and Most Desirable for Wonder Workers ♣ ♣ ♣

W. D. LEROY

(Member "Society American Magicians")

BOSTON SCHOOL OF MAGIC

103 COURT ST., BOSTON, MASS.

TELEPHONE CONNECTION

This catalogue, one of the finest ever published in America, was issued about 1910–1915. Excerpts from it are shown on the two following pages.

648. THE ENCHANTED CLOCKS.

From a borrowed hat the performer takes, one after the other, six large clocks, looking like marble, each one being large enough to fill the hat itself. One of the latest additions to the popular hat trick. Set of six, ... Price, **$6.00**

649. Same as above, but as last clock is removed and placed on table, the alarm goes off, creating roars of laughter. An improvement. The set. . . . . " **8.00**

---

605. CARD RAISING PACK OF CARDS.

A pack of cards is placed inside a glass and is set in full view of the spectators, or anywhere they may designate. Without going near the glass, chosen cards rise from pack at command from conjuror. No assistants or confederates required. Can be done in any parlor. This is the finest mechanism ever produced in self-working apparatus. . . . . Price, **$15.00**

606. THE FAIRY GARLAND.

A beautiful garland of flowers is suspended on the stage, several watches are borrowed and three cards are selected and loaded into a pistol. On shooting against the garland, the watches and cards appear instantly on latter.
Price, ... **$6.00**

No. 605.

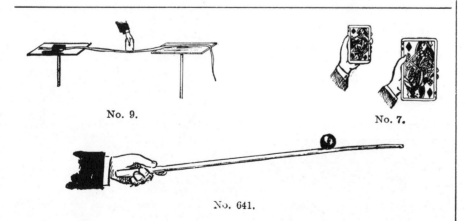

No. 9.

No. 7.

No. 641.

No. 391.

No. 116.

No. 295.

No. 386.

No. 353.

No. 714.

No. 515.

776. JAPANESE WONDER BOWL.

Holding in his hand an ornamental bowl, filled with paper clippings, performer uses a fan, causes these to fly about, revealing bowl filled with flowers, which are given to the ladies in audience. He then brings from bowl a number of flower balls on silk ribbons, which he suspends on a handsome nickel tripod stand. Bowl then suddenly transforms itself into a large, ornamented Hexagon Pagoda, which in hung on top of nickel stand. From Pagoda now streams various colored ribbons. A large, empty basin, all sides shown, is placed under Pagoda to catch the ribbons. Basin is then set on top of a handsome tabouret, pistol fired, and instantly the basin fills itself with doves, rabbits, etc. Ornamental. Done anywhere. Suitable for lady or silent act. Weight about 30 lbs. Complete, with accessories. . . . . Price, **$55.00**

THE BOSTON SCHOOL OF MAGIC, 103 COURT ST., BOSTON.

No. 929.

No. 496.

No. 271.

No. 545.

No. 327.

No. 578.

No. 422.

No. 894.

179

BELOW: A clock automaton with a figure of a magician who performs the Cups and Balls trick on the hour. The conjurer raises two of the three cups, revealing differently colored balls and dice that form five combinations. 1 foot 9 inches high. French, late nineteenth century. (*Sotheby's Belgravia*)

RIGHT: Most of the effects shown in the border of Otto Hornmann's catalogue cover of 1907 are still available in magic shops today.

RIGHT BOTTOM: This automaton depicting the levitation of Snow White was originally exhibited as a magician and his assistant. As the magician's hands rose, the prone figure of the hypnotized lady would follow, and return to the couch as his hands went back down to his side. Seven dwarfs at the bottom. 45 inches by 38 inches. Electrically operated. About 1920. (*Sotheby's Belgravia*)

OPPOSITE PAGE: Cover of Catalogue No. 11 of August Roterberg, noted Chicago magic dealer. About 1911. Items from another edition of Catalogue No. 11 appear on the two following pages.

CATALOGUE
OF
CONJURING TRICKS

No. 11

A. ROTERBERG,
151 West Ontario Street, - CHICAGO, ILL.

No. 457   Roterberg's Acme Coffee and Milk Trick.

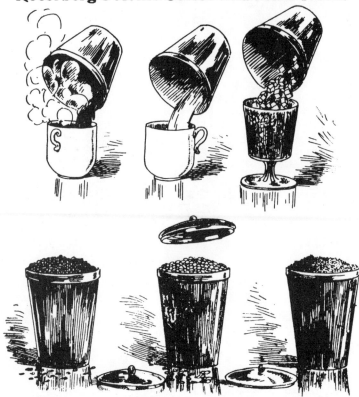

A great improvement on Prof. Kellar's method of performing this clever trick as no servante nor velvet cloths are required. A handsomely nickeled goblet of large size is visibly filled with brown paper cuttings and covered over with a small, very shallow lid. Another similar goblet is then filled with white shavings and also covered over. Upon removal of the lids, which are freely shown, hot coffee instead of brown paper shavings is discovered in the first goblet and milk in the other one. Goblets, lids, etc. are heavily spun and are seamless. Finest grade. Beware of cheaper imitations Complete. "S." Price...**$7.00**

No. 458. Do. With the addition of a third goblet, in which bran changes into lump or granulated sugar. "S." Price................................**$10.00**

No. 459   The Fairy Plant and Japanese Trays.

A splendid and novel trick, highly recommended. A shallow Japanese tray is freely shown and some moss placed on it, after which another similar tray, which is also shown, is inverted over it. Both trays are held in the performer's hand and are then covered over with a borrowed handkerchief. Upon removal of the latter and the top tray, a large beautiful bouquet is seen to have appeared on the lower tray. Performed anywhere with comparative ease. Best make. Price................**$10.00**

No. 460   The Marvelous Wine and Water Separation.

A charming experiment; easy of performance. The conjurer introduces two clear glass goblets, each standing on a china plate, one of the goblets being filled with wine and the other with water. The contents of these glasses are next emptied into a clear glass decanter which is covered with an unprepared handkerchief. Over each one of the empty goblets, a cylindrical nickeled cover, open at each end and which is first shown to be perfectly empty, is next placed. A change is now commanded to take place. Upon the handkerchief being removed from the decanter, the latter is seen to be entirely empty, whereas the first one of the glasses is found to be again filled with wine and the second one with water as in the beginning of the trick. We supply the above outfit in the latest improved form in which the nickeled tubes are shown to be empty during any part of the trick. If desired, they can even be examined beforehand. "S." Price $7.50

No. 461   The Fairy Jar and Mysterious Pictures.

Into a jar is poured a quantity of water and a number of sheets of blank paper then laid over the mouth of the jar, which together with the water is placed upside down on a small metal stand.   The performer now pulls out several sheets of paper from underneath the jar and instead of the sheets being wet, they are perfectly dry, and a pretty picture has appeared on each.   The jar is now returned to its original position and from it hundreds of yards of ribbon and other objects are then produced and finally the missing water is poured out. Superior finish, the jar being an exact imitation of the well known stone jar. Professional size. "S." Price $6.00

No. 233   **THE LATEST RISING CARD TRICK**

As performed by the late Buatier De Kolta. A number of cards are drawn and shuffled back into the pack. The pack is then placed in an ordinary drinking glass. Upon command, the chosen cards rise one by one from the pack and are instantly thrown out to the audience. But to make the trick all the more wonderful, the performer, stating that he can cause any one of the remaining cards to rise, calls out the name of some card. This also rises in like manner as the chosen cards. The same happens to a second and also to a third card; this process being continued until every card has risen out of the glass. The last cards rise in rapid succession, forming, as they spurt out, a perfect shower of cards. Complete with glass, cards, etc. Price....**$1.50**

No. 234   **THE ASTRA FLOATING BALL**

In this beautiful trick we have the very "top-notch" of the mysterious. It is unapproachable in every way as a spiritual effect and our apparatus in connection with it is the finest that can be constructed. The performer enters the stage, carrying a large ball and a hoop. He taps the ball to prove it perfectly solid and tosses it in the air to show that it is not connected with anything. Now, holding the ball in the palm of his hand and making a few mysterious passes around it, to the surprise of all it gradually commences to float and will ascend or descend at the word of the performer. Also while the ball is floating in mid-air, a hoop is passed over it to prove the impossibility of its having any connection with anything whatever. All movements connected with this fascinating trick can be done in a graceful and convincing manner. Some people are made to believe that the performer actually has access to some supernatural force. New. Can be performed anywhere. Price.............**$1.75**

LEFT AND RIGHT: Pages from Catalogue No. 17 of Roterberg's successor, Arthur P. Felsman, about 1919.

No. 236   MYSTERIOUS GLASS JAR AND FLYING COINS

An elegant trick for parlor or small stage, performed with ease by anyone. Pronounced by all who have purchased it to be the best trick of its kind ever invented. The performer introduces a pretty glass jar which he shows to be quite empty. He next exhibits a glass stopper, has it freely examined and, without exchanging it or putting anything into the hollow part, fits the examined stopper into the mouth of the empty jar, thus hermetically sealing the latter. He now takes a number of coins, say five, and commands them to leave his hand and passed into the closed glass jar. Presto! The hand is shown empty, while, at the same time, the five coins are seen and heard to arrive in the glass jar. **Now read carefully.** The conjurer then takes up the jar, still closed by the stopper, and takes it down to the company, who in turn, open the jar, take out the five coins, and examine everything very closely to prove that "there is no trickery." Unfathomable. No assistance required. Price....................$1.50

No. 237   THE CARD WAND

Suitable for Parlor or Stage. This mysterious trick never fails to score a hit wherever produced. From a plate of real eggs, one is selected by the company and then given to a spectator to hold. Next a card is chosen, torn into pieces, and one of the pieces kept by the person who drew the card. The remaining pieces are then burnt up, or are made to disappear in any other way. The egg held by the spectator is now broken. From its very center, the selected card is pulled out, the card being completely restored with the exception of the piece previously kept out. This piece is applied to the card and found to fit exactly, the latter effect being particularly appreciated. Including a slender, beautifully made, ebonized wand with nickel plated tips. Price...........$2.00

155. LATEST PRODUCTION AND COLOR CHANGE THROUGH HAND.

A very new and exceedingly clever device for showing the hands empty and then producing a handkerchief in one hand. Stroking this through the hand, the performer again shows the hands empty, and taking the handkerchief in his right hand he closes his left hand and tucks the handkerchief into it. It emerges at the other end an entirely different color. After going clear through, the hand is opened and shown empty. Requires a little practice, but is not to be called a slight of hand trick. (See price list.)

Excerpts from the catalogue of the Mysto Company appear on these two pages. This catalogue was probably issued about 1908. Although the company started in the magic field by catering to professionals, and was still doing so when this catalogue came out, it was already aiming partly at the juvenile trade. A boy magician, elegantly dressed in evening clothes, appeared on the catalogue cover, and the firm was already selling magic sets (opposite page). Later, inexpensive tricks sold in the Mysto Magic sets introduced many young people to magic.

MAGIC SETS.

UNEXCELLED CABINET OF TRICKS.

Your attention is called to these fine collections of magical tricks. The finest ever offered for sale. They are the very best tricks and as the cabinets contain such a number, the price is very low. They are encased in a handsome and beautifully made box with nickel corners. Besides the tricks and illusions from our catalog, as mentioned below, is included in every set a printed treatise, giving full instructions for performing twenty wonderful illusions and experiments in magic without apparatus and the secret of performing these stage illusions; also valuable hints to conjurors, together with an article on legerdemain.

NOTE.—These outfits in the possession of any man or boy can readily give an entertainment or show not inferior to some of the best magicians.

Set No. 1, containing seven good tricks for amateurs and the literature as described above, not put up in the large box. (See price list.)

Set No. II contains tricks Nos. 14, 16, 36, 76, 41, 39, 265, 149 and 152. A great bargain in magic. (See price list.)

Set No. III contains tricks Nos. 152, 159, 170, 41, 75, 76, 80, 164, 88 and 130. A greater bargain in magic. (See price list.)

Set No. IV contains tricks Nos. 130, 170, 88, 164, 41, 76, 110, 159, 71, 92, 116, 156, 119, 117, 152 and 162. The greatest bargain and a wonderful outfit. (See price list.)

A GUARANTEE—

We enter the magical world on a manufacturing basis, after years of successful manufacturing. We consider it worth stating that for years we have been the most successful Limousine Automobile Lock Manufacturers in the world, and we still are; during this time we have also been catering to the Master Magicians of the country for private work, and our books show that we have manufactured for nearly every magician of note, and with pride we point to an enviable reputation for fair dealing and reliability.

P-L CREATIVE SILKS
NO. 49

Probably the greatest and most amazing production effect for its size ever invented.

This astounding (real magic) creation may be performed anytime or place.

EFFECT—Performer, with sleeves rolled up, shows and passes two beautiful silver rings (2½" in dia.) and a small square of tissue paper to a spectator with the request that he place the paper between the rings and form a drumhead. The hands are casually shown empty as the drumhead is taken again from assisting spectator, and held out at arms length showing both sides of the drumhead which is immediately broken and two 16 inch silk handkerchiefs and yard upon yard of ¼ inch ribbon produced. Then picking the ribbon from the floor, another production of even greater size may easily be produced from the ribbon.

Every magician should have Creative Silks as it is one of the few big effects that can be carried in your pocket ready to perform.

Numerous additional uses will be found for the "gimmick" which can be used without the rings for a bare hand production.

Price complete (without handkerchiefs)   **$4.50**

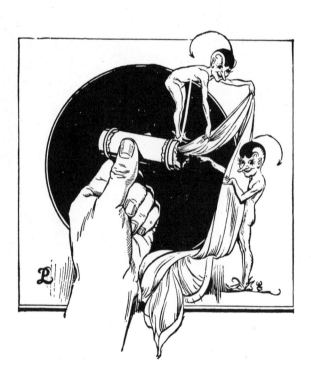

The "Goblin" Tube
NO. 48
"First A Vanish - Then - A Startling Production"

An entirely NEW and subtle method of Vanishing then Reproducing a marked handkerchief.

EFFECT—Performer passes for thorough inspection, a beautiful Nickel Tube, open at each end. He now requests a spectator to close both ends with a piece of paper (a la Drum Head) and retain it for the moment. A Silk handkerchief is now selected, marked, and passed to the performer who causes it to vanish. He now takes the Tube from the spectator and breaking the paper head, produces the marked SILK.

NO PULLS OR PALMING OF FAKES

A SENSATIONAL IMPROMPTU EFFECT and worthy of being included in the program of any performer.   **Price (without Handkerchief) $3.00**

The Petrie-Lewis Manufacturing Company, founded and headed by John N. Petrie, continued the more advanced magic line of the Mysto Company. Petrie remained in New Haven, where his new company soon earned a solid reputation for the dependable quality of its magical apparatus. The P & L symbol shown in these items from one of the firm's catalogues was stamped into most of its effects and served as a hallmark of quality. These are two excellent silk effects.

RIGHT: An exceedingly rare Petrie-Lewis effect is the Card Ladder. Four or five cards were chosen by spectators from a deck, which was then shuffled and placed in a holder at the top of the ladder. On command all the cards start sliding down the ladder, one after another. Most of them fall into a container at the bottom, but the selected cards stick to the ladder as shown. The piece was made about 1930 and then cost $100.00. About 4½ feet high. (*Clayton Albright Collection*)

BELOW: Stage-size Comedy Passe Passe Bottle and Glass trick from the Petrie-Lewis Manufacturing Company. (*Author's Collection*)

Bartl & Willmann

Vereinigte

Zauber-

Apparate-

Fabrik

Hamburg 36

Neuer
ungfernstieg 1.

LEFT: Some of the finest magical apparatus came from Germany, with its skilled mechanics, ingenious inventors of effects and a folklore peopled with witches and sorcerers. Two Teutonic-looking wizards adorn the cover of a catalogue of the Bartl and Willmann Combined Magical Apparatus firm of Hamburg, issued about the time of World War I. János Bartl later continued to manufacture and sell conjuring apparatus independent of Carl Willmann. Bartl's magic emporium on the busy Neue Jungfernstieg in the heart of Hamburg was one of the largest and finest in the world. The Zauberzentrum J. Bartl (J. Bartl Magic Center) still operates, under different management, in Hamburg.

BELOW: An ornate billiard-ball stand of solid nickel, made by Carl Willmann about 1910. Its cups enabled a sleight-of-hand artist to make billiard balls appear and disappear effortlessly. The piece is extremely rare. (*Clayton Albright Collection*)

361. The Latest Cigarette Tube.

Original Mrs. Rosa Bartl.

This pocket trick should be in the programme of every Professional or Amateur. The production is quite a simple one as the trick does not require any sleight of hand.

„The King of Tricks."

The performer takes out of a cigarette case a cigarette and lights it. He places it alight in the highly nickel plated tube. He closes this with a small cover and asks a spectator to hold it. On the command 1, 2, 3, the spectator opens the case and not a trace of the cigarette is to be seen. Only a little smoke proving that the cigarette was really placed inside. Instead of the cigarette there is a match.

The Conjurer loads the cigarette into the case and gives it to a spectator to hold. He then commands it to appear in another place, which it does, whilst a match appears in its place.

We would especially point out that our patented cigarette tube must not be confused with any other Conjuring Trick. Our cigarette tube works automatically. The cigarette is really placed inside. This seems almost incredible so startling is the vanish. To the audience it is absolutely unintelligible. This little pocket trick is a miracle to the spectators.

The trick can be performed as often as desired. $1.50

1255. The Mysterious Card and Watch Frame.

On the stage on a side table is standing an elegant nickel plated frame as illustrated. The Conjurer borrows a watch from a member of the audience, and also allows someone to to select a card from an ordinary pack. This card is torn up into little pieces and someone requested to hold one corner. As he takes back the torn pieces of card, the borrowed watch falls on the ground and breaks into a number of pieces. The Conjurer apologises explaining that it was an accident, and could not be helped. Naturally the person from whom it was borrowed does not look very cheerful. To get over the predicament the Conjurer collects the broken pieces of the watch and stuffs them into a pistol tube, and offers them to the owner. Naturally he declines them, so the Conjurer having nowhere to put them for the moment, fires them at the frame. The Conjurer next takes the pieces of card, places these in an ordinary pistol points it at the frame and fires it. Immediately the chosen card appears in the frame with the exception of one corner which a spectator is holding. Taking this corner the Conjurer throws it and immediately the card becomes whole. But the trick is not yet finished; Where has the watch got to. He commands the card to walk out of the frame and the watch to take its place. The pistol is again fired and the change quickly takes place. The card is now on top of the frame and the watch hangs in the centre. Both are now taken out of the frame and given back to the spectators. We supply the frame all parts of which are of the highest class of manufacture, with mechanism which cannot fail, complete with full instructions, so that this trick will become an ornament to anybodys programme, no matter how good it may be. $ 25.00

1231. The Latest Rose-Tree Table.

[Original Bartl & Willmann.]

On the stage stands a table the top and sides of which are completely nickel plated. The top of the table is very slender.

The Conjurer fires a pistol and instantly without any covering a massive flower pot containing a magnificent Rose—Bush appears.

The flower pot and Rose Tree are much larger and finer in appearance than the old style.

We guarantee our method to work absolutely without fail.

This most effective Conjuring Trick complete with all accessories. $65.00

German apparatus was imported into the United States and sold by Martinka's, Theo Bamberg and other dealers here. The Heaney Magic Company of Berlin, Wisconsin, handled many items that originated with Bartl, Willmann and F. W. Conradi, another German maker of choice apparatus. The effects on this page and the following one are all of this type. The Card and Watch Frame is probably a Conradi piece. The Great Fishing Trick described on page 193 was also probably imported from Germany. The items on this page and the next two are reproduced from Heaney's *Professional Catalog of Wonders*, No. 24.

No. 1286.

1286. EXCELSIOR WATCH TRICK

An elegant stand carrying four thin metal frames as per illustration, stands on stage or in a drawing-room. The performer calls the attention of the spectators to the fact that the space inside of the frames are quite free and puts his hand trough them. He bares his arms and catches a watch from the air. Which he hangs up en one of the hooks fixed to the frames. He repeats catching and produces by this way eight watches one after the other and places them on the hooks of the frames.

Performer working with sleeves rolled up and never touching his body, this trick is considered to be of entire perfection. All watches can be taken off finally.

Without assistant and back ground. Apparatus can be taken apart to accomodate packing. Complete. **$35.00**

1301. CONRADI'S ORIGINAL COIN-LADDER.

From a nicely nickeled stand is hanging down a ladder made of glass. The top part of stand is made of a thin nickeled plate provided with a hole in extension of a coin's diameter. The stand is completed by a metal cylinder with thin nickel plate on top put upon the plate of stand. After the trick „Miser's dream" is finished, performer takes some produced coins from hat and throws them in a glass, which he places on the top of the metal cylinder. The hat is placed underneath the ladder as per illustration. Performer asks audience how many coins shall come from the glass. At command the coins are seen and heard to drop down from step to step until they reache the last one, and fall into the hat suspended underneath the lowest step. Performer also can ask questions and coins will answer. By falling one coin means „yes" by two coins „no" Finally performer shows glass tobe empty, coins have left indeed. With English magic coins.

New Construction, no fail in working. Complete. **$50.00**

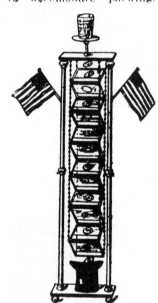

No. 1301

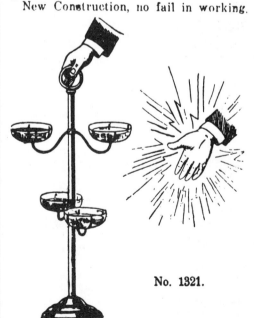

No. 1321.

1321. CONRADI'S „PHENOMENON" WATER BOWL TABLE.

Performer fills four nickeled metal bowls with water and places them on an elegant stand about 25 in. high, provided with four arms standing on a table. Performer covers a cloth over stand with bowls, only the handle of the stand is protruding through a hole in the middle of the cloth and always being visible to audience. The performer now seizes the covered stand with bowls carries them away from table and throw them into the air, when stand and filled bowls have totally vanished.

No servante, without assistant, sure automatically working. No skill at all. Complete. **$30.00**

955. „Pesco", Great Fishing Trick.

The performer enters with fishing rod, line and hook, and states that he intends to go fishing on dry land. After baiting his hook in the usual manner, he casts his line out over the heads of the audience and catches a live gold fish on the hook, from where it is removed and placed in a glass globe filled with water Again the hook is baited and another fish caught in the air and so on until three are caught in this mysterious manner. These are placed in the globe and it is passed for examination to demonstrate that they are real and very much alive No body work. Everything self-contained.

Best make. **$7.50**

No. 1C.   Heaney's Substitution Trunk
The Great Great Trunk and Bag Mystery

This is a good feature for any act. Consists of a finely made professional trunk of large size, all parts which are thoroughly examined. The performer's hands are then tied behind him and he is placed into a sack, which has been thoroughly examined and the mouth of which is then tied and sealed. In this bondage the performer is placed into the trunk, which is now surrounded on all sides by a cord. Either the trunk is placed in a cabinet or a screen is placed in front of trunk, but hardly is this done when performer steps out free. However, he is minus his coat. The trunk is opened and in the bag is found the lady wearing the performer's coat, her hands being securely tied behind her back. It only takes a few seconds for these changes to take place, in fact, so quickly does it happen, that it seems impossible. A great finish to any act as a closing feature. Our trunk is beautifully made and is not to be compared with any trunk offered by other firms. We furnish all material including the sack, and tieing feature. Price complete and put up in a shipping case, **$50.00.**

FAR LEFT: *Quality Magic Catalogue No. 7* of the Thayer Magic Manufacturing Company, 334 South San Pedro Street, Los Angeles, was issued in 1928.

LEFT: Thayer Appearing Alarm Clock. The clock appears visibly, ringing, in the previously empty frame. (*Clayton Albright Collection*)

BELOW: Illustration from the Thayer & Christianer catalogue, *Magical Woodcraft* about 1915. All items in the photo were turned out of wood—a remarkable demonstration of skilled wood turning applied to magic.

ABOVE: Display room at the Thayer plant at 334 South San Pedro Street, Los Angeles, in 1928. (*United Press photo from the Mario Carrandi Collection*)

BELOW: One of the illusions advertised that same year in Thayer's *Quality Magic Catalogue No. 7.*

No. 1320. Theo ♪ The Flying Lady

This is one of the most startling and spectacular stage effects ever offered.

The curtain goes up revealing a gorgeous back drop and setting. A lady, in bright Egyptian attire, enters and immediately without any apparent effort, she floats up gracefully from the stage and executes various movements while in mid-air, without any visible means of support.

At various times she descends to the stage to don a different costume, after which she again soars into space and executes various drills and dances, all of which are performed with the greatest of ease and gracefulness. At the finish she floats to the stage and retires. This sensation can be presented in any theatre.

Price upon application.

No. 1274. The Spirit Paintings

Here we offer what is positively one of the most beautiful and super-mystifying effects of the present age.

A number of unprepared blank canvasses, mounted upon light narrow wooden frames, are taken among the audience for examination. They may write their names or initials on these canvasses for future identification. Next the audience is given free choice in their selection of any subejct, such as that of a famous painting, or the name of any noted individual, or even that of a friend or relative, living or dead.

The performer then places two of the examined canvasses face to face, and slides them down into the front of a handsome display frame, which are thus rendered perfectly transparent due to a powerful light from the rear, so that a distinct shadow of the performer's hand, or anything placed behind, becomes clearly outlined through the canvasses.

With the house lights off and while all eyes are intent upon the white illuminated canvass, slowly and faintly at first, a dim shadow appears. Gradually this shadow grows larger and becomes more distinct. The outlines begin to take shape, colors appear, and in a few short moments, a perfect finished picture in all its brilliancy of color is before them.

The picture is then removed and passed to the person whose initial it still bears, proving that it is the very same canvass which was examined in its original blank condition. The effect may be repeated with a second and a third picture if desired, a different subject being produced each time.

It will be unnecessary for us to offer more than a brief description of the excellent features of this most wonderful of all spiritualistic illusion mysteries.

As a finished practical product for entertainment purposes it was first designed, built and perfected by us in our own shops, at a cost of much time and money. So great has been its success that others have since endeavored to copy and promote similar offerings, but they can in no way compare with our own true and original product.

This outfit comprises a very handsome and elegantly finished display frame and shadow box which mounts upon a substantial and attractive floor stand, the total height of which is 54 inches. It all takes apart for close packing. We include one special 250 watt light globe, bracket, reflector, and extension cord with a light plug to fit any standard socket.

There are four mounted blank canvasses and two beautiful colored portrait paintings of any selection desired from our lines of subjects as listed. The size of the paintings is 12x15 inches. The complete outfit, ready to work, comes with original and complete instructions.

Price $75.00
Larger size with paintings 15x18 inches. Price, complete............................$125.00

No. 1275. Special Pictures for Spirit Paintings Illusion

These pictures are especially made by our exclusive artist, and are positively the most perfect and beautiful specimens of art color hand work that can possibly be produced for this particular purpose.

The following is a partial list of our usual stock subjects:

Washington	Spirit of "'76"
Lincoln	Will Rogers
McKinley	Doug. Fairbanks
Roosevelt	Wallace Reid
Wilson	Harold Lloyd
Harding	End of the Trail
Gen. Pershing	Head of Christ
Lindbergh	Weeping Magdeline
Longfellow	Madonna and Child

We can supply practically any subject desired, or a reproduction made from any photo, print, or drawing, without extra charge, and upon reasonably short notice.

These pictures are supplied ready mounted on the regular standard frames for our "Spirit Paintings."

Price, size 12x15 inches, each..$ 8.00
Price, size 12x15 inches, two for...$15.00
Price, size 15x18 inches, each ....$ 9.00
Price, size 15x18 inches, two for...$17.00

No. 1276. Slate Writing Extraordinary

The performer seats a spectator opposite to himself at a plain table upon which are a pile of ordinary plain slates about 7x9 inches in size, and one large slate about 8x11 inches.

All the slates are freely examined and cleaned by the spectator, who is then requested to write on one of the small slates his name as well as any particular questions that he wishes to know about, and then to place his slate, with writing side down, on top of the stack of slates.

The performer then places the large slate on top of the pile, and further requests the spectator to write upon that slate the initials of some one in the Spirit World.

Regardless of the fact that to all appearances, at no time has the performer seen or touched the slate written upon by the subject, nevertheless, the performer is able to call the party by name, and to answer each and every question with the utmost ease and accuracy.

This seemingly supernatural mystery has perhaps amazed more people who have sat for private readings than any other medium slate effect known.

Price, slates complete with extensive instructions...................................$5.00

THE INVISIBLE FLIGHT

The first time in any catalogue. Positively not to be had elsewhere.

The time occupied to present trick 3 to 6 minutes. Approximate weight in packing case 350 pounds. Suitable fo La or Gentleman. Number of persons required, 2. Travels in 2 pieces of baggage.

Lady enters beautiful cabinet highly ornamented, which is suspended in mid-air where she is seen until the last moment. Front curtain is pulled to cover her for an instant only, this automatically releasing two side curtains and back curtain and immediately all curtains fly up and flowers are seen falling from cage to floor. Then without any hesitation, performer immediately raps on trunk. Right then and there, lady is heard to rap from inside trunk. This trunk stands near footlights, off the floor and during performance, has been hanging on opposite side of stage in mid-air. Trunk is now unlocked, second trunk removed. This trunk is also kept off floor and when opened a large bag is discovered. Bag is untied and the lady steps out.

Special attention is called to the following:—Cage and trunks hang in mid-air and never come in contact with one another. The transposition is done in less than three seconds. There are no traps, no special scenery or mirrors used, and only one lady required.

Price complete, with packing cases for road use, ~~$250.~~ $150.00

THE ORANGE
TREE TRANSFORMATION

PERFORMED WITH GREAT SUCCESS IN ENGLAND AND AUSTRALIA BY
CHUNG LING SOO.

The time occupied to present trick 2 to 4 minutes. Approximate weight in packing case 150 pounds. Suitable for Lady or Gentlemen. Number of persons required 2. Travels in 2 pieces of baggage.

In this brilliant effect, young lady mounts a small table several feet high. A large cone open at both ends thus enabling audience to see right through, is next proven to be empty. Cone is now lowered over young lady and upon being raised, a beautiful orange tree is seen from which real oranges are cut and distributed amongst audience. In the meantime, the lady may reappear from any part of the house that the artist may fancy.

Really a great effect and a modern success.

Price complete with packing case for road use, ~~$400.00~~.

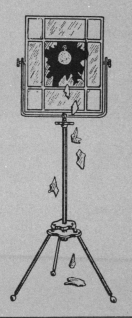

THE ENCHANTED WATCH MIRROR

A very showy and effective stage trick, consisting of a large, handsome mirror, set in a narrow nickeled frame. This is mounted on a fine nickeled base, as shown above. A watch is borrowed, and either placed in a Pistol Tube or hung from the barrel of the Latest Watch Pistol. Taking aim at the mirror, the pistol is fired, when the center of the mirror is seen to shatter into innumerable pieces which fall to the floor and disclose the borrowed watch hanging in the center of the mirror.

The outfit is portable, and beautifully made. Complete, including nickeled base. Price $30.00

HOLMES' PATRIOTIC PARADOX

A most beautiful and mystifying combination trick. It may be adapted to so many good uses that we recommend it for both parlor and stage. The outfit is thoroughly practical, being self-contained and can therefore be worked upon any table, and demands no skill.

The conjurer calls attention to a large, handsome, polygon-shaped Crystal Jar, provided with a glass lid; also two large polygon-glasses, one of which is filled with wine and one with water.

The glass of wine is now emptied into the Crystal Jar, followed by the glass of water, after which the glass lid is placed on the Jar.

Baring his arms to the elbows, the performer next magically produces three silk handkerchiefs, one red, one white, and one blue. The red silk is pushed into one of the polygon-glasses, which is placed on the right side stand, and a large covering cloth drawn over it. The blue silk is, in like manner, deposited in the other polygon-glass placed on the left side stand, and covered in a similar manner with a cloth. A borrowed handkerchief is now thrown over the Crystal Jar, containing the mixture of wine and water, and the performer's assistant holds the Jar, if desired, or the Jar, thus covered is merely placed on the center table.

Taking the remaining silk handkerchief (white), the performer rubs it smaller and smaller between his palms, until it disappears altogether; then, removing the covering from the Crystal Jar, the wine and water are found to have given place to a large silk American flag, which is removed and the Jar shown empty. Uncovering the polygon-glasses, the missing wine is found in one glass and the missing water in the other.

The beauty of this fine combination must be seen to be appreciated. As stated above, it is subject to much variation, such as working it as a straight Wine and Water Separation, or using ink instead of Wine, etc.

The only modern Wine and Water Separation Trick in existence that is absolutely self-contained, worked upon any table, and without assistance.

Complete, including a beautifully made Crystal Jar with glass lid; polygon-glasses, red, white, and blue silk handkerchiefs, 24x36 inch silk American flag etc. all of the finest make and quality.

Price, Complete $10.00
Price, without handkerchiefs or flag $7.50

THE HUMAN FLIES—Prints $25.00

The above picture illustrates human up-side-down girls dancing on the ceiling, walls and floor of a room. The girls can dance in groups or make their entrance up-side-down, one at a time, and make their exit the same way, while a group is dancing on the floor.

This illusion is perfect and requires very little rehearsal to accomplish this impossible feat without the aid of any support. The large cabinet room is easily shoved to one side out of the way. This is an attraction that will cause much talk and will increase the box office receipts of any theatre or night club. Any first class carpenter can build this apparatus with the prints and specifications.

THE THRILLING DEATH DEFYING EMPALEMENT
ATTRACTION—Built to order.

Price $350.00—Prints and Specifications $35.00

Blindfold hurling of knives through the paper wall by sound. A score of razor edged steel knives hurled through space, outlining the figure of a beautiful girl strapped on a revolving disc, rotating at a terrific speed. When the paper wall is removed from the disc, the steel knives can be seen embedded within one inch of the girl's body which has pinned her to the boarded disc. The knives are removed and the girl unstrapped, and out she steps unharmed and smiling.

This apparatus is so cleverly constructed, it can be in the open for inspection. No one will ever find the secret of how the girl remains safe.

Archery can be used with this device. A hundred arrows from a bow can be shot into the revolving disc making it very spectacular. A blacksmith or wheelwright can build this with the prints.

Another sensational effect from the catalogue of Leffell Devices.

MUSEUMS OF MAGIC

A richly rewarding experience for anyone interested in magic is a visit to one or more of the museums in the field. Pleasant and informing as it is to read about great magicians and their baffling illusions and high artistry, they become especially real and close to us when we actually see the beautiful equipment they used, admire the magnificent lithographed posters and printed playbills with which they advertised their shows, read their letters, or inspect books and periodicals from their private libraries. Actual contact with these things brings us a whole step closer to their owners than the printed page can, and their magical feats and ways of working take on concrete reality for us.

Much credit is due to the dedicated men and women whose enthusiasm, hard work and money have been devoted to collecting apparatus and memorabilia for museums of magic where future generations can see and appreciate them. A descriptive list of such museums follows.

Poster of the American Museum of Magic, due to open soon in Michigan. (*Courtesy of Robert Lund*)

of memorabilia of magic and magicians. It is the successor to the American Egyptian Hall Museum founded in Kenton, Ohio, in 1895 by W. W. Durbin. The name of the institutions was borrowed from London's famous Egyptian Hall, where the eminent British conjurer John Nevil Maskelyne rented the theater at which he presented his popular magic shows for more than three decades. Prior to the Maskelyne era Alexander Herrmann, the leading magician of his day, had also had a long run of three years at Egyptian Hall.

W. W. Durbin was a versatile powerhouse of a man who simultaneously carried on three careers—those of a professional magician, businessman and politician. He built a small local sign company into a wealthy national corporation. He did outstanding work as State Executive Committee Chairman of the Democratic Party in Ohio, greatly strengthening the party in the state and engineering the elections of many public officials. In 1933 Durbin went to Washington as Register of the United States Treasury.

Durbin served as president of the International Brotherhood of Magicians from 1926 until his death in 1937. He used his Egyptian Hall, a white-clapboarded, one-story building in Kenton, to rehearse his magic shows, entertain friends, and house his extensive collection of photographs of magicians of the era approximately from 1890 to 1930. Durbin's Egyptian Hall also

EGYPTIAN HALL MUSEUM OF MAGICAL HISTORY, 1954 OLD HICKORY BOULEVARD, BRENTWOOD, TENNESSEE 37027. TEL. 615-298-2895

The Egyptian Hall Museum of Magical History, owned and operated by David Price in Brentwood, near Nashville, Tennessee, is one of the world's largest museums

Egyptian
Hall
Museum
-31-76

David Price

David Price, of the Egyptian Hall Museum of Magical History.

a collector, preserver and archivist of magical memorabilia and publications. He moved the Durbin collection of photos and memorabilia, though not the building itself, to his Tennessee home.

The Durbin photograph collection now constitutes less than 5 percent of the vast collection Price has assembled. When his house could no longer hold all of his memorabilia, Price built a lovely new country home in Brentwood. One wing of the building contains the Prices' personal living quarters. The other is occupied by the museum.

Just beyond the entrance is the large museum hall. Here the walls are covered with colorful lithograph posters of the great magicians of every era from that of Alexander Herrmann to the present. Complementing the posters on the walls of the main exhibition hall is a collection of magicians' playbills. A large album holds more than 1500 photographs of magicians. A second large collection of photos is arranged with swinging panels, to resemble one of those giant books from whose pages Thurston, McDonald Birch and other conjurers used to materialize and step out onto the stage to begin their performances. Glass cases display three-dimensional memorabilia.

In addition to the main exhibit hall, the museum has two archives rooms, a library, and an office. Modern filing facilities can accommodate memorabilia of every size, from magicians' calling cards to huge, 24-sheet posters and even one 28-sheet giant dating from 1895. The museum walls can display posters measuring up to 8 feet in height. The larger ones are kept in special containers.

Over the years David Price's collection has grown steadily, with donations from individual magicians and the acquisition of whole collections. Among these collections now at the museum are the following, with the respective years of their acquisition: *

1954: the C. A. George Newman poster collection. In 1967 David Price also acquired the Lee Allan Estes poster collection.

1959: the large Loring Campbell collection, including scrapbooks of Eugene Laurant, Maro, Houdini and C. A. George Newman.

1965: a bequest from Eddie McLaughlin of items used by the great sleight-of-hand artist T. Nelson Downs, Ed Reno, Mock-Sad-Ali and other magicians. They include the leather prop suitcase used by Downs throughout his entire career, packed with the props he was using in his club shows. Downs carried props to his command performance at Buckingham Palace in this suitcase.

Other relics of Tommy Downs at the museum were donated by Bud Tracy. These include Downs's Coin

deserves to be remembered in magical history as the locale of what is believed to have been the very first convention of magicians to be held anywhere in the world. This was the International Brotherhood of Magicians convention organized by Bill Durbin in 1926.

After Bill Durbin's death his American Egyptian Hall was acquired by Thomas M. Dowd, now international treasurer of the I.B.M. and advertising editor of its official monthly publication, *The Linking Ring*. The hall was moved to the Dowd farm on the outskirts of Kenton. In 1953 the Egyptian Hall was purchased from Dowd by David Price, well-known magician in the Nashville area. When a foot injury sustained in World War II prevented his continuing his professional performances, David Price concentrated on a new career as

---

* For details of this list of acquisitions I am indebted to an account by John Booth in *The Linking Ring*, Vol. 56, No. 8 (August, 1976), augmented by information from David Price.

Ladder, which was too large to fit into the suitcase—probably one reason for his taking it out of his act.

These T. Nelson Downs relics were given to Bud Tracy and Eddie McLaughlin by Mrs. Downs, and by them to the museum.

1956–1966: material from Stanley Collins relating to the old Egyptian Hall in London, and British conjurers.

1962: from Emile Bamberg: treasures used by several generations of conjurers in the Bamberg family of Holland, including the set of Cups and Balls handed down in the family from the time of Tobias Bamberg (1812–1870), and the Bamberg Wonder Book made by David Tobias (Papa) Bamberg (1843–1914).

1962 and 1969: Carl Rosini's original thumb-tie rings and scrapbook.

1970: the Dante scrapbooks, presented by the magician's son, Alvin Jansen.

1971: the DeMott collection of material on Chatauqua and lyceum magicians, including a number of scrapbooks.

1972: to Egyptian Hall came items from the Thomas Chew Worthington collection: a number of wands, Mme. Adelaide Herrmann's mother-of-pearl fan, and the lifelike bust of Harry Kellar that played an important part in Kellar's Self-Decapitation Illusion.

1973: the Cliff Hard collection.

Since then contributions have continued to flow in, including the scrapbooks of Tommy Martin and apparatus used by John Booth.

Among other interesting collections at the museum are the scrapbooks of Professor Augustus Rapp, who played the small country towns, leaving his mark on the show business of his era; and the combined props for the ten "suitcase shows" of Edwin Brush, a Chatauqua magician as early as 1904. Later in his career, Brush kept ten suitcases packed with the equipment for as many different programs. When called to present a club act or other show on short notice, Brush would simply grab a suitcase he had not used before for that particular group. Thus he was always ready.

David Price writes of the unique collections of memorabilia in Egyptian Hall: "The museum is not a commercial enterprise but a permanent repository for relics of magic over which we exercise a relationship of stewardship. We collect, preserve and display such relics with the view of passing them on to future generations of magicians. . . . Egyptian Hall is open at all times by appointment to magicians and other interested persons subject, of course, to the convenience of the proprietor. Most of the visitors from out of town are magicians or magic-oriented individuals." Although it is not always possible to show the museum at the exact time requested, there is no charge for admission to Egyptian Hall.

Mrs. David Price with some of the rare exhibits at the Egyptian Hall Museum.

The Houdini Magical Hall of Fame, opened in 1968, offers a unique display of illusions, apparatus and memorabilia associated with the gerat escape artist Harry Houdini and other noted conjurers. The dedication plaque at its entrance reads: "The Houdini Magical Hall of Fame is dedicated to the unparalleled genius, the skills, the intrepidity and the brilliance of the world renowned magician Houdini. . . . Born March 24, 1872, died October 31, 1926."

Since its establishment the museum has broadened its scope. While still focused on the world's greatest escapologist, it also pays tribute to magic as a whole and its exhibits include memorabilia of other noted magical performers as well.

After the death of Houdini in 1926 much of his equipment was purchased from his estate by America's most famous mentalist, Joseph Dunninger. This material remained in a New York warehouse for almost half a century, before finally being housed in the museum. A friend and associate of Houdini's, Dunninger invented many illusions used by the great escape artist and other magicians. His collection of Houdiniana forms the core of the museum's exhibits. It includes not only equipment used by Houdini himself in his escapes and fabulous stage illusions, but also magical wonders of earlier years from the extensive collection of magical memorabilia collected by Houdini during his lifetime.

In the foyer of the museum stands the figure of an Egyptian mummy used by both Houdini and Dunninger in presenting the Sarcophagus mystery. In this illusion, a mummy was transformed into a living girl.

Within the museum proper one may view the apparatus for many other famous illusions. Here is the Flight of Karma, developed by Dunninger for Houdini, in which a girl vanished at a pistol shot from a thin, draped platform suspended high above the stage. Nearby is the Beaumont Cylinder, with which two girls were miraculously vanished and re-produced. Used by Count Beaumont, a prominent French conjurer of the nineteenth century, the cylinder was in Houdini's collection. Here, too, is the mysterious Spirit Paintings effect, which visitors can operate by pressing a button. Nearby is a massive Sword Suspension effect in which a girl lies horizontal in the air, suspended only by the point of a scimitar at the back of her shoulders. Other fascinating exhibits include a Sword Box used by the magician Jarrett in Broadway performances of the 1920s; the Trunk of Nations or Costume Trunk used by Adelaide Herrmann; Dunninger's own Cutting a Girl in Eight illusion; the Golem, a disembodied head effect related to the Sphinx illusion; and the fearsome Cremation effect invented by the Belgian conjurer Servais Le Roy, in which a girl was apparently consumed in flames and reduced to a grim skeleton. Also on display are the Chair Suspension from Harry Blackstone's show and a sensational decapitation illusion acquired by Houdini from the estate of Alexander Herrmann.

Even more intimately associated with the life and career of Harry Houdini, however, are the museum's exhibits of Houdini's handcuffs, locks, picks and other escapes. Houdini first became renowned, as we have seen, after his sensational escape from regulation handcuffs at Scotland Yard. During his career Houdini emerged successfully from hundreds of other handcuffs, leg-irons, chains and shackles. As a condition of these challenge tests, it was stipulated that Houdini would be allowed to keep the handcuffs or other restraints. Consequently he amassed a vast collection. The exhibition of locks and handcuffs at the museum is believed to be the largest in the world.

Still other exhibits include the Plate Glass Box, said to have been the earliest of Houdini's escape tricks, a precursor of his famed Chinese Water Torture illusion; and equipment associated with his escapes from straitjackets, jail cells, mailbags, milk cans and packing cases.

Not neglected is Houdini's smaller magic, including many pieces belonging to earlier magical celebrities which he bought for his collection. Here is apparatus that once belonged to Robert-Houdin, Buatier de Kolta, Kellar and Le Roy.

No less intimately associated with the memory of Harry Houdini is his long campaign against fraudulent mediums. He first became interested in the subject while studying literature exposing the methods used by fake mediums in escaping from restraints. What interested Houdini mainly at that time was how these methods could be used in his own escape work. Later in life he became greatly concerned with questions of life and death and campaigned actively against self-professed mediums who victimized the public from motives of gain or publicity.

Museum exhibits reflecting this dramatic chapter of Houdini's life include the spirit cabinet given to Houdini by the amazing medium Anna Eva Fay, and a séance room in which methods used by fraudulent mediums are revealed.

After Houdini's death, Dunninger continued his work in a similar campaign against fake mediums, and offered a reward of $31,000 for anyone who could pass an especially devised test. This test is now displayed at the museum, and the reward offer remains in effect. In a sealed glass cabinet, a pencil hangs by an elastic cord over a pad of blank paper. Anyone who claims mediumistic or psychic powers and who, without breaking the seals on the box, can use the pencil to write on the pad, qualifies for the reward.

The museum also houses a noteworthy collection of letters, pictures, programs, posters, letterheads and other memorabilia of Houdini and other magicians. There is a film showing of Houdini's exploits in the field of aviation.

For lovers of mechanical wonders, one of the finest automatons extant is also on display in the Houdini Hall of Fame. This is "Psycho," which Houdini purchased from Harry Kellar for a reported $10,000. It consists of the upper half of a man, mounted on a clear glass cylinder. Among other accomplishments, the mechanical figure could select numbers or playing cards requested by spectators.

The fascinating and educational collections on display at the museum do not reveal the secrets of Houdini's amazing escapes and other magic. That these secrets should always be kept inviolate was a stipulation agreed to before the collection was entrusted to the museum.

The Houdini Magical Hall of Fame is managed by Mr. Henry Muller. The museum is open seven days a week from 11 A.M to 7 P.M. Admission is $2.75 for adults, $2.00 for students, and $1.25 for children under twelve, with a special $5.75 family rate which covers two parents and any number of children.

JOHN MULHOLLAND COLLECTION, THE PLAYERS,
16 GRAMERCY PARK SOUTH, NEW YORK,
NEW YORK 10003. TEL. 212-228-7610

John Mulholland, magician, prolific writer on magical subjects, and for many years editor of *The Sphinx,* bequeathed his extensive magical library and much of his large collection of fine apparatus to the Walter Hampden Memorial Library at The Players in New York. The John Mulholland Collection is rich in rare books and periodicals in many languages, playbills and other memorabilia. Among the unique pieces of apparatus left by Mulholland to his club is Johann N. Hofzinser's own Miraculous Casket for vanishing coins, somewhat similar to the one described and pictured on page 202 of Professor Hoffmann's great book *Modern Magic* (1876). There is a lovely mechanical rose made of brass by Robert-Houdin and so constructed that its petals gradually unfold. Here too is a cast of the powerful hands of the great sleight-of-hand artist Nate Leipzig, a performer whose work John Mulholland especially admired. These are only a few examples of the treasures in the collection.

Although The Players is a private club, qualified investigators with a serious interest in magical research may apply for special permission to consult materials in the John Mulholland Collection. The Curator is Mr. Louis A. Rachow.

Some of the treasures in the John Mulholland Collection, The Players, New York. (*William Doerflinger Photo*)

THE MAGIC CELLAR,
EARTHQUAKE MCGOON'S SALOON,
630 CLAY STREET, SAN FRANCISCO, CALIFORNIA.
TEL. 415-986-1433

In the basement of Earthquake McGoon's popular San Francisco restaurant and night spot is a unique place of entertainment called The Magic Cellar. Here magical illusions from the repertoire of one of America's most famous magicians of the early part of this century, Carter the Great, are displayed and still used in magic shows. Visitors enjoying their drinks in The Magic Cellar can witness these unique performances and inspect memorabilia reflecting the life and career of one of America's greatest magicians.

Only drinks are served in The Magic Cellar, but

Rare Punch and Judy puppets and ventriloquial figures displayed at Flosso's. (*William Doerflinger Photo*)

dinner and dancing are available upstairs at Earthquake McGoon's.

FLOSSO HORNMANN MAGIC COMPANY, 304 WEST 34TH STREET, NEW YORK, NEW YORK 10001. TEL. 212-239-6079

In the Flosso Hornmann Magic Company, America's oldest magic shop, is a small but choice display of magical apparatus and memorabilia associated with Al Flosso, the former proprietor of the shop. After Al's death in May, 1976, the exhibits were arranged by his son, Jack Flosso, who now conducts the company's shop and mail-order business.

Items on display include personal effects of Al Flosso's: his wand, top hat, spring-laden bow tie, and the silver pail he used in his famous performances of the Miser's Dream. As a dealer, performer, and collector of magic for many years, Al was a connoisseur of antique magic and one of the pillars of the Magic Collectors Association. In the cases at his old shop are many rare pieces of apparatus used by Al; his father-in-law, Professor L. "Pop" Krieger of New York; and other magicians. Among the items on display are a magnificent set of antique Punch and Judy figures and Pip and Flip, "the world's only two-headed vent figure." The accompanying photographs include some of the objects exhibited. Among them is an interesting photograph of a ten-in-one show at Coney Island when that resort was in its heyday. From his performances with such shows in his early years as a young magician, Al Flosso developed his popular comedy role of later years, when he appeared as "the Fakir of Coney Island."

AMERICAN MUSEUM OF MAGIC, 107 EAST MICHIGAN, MARSHALL, MICHIGAN 49068

A new museum of magic is being readied for opening in the pleasant town of Marshall, Michigan, situated halfway between Detroit and Chicago. It is under the direction of Robert and Elaine Lund. Mr. Lund, who is Detroit editor of *Popular Mechanics* and *MOTOR* magazines, has been collecting magic memorabilia for almost thirty-five years. In 1974 Mr. and Mrs. Lund purchased a building in Marshall to house their collection. They have devoted most of their free time since then to transforming it into a museum of conjuring. Advance reports from those who have had a glimpse behind the scenes are enthusiastic.

The museum occupies a spacious, 100-year-old building with cast-iron pillared front, gingerbread cornices, tall, curved-top windows and airy 12- and 14-foot ceilings. The edifice has been extensively restored and redecorated.

Mr. Lund writes that his collection runs to about 250,000 items, including books—an extensive library—films, coins and tokens, newspaper clippings, letters, programs, toys, magic sets (about 350 of them), paintings and prints, apparatus, magazines and other material. Over 2700 posters, ranging in size from small handbills to three sheets, will cover the interior walls.

Special displays are planned on such themes as women magicians, black magicians, nationality groups, magicians in the movies, in fiction, in children's literature and so on. There will also be displays concerning individual performers. The Houdini exhibit, for example, will include such rare objects as the original containers Houdini used for his Overboard Packing Box and Milk Can escapes, needles he used for the East Indian Needle Mystery, a coin tray from his early magic act and a spirit trumpet from his campaign against fake mediums.

At this writing the date the museum will open to the public and admission charges have not yet been definitely set. It is suggested that visitors phone ahead to check on these points. Mr. and Mrs. Lund hope to have the first floor open before the end of 1977, and the second floor three or four months later. A newsletter detailing the progress of the work on the museum, new acquisitions and other developments is available. To subscribe to the newsletter, write to the museum at Box 5, Marshall, Michigan 49068, sending $2.00 for four issues.

THE MAGIC CASTLE (ACADEMY OF MAGICAL ARTS), 7001 FRANKLIN AVENUE, HOLLYWOOD, CALIFORNIA 90028. TEL. 213-851-3313

On display in the Magic Castle, the lavishly appointed private club on a hill overlooking the heart of Hollywood, is a collection of posters, pictures and interesting props used by magicians of years gone by. The Castle also houses a fine library of magic which may be consulted by regular members. Regular and associate members may enjoy gourmet meals in the dining rooms and attend performances by some of the world's most skillful magicians. These are held simultaneously in the Castle's

close-up room and several other show rooms. A new area opened in 1976 houses the Palace of Mystery and the Parlour of Prestidigitation. In the Palace of Mystery magical revues are presented nightly, except Mondays. On Monday evening "Guest Night" is held for magicians wishing to audition or perform for friends or agents. Also situated in the new area is a Mechanical Museum.

Almost as amazing as the magic feats performed at the Castle is the story of the two brothers who run it, Milt and Bill Larsen. In 1953 their father, William Larsen, Sr., Los Angeles attorney and magician, formed the Academy of Magical Arts, Inc., a non-profit organization dedicated to the advancement of the art of magic in America. Bill Larsen, Jr., is now president of the Academy; he is also editor of the independent magicians' magazine *Genii*. The Magic Castle is the brainchild of Milt Larsen, writer, producer, magician, and connoisseur of vintage architecture and furnishings. He had long admired the fine old Gothic-Victorian mansion, built in 1909, on a hill overlooking Hollywood, that is now the Castle. It was he who conceived the idea of restoring it as the clubhouse of the Academy. He negotiated a lease, supervised the refurbishing of the Castle, and has added to the original mansion many treasures in the form of fine parts and rare building materials from other opulent old residences.

With its many turrets and gables, the Castle is mysterious and impressive in appearance. Its carved oak door swings open to a luxurious interior. Here members assemble to enjoy cocktails, dine and watch the magic performances. In the Grand Salon is a very large bar, topped with a wooden mosaic which is part of the parquet floor from the ballroom of a mansion built in the 1880s. The wall back of the bar is decorated with what looks like multicolored stained glass, but is really bits of old "Coming Attractions" slides. In the music room is a grand piano on which the house ghost, Irma, will play any tune requested, the keys being mysteriously depressed by an unseen hand. The Castle also owns a rare contraption called an Imhof Mammoth Pneumatic Orchestration—a seven-piece mechanical band that combines the music of a pipe organ, piano, bass drum, xylophone, snare drum, cymbals and *glockenspiel!*

Magicians who have performed at the Magic Castle include many of the great names in magic today, such as Dai Vernon, Peter Pitt, Derek Dingle, Kuda Bux and Albert Goshman.

Associate membership in the Magic Castle is available to non-magicians on a limited basis. Each new member must be sponsored by two members in good standing. The admission fee is $500.00 and yearly dues are $65.00. Magicians may join at a slightly lesser fee, as regular members, but they must pass an entrance examination to prove their proficiency. Non-members are admitted to the Castle only with a member or with a

ABOVE: The Magic Castle in Hollywood, California, is the world's most luxurious club for magicians and magic lovers.

LEFT: Milt Larsen (*left*) and Bill Larsen, Jr., of the Magic Castle. (*Photos courtesy of William W. Larsen, Jr.*)

guest card signed by a member. For further information regarding membership write the Academy of Magical Arts at the address given above.

THE MAGIC CIRCLE,
84, CHENIES MEWS, LONDON, W.C. 1, ENGLAND. TEL. 01-459-1569

The Magic Circle is Britain's most prestigious conjurers' organization. The atmosphere of its London headquarters is truly magical. Chenies Mews is a tiny street so tucked away that even your London cabbie may have trouble finding it. As you enter the club, you are confronted with your own reflection in a large mirror. After a few moments the reflection mysteriously vanishes from the mirror. Beyond are the club rooms; a museum with fine exhibits of magical apparatus and memorabilia; an excellent magical library and a theater. The Magic Circle is one of the few magic clubs in the world with a permanent headquarters.

The admission standards of the Magic Circle are high and its membership consists entirely of professional and amateur magicians. Admission to the club rooms is restricted to members and their guests.

Details regarding membership and an illustrated brochure are available on request.

S.A.M. MAGICAL HALL OF FAME,
SUNSET AND VINE, HOLLYWOOD, CALIFORNIA

The Magical Hall of Fame of the Society of American Magicians is located in the Home Savings and Loan Building on the corner of Sunset and Vine in Hollywood, California. It includes galleries of photographs of famous magicians, a library, an auditorium and a museum of magic.

The museum room presents the history of magic. Life-size figures of magicians are displayed performing their most famous effects. Valuable apparatus and magic memorabilia are exhibited.

To visit the Magical Hall of Fame contact, in advance, Associate Director John Engman, 10th Floor, 3731 Wilshire Boulevard, Los Angeles, CA 90010. Tel. 213-383-1266.

MUSÉE ROBERT-HOUDIN,
BLOIS (LOIRE-ET-CHER), FRANCE

Jean Eugène Robert-Houdin, known as the "Father of Modern Magic," was born in 1805 in the city of Blois in the Loire Valley. On a steep, winding street leading to the Chateau de Blois stands the Musée Robert-Houdin, devoted to the life and work of the great magician. The museum contains a fine collection of memorabilia, including some of the magnificent automatons that Robert-Houdin constructed and used in his Soirées Fantastiques. As a young man the future magician was fascinated by watchmaking, which was his father's profession and the leading industry of Blois. He was apprenticed to a watchmaker and in this employment he sometimes had the pleasure of repairing automatons, which were then popular in the programs of conjurers. This work helped to kindle his own interest in magic and led to his building beautiful automatons in later years. These he exhibited in his theater in Paris and during his appearances in England. After leaving the stage Robert-Houdin retired to a comfortable house in the vicinity of Blois where he devoted himself to writing and scientific research. Relics of his later life in this house, Le Prieuré, are also preserved in the museum.

MAGICIANS' SOCIETIES

Magicians may tend to be closed-mouthed and clannish, but among themselves they are the most gregarious of humans. This is as it should be, for membership in a local magic club, or national or international organization, is the surest, easiest, and most companionable way to increase your knowledge of the art and sharpen your skills.

The large organizations such as the International Brotherhood of Magicians, the Society of American Magicians and the Magic Circle all publish magazines. These magazines provide news and announcements of interest to magicians, as well as magic secrets, evaluations of new tricks, and advertisements. The publications are included in the membership dues. Local magic clubs offer those who are seriously interested in the art a chance to perform and receive constructive criticism from fellow magi, as well as the opportunity to enjoy many pleasant social occasions and form lasting friendships with men and women with similar interests. When traveling, you will be welcome at a local branch of your club.

Many of these clubs also organize magic entertainment for hospitals, senior citizens' groups, and underprivileged children. The larger ones often name special committees that do important work in such fields as maintaining ethical standards, preventing the exposure of magic secrets to the merely curious, and investigating claims of ESP and supranormal phenomena.

Design by Mickey O'Malley on cover of a banquet program of International Brotherhood of Magicians Ring 26, New York.

Some of the most important magic societies are described below, and addresses are given to write to for further information. Inquire also at your local magic dealer's for information regarding a possible regional association in your area, the names of its current officers, and where they may be reached.

THE INTERNATIONAL BROTHERHOOD OF MAGICIANS

The International Brotherhood of Magicians, as its name implies, links magicians throughout the world in a bond of fraternity and cooperation. Its membership extends from New York all the way to Hong Kong and Singapore, and from the United Kingdom to China.

In 1922 three young men—Gene Gordon and Ernest Schliedge, Americans, and Len Vintus, a Canadian—conceived the idea of a correspondence society open to those interested in the art of magic. Mr. Thomas M. Dowd, international treasurer of the I.B.M., writes as follows in a letter regarding the early history of the society: "The group's directory was soon replaced by a magazine entitled *The Linking Ring*, and the first issue was published in 1923. The society held its first convention at Kenton, Ohio, in June, 1926, and more than 300 members attended. In 1927 *The Linking Ring* became a monthly, and it has not missed a publication date since that time."

Among other early members of the organization were Mr. Dowd, W. W. Durbin and H. Adrian Smith, to name only a few. The 1926 gathering is believed to have been the first large convention of magicians to be held anywhere in the world. It took place at W. W. Durbin's American Egyptian Hall. That attractive white building on the grounds of Mr. Durbin's Kenton home contained his private magic theater and extensive collection of magicians' photographs (see page 204). Mr. Durbin continued active in I.B.M. affairs for many years and was president of the society from 1926 to 1937.

Annual I.B.M. conventions continue to be held in a different city each year. They are memorable occasions lasting several days and featuring elaborate magic programs, fine dealer exhibits, and a crowded program of fun and activities.

International headquarters of the I.B.M. are located at 114 North Detroit Street, Kenton, OH 43326. The editorial offices of *The Linking Ring* are at 820 North Inverway Road, Palatine, IL 60067. The executive editor is Mr. Howard Bamman, P.O. Box 606, Palatine, IL 60067. The advertising editor is Mr. Thomas M. Dowd, 28 North Main Street, Kenton, OH 43326.

At present the I.B.M., with over 10,000 members, is the largest magic fraternity in the world. This number includes 800 junior members between the ages of fourteen and eighteen. The organization has more than 200 local groups or "Rings," ranging in size from a dozen members to the British Ring with over 700 members. Rings may be found in most larger American and Canadian cities, with the largest overseas Rings located in Great Britain, Italy, Australia, New Zealand, Singapore, Buenos Aires, France, Sweden, Holland, Belgium and Switzerland. There are individual members in thirty-two other nations, including China and four countries behind the Iron Curtain.

Application forms for admission to the international organization may be obtained by writing to its headquarters in Kenton. Candidates are required to submit on the official forms information regarding their experience in magic and any special interests they may have, and must be sponsored by two members of the I.B.M. The admission fee and annual dues are relatively inexpensive and include a subscription to *The Linking Ring*.

Each issue of this magazine usually runs to over 150 pages. *The Linking Ring* contains many features that are both interesting and helpful for magicians, including new tricks and ideas contributed by members, columns, reviews of new effects being offered commercially, news of coming events in the world of magic, and—a feature of special interest to many readers—news reports of meetings, magic performances, and activities of members of the local Rings of the I.B.M.

The Rings are one of the I.B.M.'s greatest features.

The members of each Ring elect their officers, plan the Ring activities, and organize social events, shows, and special functions. In most Rings a monthly business meeting is followed by a magic show put on by members, or a lecture on magic by an eminent magician. Some Rings, like Ring 26 in New York City, also conduct "lab" sessions once a month. At these valuable sessions, a theme is discussed—such as rope effects, tricks with coins or cards, mental effects, or whatever the topic for the month may be. Members perform before the group and constructive advice and suggestions are offered.

Applications for admission to the Ring that is closest and most convenient for you may be made directly to the local Ring. Ring members must also be members of the international organization. To belong to the international I.B.M., it is not essential to join a Ring; however, if there is a Ring anywhere near your home, your I.B.M. membership will be greatly enriched by joining it. You will learn a great deal about magic while making new friends and enjoying the society of your fellow devotees to the mystic art. Your local magic dealer can probably tell you where the nearest Ring is located and inform you regarding its meetings and officers.

THE SOCIETY OF AMERICAN MAGICIANS

The Society of American Magicians has been working for the good of magic for three quarters of a century. Its thousands of members all over the world include many of the top magical performers, both professionals and serious amateurs.

It was on May 10, 1902, that the Society of American Magicians was founded in New York City. At that time the magic shop of Martinka & Company (see pages 169 and 223) at 493 Sixth Avenue was the country's leading magic emporium. A group of prominent magicians in the city had formed the habit of gathering frequently in an inner sanctum at Martinka's known as "the little back shop," where there was a small stage. There they talked magic and discussed new effects.

The idea of establishing a formal society of magicians was first proposed by two accomplished New York amateurs, Dr. Saram R. Ellison and Dr. W. Golden Mortimer. There were thirteen in the original organizing group. In *The Sphinx* for May, 1902, there appeared a news item reading as follows:

Initial steps have been taken for the formation of a society of American magicians. A largely attended meeting was held at Martinka's establishment and preliminary arrangements made for another meeting for the enactment of by-laws. Over twenty charter members have been secured.

The following month *The Sphinx* reported that the aims of the new society were "to promote harmony among those interested in Magic, and to further the elevation of the Art." These have continued to be the major objectives of the organization.

Many of the most famous names in magic were among those who joined the S.A.M. in its initial year. They included such eminent conjurers as Dr. James W. Elliott, Frank Ducrot, Elmer Ransom, Horace Goldin, Harry Kellar, Imro Fox, Leon and Adelaide Herrmann, Henry Ridgely Evans, Chung Ling Soo, Eugene Laurant, Dr. A. M. Wilson, William Hilliar, Buatier de Kolta and Frederick Eugene Powell. Howard Thurston, Harry Houdini and T. Nelson Downs were then performing in Europe but they, too, soon entered the society. Houdini took a very active part in the society's affairs and for a number of years he served as its president. David Devant was another early member.

In the years since the establishment of the New York City organization, which is known as the Parent Assembly of the S.A.M., many other Assemblies have been organized and chartered. At present there are 99 Assemblies in the United States, Canada and other countries.

Any reputable person seventeen years of age or older, sincerely interested in magic as an art, may apply for Active Membership through any one of the Assemblies. Applicants are tested to establish their proficiency in magic. They must also apply for Active Membership in the international organization of the S.A.M. Two sponsors, both S.A.M. members, are required.

Applicants between the ages of fourteen and seventeen may also be admitted, under similar conditions, as Junior Assembly Members.

Associate Members are also enrolled in the international organization. For further information about this category of membership, for which sponsors are not required, and admission procedures in general, write to Frank Buslovich, Membership Development Chairman, Lock Drawer 789-G, Lynn, MA 01903.

The official publication of the S.A.M. is the monthly magazine *M.U.M.* This is a well-edited and printed periodical full of news, secrets and advertisements of interest to magicians. It is available only to members.

The S.A.M. Library is housed in the Lincoln Center branch of the New York Public Library. Those wishing to consult it must present an S.A.M. membership card.

The S.A.M. maintains a Magic Hall of Fame in Hollywood, California. For particulars see page 211.

THE MAGIC COLLECTORS ASSOCIATION

This is an organization for serious collectors of magic equipment, books, magazines and memorabilia as well as for students of the history of the art. The Association publishes an excellent quarterly magazine, *Magicol;* the subscription is included in dues of $5.00 quarterly. A Magic Collectors Weekend for members of the Association, with talks and exhibits, has been held annually at Magic, Inc., in Chicago. Dr. John Henry Grossman is Honorary Life President of the Association. The Executive Secretary is Walter J. Gydesen, 5103 North Lincoln Avenue, Chicago, IL 60625.

THE INTERNATIONAL GUILD OF PRESTIDIGITATORS

The American branch of the International Guild of Prestidigitators meets the third Thursday evening of each month at Freedom House, 20 West 40th Street, New York, NY 10018. A magic show featuring members of the I.G.P. is presented at each meeting. Others interested in magic are welcome to attend the shows for a nominal admission fee.

Every few months, the I.G.P. holds a magic "clinic" at which members may perform effects and receive constructive criticism and suggestions on presentation or other aspects of their work from fellow members. Both stage and close-up magic are performed at these clinics.

A good many members of the New York group are schoolteachers as well as magicians. Many of them use magic techniques and effects in the classroom and find them useful aids in their educational work.

Formerly called The Knights of Magic, the organization adopted its present name following World War II. During that war its members presented many magic shows to entertain the troops at Army camps and hospitals, and also for senior citizens' groups.

The president of the New York group at time of writing is Herb Hurwitz. A former president was his brother, Dr. Abe Hurwitz, the father of Shari Lewis.

Other units of the I.G.P. have been organized in Hawaii, Australia and Japan.

THE MAGIC CIRCLE

This prominent British organization has its headquarters at 84, Chenies Mews, London, W.C. 1, England. It possesses an excellent library and collection of apparatus and memorabilia, as described on page 211.

For information, write to:

The Magic Circle
John Salisse (Secretary)
12 Hampstead Way
London, N.W. 11, England
(Telephone 01-455-1569)

OTHER ORGANIZATIONS

Association Française des Artistes Prestidigitateurs
Decamps (Zum Pocco)
9 Rue Bénédic-Mace
Caen, France, 14000

Clowns of America, Inc.
2300 Foster Avenue
Parkville, Maryland 21234

Fellowship of Christian Magicians
Mail Center—E.T.C.
Box 385-T
Connersville, Indiana 47331

The Magic Castle
7001 Franklin Avenue
Hollywood, California 90028
(see page 209)

Magic Club
Universal Magic & Supply Company
256 South Robertson Boulevard
Beverly Hills, California 90211

Magicians Club
International Unique Magic Studios
99 Leather Lane
London, E.C. 1, England

Magical Youths International
61551 Bremen Highway
Mishawaka, Indiana 46544

Ventura County Mystics
℅ R. Huffman
3530 Ketch Avenue
Oxnard, California 93030

(13 years old and up)

Napa Valley Magicians Guild
℅ J. P. Jackson
P.O. Box 2481
Napa, California 94558

*(Has junior division for
members 12 to 16 years)*

MAGIC CONVENTIONS

Many conventions for magicians are held every year in cities and towns all over the United States, as well as in the United Kingdom and on the European continent. These get-togethers range in length from one to three, four or even five days. The largest of them attract between 1000 and 2000 registrants. Many are sponsored by magical societies. Others are organized by prominent magic dealers such as Abbott's or Tannen's. These are important events in the magic world, and magi and their families look forward to the conventions and often plan their vacations around them.

Many of the conventions change their locations and dates from season to season. Some of them, such as the annual conventions of the International Brotherhood of Magicians and the Society of American Magicians, are organized in a different city each year by the local Ring or Assembly. The best way to keep informed about upcoming conventions is to subscribe to a magic magazine. It is usually necessary to register in advance, and it is best to arrange for lodgings at a motel or hotel, or for parking space for your camper or motor home, well ahead of convention time.

Because of the changing locations, dates and management of many of these get-togethers, that information cannot be given here. And since many are similar as to their general programs, it would hardly be useful to describe them all individually. Therefore, in order to

The dealers' display room is a popular gathering place at Abbott's Get-Together at Colon, Michigan. (*William Doerflinger Photo*)

give an idea of what the conventions offer, we will explore a cross-section of them and see what takes place at some of the best known and most representative.

INTERNATIONAL BROTHERHOOD OF MAGICIANS NATIONAL CONVENTION

The I.B.M. holds its national convention each summer in a different city, under the sponsorship of that city's I.B.M. Ring, as the local chapters are called. The conventions usually take place in July. Cities in which recent I.B.M. conventions have been held include Washington, D.C.; Evansville, Indiana; and Little Rock, Arkansas. On occasion the I.B.M. and the Society of American Magicians hold a combined convention.

Particulars regarding each year's upcoming convention appear in *The Linking Ring* and other magic magazines. Non-I.B.M. members are welcome at a higher registration fee, which includes membership application fee.

SOCIETY OF AMERICAN MAGICIANS

Each summer the S.A.M. holds a convention of several days' duration in a selected city in the United States. These conventions are elaborate affairs featuring gala evening shows, lectures, magic movies, close-up demonstrations, dealers' exhibits, social events and business meetings. Junior and Teen-Age Magical Contests are held.

Other organizations which have held meetings of members attending the S.A.M. convention, in recent years, include the Clowns of America, the Puppeteers of America, and the Invisible Lodge, a Masonic group. Boston was host to the S.A.M. convention in 1974, Chicago in 1975, and Philadelphia in 1976.

ABBOTT'S MAGIC GET-TOGETHER

Every August finds hundreds of magicians and their families from all over the United States and Canada converging on Colon, Michigan, for the annual four-day Get-Together sponsored by Abbott's Magic Manufacturing Company. The fortieth Get-Together in 1977 was a magician's paradise. The pleasant village of Colon (pop. 1172) borders three lakes connected by Swan Creek. Home of a dozen noted magicians and of the long-established Abbott company, Colon prides itself as "Magic Capital of the World." Recil Bordner, president of Abbott's, organizes each year an excellently varied program. Some 1600 people pack the high school auditorium each evening for glamorous stage shows.

Abbott's and other dealers' extensive displays of magical tricks, apparatus, accessories and publications are on sale in the showroom at the Colon Elementary School mornings and afternoons and after the evening shows. The showroom, always crowded with magicians of all ages, becomes the main social center of the Get-Together. Refreshments are sold outdoors at reasonable prices, and the informal atmosphere gives amateurs a change to talk with well-known magicians.

Morning and afternoon events include lectures and a talent contest for magicians up to age twenty-one, conducted by master prestidigitator and magic editor Neil Foster. Organ accompaniment is provided for all contestants. "Ventoramas" held in the intimate theater at the Abbott office just off the main street enable young ventriloquists to show their talent.

There are baffling close-up magicians; sub-get-to-gethers and bingo for ladies; a luncheon for senior citizens; and usually a magic ministers' meeting.

Abbott's can arrange rooms for registrants in private homes in Colon at prices averaging about $8.00 to $10.00 a day. Colon also has good facilities for motor homes and camping. These amenities make it unnecessary to stay at the motels at least 15 miles away. Meals are served at restaurants, with home-cooked dinners at churches.

Registration charge for 1977 was $40.00 per person for the four days, including reserved seats for all evening shows; one-day registration, $12.00. Registration is necessary for admission to the showroom. There were 1314 people registered for the 1976 Get-Together, with more attending the evening shows.

For particulars write Abbott's Magic Manufacturing Co., Colon, MI 49040.

At the check-in desk on arriving at a magic convention. (*William Doerflinger Photo*)

LOU TANNEN'S MAGICAL JUBILEE

Magical Jubilees are sponsored each fall in the Catskills by Louis Tannen, Inc., New York magic dealers. For some years the Jubilees have been held at Brown's Hotel, a large and luxurious resort hotel at Loch Sheldrake, New York. For a summary of the events at the Jubilee, please turn to page 230.

There is a registration charge of $35.00 per person, and hotel accommodations at Brown's range from $24.50 to $45.00 per day, with slightly lower rates for Thursday if you care to come a day early and attend the Thursday Night-Before Party, as many do. Rates cover full American plan accommodations with three meals a day. For a reservation form or further information write to Louis Tannen, Inc., 1540 Broadway, New York, NY 10036.

GEORGE SCHINDLER'S ANNUAL WEEKENDS OF MAGIC AND COMEDY

For several years George Schindler of Show-Biz Services, 1735 East 26th Street, Brooklyn, NY 11229, has produced these magic weekends at Grossinger's Hotel, Grossinger, New York 12734. The gatherings offer several days of fun and magical entertainment for the whole family. There are shows featuring some of the country's top magicians, talented close-up performers, and magic seminars, plus all the regular attractions of this glamorous luxury hotel. The 1977 Weekend included a contest for young magicians, ages ten to fourteen, sponsored by *Parents Magazine*.

Registration should be made in advance. For further

information and rates, write Show-Biz Services or Gros-singer's.

HOLLYWOOD I.B.M. RING 21 CAVALCADES OF MAGIC

Conventions are sponsored not only by the international organization of the I.B.M., but also by some local Rings. Ring 21, Hollywood, California, sponsored its eighth annual Cavalcade of Magic at the Ambassador Hotel in Los Angeles in June, 1977. This was a three-day affair with an elaborate program featuring a gala public show at the Wilshire Ebell Theater.

MIDWEST MAGIC JUBILEE

The Twentieth Anniversary St. Louis Midwest Magic Jubilee was sponsored in late July, 1977, by I.B.M. Ring No. 1 and S.A.M. Assembly Eight. It was a three-day affair, with an additional Night-Before Party on the Thursday just before the convention proper. The program included three gala shows, close-up magic, contests, a banquet, lectures and dealer displays.

SOUTHEASTERN ASSOCIATION AND FLORIDA STATE COMBINED CONVENTION

This convention, lasting four days, was held in 1977 at the Sheraton-Twin Towers Hotel in Orlando, Florida, from May 27 through 30. Shows, lectures, close-up performers, contests—the whole works were offered to registrants, with special rates for couples and for junior magicians fourteen years old and younger.

P.C.A.M. CONVENTIONS

Annual conventions are held by the Pacific Coast Association of Magicians, with full programs of shows, exhibits, lectures and other events, running for four days. The 1977 convention was scheduled for a conference center at the University of Washington at Seattle. It was sponsored by the Seattle Magic Ring, Inc., in cooperation with International Magigals, Inc., the organization of women magicians.

LARRY WEEKS' ALL-DAY MAGIC CONVENTIONS

For over ten years Larry Weeks, well-known magician, master juggler, and magic dealer, has sponsored his All-Day Magic Conventions in New York City. The conventions are held four times a year, usually on the first Sundays of March, June, September and December. Recently the events have been held in the ballroom of the Hotel Diplomat, 108 West 43rd Street, New York, N.Y. The location of the conventions changes from time to time, however, so check with Larry Weeks in advance before attending.

At a typical Larry Weeks' convention, doors open at 11 A.M. Registrants find a number of magic dealers awaiting them at well-stocked booths around the ballroom. Before lunchtime some unusual movie on magic is usually screened and a children's magic show is presented. About 2 P.M. there is a dealers' show, at which the dealers' representatives describe and perform new effects that they are offering for sale at their booths.

About 3 P.M. the auction gets underway. With Larry Weeks and volunteers such as Clayton Albright, the magician and magic collector from Albany, Ace Gorham, former president of the I.B.M., and others as auctioneers, used and some new magic apparatus, books, and magazines are auctioned off. The auctions offer opportunities to find those collector's items you've been looking for, perhaps at a modest price if you're lucky. The items are usually brought for auctioning by people attending the convention. The proceeds go to the owners, less 20 percent commission. The auction usually lasts for three or four hours of spirited bidding.

After a break for dinner at one of the many nearby restaurants, a professional magic show is staged at 8:30 P.M. The program usually features acts by half a dozen performers or troupes.

The success of these conventions is clear from the years they have been running and the faithfulness of the many magicians of all ages who regularly attend them. They're a great way to keep up with what's new in magic, sell equipment you no longer need, pick up new tricks or old rarities, and enjoy magic entertainment.

The registration charge for the convention in June, 1977, was $7.00 in advance, $8.00 at the door. Notices of upcoming conventions will be sent to those requesting them, at a nominal yearly charge of $1.00 to help cover costs of multigraphing and postage. For further information write to Larry Weeks, 456 Brooklyn Avenue, Brooklyn, NY 11225.

GARDEN STATE MAGICALE

The Garden State Magicale is presented three times a year by Doug Keller of the House of Magic in Red Bank, New Jersey, and Carl Bajor. These one-day conventions are held at the Coachman Inn in Cranford, New Jersey, near the Garden State Parkway. This is a modern, attractively appointed motel with large public rooms and excellent dining facilities. A number of magic dealers from the eastern states display their products for sale at booths and stands around a large room adjacent to the auditorium. In the auditorium movies on magic are shown in the morning, followed by a lecture; a dealers' demonstration show and a special ladies' event; a large auction of magic apparatus, books and magazines; and a magic show of many acts in the evening.

The Magicales are presented on the second Sunday

Magic collector and volunteer auctioneer Clayton Albright (*right*) recognizes a bid from the floor while Larry Weeks holds the next item to be auctioned at an All-Day Magic Convention in New York. (*William Doerflinger Photo*)

in March, the second Sunday in June, and the third Sunday in September. For further particulars write to Doug Keller's House of Magic, 12-14 White Street, Red Bank, NJ 07701 or phone 201-842-2255.

SUPER SUNDAY FOR SUPER MAGICIANS

One of the most enjoyable ways to sharpen your magic skills is to attend this unusual, all-day convention sponsored four times yearly by the Guaranteed Magic Company in Hatboro, Pennsylvania. Its colorful setting is Hatboro Manor, a Victorian mansion at 122 North York Road, whose architecture suggests some legendary castle of Merlin or King Arthur.

The program gets under way at noon with a series of four 15-minute teaching sessions, each led by an expert magician who gives instruction in his special field, such as magic with silks, ropes, cards, canes, etc. Half a dozen salesmen demonstrate and sell Guaranteed Magic equipment, and a magic auction is held.

The big feature of the afternoon is a lecture, demonstration and instruction given by the Super Star of the day, who is always a nationally-known magician.

From 5 to 7 P.M. a gourmet smorgasbord is served. Other restaurants nearby provide simpler snacks.

A gala, two-hour Concert of Magic, featuring four or five top-notch acts, is presented in the evening. The convention closes at midnight.

Super Sundays are held in March, June, September and December, on the first Sunday in each of these months, except that in September a later Sunday is sometimes chosen. Registration fee is $8.00; the optional smorgasbord is $6.50 additional. For complete details

drop a postcard to Bob Little, Guaranteed Magic, 27 Bright Road, Hatboro, Pennsylvania 19040; telephone 215-672-3344 (see also pages 225–226).

I.B.M. BRITISH RING CONVENTION

The large British Ring of the I.B.M. holds an annual convention in the late summer or autumn. The 1976 convention was held at the famous watering place of Brighton, a favorite spot for such events.

WORLD CONGRESS OF THE FÉDÉRATION INTERNATIONALE DES SOCIÉTÉS MAGIQUES

One of the great events of the international magic scene is the triennial Congress of the F.I.S.M. a gala affair held in one of the major capitals of Europe. In 1976 representatives of magic societies in many countries gathered in Vienna for this five-day convention. At the Vienna Concert House magicians from many lands appeared in competition for the highly coveted international trophies. The F.I.S.M. Congress is attended by a good many Americans and offers a rare opportunity to witness the performing styles of the finest European and Oriental magicians. Over 1800 registrants attended the latest Congress.

There are many more magicians' conventions being held in the United States, Britain and on the Continent. For the latest information, consult your local magic dealers or a conjurers' magazine such as *Genii, The Linking Ring* or *M.U.M.* There is an excellent chance of your finding a gala magic convention scheduled for your own home region.

MEET SOME DEALERS *

ABBOTT'S MAGIC MANUFACTURING COMPANY

Abbott's Magic Manufacturing Company is one of the oldest manufacturers of magical apparatus in the United States. It is located in Colon, a village of about 1200 population in the beautiful lake and farming country of southwestern Michigan. This lovely village, which is surrounded by three lakes and has a waterfall a few yards from its main street, is known as "The Magic Capital of the World."

The company was founded in 1934 by Percy Abbott, an Australian magician who had previously operated a magic business in Sydney. Abbot had first come to Colon in 1927 as a guest at the summer home there of the celebrated American magician Harry Blackstone. The vaudeville conjurer from "down under" promptly fell in love with the village of Colon and also with one of its prettiest girls, Gladys Goodrich. For about eighteen months Percy Abbott was associated with Blackstone in the Blackstone Magic Company. He then returned to the road, working as a magician in shows and carnivals. He and Gladys were married and when their first child was born they realized that life on the road was not right for a youngster and decided to settle down—permanently, they hoped—in Colon.

There, in January, 1934, Percy Abbott started the magic company that still bears his name. After renting

(William Doerflinger Photo)

space above the A. & P. grocery store, he had so little money left that he had to have his first catalogue, a booklet of twenty pages, printed on credit.

A few months later, Percy Abbott invited a new partner to invest in a half share of his fledgling business. The new member of the company, a young man named Recil Bordner, had a very different background from that of the Australian magician. The son of a respected farmer of Eaton, Ohio, he had taken magic lessons from Abbott and had then spent two years giving shows in Michigan and Ohio communities.

From the moment that Recil Bordner and Percy Abbott teamed up together, their business forged ahead steadily. They leased a building which had been a carriage factory. An office and workshop occupied the ground floor, with a small theater on the second floor. Here the magic effects they planned to produce would be demonstrated. With its black-painted walls decorated with silhouettes of skeletons in white, the Abbott plant stood out in contrast to its quiet village surroundings.

At this factory, in September, 1934, Abbott and Bordner held an open house for magicians from Michigan and Ohio. This was the start of the famous Abbott Get-Togethers for magicians. The eighty conjurers who attended the one-day affair bought $88.00 worth of magic. This so encouraged the partners that they decided

* In alphabetical order.

to make it an annual event. A Second Annual Get-Together was held in 1935 and since then there have been Get-Togethers each year, with few exceptions. In 1937, over 500 magicians attended the Get-Together. The theater was enlarged, and a Night-Before Party for magicians and a show for the general public were added to the program. Later the Get-Togethers were held in a large tent with a seating capacity of 1200 people. They were subsequently moved to the Colon High School. The 1977 Get-Together, as already mentioned (page 217), included four elaborate evening shows. A special children's magic show was co-sponsored by the Colon Lions' Club. Lectures, magic talent contests, and close-up sessions are also regular features of the present-day Get-Togethers.

A creative magician, Percy Abbott invented many new effects to help swell the size of the firm's catalogue. As their sales of magical apparatus increased in volume, the partners opened branch retail shops in Detroit, Indianapolis, Chicago, New York and Los Angeles, which they operated for some years. They instituted an active publishing program and over the years have published many outstanding hardbound and softcover books on various branches of magic. A monthly magazine of magic, *The Tops,* was published from 1936 to 1941 under Percy Abbott's editorship and from 1941 to 1951 under the editorship of Mel Melson. Publication was then suspended owing to a temporary decline in public interest in magic during the 1950s. January, 1961, however, saw the publication of the first issue of *The New Tops,* edited by the talented prestidigitator and artist, Neil Foster. This monthly magazine, printed at the Abbott plant, now has about 4000 subscribers all over the world. Among its regular contributors are Bruce Posgate, who writes on magic for children; Frances Ireland Marshall on women in magic; Nick Trost on card conjuring; Micky Hades on mentalism; Sid Lorraine with an entertaining column of magic news, and many others.

In 1959 Percy Abbott decided to retire and Recil Bordner bought his share of the business. The following year the magic world was saddened by the news of Percy Abbott's death.

Under the leadership of Recil Bordner, Abbott's has continued to grow and to flourish. A new building where many of the manufacturing processes are carried out was acquired in 1974. The Abbott plant now occupies some 42,000 square feet of floor space. It provides full-time employment for about twenty-five people. It includes facilities for precision metal work, tool and die making, silk dyeing, blacksmith shop, woodworking, printing, art, silk-screen processing, and many others. The latest Abbott catalogue has over 500 large pages, which is more than twenty times the size of that first one of 1934. So far forty summer Get-Togethers have been organized, most of them in Colon, and the town can point to Abbott's,

The main office building at Abbott's Magic Manufacturing Company, Colon, Michigan. (*William Doerflinger Photo*)

as well as to a dozen well-known magicians, in support of its proud claim to be the Magic Capital of the World.

Mario Carrandi

Unlike most magic dealers, Mario Carrandi confines himself to a single field: antique magical apparatus, posters, books and memorabilia. He buys and sells old and rare magic as a hobby, because he loves the beautifully made, precision apparatus and colorful graphics of an earlier era. A collector at heart, he often finds himself unable to part with a particularly choice piece. In his home in Kendall Park, New Jersey, this young NBC executive has built one of the country's leading collections of magic posters, apparatus and publications. Its quality testifies to the enthusiasm and natural good taste he brings to his avocation of magic collecting.

Mario Carrandi's fascination with magic dates back to 1948, when as a small boy he saw the full evening show of Fu Manchu (David Bamberg) in Havana, Cuba, where his family then lived. Mario was convinced that Fu Manchu's illusions were real, until his father took him backstage to meet the magician. Fu Manchu showed him some card tricks, explaining that they were done by sleight-of-hand and that his stage illusions had been done by trickery too. Mario was reassured—and forever after enthralled by the world of magic. In later years he regretted that he had not seized the opportunity to ask Fu Manchu for some of his mysteriously dramatic posters, which covered the walls of the city with pictures of demons and other supernatural marvels.

Mario Carrandi, magician, magic collector and dealer in the unusual. (*William Doerflinger Photo*)

Not long after this event the Carrandi family moved to New York, where Mario became a customer of Al Flosso and Lou Tannen. In time he graduated from St. John's University. In 1964 he joined the Marine Corps, in which he served for six years.

After leaving the Marines, Mario and his wife, Susan, settled in Queens. It was to decorate their new apartment that Mario acquired his first magic poster from Paul Fleming, that fine magician from Swarthmore, Pennsylvania. This first real magical investment was the Strobridge poster of Harry Kellar with imps on his shoulders. Today, at auction, that poster would probably bring from six to ten times the $25.00 that Mario paid for it. He has it today and says he would not part with it at any price. After that his poster collection grew rapidly until he owned forty to fifty—far more than he could display in the apartment.

It was another development, however, that was to launch Mario Carrandi in his role as a dealer in old and rare magic. Late in 1969 he read in *The Linking Ring* a small advertisement announcing that the estate of the late Warren Hamilton of Tampa, Florida, manufacturer and dealer in magical apparatus, would be offered for sale.

"I didn't know what it consisted of," Mario related

recently, "so I wrote the trustee, a bank in Tampa, and received a huge inventory of apparatus, posters, memorabilia and books. I wanted them, badly. It was a sealed-bid proposition, and I was able to persuade my father-in-law to go along with me and advance me the money. I placed my sealed bid, and two days later I was notified that I had the collection.

"I was really scared," Mario continued, "especially since it wasn't my money! I drove down to Tampa and paid the bank. My cousin went down with me, and he helped me load the stuff. We had a huge Ryder truck—a big twelve-speed truck with a hydraulic lift at the end, and we started loading the Hamilton estate into the truck. There was so much of it that we filled seventy-five moving cartons, the real big ones. It took us two days, eighteen hours a day, packing without stopping in 90-degree weather, humid, in a very old, musty house, full of dust. The heat was unbearable, and my cousin and I both broke out in a rash. Finally we finished loading the truck, and set out for New York.

"After I got the collection," Mario went on, "I said to myself, 'What am I doing with all this?' I decided that I would keep the best pieces and try to sell the rest. At that time I used to get lists of used magic from Harold Martin in Peoria, Illinois. I figured, 'What have I got to lose? I will put a little block ad in *The Linking Ring*, make up a list, and try to dispose of my excess.'

"And that's exactly what I did. I started selling off the excess material. And before I knew it I was involved in buying collections and estates, and dealing in antique magic."

Since that first list Mario Carrandi has been sending out others, once or twice a year, to collectors. His success in finding these rare items is due partly to his willingness to travel hundreds of miles, if need be, to secure them. Preparing the lists involves research and careful study, for each includes hundreds of pieces of magical apparatus, posters, books, magazines, photographs, letters and other memorabilia. To help cover costs of duplicating and mailing, there is a charge of $1.00 per list. Such lists are the favorite reading of magic collectors. No time is lost in studying them from end to end, for the most desirable items go fast . . . and may never be duplicated in a collector's lifetime.

Mario Carrandi also exhibits fascinating selections from his holdings of antique magic at magicians' conventions. A crowd of magicians of all ages usually surrounds his booth, studying and admiring the unusual items offered for sale. Among these treasures one may perhaps find an intricate Watch and Card Target made in Germany by Conradi some seventy-five years ago. Beside it may be an old French Spirit Clock, a crystal dial with inlaid gold numerals, on any one of which the freely spinning hand will come to rest at the will of the operator. At the back of the table will be, perhaps, a magnificent stand of ornate bronze work, made by János Bartl of Hamburg, to cause billiard balls mysteriously to vanish and reappear in its many shallow cups. There are materializing birdcages made by Floyd Thayer of Los Angeles half a century ago; rare palming coins from the great Roterberg shop in old Chicago and the act of T. Nelson Downs; production boxes beautifully decorated in Oriental style by Fu Manchu's father, the great Okito . . . and who knows what else? No one can predict what may appear in Mario Carrandi's collection to bring the spirits of great wizards of the past clustering around again, and blow away the dust from the pages of old catalogues eloquent with the secrets of magic.

THE FLOSSO HORNMANN MAGIC COMPANY

Of all America's rapidly increasing number of magic dealers, the one carrying on the longest continuous record of operations is probably the Flosso Hornmann Magic Company, the "Little Old Magic Shop" at 304 West 34th Street in New York City. For almost forty years the shop was presided over by Al Flosso, the "King of Koins," one of the most knowledgeable and original magicians of his day. Since Al's death in 1976, the shop's historic tradition has been carried on capably by his son Jack, also a talented magician, who was associated with his father in the store and has toured the world with his own magic revue.

But Al was one of the shop's later owners. Despite the Flosso Hornmann name on the glass street door, on the second-story window of Flosso's a weathered sign in black and gold Victorian lettering still reads:

MARTINKA & CO.
MAGIC TRICKS

This modest reminder recalls the origin of the enterprise in New York's most legendary magic emporium of the nineteenth and early twentieth centuries. Established in 1873, according to its 1898 catalogue, Martinka & Company occupied premises with over 5000 square feet of floor space at 493 Sixth Avenue. Its founders, the brothers Francis and Tony Martinka, ranked among the world's top magical designers and mechanics. Their thick catalogues, beautifully illustrated with fine engravings, are now collectors' items, like the fabulous magical apparatus and illusions described and depicted in their pages. Antique Martinka equipment is now all but unobtainable and commands premium prices from collectors. Many of the Martinkas' creations were bought by such headliners as Harry Kellar and Herrmann the Great and used in their full evening shows.

An intriguing feature of the old Martinka catalogues reflects a tradition that went back to the magic performances of the seventeenth and eighteenth centuries and was brought to its all-time high by the great French conjurer Robert-Houdin. This was the exhibition of marvelous mechanical automatons. The Martinkas made to order a turbaned chess-playing automaton that rivaled the automatic grand master of Maelzel, which Edgar Allan Poe had analyzed (not entirely correctly) in a famous essay.

The back room at Martinka's, with its small theater, was the locale where the Society of American Magicians was organized, as previously described, in 1902. Francis Martinka was one of the moving spirits in the founding of the society. His brother Antonio was also an early member.

In 1917 Martinka & Company was purchased by the famous Carter the Great, the American magician who made eight world tours with his impressive illusion shows. One of Carter's most startling illusions was 'The Lion's Bride.' In this effect Carter threw a beautiful maiden into a cage holding a ravenous lion. Luckily for the girl the King of Beasts changed at the last moment into Carter himself, draped in a lion's skin. Between tours this illusion was stored in the back room at Martinka's. "The illusion slept quietly," says an account in the Flosso Hornmann catalogue, "but 'Monty' the lion, star of the show, used to roar like the devil when business was slow. Monty's roars always stimulated the customers. In those golden days they'd buy anything—just to get out, and fast!"

Carter the Great seems to have been unable to abandon the stage to adopt the more settled life style of a magic dealer. In 1919 the company was sold again to none other than Harry Houdini and two associates. A stock certificate dated April 29, 1919, and signed by Houdini as president, is now on display in the shop.

The following year, according to a recently-published Flosso Hornmann catalogue, Houdini merged Martinka & Company with the Hornmann Magic Company. Professor Otto Hornmann had been active in the magic business in New York for a number of years. He had the reputation of being a gifted inventor of tricks and illusions, some of which are still being performed today. A catalogue in the writer's collection shows that in 1907 his Magic Company was located at 270 West 39th Street. By 1920, Hornmann's was at 304 West 34th Street, and there the combined business continued. It is still there today.

When I, as a youngster in the 1920s, first climbed the single flight of stairs and doubled back down the hallway to enter the enchanting Hornmann/Martinka showroom, there was a new proprietor—rotund, jolly Frank Ducrot, a clever and popular society and club magician who wore a flowing black silk bow tie and possessed an exhaustive knowledge of all things magical. Associated with Ducrot at one time, some years earlier, had been William E. (Billy) Robinson, the native New Yorker better known as Chung Ling Soo, the name under which he appeared in his world-renowned Chinese magic act. Ducrot and Robinson collaborated in inventing and improving effects, including the Ducrot Thumb Tie, one of Frank's most impressive specialties. In 1918 Robinson died in London, shot down on the stage when his Bullet-Catching Trick went wrong.

Among the countless New York boys who had been drawn irresistibly to Martinka's, back in the 493 Sixth Avenue days, was a nine-year-old lad from Brooklyn named Albert Levinson, who was later to be better known under his professional name, Al Flosso. To save carfare, Al walked all the way from his Brooklyn home across the Williamsburg Bridge, uptown to Martinka's and back. The Martinka brothers, unlike most dealers today, never encouraged juvenile trade. Youngsters were tolerated in their showroom only to the extent of being permitted to pay a small sum and receive in return a sealed package which they were not allowed to open in the store. Only when a young customer was outside on the sidewalk again did he find out what trick he had bought. When Al tore open his 25-cent package on Sixth Avenue he was pleased to find that it contained the well-made wherewithal to produce from one's mouth yards and yards of paper ribbons followed by a long, slender, red-and-white-striped Barber's Pole.

By age thirteen Al Flosso was working full-time in a Coney Island ten-in-one show, presenting a coin act featuring the Miser's Dream, always one of his most brilliant effects. At fifteen he went on the road and for some years traveled the country over with such circuses as Al G. Barnes' (Flosso managed its sideshow, besides doing his magic act), Sells-Floto, Ringling Brothers-Barnum and Bailey, Miller's 101 Bar Ranch, and many others.

When Frank Ducrot died in 1938, Al Flosso bought the Hornmann/Martinka Company and settled down in New York. Besides operating the shop, he continued to appear frequently as one of the country's cleverest and most beloved magicians, presenting his uproarious comedy act and coin manipulations as "the Fakir of Coney Island." His costume was always the same—top hat, black coat with outsized boutonniere, and spring-loaded black-and-yellow bow tie that sprang open to a majestic wing-spread at the height of the fun.

Hundreds of small boys made their first appearance in a magic show as volunteers for Flosso's incomparable Miser's Dream. "Stand up straight, my boy!" he would admonish them as he plucked coins from their ears and collars and half-dollars rained from their noses and mysteriously filled their pockets. "Watch the perfessor! He'll be here in a minute!"

Al Flosso's shop was a gathering place for professional and amateur magicians, all of whom were his friends as well as his customers, or soon became so. There of a Saturday it was common to find such top magicians as Dunninger, John Scarne, the Amazing Randi and Martin Gardner chatting and browsing through Al's stock of magical books and apparatus old and new, while Al overhauled people's obstinate gimmicks and talked magic. Somehow Al made every visitor feel better when he belatedly departed than he had when he sounded the buzzer at the street door and walked upstairs. "There is only one true, non-commercial magic shop left in the world," the Great Virgil once said. "It belongs to Al Flosso. It's a magician's 'heaven on earth' for me."

Al was active both as a dealer and as a performer until he was past the age of eighty. He died, after a short illness, on May 13, 1976.

Today the Flosso Hornmann Magic Company, under Jack Flosso, continues much as it was, except that Jack has dusted, cleaned house, rearranged the showcases and installed new exhibits. Like a small but distinguished museum of magic, the shop now houses a remarkable collection of magic memorabilia and beautifully made, one-of-a-kind pieces of antique apparatus lovingly arranged by Jack Flosso. Glass cases are filled with priceless things that belonged to his father, mementoes of a lifetime in magic. Here is an early pair of Houdini's handcuffs, next to the Martinka & Company stock certificate bearing the signature of the immortal escape artist. Here is a letter written in longhand by Chung Ling Soo on one of his full-color letterheads. Here is a rare, amber glass wand presented to Al Flosso by a famous magical society, alongside mounted testimonial plaques awarded him by a dozen I.B.M. Rings and S.A.M. Assemblies. Here are a pair of beautifully executed bronze hands perched on costly bases and holding fans of sculptured playing cards, commissioned and presented by the Magicians' Guild to honor Al Flosso. And here is an old, yellowed, red-and-white-striped paper Barber's Pole from Martinka & Company.

U. F. GRANT AND THE MAK-MAGIC COMPANY

"I consider U. F. Grant one of the outstanding inventors of magical effects of the past twenty-five years," wrote John Northern Hilliard, the famed author of *Greater Magic,* some years ago. A contemporary magician, Russell Swann, was even more unreserved in his praise. "I consider U. F. Grant," he said, "the greatest creator of magical effects in the world."

For sixty years "Gen" Grant—the nickname by which he is best known to his many friends throughout the world of wonder-working—has been performing, originating and selling magic. His full name is Ulysses Frederick Simpson Grant and he is a great-great-grandson of General U. S. Grant. His "Popular Magic" catalogues and handsomely designed, sturdy, yet reasonably priced apparatus and illusions have long been familiar to most magicians. A deluxe line of U. F. Grant's Popular Magic is now manufactured and distributed by the Mak-Magic Company of Columbus, Ohio. Mak-Magic is operated by Mr. Grant's son, Joseph T. Grant, and daughter, Mary Ann King. Mak-Magic effects and illustrated catalogues are available not only from the company itself but also from some 200 other dealers whom it supplies throughout the world.

Mr. Grant has written and produced countless tricks and manuscripts on original ideas or variations in practically every field of magic: pocket tricks, card effects, club magic and illusions, mental magic and others. He has performed as a guest on the programs of many of the "greats," including Houdini, Thurston and Blackstone. He has created over 14 types of levitations and suspensions. He was a pioneer in creating and developing "illusionettes," such as the Dagger Head Chest, in which a chest is placed over a volunteer's head and daggers are thrust through it in all directions. The front of the chest is then opened and the head has vanished. Eventually the volunteer returns to his seat intact.

Another favorite creation of Mr. Grant's is the Farmer and the Witch illusionette. This is worked with two unrehearsed children from the audience. The boy is dressed in a farmer's costume and the girl in a witch's outfit. They mysteriously change places, without the use of any cabinet.

Mr. Grant has also created a number of other illusions that can be performed without the use of heavy stage props. He has lectured widely before magic clubs and issued a series of 16-millimeter sound films to demonstrate and teach over twenty-four tricks with ordinary objects.

Recently U. F. Grant, who is now aged seventy-six, was flown from his Ohio home to Hollywood, where he was acclaimed and honored with the award of the Academy of Magical Arts for his outstanding work as a magical inventor and producer of original material. His career has been exceptional indeed for the extent and variety of his contributions to magic over the years.

BOB LITTLE'S GUARANTEED MAGIC

An hour's drive from Philadelphia in the southeastern hills of Pennsylvania there is an enchanted village whose 300 people all "eat, sleep, and drink magic." Hatboro, Pennsylvania, was founded in the eighteenth century by a colony of some seventeen hat makers from England who later made tri-corner hats for George Washington's Continental Army. Hat making continued to be the town's chief industry until shortly after the Civil War. Now Bob Little, dynamic young head of the Guaranteed Magic Company, has brought the hat business back to Hatboro with the making of magic hats which materialize mysteriously out of torn-up tissue paper. These beautifully crafted, colorful hats are made, Bob Little

Memorabilia of Al Flosso on exhibition at the Flosso Hornmann Magic Company. (*William Doerflinger Photo*)

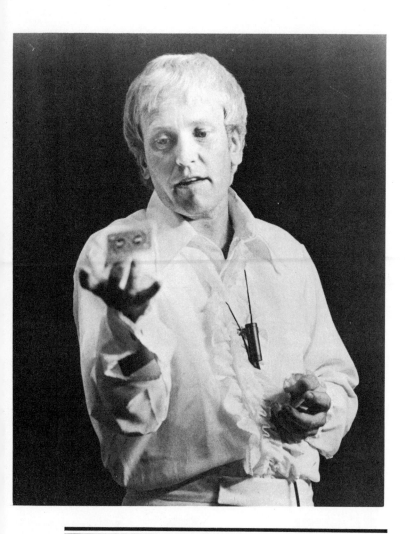

Bob Little of Guaranteed Magic.

ucts are sold, as well, by many other dealers, for much of the company's business is wholesale.

As a performer himself, Bob Little especially enjoys doing close-up, after-dinner magic with cards and coins. Business in Hatboro has "been growing by leaps and bounds," he says, "because magic is such a great hobby. It makes an extrovert out of you. It boosts your own ego and for the general public, its effect is amazing and mind-boggling. You can entertain anyone from children in Sunday school right up to a nightclub audience. More people are taking up magic all the time. It's an 'in' thing right now; how long it'll be up like this I don't know, but it's a good thing for our town and everybody that's making magic."

Tours of the Guaranteed Magic plant are arranged by Mr. John Soloway on weekends, by appointment. The address is 27 Bright Road, Hatboro, PA 19040. Tel. 215-672-3344.

Guaranteed Magic's Super Sundays for Super Magicians, all-day magic conventions held four times yearly, were described on page 219.

Magic, Inc.

One of America's oldest magic dealers is the Chicago firm simply and aptly known as Magic, Inc. It was founded in 1926 by Laurie Ireland and was called the Ireland Magic Company until 1963, when the present owners incorporated it and adopted the new name.

Frances Ireland Marshall, one of the owners, was formerly married to Laurie Ireland. After his death she married the well-known magician Jay Marshall, and they have since operated the business together. Jay Marshall is president of the company and his wife is secretary-treasurer.

Magic, Inc., occupies its own two-story building at 5082 North Lincoln Avenue, on the north side of Chicago. On the ground floor is the display room of its magic store, which is managed by Walter J. Gydesen. Here, too, is the Punch and Judy Bookshop, operated by Jay Marshall personally. Offices and the shipping department occupy the middle of the building, and the printing and binding departments are in the rear. In an extension to the south is a small theater and meeting room. Altogether the firm has some 13,000 square feet of space.

In the Magic, Inc., theater, among other events, the annual Collectors' Weekends of the Magic Collectors Association, of which Walter Gydesen is executive secretary, take place. The Mazda Mystic Ring and the Wizards' Club, independent magic clubs, and the Junior Magicians' Circle also hold their meetings in the company's theater.

Magic, Inc., carries an extensive line of magic equipment and supplies, as well as books and other publica-

explains, "with tender, loving care. They're all hand-made, hand-folded, and the Hatboro women do this in their homes while they're watching TV. We make more magic hats now than anyone in the world" (see page 104).

When you cross the old drawbridge leading into this rural village, you enter a twilight zone of yesteryear. Its cobbled streets are dominated by an antique castle and the buildings of the Guaranteed Magic plant. The company started manufacturing magic effects in 1962. It produces and imports a wide range of magic goodies, including the hats. Two German jewelers turn out precision-cut magic coins and coin boxes for the company. Tricks are made with silks, ropes, playing cards, metal and plastics. Books and an attractive catalogue are printed. Bob Little goes out to some thirty magic conventions a year around the country to sell tricks and bring orders back to Hatboro. Guaranteed Magic prod-

tions. It has a well-written magic catalogue of 258 pages, and two book catalogues. The older of these contains books of all publishers in the field of magic and related arts. It also contains a number of interesting short articles on magic books and book collecting, by experts in the field.

Prices have been brought up to date in the newer book catalogue, which includes all titles published by Magic, Inc.

Jay Marshall, the head of Magic, Inc., is one of the country's most talented magicians and ventriloquists. He is in demand at magic conventions in all parts of America, and also frequently entertains at trade shows, parties and other events. For some years his ventriloquial figure was, in fact, one of his own hands, with a white glove and two buttons, and Mr. Marshall's thumb for lower jaw. "Lefty" exhibited a thoroughly independent personality. He has recently been augmented by an oversized white rabbit with a large mouth and irrepressible habit of arguing. The rabbit also likes to sing, in a voice that inimitably combines stridency and sentiment.

Jay Marshall has brought together a large collection of rare magic posters, books, and memorabilia. His Punch and Judy Bookshop sells new and old magic books and buys libraries, magazine files and interesting old books. Anyone wishing to buy or sell is invited to write or telephone. This should always be done before mailing in books. The bookshop will also try to help customers find the old magic books for which they are hunting.

Frances Ireland Marshall is one of America's most prolific, best informed and most entertaining writers on magic and magicians. She is associate editor of *The Linking Ring,* the official magazine of the International Brotherhood of Magicians; in addition, she contributes a column on magic in the Chicago area to *The Linking Ring* and one on women in magic to *The New Tops.* Her popular book, *With Frances in Magicland,* is filled with reminiscences of magicians she has known, and is written with the light touch she made popular in an earlier book, *You Don't Have To Be Crazy.* An important work on which Jay and Frances Marshall have recently collaborated is *The Success Book,* a comprehensive guide to the business side of magic. Frances Marshall is also co-author with Gene Anderson of *Newspaper Magic,* an outstanding book in that field as previously mentioned.

In the Magic, Inc., building there is a bulletin board giving the news of magicians in the Chicago area and where they are working. All magi traveling to Chicago are invited to pay a visit to Magic, Inc., during their stay in the Windy City. So if you're planning a trip, write ahead for a map showing just how to find your way to Magic, Inc., a Chicago institution well known in all fifty states.

THE MYSTICAL MAGIC TOWNE HOUSE

Want to enjoy a buffet dinner while watching several of New York's cleverest close-up magicians perform their miracles? Take a child to a magic show? Browse among tricks for sale in a modern magic shop? Or arrange a gala children's birthday party complete with magic clowns, ice cream, cake, balloons and a magic show staged especially for your guests in an intimate little theater?

All these attractions are available under one roof at the Magic Towne House, 1026 Third Avenue, near 61st Street, New York. The Towne House is the brainchild of two young magicians, Ray Carter and Dorothy Dietrich, who operate it and sometimes appear on its programs.

Buffet dinners are served on Friday and Saturday evenings, starting at 9:00 P.M. The first magic act goes on at 9:30. The magi work at a large round table at one end of a long room, with the spectators sitting around them on chairs and perched on comfortable stools. The other half of the room is lined with tables for diners, which are occupied mostly during the intervals between performers.

On Friday evenings the crowd is mostly singles, on Saturday young couples, plus a representation of older magic buffs. Cost for dinner and entertainment is surprisingly reasonable, about $6.00 per person. There is an additional charge of $4.00 for a special appearance at midnight Saturdays by Theodore, the diabolical comedian.

Children's shows are staged in the theater on a lower floor of the Towne House on Saturdays, Sundays, and any holiday when the New York public schools are closed. Performances start at 1:00, 2:30 and 4:00 P.M. Advance reservations are necessary for the kiddies' shows. They can be made by phoning (212) 752-1165.

Dorothy Dietrich, who hails from Erie, Pennsylvania, is one of the East's most active lady magicians. She does general magic, dove productions, even straitjacket escapes. She claims to be the only magician who saws a man in half as a feature illusion. The victim is usually a volunteer from the audience, but Dorothy has also neatly bisected Garry Moore on TV.

Her partner, Ray Carter, performs a wide range of magic effects also, and is well known for his demonstrations of ESP and mind reading. The Towne House is a discovery for magic lovers and the parents of magic lovers.

D. ROBBINS & COMPANY AND ITS "E-Z" MAGIC

West 17th Street between the Avenue of the Americas and Seventh Avenue in New York is a busy, hardworking neighborhood. Trucks load and unload merchandise along the curb. Workaday buildings line the block, some of them old, with show windows drably painted over, others modern and brightly lighted. For the passer-by there is nothing mystical about the plain building on the north side of the street, about halfway down the block. No one who wasn't familiar with the world of hocus pocus would suspect that this unassuming edifice held a treasure house of conjuring wonders. Yet such is the case, for here one will find the headquarters of D. Robbins & Company, Inc., one of the oldest firms in the magic trade.

It is also one of the most versatile. Paul Fried, president of D. Robbins, describes his company as a "wholesaler, distributor, manufacturer and publisher." D. Robbins brings together magic tricks and supplies from all over the world and redistributes them to retailers in the United States and abroad. Its line is familiar to most magicians under the trade name "E-Z" Magic. "E-Z" tricks form an important part of the stock of many smaller magic shops, and are also carried by many larger retail dealers.

Recently D. Robbins celebrated its fiftieth anniversary. The company was established by David Robbins, a well-known magician and dealer, in 1926. Mr. Robbins ran the business for thirty-four years. On his retirement in 1960 the company was purchased by Paul Fried. Thus the firm has had only two presidents in over fifty years of operation.

From a busy office at the entrance to a huge stockroom with capacious shelves reaching from floor to ceiling, Paul Fried corresponds with his widely distributed sources of supply. He and his staff fill a steady flow of orders from magic dealers all over North America, as well as many in other countries, and keep watch over a complex inventory. The "E-Z" Magic line ranges from pocket tricks of all kinds to apparatus for "club and stage" magic, from spring-animated bunnies to be produced from hats to secrets of mentalism and clairvoyance. In all, the company at present stocks about 2000 different items.

D. Robbins & Company itself publishes many of the books on magic that it distributes. It also issues, at frequent intervals, catalogues of "E-Z" Magic which are sold in quantity to retail dealers and released by them to the public.

D. Robbins sells only to stores, to pitchmen, or others who buy in large quantities for promotional or advertising purposes. Because it is so fully occupied with its wholesaling work, the company does not sell to individuals. Its products are available, however, at most magic shops in the United States.

Individuals who wish to purchase "E-Z" Magic tricks should not, therefore, order them directly from D. Robbins & Company. Instead, ask your nearest retail magic dealer for the "E-Z" Magic items you need.

He will know all about D. Robbins & Company and the varied line of dependable magic that it makes available from all over the world.

Louis Tannen, Inc.

Seventeen stories above Times Square in New York's theatrical district, one of the country's largest magic dealers has its showroom and offices. Louis Tannen, Inc., have been manufacturers, wholesalers and retailers of magic effects for nearly half a century. They are also one of the major publishers of magic books. The Tannen shop and offices are, with design, located off the street and away from casual curiosity seekers. Nevertheless, they are the crossroads of professional and amateur magic in New York and a favorite gathering place for magicians in both categories.

Since its founder, Louis Tannen, retired to Florida a few years ago, the company has continued to flourish under the management of his younger brother, Irving Tannen, and two other partners, Tony Spina and Jack Ferero. Tannen's employs a staff of more than twenty people who demonstrate effects to customers, process mail orders, ship from five to seven large mailbags of magic daily, and manufacture a wide variety of "engineered magic" items ranging from pocket tricks to glamorous illusions.

Almost always, it seems, the Tannen company has operated next door to a theater. Lou Tannen founded the business about 1929, starting with what his brother Irv describes as "a tiny little store in Brooklyn," next door to the Fabian Fox Theater at Flatbush Avenue and Nevins Street. It was called The Nat Louis Fun Shop, combining Lou's name with that of his wife, Natalie. Despite his youth, red-headed Lou had already been active in magic for some years. He had worked for a dealer on Manhattan's Park Row and had toured the country doing magic shows under the professional name of The Great La-Dan.

Selling magic and novelties, the Fun Shop prospered, and in the early 1930s Lou opened a magic manufacturing plant in Brooklyn, near Loew's Metropolitan Theater. Irv Tannen went to work there for Lou in 1933, as a machinist making magic apparatus.

"Then," Irv recalled in an interview, "in the mid-thirties we moved to Manhattan—moved the shop to the arcade in 52nd Street, and the manufacturing plant to Eighth Avenue, near Stillman's Gym." In the 1930s Lou also opened branch stores in various cities around the country, including one in Boston and others in Texas and California.

In 1941 Lou Tannen made the momentous decision to move "off the street." Closing the shop in the busy arcade, he leased a secluded, windowless showroom and publishing office high in the old Wurlitzer Building at

Lou Tannen in his first shop, the Nat Louis Fun Shop in Brooklyn. (*Courtesy of Irving Tannen*)

120 West 42nd Street, just west of Sixth Avenue. There he laid out his apparatus and books and waited, without even the benefit of a show window or any street display, for the world to beat a path to his door, although it was quite a plain wooden door, opening into a prosaic corridor.

To move "off the street," as Irv Tannen explained, was "a very difficult thing to do in those times, because you had to establish a following. But it was a very clever thing to do, because street trade is OK, but it's difficult to control. Up here, we get a very nice clientele. We trust them; they're just honest and nice and it's a warm, close feeling. It's a much nicer feeling when you get off the streets. And over the years, the business got bigger and more profitable."

In 1969 came another move. The Wurlitzer Building—which, incidentally, had a theater in the basement —passed into history. "They tore the building down," said Irv Tannen. "We're not that great magicians, to keep ourselves suspended in midair."

Consequently Louis Tannen, Inc., moved to its present location at 1540 Broadway, in the Loew's Theater Building. "It was the best move we ever made," Irv continued, "because we're so beautifully located here. We've doubled the size of our quarters and can now keep the big illusions right on the premises."

Tannen's is able to build almost any illusion the customer may desire. This imaginative work is done at their manufacturing plant in New Jersey. There they create many of the colorful effects they sell. Others come from out-of-town suppliers or are imported from abroad.

Tony Spina, the illusionist and inventor of magical effects, became a Tannen partner in the late 1960s. Jack Ferero, dedicated magician and prestidigitator, joined the partnership in 1975. Both are active in magic affairs and are past presidents of Harry Roz-On Ring No. 26 of the International Brotherhood of Magicians.

A substantial part of the Tannen business is its publishing program. Leading item on the Tannen book list is *The Tarbell Course in Magic*, in seven volumes (vol. I, $12.50; vols. II–VI, $15.00 each; vol. VII, $20.00). Lou Tannen took over the publishing of the famous course from its author, Dr. Harlan Tarbell. Tarbell originally distributed it in smaller units by subscription. Lou republished the course in book form. Irv Tannen considers the Tarbell course "the greatest set of books ever put out, as far as actually learning goes, for any age group. In fact, magic has no age groupings. A ten-year-old can talk to a seventy-year-old about magic and both can enjoy the same things on the same level."

Tannen's best-selling books also include three volumes containing the 151 issues of *Jinx* magazine, edited by Ted Annemann ($15.00 per volume); the six volumes of the *Phoenix* magazine, edited by Bruce Elliott (vols. I–V, $12.50 each; vol. VI, $15.00); *Stars of Magic* ($15.00), a photo-illustrated collection of favorite effects by noted magicians; and Harry Lorayne's books on card magic. These are all exceptionally good, steady sellers.

There are over 325 hardbound and softbound books listed in Tannen's *Catalog No. 11* (revised edition, 1976), and the company owns over 200 copyrights. The catalogue itself has 648 pages and can be had for $3.50.

Irv Tannen (*left*) and Tony Spina. (*James J. Kriegsmann Photo, courtesy of Louis Tannen, Inc.*)

In the back of the 1976 edition is a bonus, a whole book of magic, Annemann's *The Book Without A Name*. The catalogue contains descriptions of over 3000 tricks and gimmicks.

Irv Tannen, Tony Spina and Jack Ferero revise the catalogue every year, a task that takes about six months.

Publishing the catalogues is expensive for the company. "That's the whole story of our business," Irv Tannen says, "advertise, advertise, advertise. I think we're about the biggest advertisers in the magic field in the world." Tannen ads appear in magic and boys' magaines and they also publish a bulletin, *Tannen's Topics,* every few months. This is mailed free to customers.

Each October Tannen's sponsors a gala four-day jubilee for magicians and their families at a luxury hotel in the Catskills. These get-togethers now take place at Brown's, a large, inviting resort hotel at Loch Sheldrake, New York. From 1000 to 1500 people register for the four-day program of evening magic shows and matinees, close-up demonstrations, lectures and displays of magic and books by a score of dealers. Fifteen jubilees have now been held. For further information, prospective registrants should write to Louis Tannen, Inc., 1540 Broadway, New York, NY 10036.

Another Tannen enterprise is its summer magic camp program for boys at La Salle Military Academy at Oakdale, on the south shore of Long Island. Here from 150 to 200 campers receive instruction in magic and enjoy swimming, baseball and other recreations.

Among Louis Tannen's steady customers are such headliners as Siegfried and Roy, the Las Vegas illusionists; Doug Henning, the first star of *The Magic Show,* whose magic has been featured in TV specials; and many other leading professionals. "But anybody and everybody can enjoy magic," Irv Tannen says. "If you like skills, you can learn skills. If you don't want to learn skills, you do mechanics. If you just want to read about it, there are hundreds of books you can turn to. It's inexhaustible. The clientele that come to us are varied—and very nice. We get a lot of professional people: doctors, lawyers, engineers, who look for a little relief from the tasks they do. Magic has great therapeutic values. You can get lost in it. You don't even have to have company; you can sit by yourself and enjoy it. I think it's more popular now than it's ever been. It's a very busy life, but we like it."

DIRECTORY OF DEALERS AND CATALOGUES

(A Catalogue of Catalogues)

The addresses of representative magic dealers whose catalogue descriptions or advertisements are reproduced in this book, and others from whom catalogues and lists are available, are listed below. Charges for catalogues are given, if known. If you wish to order an item listed in the book, it is suggested strongly that you write first to the dealer indicated, enclosing a self-addressed, stamped envelope for his reply, to check the price and continued availability of the item. This is advisable owing to the frequent changes in prices; in view of which, prices mentioned in *The Magic Catalogue* are subject to change and can only be considered a general guide.

Abbott's Magic Manufacturing Company
Colon, MI 49040
Catalogue $4.00

Abracadabra Magic Shop (Retail Shop)
Colonia Shopping Plaza
Highway 27
Colonia, NJ 07067

Send mail orders to:

Abracadabra Magic Shop
Dept. EP,
280 Hamilton Street
Rahway, NJ 07065

SPECIAL OFFER! *The Abracadabra Magic Shop will send readers of this book both its Professional Magic Catalogue (regular price $2.00) and its Giant Magic Catalogue, and will also place them on its mailing list for its quarterly "What's New in Magic"—all for $1.00.*
To take advantage of this offer, please mention this book and address your inquiry to Abracadabra Magic Shop, Dept. EP, 280 Hamilton Street, Rahway, NJ 07065.

Al's Magic Shop
1205 Pennsylvania Avenue, NW
Washington, D.C. 20004
Catalogue available

Aladdin's Magic Lamp
3026 San Bruno Avenue
San Francisco, CA 94134
Catalogue $1.50

Alakazam Magic Castle
100 West Lincoln Avenue
Roselle Park, NJ 07204
Catalogue $.35

Samuel Berland
517 South Jefferson Street
Chicago, IL 60607
Original effects

Black Magic Company
441 Godfrey Road
Weston, CT 06880
Catalogue $1.00

Boomerang Magic
P.O. Box 16
Castle Hill 2154
N.S.W., Australia
List $1.00

Mario Carrandi
29 Virginia Street
Kendall Park, NJ 08224
Lists of rare and used apparatus, books and memorabilia available, $1.00

Cassini Magic Creations
124 Eileen Circle
Burnsville, MN 55337

Chu's Magic Studio
401 Chatham Road
T.S.T.
P.O. Box 5221
Kowloon, Hong Kong
Catalogue in full color, $6.00;
Airmail, $10.00

Glenn Comar
353 East 6th Avenue
Roselle, NJ 07203
Catalogue $.75

Creative Magic Products, Inc.
786 Merrick Road
Baldwin, NY 11510
Catalogue $1.00

Deceptions Unlimited
6743 Ewing Avenue North
Minneapolis, MN 55429
Catalogue $.50

Delben Company, Inc.
Box 3535
Springfield, MO 65804
List available

Dragon Mysteries
The Lodge
Ayot Bury
Welwyn
Herts, England
Chemical magic, catalogue $1.00

El Duco's Magic
Lergoksgatan 18S
214 79 Malmo, Sweden
Brochure available

Eagle Magic Store
708 Portland Avenue
Minneapolis, MN 55414
Catalogue $1.00

Emerson & West
   (Arthur J. Emerson, Jr.)
590 Bond Court
Alexandria, VA 22310
Original card and other effects

The Emporium of Magic
17220 West Eight Mile Road
Building A, Suite 110
Southfield, MI 48075
*Catalogue $3.50, refunded on first
purchase for $10.00 or more
Minimum order $5.00*

Fabjance Studio, Inc.
P.O. Box 123
Bethalto, IL 62010
Catalogue $1.00

Fabulous Magic Company
3319 East Charleston Blvd.
Las Vegas, NV 89104
Catalogue $1.00, magic club

Joseph Fenichel
4714 Avenue I
Brooklyn, NY 11234

Flosso Hornmann Magic Co.
304 West 34th Street
New York, NY 10018
Catalogue $1.00

Dan Garrett
4929 Salem Road
Lithonia, GA 30058

Gem Production, Inc.
1900 Franklin Avenue East
Seattle, WA 98102
Catalogue available

Eddie Gibson
73 James Street
Preston
Lancashire, PR1 4JX, England
Coin magic, list available

Gibson Magic
7 Amherst Street
Nashua, NH 03060

Goodliffe the Magician
Arden Forest Industrial Estate
Alcester, Warwickshire, England
Books, list $1.00

U. F. Grant (Mak-Magic)
P.O. Box 44052
Columbus, OH 43204
Catalogue $1.00

Guaranteed Magic
27 Bright Road
Hatboro, PA 19040
*Catalogue $2.00
Minimum order $2.00*

Micky Hades International
Box 476
Calgary
Alberta, Canada T2P 2J1

*Book-a-Log No. 13, $2.00
with coupon redeemable
for purchase price*

Micky Hades International
110 Union Street, Suite 500
Box 2242
Seattle, WA 98101

Haenchen & Co.
Route 1, Box 1650
Harrah, OK 73045

Haines House of Cards
P.O. Box 12527
2044 Ross Avenue
Norwood, OH 45212
Catalogue $2.00

Robert Healey, Jr.
1612 Dickson Avenue
Scranton, PA 18509
*Custom built illusions & magic
Catalogue $1.00*

Hollywood Magic, Inc.
6614 Hollywood Boulevard
Hollywood, CA 90028
Catalogue $2.50

The House of Hocus Pocus, Inc.
1344 Coney Island Avenue
Brooklyn, NY 11230
         and
942 East 78th Street
Brooklyn, NY 11236
Catalogue available

The House of Magic
2025 Chestnut Street
San Francisco, CA 94123

Hughes House of Magic
The Grange
Willow Park
King's Lynn
Norfolk, PE30 IEJ,
England
List $.50

Imperial Products, Inc.
Box 623
Federal Building
Worcester, MA 01601
Catalogue $2.00

Lee Jacobs Productions
P.O. Box 362
Pomeroy, OH 45769
*New and used magic
 & books
Catalogue $1.00*

Jan's Magical Manufacturing Company
55 West 19th Street
New York, NY 10011

Johnson Products
P.O. Box 734
Arcadia, CA 91006
Catalogue $.50

Jose's Studio
17 Wallace Street
Belleville, NJ 07109

Kanter's Magic Shop
200 South 13th Street
Philadelphia, PA 19107
Minimum order $2.00

Doug Keller's House of Magic
12–14 White Street
Red Bank, NJ 07701

Kenzini's Magic Palace
28 East Colfax Avenue
Roselle Park, NJ 07204
Catalogue available

Yutaka Kikuchi
10-16 Befu 5 Chome
Nishi-Ku Fukuokashi
Fukuokaken
814 Japan

George W. Kirkendall
2180 Jervis Road
Columbus, OH 43221

KKK Magic Shop
815 West Court Street
Kankakee, IL 60901
*Catalague $1.00
Discount card available*

Kovari Magic Productions Ltd.
465 Watford Way
London, N.W. 4, England
List $1.00

LaWain House of Magic
P.O. Box 160
Monmouth, IL 61462
*Periodical lists available, of used, antique
and new magic, books, etc., $1.00*

Lee's Studio of Magic
116 High Street
Millville, NJ 08332
Catalogue $2.00

Hank Lee's Magic Factory
24 Lincoln Street
Boston, MA 02111
Catalogue $1.00
Minimum order $2.00

Nat Litt's Magic Shop
(Nathaniel Litt, Inc.)
227 North 13th Street
Philadelphia, PA 19107

Jack London
1937 A Barnes Avenue
Bronx, NY 10462
Mental effects

Luna Magic
Southend House
The Southend
Ledbury
Hertfordshire, England
List $1.00

Magic Art Book Co.
137 Spring Street
Watertown, MA 02172
New and antique magic, books
List available

Magic by Gosh, Inc. (Albert Goshman)
11226 Kamloops Street
Lakeview Terrace, CA 91342
List available

Magic Center
739 Eighth Avenue
New York, NY
Catalogue available

Magic Center
144 North 13th Street
Philadelphia, PA 19107
Catalogue available

Magic Emporium
19554 Ventura Boulevard
Tarzana, CA 91356

Magic Emporium
P.O. Box 385
Hawthorne, CA 90250

The Magic Hands
Donaustrasse 21
D-7033 Herrenberg
West Germany
Catalogue in English DM 10

The Magic House
Box 70
Fontana, WI 53125
Catalogue $1.00

Magic, Inc.
5082 North Lincoln Avenue
Chicago, IL 60625
Catalogue $2.00
Book catalogue $3.00

Magic Masters
766 Carman Avenue
Westbury, NY 11590

Magic Methods
P.O. Box 4105
Greenville, SC 29608
Catalogue $2.00

The Magic Shop
P.O. Box 744
10919 Los Alamitos Boulevard
Los Alamitos, CA 90702
Catalogue $.50

The Magic Shop
P.O. Box 5215
Cresaptown, MD 21502

The Magic Towne House
1026 Third Avenue
New York, NY 10021
Catalogue available, classes

Magic Unlimited
14 Whitman Drive
Denville, NJ 07834
Catalogue $1.00

Magic Unusual
Box 112
Boise, ID 83701
Catalogue available

Magic Workshop (Jim Zee)
P.O. Box 314
Rocky Hill, CT 06067
Catalogue $1.00

Mak-Magic (U. F. Grant)
P.O. Box 44052
Columbus, OH 43204
Catalogue $1.00

Robert Mason Productions
99 Fernwood Avenue
Dayton, OH 45405
Catalogue available

Mephisto-Huis
Veldstraat 156D
8500 Kortrijk
Belgium
Bulletins available

Miami Magic (The Performer)
9734 Bird Road
Miami, FL 33165
Catalogue $.75

Mickey "O" Enterprises
606 Fifth Avenue
Brooklyn, NY 11215
Escapes

Mollo Magic
43 Wright Street
Stamford, CT 06902

Moorehouse Magic Warehouse
516 East William
Ann Arbor, MI 48108

Herb Morrissey Products
Morrissey Magic Ltd.
1475 Decelles Street
Suite 1
Ville St. Laurent 379
Quebec, H4L 2C8, Canada
Catalogue available

Mosley Electronics, Inc.
4610 North Lindbergh Boulevard
Bridgeton, MO 63044
Catalogue $1.25

Mystic Myron's Magic Mart
109 West South Orange Avenue
South Orange, NJ 07079
Circular & mailing list $.25

NBK Distributors, Inc.
P.O. Box 10718
Winston-Salem, NC 27108
Catalogue $3.00
Minimum order $2.00

Robert Nelson
470 Forest Lake Circle
Kernersville, NC 27284
New and used magic and books

Lee Noble
155 Greenbelt Lane
Levittown, NY 11756
List available

Owen Magic Supreme
1240 South Chapel Avenue
Alhambra, CA 91801
Catalogue $12.50

Paul's Magic and Fun Shop
903 Federal Highway (US 1)
Searstown
Fort Lauderdale, FL 33304
Catalogue $1.00

Pavel
P.O. Box 42
1212 Grand Lancy 1
Geneva, Switzerland
Original magic

Repro 71
48 Emu Road
London S.W. 8, England

Rings 'n' Things Magic Co.
P.O. Box 3982
St. Louis, MO 63136
Catalogue available

Ripley's Believe It or Not Magic Shop
600 Parkway
Gatlin, TN 37738
Catalogue $1.00

D. Robbins & Company, Inc.
127 West 17th Street
New York, NY 10011

D. Robbins & Co., Inc., sells only to stores, pitchmen or others who buy in large quantities for promotional or advertising purposes.

Show-Biz Services
1735 East 26th Street
Brooklyn, NY 11229
Catalogue $1.00

Silk King Studios
640 Evening Star Lane
Cincinnati, OH 45220
Catalogue available

Simplex Magic
James Rainho Products
16 Windsor Road
Medford, MA 02155
Catalogue available
Minimum order $3.00

Sorcerium, Inc.
P.O. Box 2
Plainsboro, NJ 08536
Catalogue $1.00

Sorcerer's Apprentice
P.O. Box 9991
Atlanta, GA 30319

The Sorcerer's Apprentice
Suite 243, West Village
Crown Center
Kansas City, MO 64108

Stevens Magic Emporium
3238 East Douglas
and 6004 East Douglas
Wichita, KS
List $1.00

The Studio
4765 North Lincoln Avenue
Room 210
Chicago, IL 60625
Brochure $5.00

Sun Rise Magic
601 N.E. 21st Street
Washington, IN 47501
Silk list $1.00

Supreme Magic Company
64 High Street
Bideford
Devon, England

James Swoger (House of
   Enchantment, Inc.)
Lake Road, RD #5
Somerset, PA 15501
Catalogue available

Louis Tannen, Inc.
1540 Broadway
New York, NY 10036
Catalogue $3.50

Tigner Magic Supply Company
P.O. Box 7149
Toledo, OH 43615
Escapes, magic
Catalogue available

Nick Trost
1382 Virginia Avenue
Columbus, OH 43212
Card effects, list $.50

Universal Magic & Supply Co.
256 South Robertson Boulevard
Beverly Hills, CA 90211
Catalogue $1.00
Discount card, newsletter available

U.T.C. Import
P.O. Box 1651
Idaho Falls, ID 83401
Catalogue $.75

Anthony A. Vander Linden
R.F.D. #2
Oyster Bay, NY 11771
Books on magic and related subjects
Catalogue $2.00

Henk Vermeyden
Kloveniersburgwal 113
Amsterdam C, Holland
List $1.00

Warner's Magic Factory
Box 455
Hinsdale, IL 60512
Catalogue available

Prynce E. Wheeler
P.O. Box 349
Great Falls, MT 59403
Escape
Illustrated price list available

Wilcox Magicrafters
Magic Manor
Altus, AR 72821
Illusions, unusual magic tables
List available

The Wizard Magic Shop
1136 Pearl Street
Boulder, CO 80302
Catalogue $1.00

LISTS OF ADDRESSES

The Mister E List
Researched by James P. Zorn
Distributed by Mister E Enterprises
P.O. Box 8883
Rochester, NY 14624 $5.00
Includes magic shops, dealers, mail order dealers, publications, clubs, organizations, specialists, etc.

Sid Lorraine's New Reference List
Compiled and distributed by Sid Lorraine
781 Coxwell Avenue
Toronto, Canada M4C 3C8 $3.50
Includes magazine, club publications, magic dealers, magic shops, mail order dealers, dealers in magic books, specialists.

COURSES IN MAGIC

Courses in magic are of various types, ranging from personal instruction to lessons by correspondence or, in one case, a remarkable set of books so rich in material and so comprehensive that they must be included among the best sources of instruction. This is *The Tarbell Course in Magic,* a monumental work written and compiled by Dr. Harlan Tarbell and originally issued by him to subscribers, in parts, as a correspondence course. It is now published in book form, in seven volumes (the last volume written and edited by Harry Lorayne), by Louis Tannen, Inc., 1540 Broadway, New York NY 10036. Volume I is priced at $12.50, vols. II–VI at $15.00 each, and vol. VII at $20.00; or the whole seven-volume set may be ordered for $97.50. Each volume contains over 400 pages. Details of the contents of the various volumes are given in the Tannen catalogue.

Chavez Studio of Magic, Marion Chavez, Director, Suite 202, 8727 Van Nuys Boulevard, Panorama City CA 91402, gives personal instruction in magic. It also offers a correspondence course. For information regarding the course, write the studio at 8706 Colbath Avenue, Panorama City, CA 91402.

Doug Keller's House of Magic, 12–14 White Street, Red Bank, NJ 07701, conducts classes in magic for beginners and advanced students each spring and fall. Each class meets for 2½ hours one evening a week, usually Thursdays, for five weeks, making a total of 12½ hours of instruction in each course. Tuition for the beginners' course is $65.00 and for the advanced course, $85.00. For further particulars contact the House of Magic.

Magic Towne House, 1026 Third Avenue, New York, NY 10021. Instruction in magic is available by arrangement at the Magic Towne House (see page 227). Inquire for further details.

New York School for Magicians. Conducted by Show-Biz Services, 1735 East 26th Street, Brooklyn, NY 11229. Write them for details.

Col. F. M. Seymour, S.C.C. School of Magic, 5200 West 29th Street, Little Rock, AR 72204, offers instruction. Newsletter, $1.00.

Tannen's Magic Camp. A summer camp session for boys, with instruction in magic, conducted by Louis Tannen, Inc., New York magic dealers, at Oakdale, Long Island, NY. See page 230. Write Louis Tannen, Inc., for further details.

The *Mark Wilson Course in Magic,* P.O. Box 440, North Hollywood, CA 91603. This comprises over 450 pages of instructions, bound in a heavy vinyl cover. An optional kit of props is available with the instructions, if desired. There is a Special Collector's Edition priced at $45.00 plus $2.00 postage and handling (California residents add $2.70 sales tax); a regular edition at $39.95 plus $2.00 postage and handling (California residents add $2.40 sales tax); and the regular edition without the props at $29.95 plus $2.00 postage and handling (California residents add $1.80 sales tax).

MAGAZINES FOR MAGICIANS

The best way to keep up with the march of ideas and events in the world of magic is to subscribe to a good magic magazine. Here are a number of periodicals, with brief notes of any special emphases they may reflect.

Bulletin for Friends of Magic History
Quarterly, $5.00 yr.
Steven Tigner, Pub.
Tigner Magic Supply Co.
P.O. Box 7149
Toledo, OH 43615
Scholarly information and intriguing novelties and memorabilia related to the history of magic

Club 71
Repro 71
48 Emu Road
London, S.W. 8, England
General magic and mentalism

The Cheat Sheet
Deceptions Unlimited
6743 Ewing Avenue North
Minneapolis, MN 55429

Epilogue, 3 times yearly, $4.50
Karl Fulves, Pub.
Box 433
Teaneck, NJ 07666
Sleight-of-hand

Genii, monthly, $12.00 yr.
William Larsen, Jr., Ed. & Pub.
P.O. Box 36068
Los Angeles, CA 90036
General magic

The Hierophant
Jon Racherbaumer, Pub.
P.O. Box 1142
Metairie, LA 70001

Invocation, quarterly, $5.50 yr.
Bob Lynn, Pub.
P.O. Box 169
Waldwick, NJ 07463

Le Journal de la Prestidigitation
Decamps (Zum Pocco)
8 Rue Bénédic-Mace
14000 Caen, France

Legerdemain, monthly, $11.00 yr.
Fabjance Studio, Inc.
130 West Central
Bethalto, IL 62010

The Levitator, bimonthly
The Society of Canadian Magicians
Mrs. Maureen Wyvern, Ed.
7470 Redstone Road
Malton, Ont., Canada

The Linking Ring, monthly
The International Brotherhood of Magicians
114 North Detroit Street
Kenton, OH 43326

The Magic Magazine, monthly, $10 yr.
SUBSCRIPTION CORRESPONDENCE:
1808 West End Avenue,
Suite 1500,
Nashville, TN 37203
EDITORIAL CORRESPONDENCE:
801 Second Avenue,
New York, NY 10017
General magic

The Magic Shop Newsletter, $4.00 yr.
P.O. Box 744
10919 Los Alamitos Bolevard
Los Alamitos, CA 90720

Magick, biweekly, $10.00 yr.
Bascom Jones, Pub.
1065 La. Mirada Street
P.O. Box 334
Laguna Beach, CA 92651
Mentalism and close-up magic

The Magigram, monthly, $10.00 yr.
Supreme Magic Company
64 High Street
Bideford, Devon, England
General magic

Magische Welt
W. Geissler-Werry, Pub.
516 Dueren
In den Benden 13
Federal Republic of Germany

M.U.M., monthly
Society of American Magicians
Lock Drawer 789
Lynn, MA 01903

Mystic Quarterly
James Hagy, Ed. and Pub.
565 East 266th Street
Euclid, OH 44132
Magic history, collecting

Quarterly News Sheet, $2.00
Robert Lund
American Museum of Magic
Marshall, MI 49068

The New Tops, monthly, $11.00;
Canada & Mexico, $14.00
Neil Foster, Ed.
Abbott's Magic Mfg. Co.
Colon, MI 49040
General magic

The Pallbearers' Review, monthly,
$11.00 yr.
Karl Fulves, Ed. & Pub.
P.O. Box 433
Teaneck, NJ 07666
Sleight-of-hand

The Pentacle, monthly
Cincinnati Academy of Magic and Allied Sciences
1698 Montrose Street
Cincinnati, OH 45214

The Spellbinder
(Parent Assembly No. 1, S.A.M.,
New York)
Lawrence Arcuri, Ed.
3 Stuyvesant Oval
New York, NY 10009

Tricks, monthly
Kloveniersburgwal 113
Amsterdam C, Holland

Zauberkunst
Zentralhaus fuer Kulturarbeit der DDR
Dittrichring 4, P.S.F. 1051
701 Leipzig
East Germany

A SELECTED BIBLIOGRAPHY

The art of magic has an exceptionally rich and extensive literature. This is fortunate, for short of personal instruction, the best way to become an accomplished magician is to study good books and magazines on the art, practice intensively, and seek constructive criticism of your work from fellow magi.

To help the reader build a good magical library that will serve him well as a performer, the following selected bibliography of about 100 titles is offered. Such a selection must, inevitably, be influenced by the individual compiler's personal interests and knowledge. I do not wish to imply that the books listed below are necessarily the 100 "best" books in the field: in order to cover a number of different branches of magic in the space available, many fine books have had to be omitted. Readers are urged to consult also the fuller bibliographies listed below.

Since the following selection is designed primarily for the practical performer or student who is building up his library, I have included mainly books that are currently available. If some are no longer actually in print on their publishers' lists, one can reasonably hope to acquire used copies sooner or later from magic dealers, or to locate them at the library. Titles that I have consulted in preparing the present book are also included. Because of their outstanding quality, I have included a very few books, such as John Northern Hilliard's *Greater Magic,* which are admittedly now hard to find, yet definitely worth looking out for. The list does not, however, attempt to deal with old and rare magic books as collectors' items. Collectors in that field will wish to consult the bibliographies of Gill, Hall, Heyl and Price, listed below in the section on "Bibliographical Works."

Pleasant reading!

GENERAL

Anderson, George B., *Magic Digest.* Chicago: Follet Publishing Co., 1972.

Annemann, Theodore, *The Jinx.* 3 vols. New York: Louis Tannen, Inc., vol. I, 1963; vol II, 1964; vol. III, 1964.

Booth, John, *The John Booth Classics.* Bideford, Devon: Supreme Magic Co., 1975. Comprises three books by Booth: *Forging Ahead in Magic, Marvels of Mystery,* and *A Conjurer's Reminiscences.*

De la Torre, Jose, *Magicana of Havana (in New York),* ed. Marc Tessler. Belleville, N.J.: Jose's Studio, 1975. Magic routines with cards, coins and ropes.

Downs, T. Nelson, *The Art of Magic,* ed. John Northern Hilliard. Chicago: Arthur P. Felsman, 1909.

Elliott, Bruce, *Phoenix.* 6 vols. Berkeley Heights, N.J.: Fleming, 1952–1954.

Fischer, Ottokar, *Illustrated Magic.* New York: The Macmillan Co., 1931.

Ganson, Lewis, ed., *The Art of Close-Up Magic.* Vol. I. London: Unique Studio, 1961. Vol. II. Bideford, Devon: Supreme, 1973.

————, *The Dai Vernon Book of Magic.* London: Unique, n.d.

————, *The Magic of Slydini.* Bideford: Supreme, n.d.

————, *Routined Manipulation,* Part I. New York: Tannen, n.d.

————, *Routined Manipulation,* Part II. New York: Tannen, n.d.

————, *Routined Manipulation, Finale.* New York: Tannen, n.d.

Gaultier, Camille, *Magic without Apparatus,* trans. Jean Hugard. Berkeley Heights, N.J.: Fleming, 1945.

Hay, Henry, *The Amateur Magician's Handbook.* New York: Thomas Y. Crowell Co., 1965.

————, *Cyclopedia of Magic.* New York: Dover Publications, Inc., 1975.

Hilliard, John Northern, *Greater Magic.* Revised ed. Minneapolis: Carl Waring Jones, 1945.

Hoffmann, Professor [pseud. of Angelo Lewis], *Modern Magic.* London and New York: George Routledge and Sons Ltd., 1876.

————, *More Magic.* London: Routledge, 1890.

————, *Later Magic.* London: Routledge, 1904; New York: E. P. Dutton and Co., 1904.

Hugard, Jean, *Modern Magic Manual*. Paper-covered ed. London: Faber & Faber Ltd., 1973.

Ireland Magic Co. (later became Magic, Inc.), *The Ireland Yearbooks*. Chicago: Magic, Inc., 1934–1970. Tricks, routines, building plans, articles, etc. Bi-annual after 1962.

Kaplan, George G., *The Fine Art of Magic*. York, Pa.: Fleming, 1948.

Nathanson, Leon, M.D. *Slydini Encores*. New York: Slydini's Studio of Magic, 1966.

Neil, C. Lang, *The Modern Conjurer*. New York: Wehman Brothers, 1917.

Sachs, Edwin T., *Sleight of Hand*. Ed. Paul Fleming. Berkeley Heights, N.J.: Fleming Book Co., 1946.

Starke, George, ed., *Stars of Magic*. New York: Tannen, 1961.

Tarbell, Harlan, *The Tarbell Course in Magic*. 7 vols. New York: Tannen, 1941–1972.

Warlock, Peter, *The Magic of Pavel*. Bideford: Supreme, 1971.

BIBLIOGRAPHICAL WORKS

Gill, Robert, *Magic as a Performing Art: A Bibliography of Conjuring*. Epping, Essex: Bowker Publishing Co. Ltd., 1976.

Hall, Trevor H., *A Bibliography of Books on Conjuring in English from 1580 to 1850*. Minneapolis: Carl Waring Jones, 1957.

————, *Old Conjuring Books: A Bibliographical and Historical Study*. London: Duckworth, 1972.

Heyl, Edgar, *A Contribution to Conjuring Bibliography, English Language, 1580–1850*. Baltimore: Edgar Heyl, 1963.

————, *Cues for Collectors*. Chicago: Magic, Inc., 1964.

Potter, Jack, *The Master Index to Magic in Print*. 14 vols. Calgary: Micky Hades, 1967–1975.

Price, Harry, *Short Title Catalogue from Circa 1450 A.D. to 1929 A.D.* London: National Laboratory for Psychical Research, 1935.

BIOGRAPHICAL WORKS

Bamberg, Theo, *Okito on Magic*. 2nd ed. Chicago: Magic, Inc., 1968.

Christopher, Milbourne, *Houdini: The Untold Story*. New York: Pocket Books, 1970.

Dexter, Will, *The Riddle of Chung Ling Soo*. London and New York: Arco, 1955.

Frost, Thomas, *The Lives of the Conjurers*. London: Chatto and Windus, 1881.

Gibson, Walter B., *The Original Houdini Scrapbook*. New York: Corwin Sterling Publishing Co., 1976.

Marshall, Frances Ireland, *With Frances in Magicland*. Chicago: Ireland Magic Co., 1952.

Robert-Houdin, Jean Eugène, *Life of Robert Houdin* [sic], *The King of the Conjurers*, trans. Dr. R. Shelton MacKenzie. Philadelphia: Henry T. Coates and Co., copyright 1859. Many editions published.

Seldow, Michel, *Vie et Secrets de Robert-Houdin*. Paris: Fayard, 1971.

CARD TRICKS

Annemann, Theodore, *Miracles of Card Magic*. New York: Max Holden, 1945.

Erdnase, S. W., *The Expert at the Card Table*. See MacDougall, *Card Mastery*.

Fischer, Ottokar, *Hofzinser's Card Magic*, ed. and rev. with notes by S. H. Sharpe. Teaneck, N.J.: Gutenberg Press, 1974.

Ganson, Lewis, *Card Magic by Manipulation*. Bideford: Supreme, 1971. Deals with bare-handed production of cards and card fans.

————, *Dai Vernon's Further Secrets of Card Magic*. Bideford: Supreme, 1972.

————, *Dai Vernon's Inner Secrets of Card Magic*. Bideford: Supreme, 1972.

————, *Dai Vernon's More Inner Secrets of Card Magic*. Bideford: Supreme, 1972.

————, *Dai Vernon's Ultimate Card Secrets*. Bideford: Supreme, 1972.

Garcia, Frank, *Million Dollar Card Secrets*. Ed. George Schindler. New York: Million Dollar Productions, 1972.

————, *Super Subtle Card Miracles*. Ed. George Schindler. New York: Million Dollar Productions, 1973.

Hugard, Jean, *Encyclopedia of Card Tricks*. New York: Dover, 1975.

Hugard, Jean, and Frederick Braue, *Expert Card Technique*. 3rd ed. London: Faber and Faber, 1950.

LePaul, Paul, *The Card Magic of Brother John Hamman*. Chicago: Magic, Inc., 1958.

Lorayne, Harry, *Close-Up Card Magic*. New York: Tannen, 1962.

————, *Dingle's Deceptions*. Norwood, Ohio: Haines House of Cards, n.d.

————, *Reputation Makers*. New York: Author, 1971.

MacDougall, Michael, *Card Mastery*, with which is combined S. W. Erdnase, *The Expert at the Card Table*. New York: Tannen, 1944.

Marlo, Edward, *The Cardician*. Chicago: Magic, Inc., 1966.

Scarne, John, *Scarne on Card Tricks*. New York: Crown, 1950. Deals with card tricks that do not involve sleight-of-hand.

Searles, Lynn, *The Card Expert*. Colon, Mich.: Abbott, 1938.

CHILDREN'S SHOW MAGIC

Kerns, Ernie, *How To Be a Magic Clown*. Chicago: Magic, Inc., 1960.

Lewis, Eric C., and Wilfred Tyler, *Open Sesame*. Birmingham: Goodliffe, 1947.

Marshall, Frances Ireland, *Kid Stuff*. Vols. 1–6. Chicago: Magic, Inc., 1954–1974.

Posgate, Bruce, *Kid Show Showmanship*. Colon, Mich.: Abbott, 1961.

COIN TRICKS

Bobo, J. B., *Modern Coin Magic*, ed. John Braun. Minneapolis: Carl Waring Jones, 1952.

Hugard, Jean, *Coin Magic*. New York: Holden, 1935.

THE CUPS AND BALLS

Ganson, Lewis, *The Dai Vernon Cups and Balls Routine*. Bideford: Supreme, 1971. Also included in the same author's *The Dai Vernon Book of Magic* [q.v.].

Ireland, Laurie, *Ireland's Original Cups and Balls Routines*. Chicago: The Ireland Magic Co., 1961.

Joseph, Eddie, *Advanced Lessons in Cups and Balls*. 2nd ed. Colon, Mich.: Abbott, n.d.

————, *The Last Word on Cups and Balls.* Colon, Mich.: Abbott, 1942.

————, *A Practical Lesson in Cups and Balls.* Colon, Mich.: Abbott, n.d.

ESCAPES

Gibson, Walter B., and Morris Young, eds., *Houdini on Magic.* New York: Dover, 1953.

Gibson, Walter B., *Houdini's Escapes and Magic.* New York: Funk and Wagnalls, 1976.

HISTORICAL WORKS

Burlingame, H. J., *Leaves from Conjurers' Scrap Books.* Chicago: Donohue, Henneberry and Co., 1891.

Christopher, Milbourne, *The Illustrated History of Magic.* New York: Thomas Y. Crowell Co., 1973.

————, *Panorama of Magic.* New York: Dover, 1962.

Evans, Henry Ridgely, *The Old and the New Magic.* Chicago: Open Court Publishing Co., 1906.

Pecor, Charles Joseph, *The Magician on the American Stage, 1752–1874.* Washington, D.C.: Emerson and West, 1977.

ILLUSIONS

Ayling, Will, *The Art of Illusion.* Bideford: Supreme, 1971.

Dart, Edward W., ed., *The Conjurers' Book of Stage Illusions.* Calgary: Micky Hades, 1974.

Foster, Neil, ed., *Tops Treasury of Illusions.* Colon, Mich.: Abbott, 1965.

MENTALISM AND PSYCHIC INVESTIGATION

Annemann, Theodore, *Practical Mental Effects.* New York: Max Holden, 1944; Tannen, 1963.

Corinda, Tony, *Thirteen Steps to Mentalism.* New York: Tannen, 1968.

Houdini, Harry, *A Magician Among the Spirits.* New York: Arno Press, 1972; copyright 1924.

Hull, Burling, *The Encyclopedic Dictionary of Mentalism.* 3rd ed., rev. and enlarged, ed. Micky Hades. Calgary: Hades, 1973.

Kolb, Fred, *Exciting Experiments in E.S.P.* Bideford: Supreme, 1970.

Nelson, Robert A., *The Encyclopedia of Mentalism and Allied Arts.* 2nd ed. Calgary: Hades, 1971.

MISCELLANEOUS

Adair, Ian, *Encyclopedia of Dove Magic.* Bideford: Supreme, vol. I, 1968; vol. II, 1972; vol. III, 1973.

Albenice & Spalding, *Reel Magic and the Penetrable Silk* (ed. Ralph W. Read). New York: Tannen, 2nd rev. ed., 1950.

Annemann, Theodore, *Two Hundred and Two Methods of Forcing.* New York: Holden, 1933. Covers forcing of cards, colors, numbers, etc.

Clark, Keith, *Encyclopedia of Cigarette Tricks.* New York: Tannen, 1952.

Holden, Max, *Programmes of Famous Magicians.* 2nd ed. Chicago: Magic, Inc., 1968.

Hutton, Daryl, and Micky Hades, *The Dove Worker's Handbook.* Calgary: Hades, vol. I, 1966; vol. II, 1969.

Marshall, Frances Ireland, and Jay Marshall, and a panel of experts, *The Success Book.* Chicago: Magic, Inc., 1973.

————, *The Table Book.* Chicago: Magic, Inc., 1961.

Martineau, Francis B., *Walsh Cane Routines.* Cincinnati: Silk King Studios, 1945.

Maskelyne, Nevil, and David Devant, *Our Magic.* Berkeley Heights, N.J.: Fleming, 1946.

Posgate, Bruce, *Dove Pan-Orama.* Montreal: Morrissey, 1972.

PAPER MAGIC

Anderson, Gene, and Frances Ireland Marshall, *Newspaper Magic.* Chicago: Magic, Inc., 1968.

De Courcy, Ken, *Troublewit Routines.* Bideford: Supreme, 1965.

ROPES

Fitzkee, Dariel, *Rope Eternal.* New York: Tannen, n.d.

James, Stewart, comp., *Abbott's Encyclopedia of Rope Tricks.* Colon, Mich.: Abbott, vol. I, 1941; vol. II, 1962.

SILKS

Hugard, Jean, *Silken Sorcery.* New York: Holden, 1937.

Rice, Harold R., *The Encyclopedia of Silk Magic.* Cincinnati: Silk King Studios, vol. I, 1948; vol. II, 1953; vol. III, 1962.

Rice, Harold R., and W. T. van Zandt, *Thru the Dye Tube.* Wynnewood, Pa.: Silk King Studios, 1943.

LOU TANNEN ULTRASILK DESIGNED BY ED MISHELL

INDEX